THE NAVY

THE
NAVY

Rear Admiral W. J. Holland, Jr., USN (Ret)
Editor-in-Chief

NAVAL HISTORICAL FOUNDATION
HUGH LAUTER LEVIN ASSOCIATES, INC.

Naval Historical Foundation

Seventy-five years ago, Commodore Dudley Knox wrote in the U.S. Naval Institute *Proceedings* about the "glaring deficiencies" in collecting and preserving the Navy's written records. Knox's article on "Our Vanishing History and Traditions" gave birth to the Naval Historical Foundation in 1926 under the sponsorship of the Secretary of the Navy. From its initial focus on safeguarding the material culture of the Navy, the Foundation has developed into a non-profit organization dedicated to preserving and promoting the full range of naval history. Today, in addition to providing much-needed support to the Navy's historical programs and its flagship United States Navy Museum in Washington, D.C., the Foundation collects oral histories of Navy veterans from World War II through the Cold War, and publishes articles and sponsors symposiums on important naval history topics. To provide increased access by the public to the Navy's historical collections of art, artifacts, documents, and photographs, the Foundation provides historical research and photo reproduction through its Historical Services Division.

USS Constitution *underway in Massachusetts Bay as the Blue Angels fly over. (Photo: Dick Arthur, Sippican, Inc.)*

Naval Historical Foundation
1306 Dahlgren Avenue, S.E.
Washington Navy Yard, D.C. 20374-5055
(202) 678-4333; fax (202) 889-3565
nhfwny@msn.com
http://www.mil.org/navyhist/

Published by Hugh Lauter Levin Associates, Inc.
© 2000 Naval Historical Foundation
Design: Lori S. Malkin
Project Editor: James O. Muschett
ISBN 0-88363-100-8
Printed in Hong Kong
Distributed by Publishers Group West

Contents

Preface 6
Rear Admiral W. J. Holland, Jr., USN (Ret)

The Prerogative of Sea Powers 8
Rear Admiral Alfred Thayer Mahan, USN

1775–1865

We Have Met the Enemy and They Are Ours
1775-1815 12
William M. Fowler, Jr.

Whose Flag Has Displayed in Distant Climes
1816-1860 28
Michael J. Crawford

Damn the Torpedoes! Full Speed Ahead!
The Civil War 44
Craig L. Symonds

1865–1941

You May Fire When Ready, Gridley
1865-1922 62
James C. Bradford

A Navy Second to None
1922-1941 74
Thomas C. Hone

1941–1945

Winning a Two-Ocean War
1941-1945 94
Paul Stillwell

1945–1991

Cold War to Violent Peace
1945-1991 144
Edward J. Marolda

THE FLEET TODAY

Today's Fleet—Forward from the Sea 202
Vice Admiral Robert F. Dunn, USN (Ret)
President, Naval Historical Foundation

Surface Action Starboard! 206
Captain Bruce R. Linder, USN (Ret)

Two Block Foxtrot!—U.S. Carrier Aviation 228
Captain Rosario Rausa, USNR (Ret)

Dive! Dive!
Submarines in the New World Order 250
Captain James H. Patton, USN (Ret)

Land the Landing Force!
Amphibious Assault at the Turn of the Millennium 266
Captain George Galdorisi, USN (Ret)

Mare Nostrum
Ocean Surveillance, Maritime Patrol, and Intelligence 278
Captain Andrew C. A. Jampoler, USN (Ret)

Weapons That Wait
Mine Warfare in the 21st Century 284
Rear Admiral Charles F. Horne III, USN (Ret)

Stealth from the Sea 288
Rear Admiral George R. Worthington, USN (Ret)

The Supporting Cast
Doctors . . . Lawyers . . . and Storekeeper Chiefs 292
Captain John Edward Jackson, Supply Corps, USN (Ret)

THE HERITAGE

Partakers of the Glory—Customs and Traditions . . . 314
Vice Admiral William P. Mack, USN (Ret)

Lest We Forget—Museums and Memorials 332
Rear Admiral Henry C. McKinney, USN (Ret)

Acknowledgments 344
Suggested Reading 345
Authors and Editors 346
Index 348

Preface

This book is a labor of love for the authors—most of whom have been associated with the United States Navy for most of their working lives. They endeavor to pay tribute to the people who have made the history, built the traditions, and continue to operate a grand institution that inspires their dedication and devotion.

The Navy is a big organization with many facets and a long, proud history. No one can know or tell the whole story. Each author tells his part in his own way. The common elements are the sea and the people.

The book aims to rekindle dreams and satisfy memories.

Welcome aboard!

Jerry Holland

"*I can imagine no more rewarding career. And any man who may be asked in this century what he did to make his life worthwhile, I think can respond with a good deal of pride and satisfaction: 'I served in the United States Navy.'*"

—PRESIDENT JOHN F. KENNEDY

Left: *(Photo: Harry Gerwien/MAI)*

Below: *USS* Pintado *(SSN 672) turns in the San Diego entrance channel off Ballast Point at dawn. North Island Naval Air Station is in the background, and the crib of the Degaussing Facility, Naval Station, San Diego, looms in the foreground. (Photo: Yogi Kaufman)*

The Prerogative of Sea Powers

"It is not the taking of individual ships or convoys, be they few or many, that strikes down the money power of a nation; it is the possession of that overbearing power on the sea which drives the enemy's flag from it, or allows it to appear only as a fugitive; and which, by controlling thee great common, closes the highways by which commerce moves to and from the enemy's shores. This overbearing power can only be exercised by great navies . . . when a question arises of control over distant regions, . . . it must ultimately be decided by naval power, by the organized military force afloat, which represents the communications that form so prominent feature in all strategy."

—ALFRED THAYER MAHAN, *THE INFLUENCE OF SEA POWER UPON HISTORY, 1660–1783*, 1890.

"Communications dominate war; broadly considered, they are the most important single element in strategy, political or military. In its control over them has lain the pre-eminence of sea power—as an influence upon the history of the past; and in this it will continue, for its attribute is inseparable from its existence. . . . The power, therefore, to insure these communications to one's self, and to interrupt them for an adversary, affects the very root of a nation's vigor. . . . This is the prerogative of the sea powers."

—ALFRED THAYER MAHAN, *THE PROBLEM OF ASIA*, 1900.

Top: *Rear Admiral Alfred Thayer Mahan, USN (1840–1914) is the intellectual father of the theories of sea power. Henry L. Stimson, Secretary of War during World War II, characterized his legacy as ". . . the peculiar psychology of the Navy Department, which frequently seemed to retire from the realm of logic into a dim religious world in which Neptune was God, Mahan his prophet, and the United States Navy the only true church."* (Photo: Naval Historical Center)

Left: *USS* Kansas *(BB 21) and USS* Vermont *(BB 20) lead the United States Fleet out of Hampton Roads, Virginia, in December 1907 on the first leg of a cruise around the world. The "Great White Fleet" marked the culmination of Mahan's exhortations and emphasized the entry of the United States into affairs beyond the Western Hemisphere.* (Photo: Naval Historical Center)

"We conduct forward naval operations both to ensure unimpeded use of the seas and to project American influence and power into the littoral areas of the world."

—ADMIRAL JAY JOHNSON, USN, CHIEF OF NAVAL OPERATIONS, *FORWARD . . . FROM THE SEA*, MARCH 1997.

Above: *The United States Third Fleet at anchor in Ulithi Atoll, Caroline Islands, shortly after the Battle of Leyte Gulf. This largest concentration of warships in history includes the battleships USS* New Jersey *(BB 62) and USS* Iowa *(BB 61) in the center and five* Essex-class *aircraft carriers moored in line beyond them. (Photo: Naval Historical Center)*

Right: *USS* Ohio *(SSBN 726) inbound to her homeport from a deterrent patrol at Submarine Base, Bangor, Washington, passes through the Hood Canal bridge. The ultimate in national influence and power, the Navy's ballistic missile submarines' role in the nation's strategic nuclear forces has continually increased since Admiral Arleigh Burke set in motion the design and construction of the ships and the missiles in 1958. Since well before the turn of the century, over half of all America's nuclear weapons have been based in these ships.*

1775-1865

We Have Met the Enemy and They Are Ours
1775-1815

William Fowler

The Revolution

Americans are a sea-minded people. From the earliest days of settlement they were drawn as much to the sea as to the land. The Atlantic was the green pasture where they went to fish. The sea was a barrier to enemies and an avenue to the mother country. They went to sea in wartime when merchants took commissions from royal governors and armed their ships to go "a privateering," attacking the enemies of the king in a mad scramble to grab rich prizes. By the eve of the American Revolution, one-third of all the tonnage in the British Empire was American built. Places such as Boston, New York, and Philadelphia were among the most important trading centers in England's Atlantic world.

In the tumultuous years leading to the Revolution merchants and sailors were the first to endure the brunt of Parliament's new taxes and onerous regulations, so it is not surprising that the seafarers were among the first to argue for American rights. It was natural that when protest turned to war Americans looked to the sea in their struggle for independence.

On 3 July 1775, George Washington took command of the American army at Cambridge, Massachusetts. A quick survey of the situation convinced the commander in chief of the need for naval action. As the general reflected on his naval options, elsewhere Americans were striking. Three hundred miles northeast of Boston at Machias, Maine, a group of "Sons of Liberty" led by Jeremiah O'Brien seized a royal survey vessel *Margaretta*. Buoyed by such boldness, Washington launched his own naval offensive.

Cut off on the land side by American forces, the British in Boston depended entirely upon the sea for supply. At his Cambridge headquarters, Washington read reports of unarmed British supply vessels carrying in food and munitions. By capturing these vessels he could supply his own army and starve the enemy. The general moved quickly. Colonel John Glover of the Marblehead regiment, a sea captain and merchant himself, offered the charter of his schooner *Hannah*. Men from Glover's "Webfoot regiment" rushed to sign on to crew the schooner. On the

Commissioned by Washington on 2 September 1775, Hannah *was the first vessel to sail under the authority of the Continental Congress. Her owner, John Glover, was organizer and colonel of the famous Marblehead Regiment that ferried Washington's forces across the Delaware to the victories at Trenton and Princeton. (Naval Historical Center)*

A delegate to the Continental Congress from Massachusetts, John Adams was a strong proponent for the creation of a navy. He wrote "Rules for the Regulation of the Navy of the United Colonies." He would continue to be a strong supporter during his term as second president of the United States (1797–1801). (Naval Historical Center)

Top: *Continental sailors and Marines landed on New Providence Island, Bahamas, on 3 March 1776. Their initial objective, Fort Montague, is in the left background. Close to the shore are the small ships that brought the landing force to the vicinity of the beach. From left, they are two sloops captured by the squadron, the schooner* Wasp, *and the sloop* Providence. *Other ships of the fleet are visible in the right distance. ("New Providence Invasion," V. Zveg, Navy Art Collection)*

Above: *Member of a prominent Rhode Island family, Ezek Hopkins was appointed commander in chief of the American fleet on 22 December 1775. He commanded the American expedition that raided Nassau, Bahamas, in March 1776.*

morning of 5 September 1775, *Hannah* hoisted sail under command of Nicholas Broughton and stood out from Beverly, bound east toward Cape Anne to prowl for British prey. *Hannah* was the first vessel to be commissioned in the Continental cause. Two days later she took her first prize, the British vessel *Unity*.

Hannah's triumph led Washington to commission additional vessels. Caught unaware, the British scrambled to defend their supply lines, but in the meantime Washington's pesky squadron took fifty-five prizes.

Encouraged by what was happening in the north, New England delegates in the Continental Congress pushed for the creation of an American fleet. John Adams was the leading advocate, but others in Congress, particularly southern delegates, thought the idea was mad, viewing it as a cynical scheme by which New Englanders sought to enrich themselves. As a compromise on 18 July 1775, Congress resolved that "each colony, at their own expense, make such provisions by armed vessels or otherwise for the protection of their harbours and navigation on their coasts." Eventually nearly every colony would create its own state navy, but these efforts were too weak and ineffectual to satisfy the more naval-minded Americans. Finally, after witnessing the success of Washington's efforts, Congress agreed to the formation of a Continental Navy, and on Friday, 13 October, they voted to dispatch two vessels to "cruise eastward." John Adams was joyous, and reported to his friend, James Warren, that in Congress he saw a "Seafaring Inclination."

John Adams was right, Congress did have a "Seafaring Inclination." Later in October they authorized additional ships. In November 1775 Congress created the Marine Corps and approved the first "Navy Regulations." In December they appointed Esek Hopkins commander in chief of the Continental Navy and appropriated money for the construction of thirteen frigates.

Congress's quick action caught the Royal Navy unaware, with few ships on the North American station. The Americans took quick advantage, and in March a Continental squadron under Hopkins raided Nassau in the Bahamas.

GREAT
ENCOURAGEMENT
FOR
SEAMEN.

ALL GENTLEMEN SEAMEN and able-bodied LANDSMEN who have a Mind to diftinguifh themfelves in the GLORIOUS CAUSE of their COUNTRY, and make their Fortunes, an Opportunity now offers on board the Ship RANGER, of Twenty Guns, (for FRANCE) now laying in PORTSMOUTH, in the State of NEW-HAMP-SHIRE, commanded by JOHN PAUL JONES Efq; let them repair to the Ship's Rendez-vous in PORTSMOUTH, or at the Sign of Commodore MANLEY, in SALEM, where they will be kindly entertained, and receive the greateft Encouragement.---The Ship RANGER, in the Opinion of every Perfon who has feen her is looked upon to be one of the beft Cruizers in AMERICA.----She will be always able to Fight her Guns under a moft excellent Cover ; and no Veffel yet built was ever calculated for failing fafter, and making good Weather.

Any GENTLEMEN VOLUNTEERS who have a Mind to take an agreable Voyage in this pleafant Seafon of the Year, may, by entering on board the above Ship RANGER, meet with every Civility they can poffibly expect, and for a further Encouragement depend on the firft Opportunity being embraced to reward each one agreable to his Merit.

All reafonable Travelling Expences will be allowed, and the Advance-Money be paid on their Appearance on Board.

IN CONGRESS, MARCH 29, 1777.

RESOLVED,

THAT the MARINE COMMITTEE be authorifed to advance to every able Seaman, that enters into the CONTINENTAL SERVICE, any Sum not exceeding FORTY DOLLARS, and to every ordinary Seaman or Landfman, any Sum not exceeding TWENTY DOLLARS, to be deducted from their future Prize-Money.

By Order of CONGRESS,

JOHN-HANCOCK, PRESIDENT.

DANVERS: Printed by E. RUSSELL, at the Houfe late the Bell-Tavern.

A broadside used to recruit seamen to sail aboard Ranger; *this poster quotes the authorization of the Continental Congress for advance payments "to be deducted from future prize money." This kind of advance, known as a "Dead Horse," still exists—now repaid from salary since prize money is extinct. Built in Portsmouth, New Hampshire,* Ranger *was commanded by John Paul Jones. (Library of Congress)*

Created by the French sculptor Jean Antoine Houdon, this is reputed to be the best likeness of John Paul Jones. Jones sailed to Europe in command of Ranger *and conducted a very successful campaign along the coasts of England and Scotland that included a raid on Whitehaven, close to his birthplace. (Naval Historical Center)*

Other Continental vessels sortied as well. Congress, however, chronically short on cash, had great difficulty finding resources to build and man the navy. While Congress grappled with these problems, the Royal Navy recovered from their unpreparedness, and the Admiralty dispatched additional forces to hunt down and destroy American vessels.

Continental vessels did not confine their cruising to American waters. In November 1776, *Reprisal*, under the command of Lambert Wickes, entered Quiberon Bay carrying the newly appointed minister to France, Benjamin Franklin. After landing Franklin, Wickes cruised European waters taking several enemy prizes. Other Continental captains ventured across the Atlantic, none achieving more fame and success than John Paul Jones.

On 23 September 1779, Jones, in command of the converted French East Indiaman *Duc de Duras*, renamed *Bonhomme Richard* in honor of his friend, Benjamin Franklin, encountered the Baltic fleet under the escort of HMS *Serapis* and HMS *Countess of Scarborough*. In a fierce battle Jones managed to come alongside and grapple with *Serapis*. In the midst of the carnage *Serapis*'s captain, Richard

15

Top: *William Elliott's famous painting depicts the conflict off the east coast of England near Flamborough Head in September 1779.* Bonhomme Richard *(left) under John Paul Jones met HMS* Serapis. *In a furious battle, Jones took* Serapis *even though the* Bonhomme Richard *later sank. (Naval Academy Museum)*

Above: *A sea captain from Rhode Island, Abraham Whipple commanded the Continental frigate* Providence. *In July 1779, he made one of the richest captures of the war when he intercepted a British convoy homeward bound from Jamaica. (Naval Academy Museum)*

Pearson, called over to ask if Jones intended to strike. The answer came back, "I have not yet begun to fight." Jones gained the victory even though he lost his ship.

Jones, Wickes, Hopkins, Whipple, and other Continental captains launched America's naval traditions. While the Continental Navy did not play a decisive role in the Revolution, these men set an example of skill, bravery, and dedication that would serve as a foundation not only for the establishment of the navy in the new republic but as the hallmark of that navy in the years afterward.

The Quasi War

The American Republic was born into a hostile world. Great Britain sought revenge, while the old ally, France, slipped into revolution and chaos. On the high seas American ships were harassed and attacked. Chief among the new enemies were the Barbary corsairs.

For generations North African seafarers sailing from Morocco, Algiers, Tunis, and Tripoli seized foreign merchantmen. Those who wished to pass through the Mediterranean had the choice of either paying tribute or fighting. American ships were not excepted. Since no American fighting ships existed, merchant ships were seized and their crews imprisoned and held for ransom. After several years of enduring these insults, Congress, prodded by President Washington, finally voted to build a navy to defend commerce, and on 27 March 1794 approved the construction of six frigates. Designed by Joshua Humphreys of Philadelphia, these ships were intended to be stronger and faster than any ships of their size in any navy.

Congress approved the frigates reluctantly, providing that should Algiers cease its depredations against American ships, construction on the frigates would cease. Less than a year after the six keels had been laid, word arrived that Algiers

had signed a treaty with the United States agreeing to allow American ships to pass unmolested. While peace may have been achieved with Algiers, Washington and others realized there was a continuing need to protect American trade, and so with some difficulty the president managed to effect a compromise. Congress agreed that three of the six frigates could be completed.

On 10 May 1797 the first of the frigates, USS *United States*, a frigate of forty-four guns, slipped into the water at Philadelphia. In September, USS *Constellation* was launched at Baltimore, and in October, USS *Constitution* went down the ways at Boston. The three remaining hulls were left on the stocks.

For the time being peace prevailed in the Mediterranean, but elsewhere more trouble brewed. The eruption of war between France and England in 1793 threw the world into turmoil. American policy was to remain neutral. Yet neither France nor Great Britain was inclined to respect American neutrality and both

Right and middle: *USS* Constellation *under the command of Captain Thomas Truxtun captured the French frigate* L'Insurgente *during a battle fought in the waters between the islands of St. Kitts and Nevis in the Caribbean. It was the most important naval battle of the Quasi War and is commemorated as part of the decoration in Memorial Hall at the U.S. Naval Academy. A display case below the painting contains the colors taken from* L'Insurgente *and other prizes during the Navy's early years. (Top: "USS* Constellation v. L'Insurgente," *Lithograph of a painting by John W. Schmidt, Naval Historical Center)*

Above: *Born in County Wexford, Ireland, John Barry was the senior captain in the Navy. He commanded the frigate* Alliance *in the last two years of the Revolutionary War. In 1781* Alliance *fought a brilliant action with two smaller British ships off Nova Scotia, capturing both. In the final action of the war, Barry successfully defended a specie convoy against two frigates. He commanded USS* United States *in the Quasi War. (Naval Historical Center)*

took every opportunity to harass American trade. The critical flash point was in the Caribbean where French privateers often fell upon American vessels. When American diplomats arrived in Paris seeking to negotiate a diplomatic relationship with the new French Republic, they were confronted with a series of humiliating demands, including one that insisted President Adams pay a "sweetener" to facilitate negotiations. The president angrily refused and set the nation on a course to defend its trade and honor by force.

Secretary of the Navy Benjamin Stoddert dispatched a number of vessels to the Caribbean to protect American trade. Among the ships sent south was the new frigate USS *Constellation* under the command of Captain Thomas Truxtun. On 9 February 1799, *Constellation* was running down toward the island of Nevis when at noon her lookout spotted a large vessel ten miles to the west-southwest. As Truxtun bore down on the stranger, he recognized her as the French frigate *L'Insurgente*. Truxtun maneuvered *Constellation* into a "Position for every shot to do Execution." The battle raged for an hour and a half before *L'Insurgente* struck. Almost a year later Truxtun distinguished himself again when *Constellation* engaged and defeated another French frigate, *La Vengeance*, off Guadeloupe.

By every measure the naval war with France was an outstanding success for the United States. More than eighty French ships had been taken, with the loss of only one American vessel. Such a succession of triumphs convinced the French of the futility of continuing the conflict, and on 30 September 1800, a convention was signed ending the war.

With peace restored, Congress wasted no time in dismantling the squadrons that had served so well. The new president, Thomas Jefferson, viewed the Navy as a needless and costly expense, preferring gunboats to frigates. At the very moment the president was urging naval reduction, however, an old adversary once again began to disrupt trade.

Barbary War

Peace with the Barbary States was always a fragile affair. Claiming that insufficient tribute had been paid, the bashaw of Tripoli declared war on the United States on 10 June 1801. Jefferson responded to the Tripolitans by dispatching Commodore Richard Dale with a squadron to the Mediterranean. Dale attempted to blockade Tripoli, but lack of water, spoiled provisions, and a growing sick list made his job difficult.

Dale achieved very little, and his successor Richard Valentine Morris managed to accomplish even less. But with the arrival of Commodore Edward Preble, the American squadron began to press hard on the Tripolitans. Preble's command consisted of the frigates *Constitution* and *Philadelphia* along with four smaller vessels, *Argus*, *Siren*, *Nautilus*, and *Vixen*. On 12 September 1804, *Constitution* with Preble on board arrived at Gibraltar. Having sent *Philadelphia* ahead to cruise off Tripoli on 12 November, Preble declared that port in a state of blockade. He then got underway to join the force sailing off Tripoli. En route he spoke with the British frigate HMS *Amazon*. She bore news of an American disaster.

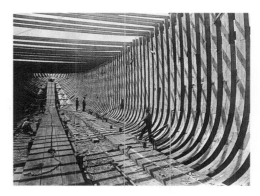

Constitution under construction in Boston. More than 1,500 trees were felled from Maine to Georgia to furnish materials. The scantlings or ribs were larger than other frigates, giving her a structural strength that led to the appellation, "Old Ironsides." (Photo: Library of Congress)

Grounded in Tripoli harbor in 1804, the frigate Philadelphia *was taken by the Tripolitans. A crew of volunteers commanded by Lieutenant Stephen Decatur sailed into the harbor, boarded the frigate and blew her up to prevent her from being used by the Tripolitans. Nelson characterized this action as, "the most bold and daring act of the age." ("Burning of the Frigate* Philadelphia," *Edward Moran, U.S. Naval Academy Museum)*

Edward Preble's aggressive actions against Tripoli pleased the American public. Like Nelson, he embued his junior officers with spirit and sense of "brotherhood." ("Edward Preble, Commodore USN," Rembrandt Peale, U.S. Naval Academy Museum)

Manned by a volunteer crew under the command of Richard Somers, Intrepid, *loaded with powder, sailed into Tripoli Harbor aiming to destroy shipping and injure the forts. Something went wrong; the ship exploded prematurely and all the crew were killed.*

Bottom, left to right: Probably Preble's most long-lasting contribution to the United States Navy was the example of courage, discipline, and training he set for the officers serving under him. These officers following the commodore's traditions became known as "Preble's Boys," and later each became famous in his own right.

ISAAC HULL (1773–1843). Hull served as a young lieutenant under Preble. He commanded USS Constitution *at the beginning of the War of 1812 and was her captain during her victory over HMS* Guerriere.

CHARLES STEWART (1778–1869). Stewart was another one of "Preble's Boys" serving in the Mediterranean. He later commanded USS Constitution *during her battle with HMS* Cyane *and HMS* Levant.

JAMES LAWRENCE (1781–1813). Lawrence was with Decatur at the burning of USS Philadelphia. *He died while commanding USS* Chesapeake *in her battle with HMS* Shannon, *1 June 1813.*

THOMAS MACDONOUGH (1783–1825). During the War of 1812 Macdonough commanded the American squadron on Lake Champlain and was the victor at the battle of Plattsburg, one of the most decisive naval victories in American history.

DAVID PORTER (1780–1843). Porter was among those captured when Philadelphia *fell into Tripolitan hands. He commanded the frigate USS* Essex *during the War of 1812 and took her into the Pacific Ocean.*

STEPHEN DECATUR (1779–1820). Perhaps the most well known of "Preble's Boys," Decatur became famous for his daring expedition to burn USS Philadelphia. *Commanding* United States *in the War of 1812, he took HMS* Macedonian *in a one-sided battle.*

WILLIAM BAINBRIDGE (1774–1833). Captain of USS Philadelphia *at the time of her capture, Bainbridge later commanded USS* Constitution *in her battle with HMS* Java *during the War of 1812. After the war he was assigned to command the Mediterranean squadron on board the seventy-four-gun USS* Independence.

USS *Philadelphia* under the command of William Bainbridge had entered Tripoli harbor in pursuit of a fleeing corsair. The wind was from the east and the American frigate was making a good eight knots. Running before the wind, cannons echoing, and an enemy about to be taken, all on board were drawn into the excitement. As his quarry scurried under the protection of Tripolitan shore batteries, Bainbridge came about and headed back toward open water. As he did so, he felt his ship shudder and grind to a stop. She was hard aground on a sloping ledge.

For hours Bainbridge did all he could to free his ship. Fire from the Tripolitans was intense, and finally, with no hope of getting off the shoal, Bainbridge ordered the colors struck. He and his crew were taken ashore and thrown into confinement.

In Tripolitan hands *Philadelphia* posed a serious threat. Considering it too risky to try to capture and bring her out, Preble's only alternative was to destroy her. Lieutenant Stephen Decatur stepped forward with a bold plan that called for slipping into the harbor on board the ketch *Intrepid*. At dusk *Intrepid* entered the harbor. Decatur and his men hid below while several crewmen, including an Italian pilot, stayed on deck disguised as Arab sailors. As they drew within hailing distance, the watch on the frigate challenged. The pilot responded in Arabic that they were from Malta and had lost their anchor in the recent gale and asked permission to tie up alongside the frigate until they could safely proceed. Foolishly the Tripolitans passed a hawser down to *Intrepid* and in a moment fifty American seamen were over *Philadelphia*'s gunwales. Within fifteen minutes Decatur and his men took the ship and set her afire. Escaping, Decatur and his shipmates could revel in what Admiral Lord Nelson called "the most bold and daring act of the age."

Preble tightened the blockade of Tripoli, launching a series of five attacks

against the port bringing his ships in close enough to deliver a series of devastating broadsides against shipping and the harbor's defenses. During this campaign, however, the squadron suffered another severe loss. Plucky *Intrepid* had been given a new mission. Under the command of Lieutenant Richard Somers, she was loaded to the gunwales with powder and sent into Tripoli harbor. The plan was for the crew to set the fuse and escape but something went awry. *Intrepid* blew up prematurely killing Somers and his entire crew.

Preble's determined assaults had weakened the Tripolitans. His successor, the new squadron commander Samuel Barron, set in motion the final campaign which involved an overland march from Egypt led by Marine Corps Lieutenant Presley O'Bannon and the American consul William Eaton. Faced with a threat from the land as well as bombardment from sea, the bashaw decided to parley. On 3 June 1805, a treaty of peace was signed in Barron's quarters on board *Constitution*.

War of 1812

Although President Thomas Jefferson was willing to take stern measures against threats from the Barbary corsairs, he was far less willing to support similar measures against the increasing hostile acts of Great Britain. Having virtually destroyed the French navy and merchant marine, Great Britain had command of the seas. The British goal was to isolate France and destroy her trade. Neutral nations such as the United States threatened this objective since they continued the trade once carried in French bottoms. Ships of the Royal Navy were ordered to intercept and seize suspected neutral traders.

The issue of impressment added to the rising distress between the United States and Great Britain. With the world's largest fleet, the Royal Navy had an insatiable appetite for men. Volunteers might be expected to fill some portion of this need, but they could never supply it completely. The only way for the service to maintain itself was by an age-old but detested custom of impressment, that is, forcing men into service.

Few questioned the right of the king's officers to impress British subjects off British ships; however, extending that right to American ships was a clear violation of sovereignty. Nonetheless, British warships stopped American merchant vessels on the high seas and forcibly removed American seamen. They justified their actions on the grounds that they were only removing men who had deserted from the Royal Navy.

While officers of the Royal Navy violated American rights at sea, on the western frontier British agents were busy instigating Indian attacks on American settlements. Both Presidents Jefferson and Madison tried through peaceful means to find solutions to the escalating crisis, while in Congress a rising chorus of "War Hawks" demanded stronger measures. Faced with British intransigence, the United States declared war on 18 June 1812. With a force of ten frigates, two sloops, six brigs, and a ragged assortment of schooners and gunboats the United States Navy faced the world's greatest seapower. The Royal Navy had nearly 1,000 ships.

Two weeks before the declaration of war, USS *Constitution* got underway from Annapolis bound for New York. The July winds were light off the New Jersey shore and the frigate was having difficulty keeping a northerly course. Informed that a British squadron was cruising the coast, *Constitution*'s captain Isaac Hull kept a keen watch. Early in the afternoon, *Constitution*'s lookout saw four sails to the north. When the strangers failed to answer recognition signals, Hull knew they were British. He ordered the frigate about and headed on a southeasterly course away from the enemy. The British took up the chase. Hull set every inch of

canvas, but the British gained. The frigate's small boats were lowered and the ship moved by kedging, dropping anchors far ahead and pulling in to make way. Through the night the men pulled on their oars. On the second day of the chase a squall line approached. Hull ordered the crew aloft, ready to take in sail, but only at the last possible moment so as to squeeze every zephyr available. The wind and rain hit, the sails were taken in, then just as quickly, the squall passed and Hull set sail again. As the squall moved astern of *Constitution*, it hid her from the enemy. The British did not react as fast or as well. They were quick to take in sail but slow to reset; their slackness left them farther astern. By the third day the British were nearly over the horizon. They gave up the pursuit. Hull tacked and headed north, wisely avoiding New York and sailing instead for Boston.

Having acquitted itself well in the first weeks of the war, the American navy was about to enjoy a streak of victories unknown to it in the past and rarely equaled since. From August through December 1812, the navy managed to humiliate the British in a series of battles that sent Britannia reeling. While Isaac Hull outsailed the British squadron, Captain David Porter, commanding USS *Essex*, wreaked havoc on British trade. Sailing from New York, *Essex* cruised for two months between Bermuda and Newfoundland and in that time took nine prizes including HMS *Alert*, the first British warship to surrender to the Americans.

Isaac Hull in USS *Constitution* forged an early link in this chain of victories. On Sunday, 2 August, with clear weather and a kindly tide *Constitution* slipped down Boston harbor bound north to cruise the waters off Newfoundland and the Gulf of St. Lawrence and then south to Bermuda. On the afternoon of 2 August

In the war's first battle between frigates, USS Constitution *gained a decisive victory over HMS* Guerriere. *The loss of* Guerriere *was a shock to the British. The sense of shock was compounded by subsequent defeats in frigate and sloop actions. ("USS* Constitution *and HMS* Guerriere," *Michael F. Corne, U.S. Naval Academy Museum)*

David Porter took the frigate USS Essex *into the Pacific in February 1813. For over a year he terrorized the British whaling fleet. HMS* Cherub *and HMS* Phoebe *finally caught up and overwhelmed* Essex *in Chilean waters outside Valpariso. Porter had complained without success about outfitting* Essex *with short-range carronades vice long guns. The desire to save money cost Porter any chance of putting up a battle with foes who remained out of range of his guns while battering* Essex *into splinters. (Capt. William B. Hoff, Naval Historical Center)*

Constitution's lookout identified a large ship to leeward. Hull closed on her. The stranger was the British frigate HMS *Guerriere*, commanded by Captain James Dacres. For more than two and a half hours *Constitution* and *Guerriere* slugged it out. Maneuvering around his opponent Hull managed to deliver a series of smashing broadsides. The carnage was horrendous. Within a few minutes, *Guerriere* lost her mizzen mast. At 6:20, according to Dacres's account, *Guerriere* lost her fore and main masts. She was, Dacres wrote, "a perfect, unmanageable wreck." A few minutes later *Guerriere* struck. In the midst of the battle an American seaman is reported to have seen a British ball strike *Constitution*'s side and fall harmlessly into the water. Upon which he yelled, "Huzzah, her sides are made of iron!" From that came "Old Ironsides."

Hull's victory set the example for other American officers and helped charge them with an aggressive spirit. On 25 October the frigate USS *United States*, commanded by Stephen Decatur, captured HMS *Macedonian*, and on 29 December, *Constitution*, now commanded by William Bainbridge, took HMS *Java* off the coast of Brazil. David Porter, still commanding the frigate USS *Essex*, took the war around Cape Horn into the Pacific, where he virtually destroyed the British whaling fleet.

Stung by these American victories, the Royal Navy dispatched more ships to the North American station and gave strict orders that no British frigate was to engage an American frigate alone. Gradually the weight of numbers began to tell, as additional British vessels took up their blockading stations off the American coast, making it increasingly difficult for the U.S. Navy to get to sea.

USS Porter *(DDG 78) is the fifth ship named after David Porter, hero of the War of 1812, and his son, David Dixon Porter, last commander of the Federal riverine flotilla during the Civil War. With few exceptions, American destroyers have been named for naval heroes. These names perpetuate a heritage of courage, accomplishment, and commitment.*

Above: *This reproduction of the figurehead of HMS* Macedonian *sits in front of Mahan Hall at the U.S. Naval Academy. The guns on the monument are carronades from the* Macedonian; *her British colors are now displayed in Mahan Hall.*

Right: *Anchored bow to stern in Plattsburg Bay, New York, Macdonough's squadron awaited the British attack. At a severe tactical disadvantage, the British took heavy losses and were forced to retreat on both the lake and the land, ending the threat of invasion from Canada. ("Battle of Plattsburg," Edward Tufnell, Naval Historical Center)*

Perry's flagship at the Battle of Lake Erie wore a banner bearing Lawrence's words. This flag is now enshrined in the Memorial Hall at the U.S. Naval Academy.

HMS *Shannon*, commanded by Captain Philip Vere Brooke, blockaded Boston. On 1 June 1813, the American frigate *Chesapeake*, under the command of James Lawrence, left the port to challenge *Shannon*. From her masthead *Chesapeake* flew a pennant proclaiming "Free Trade and Sailors' Rights." Just outside the harbor the two frigates engaged. At a distance of less than 150 feet they exchanged furious broadsides. In the midst of the battle *Chesapeake* lost headway, *Shannon* sailed into a raking position and sent devastating fire along the full length of *Chesapeake*'s spar deck. Lawrence fell mortally wounded and was taken below issuing his last command, "Don't Give Up the Ship." Within a few minutes however, *Chesapeake* surrendered.

Chesapeake's loss was a severe blow to the American navy, but Lawrence's heroism inspired his brother officers, including the American commander on Lake Erie, Oliver Hazard Perry. At the outbreak of the war both the Americans and the British planned invasions across the Canadian border. For both, the key to moving men and material in either direction was control of the Great Lakes, particularly Lakes Ontario, Erie, and Champlain. On Ontario the British established their base at Kingston. Across the lake the Americans, under the command of Isaac Chauncy, built their establishment at Sackett's Harbor, New York. In their race to control Lake Ontario the British and Americans reached a rough balance, neither could build enough ships to overwhelm the other. In the face of such a stalemate both sides saw more advantage to preserving their fleets than in risking them in a climactic battle. Such was not the case on Lake Erie, where an aggressive and able American commander, Oliver Hazard Perry, faced a British force with no choice but to fight or die.

Perry arrived at Erie, Pennsylvania, on 27 March 1813. There he found a bustling yard with several vessels already under construction. Under his direction work proceeded briskly, and by early August Perry had his fleet on the lake and ready for service. Opposing him was a British squadron under the command of Captain Robert Barclay. On the afternoon of 9 September, the British left their base and sailed out onto the lake seeking battle.

After dawn on 10 September the two fleets came into sight of one another near Put In Bay. Barclay bore up to the Americans, but then the wind shifted, giving the Americans the weather gage. From the topmast of his flagship USS *Lawrence* Perry flew a pennant emblazoned with the motto, "Don't Give Up the Ship."

For more than two hours the battle raged, in the words of Captain Barclay, "with great fury." *Lawrence* took the brunt of the combat on the American side and

in the midst of battle Perry had to shift his flag to USS *Niagara*. Although *Lawrence* was put out of action, when *Niagara* came up, the Americans quickly gained the advantage. By three in the afternoon, Barclay realized his situation was hopeless. To continue resistance in the face of such overwhelming force was suicide. He hauled his flag down from his flagship HMS *Detroit*. The rest of his squadron followed suit. Within an hour of his victory Perry wrote the area commander, General William Henry Harrison, "We have met the enemy and they are ours."

Unlike Ontario and Erie, where very little of crucial naval importance took place before the War of 1812, Lake Champlain had a colorful and violent past. It was a critical link in the Hudson River–Lake Champlain corridor running between Canada and the United States. In the summer of 1814 the British launched a major invasion along this route. The American naval force on the lake was commanded by Lieutenant Thomas Macdonough. Since his arrival in late 1812, he had been busy building vessels and engaging the enemy. British General George Prevost was a cautious man who demanded that his naval forces take control of the lake before he would commit his troops. George Downie, the British naval commander on the lake, was reluctant to sail with a squadron he felt was unequal to the task. Prevost, however, would hear no excuses and the general ordered Downie down the lake. Anticipating the British movement, Macdonough had wisely taken his squadron

Oliver Hazard Perry's squadron met the British under Captain Robert Barclay near Put In Bay, Ohio, on Lake Ontario. Every ship in the British squadron was taken, prompting Perry to send his famous message, "We have met the enemy and they are ours." (Naval Historical Center)

Below, left: *Leading the American squadron, USS* Lawrence, *Perry's flagship, was battered for nearly two hours. Lawrence was so badly damaged that Perry was forced to shift his flag to USS* Niagara. *("Battle of Lake Erie," William H. Powell, Naval Historical Center)*

Below, right: *The United States Brig* Niagara, *Perry's final flagship in the Battle of Lake Erie was scuttled in 1820 but raised in 1913 and rebuilt three times since. Returned to the water as an active sailing ship in 1990, she now operates out of the Erie Maritime Museum, Erie, Pennsylvania.*

180 miles east of Madeira, Captain Charles Stewart in USS Constitution *defeated HMS* Cyane *(right) and HMS* Levant *(left). Stewart displayed remarkable seamanship in outmaneuvering his two adversaries. ("USS* Constitution *Capturing HMS* Cyane *and HMS* Levant," *Carlton T. Chapman, Naval Historical Center)*

Memorial Hall at the Naval Academy contains this mural of USS Constitution's *victory over HMS* Cyane *and HMS* Levant. *Colors captured from these ships are displayed below the murals.*

into the confines of Plattsburg Bay to await the arrival of the enemy. When British troops reached a point near Plattsburg, Prevost halted and insisted that Downie attack Macdonough before he would move his army any farther.

On Sunday morning, 11 September 1814, the wind was light from the north, the sky was clear, and there was a bit of an early fall chill in the air. Not long after breakfast Macdonough received a signal from his lookout—"Enemy in sight." Macdonough was in a strong position. The British squadron would have to tack north into the wind to come alongside him. As a result only a few of their cannon could be brought to bear on the Americans while Macdonough, having rigged spring lines, could turn his ships allowing him to use all his guns to rake the advancing enemy ships. The British were mauled badly. One of their vessels ran aground while a second lost control and drifted through the American fleet. Downie was among the first to be killed. By noon the battle was over and the entire British squadron was in American hands. Prevost wasted little time in retreating back to Canada.

Perry and Macdonough had slammed the northern doors shut to British invasion. Two other possibilities remained—Chesapeake Bay and New Orleans. In September 1814, a British amphibious force landed and burned Washington, but then failed to take Baltimore's Fort McHenry and had to retreat. On 8 January 1815, the last entry to America was denied the enemy when General Andrew Jackson thrashed the British army at New Orleans and sent them scurrying back down to the Gulf of Mexico.

Jackson's victory came after the treaty of peace ending the war had been signed Christmas eve in Ghent, Belgium. Since it would take months for the news to reach American ships on distant stations, New Orleans was not the only battle to take place after the signing of the treaty.

On 20 February 1815, USS *Constitution* under the command of Charles Stewart was sailing off the Madeira Islands. At one in the afternoon the frigate's lookout sighted a sail toward the southwest. Stewart took up the chase and within an hour another sail was spotted. The first vessel sighted was HMS *Cyane*, a small frigate of thirty-four guns. The second was HMS *Levant*, a corvette of twenty-two guns. Taken together these two vessels could muster a slight advantage over *Constitution* in broadside weight, but such an edge hinged entirely on their being in complete cooperation and concert during the battle.

Without hesitation Stewart set out in chase. *Levant* and *Cyane* maneuvered for the windward position; failing that, they shortened sail and went into a line formation to await *Constitution*'s arrival. At 6:05 Stewart ranged up along the starboard side of *Cyane* and let loose with a broadside, which was ably answered by both enemies. For fifteen minutes the battle raged, "then [with] the fire of the enemy beginning to slacken and the great column of smoke clearing away we found ourselves abreast of the headmost ship, the sternmost ship luffing up for our larboard quarter." At this point Stewart was in danger of being pinned between the two. He acted quickly, pouring a broadside into the forward ship; then, backing his sails, he moved his frigate rearward to come abreast the ship astern, filling her with a broadside. The ballet continued, with Stewart displaying extraordinary ship handling, maneuvering between the two ships while hammering them with his guns. At 6:50 *Cyane* lowered her flag. With her consort lost, *Levant* made her best to leeward. By eight Stewart had finished his business with *Cyane* and took up the chase. *Cyane* crowded all sail and tried to make good an escape. With her bow chasers thundering, *Constitution* took up the pursuit. The American gunners did their work skillfully, and repeatedly sent well-directed shot tearing through the rigging. It was hopeless. At ten *Levant* signaled surrender. Stewart's masterful ship-handling had won an extraordinary victory.

The final naval battle of the war took place on the most distant station possible. On 30 June 1815, in the Straits of Sunda the American brig USS *Peacock*

fell upon the British East India Company armed vessel *Nautilus*. *Peacock*'s captain, Lewis Warrington, refused to listen when the East Indiaman tried to explain that the war was over. Warrington suspected a ruse and delivered a broadside. *Nautilus* struck. After examining papers on board *Nautilus*, Warrington was convinced that indeed the war was over and he returned *Nautilus* to her captain.

Algiers

Taking advantage of America's preoccupation, early in 1815 the dey of Algiers once more let loose his corsairs to molest American ships. Less than a week after proclaiming peace with Great Britain, President James Madison asked Congress to declare war against Algiers. They complied, expecting a quick and easy victory. With several ships ordered during the war now ready, and those blockaded finally released, Madison had at his disposal enough vessels for two powerful squadrons. One was put under the command of Commodore Stephen Decatur, and the other under Commodore William Bainbridge, who was to hoist his flag in the new seventy-four-gun USS *Independence*, the first American ship of the line to get to sea.

Decatur got underway ahead of Bainbridge. Led by the new frigate USS *Guerriere* sailing as flagship, his squadron included USS *Constellation*, USS *Macedonian*, and a number of smaller vessels. On 17 June, off Cape de Gata, *Constellation*'s lookout called down to the deck that he saw a large ship in the distance, soon identified as the Algerian frigate *Meshuda*, forty-six guns. Three of the American squadron were able to draw within range and engage. Shortly after their captain was cut in two by a shot from *Guerriere*, the crew of *Meshuda* hauled down their flag. *Meshuda*'s capture was the only important battle of this very short war. On 30 June Decatur signed a treaty, and after a few port visits in the Mediterranean he was back in New York by early November. Matters had gone so well and so quickly that Bainbridge's force was never involved.

The return to America of Decatur's squadron marked the end of an era. Since its founding the United States had been almost constantly embroiled in war, wars that imperiled the very existence of the nation. That was now past, independence was vindicated, and the American Republic was firmly established as a national entity with which to be reckoned. Much of the credit must go to the navy of the new republic.

The last act of the era of sailing-ship warfare ended with the American Mediterranean Squadron anchored off Algiers during negotiations with the dey of Algiers. The show of force resulted in a peace treaty and ended the wars with the Barbary States. USS Guerriere, *flagship of Commodore Stephen Decatur, is in the center. ("Decatur at Algiers, 1815," The Mariners' Museum, Newport News)*

President James Madison dispatched a powerful squadron under Decatur after Algeria declared war on the United States in 1815. After Decatur's squadron, led by USS Guerriere *(left), captured the Algerian ship* Meshuda, *on 17 June 1815, Tripoli quickly made peace. ("Capture of* Meshuda," *Irwin Bevan, The Mariners' Museum, Newport News)*

Whose Flag Has Displayed in Distant Climes
1816-1860

Michael J. Crawford

B etween the end of the War of 1812 and the beginning of the Civil War, the United States underwent remarkable growth. U.S. territory increased from 1.8 to 3 million square miles; U.S. population rose from 8.5 to 31.5 million; and the value of U.S. exports escalated from 82 million to 400 million dollars. During the same era, the United States Navy expanded modestly, while maturing into an organization capable of serving the needs of a dynamic and ambitious people. President Andrew Jackson lauded the Navy for the way it represented America's glory abroad in peaceful and warlike pursuits alike, when, in his first inaugural address on 4 March 1829 he spoke with poetic cadence of "our Navy, whose flag has displayed in distant climes our skill in navigation and our fame in arms."

American presidents dispatched naval forces worldwide to protect and promote the national interests, in particular the nation's expanding maritime commerce. The secretaries of the Navy entrusted naval officers with wide discretion to exercise diplomacy or force in the pursuit of national goals. The most impressive result of that exercise was the opening of Japan, which had been closed to foreign influence for centuries. U.S. squadrons established a regular presence in the Mediterranean, off Africa and South America, in the Pacific, and in Asia. The Navy carried out a variety of combat missions, suppressing piracy, enforcing anti-slave trade laws and international agreements, fighting the Seminoles in the swamps of Florida, and winning the war with Mexico.

Possessing a diversity of skills and interests, members of its officer corps made significant contributions to science in the fields of geography, astronomy, navigation, oceanography, and ordnance. During this period, reformers sought to keep the Navy progressive: giving younger officers better hope for promotion; making enlisted service more attractive; improving training; strengthening the administrative structure; and modernizing propulsion, ordnance, and ship design.

This painting of the frigate USS Congress *and the sidewheel steamer USS* Susquehanna *at Naples, Italy, in 1857—the frigate launched in 1841 and the steamer in 1850—illustrates the U.S. Navy's gradual and unhurried transition from sail to steam. (Tomas De Simone, Navy Art Collection)*

Opposite: *Ship of the line USS* Pennsylvania, *anchored off Norfolk Navy Yard. Carrying 120 guns,* Pennsylvania *was the largest sailing ship built for the U.S. Navy. Although her keel was laid in 1821, she was not launched until 1837. During her career, she made only one voyage on the high seas. (Naval Historical Center)*

Above: *Commissioned captain in 1806, Charles Stewart (1778–1869) became the senior officer in the U.S. Navy in 1851, when he was seventy-three years old. He retired as a rear admiral at age eighty-four. (Naval Historical Center)*

Above, right: *In this daguerreotype taken while he was attending the Naval Academy (1853–1856), John Grimes Walker wears the regulation uniform of a midshipman. (Naval Historical Center)*

The War of 1812 convinced Americans of the value of the Navy to the nation's defense, and the burgeoning of seaborne commerce persuaded most that a navy was essential to her economy. Thus, Congress provided for the gradual increase of the Navy. Yet, because few Americans saw a need of a fleet any larger than sufficient to protect commerce in peacetime, naval expansion remained modest. By 1854, when the Navy built its last sail-only warship, the sloop of war *Constellation*, the fleet had grown to include ten ships of the line, thirteen frigates, twenty sloops of war, four brigs, a schooner, and fifteen steam frigates. The authorized personnel strength of the Navy increased proportionately with the size of the fleet, more than doubling from 4,000 in 1820 to nearly 8,900 in 1854.

Recognizing the burden of work that war lay on the Secretary of the Navy, in 1815 Congress established a Board of Navy Commissioners to assist with the administration of naval affairs. The board consisted of three senior naval officers, on whose technical expertise the civilian head of the Department of the Navy could call. Under the Secretary of the Navy, the board was responsible for the procurement of naval stores and materials; the building, arming, equipping, and repairing of warships; and the superintending of navy yards and stations. The Secretary retained direct responsibility over personnel, discipline, and operations.

The conservative board eventually became a hindrance to efficiency and innovation. In 1842, Congress replaced it with a structure more fitted to the management of a complex organization in the course of adopting new technology. Throughout the remainder of the nineteenth century, the Secretary of the Navy would administer the department through experts, either civilians or naval officers, at the heads of bureaus. In 1842, the bureaus numbered five: Navy Yards and Docks; Construction, Equipment, and Repair; Provisions and Clothing; Ordnance and Hydrography; and Medicine and Surgery.

During the decades preceding the Civil War, officer promotion proceeded at a glacial pace. Congress, fearing aristocratic tendencies in the Navy, refused to create the rank of admiral, leaving captain the highest rank in the naval service. Since no system of retirement existed to clear the way for officers with less seniority, officers of the War of 1812 monopolized the upper echelons of the Navy into old age. By the 1850s, Navy rolls listed commanders sixty years of age and men in their fifties still in the rank of lieutenant.

Addressing a rising chorus of criticism, in 1855 Congress provided for the so-called Plucking Board, the Naval Efficiency Board, consisting of fifteen officers selected from every grade between commodore and lieutenant. The board examined the qualifications of line officers from captains down to passed midshipmen and recommended to the president those it deemed "incapable of performing promptly and efficiently all their duty both ashore and afloat." The board recommended removal of some officers from the rolls, and some others for a newly created reserve list. Those on the reserve list, as well as those removed, were not counted against the total for each grade, thus opening a position for the promotion of a deserving junior. The result, after the affected officers took the opportunity to appeal the board's decisions, was that 137 officers were removed from the active list, creating the potential of promoting an equal number.

In 1861, Congress allowed officers to retire after forty years of duty and required them to do so after forty-five years or on attaining the age of sixty-two. Under this system, the Department of the Navy could assign officers on the retired list to shore duty.

Discontented staff officers lobbied for assimilation of rank and uniform with those of the line, who, for their part, opposed assimilation as an affront to their own rank. Eventually, secretaries of the Navy sided with the staff officers, granting rank to members of the Medical Corps in 1846, to pursers in 1847, and to engineers in

The U.S. Naval Academy was founded by George Bancroft in 1845 on the site of Fort Severn, Annapolis, Maryland. Thus began the systematic training of officers which before then had been the responsibility of individual ship captains. ("Naval Academy, Annapolis, Maryland, c. 1855," W.R. Miller, Naval Historical Center)

During the antebellum period, petty officers like Quartermaster Frederick Boyer, USN, were the backbone of the Navy. Yet little is known about them as a group. (Henry C. Flagg, U.S. Naval Academy Museum)

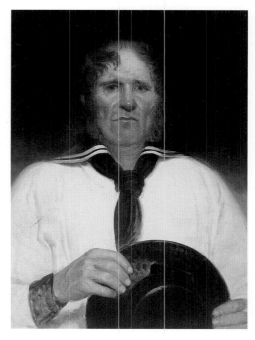

USS Colorado *and USS* Hartford *are followed by USS* Franklin *and USS* Powhatan *in this painting by Fred S. Cozzens. The ships reflect the transition from sail to steam just before the start of the Civil War. Coal fired propulsion plants required prodigious amounts of fuel so most cruising was done under sail. (U.S. Naval Academy Museum)*

A sailor from USS Constitution *and a new recruit exchange toasts. In the antebellum Navy, officers of each ship recruited their own crews by setting up rendezvous in port towns, typically at inns, taverns, and saloons. ("Toasting the New Recruit," George H. Comegys, Naval Historical Center)*

1859. Naval constructors would receive rank and pay as U.S. naval officers in 1866.

In 1842, after three successive secretaries of the Navy had appointed a record 219 midshipmen, raising the total to an unprecedented 490, Congress prohibited the appointment of midshipmen until the number had been reduced to 260. Up to that time, the educational program for midshipmen had been loosely structured. Their principal education derived from practical experience on board ship and from professors of mathematics, who gave training in navigation.

In 1845 a movement for the systematic training of aspiring naval officers led to the establishment of the United States Naval Academy at Annapolis.

After the War of 1812, increasingly harsh working conditions drove middle-class Americans away from the merchant marine. These changing conditions elicited the sympathies of social reformers who sought to improve the lot of sailors through temperance boarding houses, seamen's savings banks, employment registers, schools for seamen and their children, and religious services specifically for sailors. Social reform in the Navy related closely to the movement to improve the lot of the merchant sailor. Naval reformers sought to make naval service more attractive to Americans of the respectable classes. Reforms touched the enlisted men in the areas of education, temperance, and discipline.

The Navy experimented with a system of apprenticeship to attract American boys to naval service and increase the reservoir of trained American-born seamen. With parental consent, boys between the ages of thirteen and eighteen enlisted until they attained the age of twenty-one. Commanding officers were to see that they were instructed in reading, writing, and arithmetic, and employed in such a manner as to learn seamanship.

Until 1842, every seaman in the United States Navy was entitled to a half-pint of distilled spirits each day. Usually, the Navy issued the spirit ration in the form of grog, whisky mixed with water. Temperance advocates held that the spirit ration

Left: *Flogging a crewman, 1848. Sketch by Captain's Clerk Charles F. Sands, from his journal kept on board USS* Porpoise. *(Naval Historical Center)*

Philosophically opposed to corporal punishment, Commodore Uriah P. Levy experimented with alternative, and often controversial, forms of discipline. In this portrait, he holds a scroll attesting to his leading role in the abolition of flogging in the Navy. (Naval Historical Center)

encouraged inebriation and alcoholism, which drew in their wake a host of evils, personal and social. To encourage temperance on board naval vessels, in 1831 Secretary of the Navy Levi Woodbury allowed sailors to receive a money payment in place of the spirit ration. In 1842 the Navy reduced the spirit ration to a quarter pint and denied it to men under twenty-one years of age. Finally, in 1862, Congress put an end to the spirit ration.

Corporal punishment was the most common means of enforcing discipline in the early U.S. Navy. In flogging, the chief form of corporal punishment, a cat-o-nine-tails, a whip composed of nine knotted ropes, was applied to the bare back. Its defenders considered flogging swift and effective, while, in contrast to confinement, it quickly returned a sailor to duty. The majority of naval officers, and probably most enlisted as well, believed that flogging was the only practical means of enforcing discipline on board ship. Reformers, on the contrary, maintained that seamen were rational beings capable of being persuaded to obedience by appeals to patriotism and pride. Punishments that degraded men, reformers contended, were undemocratic and encouraged sullen compliance rather than ready obedience. Congress abolished corporal punishment in the Navy in 1850. In 1855 Congress provided the summary court-martial as a means of administering prompt justice for minor offenses, and created the honorable discharge as a way to recognize good behavior.

During the antebellum period, innovations in propulsion and ordnance began the revolutionary transformation of the Navy. The Navy entered the era using the

traditional technology of wooden sailing ships, armed with smoothbore cast-iron guns firing solid shot. On the eve of the Civil War, the Navy was in the course of adopting the new technology of iron-hulled steamships, armed with rifled wrought-iron shell guns.

The Navy built its first steam-powered warship during the War of 1812. This was the *Demologos*—renamed *Fulton* following the death of its designer, Robert Fulton—a catamaran with the steam engine and paddle wheel located between the two hulls. Not until 1837, however, did the Navy build its second steam warship, *Fulton II*, and only in 1842 did it launch steam warships capable of service at sea, USS *Mississippi* and USS *Missouri*. Even then, steam remained a form of propulsion auxiliary to the wind-powered sails. Early steam warships cruised under sail, conserving coal, but fought under steam. Steam power revolutionized naval tactics, for maneuvering no longer depended on the direction and strength of the wind.

Although by the 1840s thousands of commercial steam vessels plied America's waters, the Navy had practical reasons for delaying its adoption of steam power. Early steam engines were unreliable and dangerous, and coal consumption was so inefficient as to limit severely a ship's cruising range. Moreover, paddle wheels interfered with placement of armament in broadside, were vulnerable to enemy fire, and made vessels ungainly sailers.

More reliable and efficient engines and the screw propeller, which did away with the awkward paddle wheels, eventually made steam power practical for naval vessels. In 1843, the Navy commissioned USS *Princeton*, the world's first screw-propelled naval steam ship. Because her screw as well as all her steam machinery were below the water line—another "first"—*Princeton*'s means of propulsion were protected from enemy shot and out of the way of her own broadside.

Above: *Launched in 1843, USS* Princeton *was the first warship in the U.S. Navy equipped with a screw propeller. This allowed placing all machinery below the water line. Other innovations included steam driven blowers, anthracite coal as fuel, and a telescoping funnel. (Library of Congress)*

Opposite, top: *U.S. steam frigate* Mississippi *is depicted here in the Gulf of Mexico, in March 1847, during the campaign against Vera Cruz in the Mexican War.* Mississippi *later served as Matthew C. Perry's flagship on his mission to open Japan to trade with the United States, 1852–1854. (Naval Historical Center)*

Opposite, bottom: *Drydock Number 1 in the New York Navy Yard, shown here under construction in 1849, could accommodate ships up to 350 feet in length, 66 feet in beam, and 26 feet in draft. (Naval Historical Center)*

The introduction of steam propulsion stimulated innovation in ordnance. Because the paddle wheel limited the number of guns that could be placed in broadside, navies sought ways to make the fewer guns more powerful. The traditional cast-iron gun was liable to burst with powder charges larger than needed for shot greater than thirty-two pounds. In the 1840s, the U.S. Navy experimented with large wrought-iron guns, with mixed results. In the early 1850s, Commander John A. Dahlgren found a solution to the problem of building a powerful gun that possessed sufficient strength without being excessively heavy. The gun he developed was thickest at the breech, where the pressure of the expanding gases produced by the exploding powder was greatest. The barrel tapered toward the muzzle, as the pressure diminished, thus lessening the weight of the gun. By the end of the decade, the Navy had adopted Dahlgren's 9- and 11-inch, smoothbore, "bottle-shaped" guns, capable of firing solid shot or shell, as the major armament of many of its ships. Pivot guns, rifled cannon, and improved exploding shells were other naval ordnance innovations introduced in the years before the Civil War.

During the antebellum era, with peace prevailing in Europe, the principal missions of the U.S. Navy proved to be the protection of commerce, suppression of piracy, enforcement of anti-slave trade laws and agreements, and the promotion of diplomacy. For these missions, not ships of the line but maneuverable sloops and schooners that could operate in shallow bays and streams were best suited.

To protect the nation's world-ranging merchant ships, as well as whalers, the Navy stationed squadrons in the Mediterranean, in the West Indies, off west Africa, in the Pacific, off Brazil, and in the East Indies. Vessels of the squadrons generally did not act in unison, but patrolled individually, reporting regularly to the flagship.

Pirates infested the Caribbean and Gulf of Mexico, important markets for U.S. products, during the disorders of the wars of independence in Spanish America. Beginning in 1821, the U.S. West Indies Squadron pursued a vigorous campaign that by 1826 effectively suppressed West Indian piracy.

Congress in 1800 outlawed the participation of U.S. ships and crews in the transportation of Africans as slaves to Cuba and Brazil; in 1808 it forbade the importation of slaves into the United States; and in 1820 it made involvement of U.S. citizens in the international slave trade an act of piracy punishable by death. Congress assigned the U.S. Navy the responsibility of enforcing these laws, which became a primary task of the African and Brazil squadrons. In 1819, the Slave Trade Act authorized the president to cooperate with the private American Colonization Society in the resettlement in Africa of Africans found in illegal slavers. As a consequence, U.S. naval officers Robert F. Stockton, a founding member of the society, and Matthew C. Perry were directly involved in the establishment of the black republic of Liberia in West Africa. After 1842, the Navy stepped up its anti-slavery patrols, in accordance with the Webster-Ashburton Treaty between the United States and the United Kingdom. Under the treaty's terms, each nation pledged itself to maintain a certain number of anti-slavery

Above, left: *U.S. sloop of war USS* Constellation, *as flagship of the African Squadron from 1859 to 1861, captured three slavers, the brigs* Delicia *and* Triton, *and, depicted here, the bark* Cora. *(Arthur Disney, Naval Historical Center)*

Above: *Robert F. Stockton (1795–1866) served as a naval officer in the War of 1812, the war with Algiers, and the anti-piracy and anti-slave trade campaigns. During the Mexican War, he took a leading part in the conquest of California. He promoted advances in naval ordnance and steam propulsion. After resigning his commission, Stockton was elected to the U.S. Senate, where he introduced the bill abolishing flogging in the Navy. (H.B. Hall, Naval Historical Center)*

Above: *On 11 July 1853 USS* Mississippi's *cutter forced its way through a fleet of Japanese boats while surveying the Bay of Tokyo, Japan. This and similar displays of firmness helped convince Japanese authorities of Commodore Matthew C. Perry's seriousness of intent in negotiating a treaty. ("Perry Expedition to Japan," W.H. Brown, Naval Historical Center)*

Right: *Halftone of a sketch by a Japanese artist of a meeting between the Japanese and the Americans, 8 March 1854. Commodore Matthew C. Perry is fifth from the left. (Naval Historical Center)*

The Jeanette Monument in the U.S. Naval Academy Cemetary commemorates the heroism of the Navy personnel during an Arctic exploration expedition in 1879. After the ship foundered, only one boat, commanded by Chief Engineer George Melville, reached safety in Siberia. Melville became the Chief Engineer of the Navy in 1887 and served until 1903.

cruisers off West Africa. The British found such an agreement desirable because the United States objected to the Royal Navy's stopping and examining vessels flying the U.S. flag.

The Navy employed force to protect, and diplomacy to promote, the interests of American merchants. In a typical punitive expedition, a force of 282 seamen and marines from the frigate *Potomac* landed at Quallah Battoo, on the west coast of Sumatra, in 1832. They killed more than one hundred of the defenders and burned the town as punishment for the massacre of many of the crew of the merchant ship *Friendship*, of Salem, Massachusetts, and the plundering of the ship the previous year. In 1856, Chinese officials interpreted the landing of American forces to protect the American warehouses in Canton as cooperation with the British, with whom the Chinese were then in armed conflict. In retaliation, the barrier forts on the Pearl River between Canton and Wampoa opened fire on USS *San Jacinto*, flagship of the East India Squadron. The squadron's guns and landing parties of sailors and Marines silenced the guns of the forts.

Above: *Commodore Matthew C. Perry brought to Japan official gifts from the United States intended to highlight the advantages Japan would derive from access to American technology. Among the gifts were a miniature steam railroad, complete with locomotive, tender, coach, and track, a daguerreotype camera, and a telegraph, as well as firearms and farm implements. (Naval Historical Center)*

Left: *Commodore Matthew C. Perry meeting the Japanese imperial commissioners at Yokohama. (W.T. Peters, Naval Historical Center)*

Throughout the era, the United States employed its naval forces in seeking agreements that would protect American sailors stranded abroad and that would open foreign commerce to the United States. Early successes of such efforts came in 1833, when the king of Siam and the Sultan of Muscat both signed commercial treaties with the United States. In 1845, after the American envoy to China fell ill en route and returned home, Commodore James Biddle made the formal exchange of ratification of a commercial treaty and established the United States' first legation in Canton.

Above: *A painting of USS* Vincennes, *flagship of the U.S. Exploring Expedition (1838–1842), in Disappointment Bay, Antarctica, after a sketch by the expedition's commander, Lieutenant Charles Wilkes. (Naval Historical Center)*

Opposite, top: *Charts, like this one of Vanua Levu Island in the Fiji Islands, issued by the Navy based on the surveys of the U.S. Exploring Expedition, continued in use as late as World War II. (Naval Historical Center)*

The greatest diplomatic triumph of the era was the treaty of Kanagawa between the United States and Japan, negotiated by Commodore Matthew C. Perry in 1854. The shogunate had closed Japan to all foreign intercourse since the beginning of the seventeenth century. Access to Japanese ports became important to the United States with the growing activity of American whalers off Japan, the acquisition of ports on the west coast of North America, and the expansion of trade and development of American steamship lines across the Pacific Ocean. Perry arrived in Tokyo Bay in July 1853 with two paddle frigates and two sailing sloops of war. He refused to deal with minor officials or to depart until he had delivered, in an impressive ceremony, a letter from President Millard Fillmore to a direct representative of the emperor. Early in 1854 he returned, his squadron strengthened by an additional paddle frigate and two sailing vessels. Through a combination of firmness, dignified behavior, and display of force, Perry won a Japanese guarantee of protection for U.S. citizens and access to two ports for American shipping. Two years later, persuaded of their need for western technology, the Japanese permitted trade.

In the forefront of the antebellum Navy's notable contributors to scientific knowledge stand Matthew Fontaine Maury, called the "Pathfinder of the Seas," and Charles Wilkes, leader of the famed United States South Seas Exploring Expedition.

As director of the Naval Observatory in Washington, D.C., beginning in 1842, Lieutenant Maury worked to advance both pure and applied science in

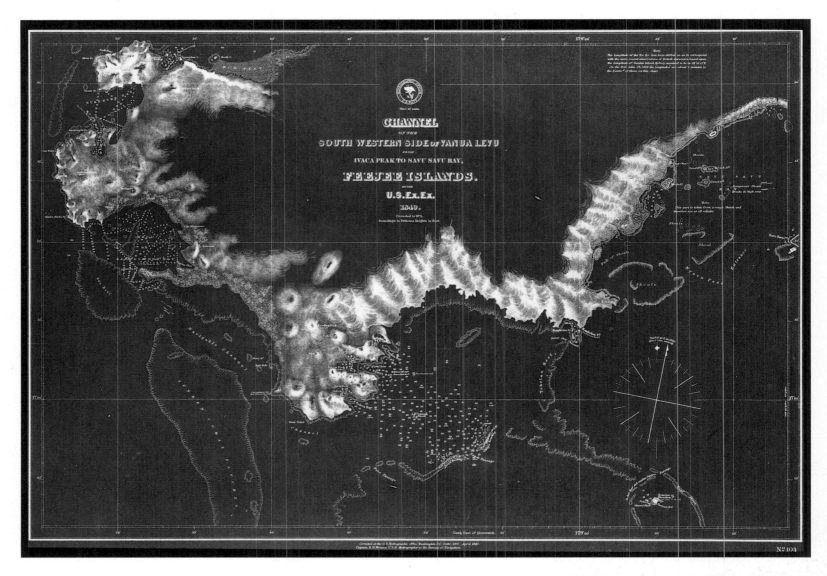

meteorology and hydrography. He produced charts of reefs, shoals, and other navigational hazards. His charts of seasonal changes in winds and currents enabled sea captains to select routes that sped their journeys. The information he collected on ocean depths helped determine the best track for the laying of the first transatlantic cable. His *Physical Geography of the World* was the first modern work on oceanography.

An expedition of six U.S. naval vessels, known informally as the Wilkes Expedition after its commanding officer, explored the Antarctic and the Pacific Oceans between 1838 and 1842. As mandated by Congress, the sailors and the nine civilian artists and scientists made hydrographic surveys and astronomical observations, and charted navigational hazards. Among the squadron's accomplishments were surveying 280 islands, charting the coast of Oregon Territory, and demonstrating that Antarctica is a continent. The expedition's collection of natural history specimens and ethnographic artifacts became the nucleus of the Smithsonian Institution's museum collection in 1858.

The Wilkes Expedition became the model for several scientific explorations undertaken by the Navy in the 1850s, including ones to the River Jordan and the Dead Sea, the western Pacific, the Isthmus of Darien, the west coast of Africa, and La Plata River in South America.

The Second Seminole War, 1835–1842, was the longest and costliest Indian war that the United States fought east of the Mississippi. While the Army carried out most of the fighting during this conflict, the Navy made a significant contribution to subduing the Seminoles. A naval blockade of the Florida coast prevented gunrunners from supplying weapons to the Native Americans. The Navy also conducted amphibious operations against the Seminoles. The Navy assembled a special squadron of shallow-draft vessels, the "Mosquito Fleet," to

The Navy's Efficiency Board of 1855 placed Matthew Fontaine Maury (1806–1873), a naval officer with an international scientific reputation, on the inactive list because an injury prevented him from serving at sea. Nevertheless, because of Maury's pioneering work in oceanography, the Secretary of the Navy retained him on active duty as head of the Naval Observatory. (E. Sophonisba Hergesheimer, Naval Academy Museum)

Top: *U.S. sailors and Marines operating in the Florida Everglades on an expedition against the Seminoles. (Naval Historical Center)*

Above: *Sailors and Marines from USS* Cyane, Savannah, *and* Levant, *under command of Commodore John Drake Sloat, raised the flag at Monterey, 7 July 1846, claiming California for the United States, during the war with Mexico. (Naval Historical Center)*

mount expeditions into the interior by way of Florida's inland waterways. Riverine warfare, sometimes conducted in conjunction with the Army, helped bring the war home to the enemy. The Seminole War demonstrated to naval officers the link between close cooperation and success in joint operations, as well as the strategic possibilities of amphibious warfare.

In the Mexican War, 1846–1848, combined American arms won for the United States the nation's most decisive victory before the Civil War. The Navy played a major role in securing that victory. By blockading Mexico's port cities, the Navy strangled Mexico's maritime trade and prevented its forces from threatening U.S. operations from the sea. The Navy also performed an essential service in transporting men and materiel for the Army. The Navy directed the landing of General Winfield Scott's troops at Veracruz and participated in the bombardment of that city. By establishing and maintaining sea control, the Navy enabled the Army to seize and garrison enemy territory. Naval forces,

Above: *Naval bombardment of Vera Cruz, Mexico, March 1847. The U.S. squadron under Commodore David Connor landed General Winfield Scott's army of 12,000 soldiers three miles from Vera Cruz, Mexico. The squadron, now under command of Commodore Matthew C. Perry, commenced the bombardment of the city eleven days later. After three days, the city surrendered opening the way to advance on Mexico City. (Naval Historical Center)*

Left: *The Mexican Monument, in the center of the Yard at the Naval Academy commemorates the four midshipmen killed at Vera Cruz: Henry Clemson, John Hynson, Wingate Pillsbury, and Thomas Shubrick. Cannon captured at Vera Cruz are mounted in the courtyard of Bancroft Hall, the midshipmen's dormitory.*

assisted by a relatively small number of soldiers, seized California for the United States.

The Mexican War left the nation with two sea coasts to defend, propelled the United States into Pacific affairs, and provided impetus for the Navy's expansion. The war also left a body of tactical experience on which officers in the Northern and Southern navies would draw during the Civil War.

Damn the Torpedoes! Full Speed Ahead!
The Civil War

Craig L. Symonds

"An August Morning with Farragut" dramatizes the final moments of the Battle of Mobile Bay as the flagship USS Hartford *closely engages CSS* Tennessee. *Farragut oversees the action from the rigging.* Tennessee, *commanded by Admiral Franklin Buchanan, held out against the Union squadron for an hour before striking her colors. (William H. Overend, Wadsworth Atheneum)*

The Civil War was America's most pervasive conflict, and by far its bloodiest. Twice as many Americans died in the Civil War as in World War II, which was the nation's second bloodiest war. While on the one hand casualty figures from the Civil War are inflated by counting the losses from both sides (they were all "Americans" after all), those losses came from a considerably smaller population than those of World War II, and the impact of those losses, plus the fact that the Civil War took place on American soil, made the Civil War the greatest trauma in the nation's history. While naval forces did not determine the outcome of the war, they did affect both its direction and its timing, and it is clear that without overwhelming Union naval superiority, the war would have run a different course.

Within days of the firing on Fort Sumter in April 1861, President Abraham Lincoln turned to his senior army officer, Major General Winfield Scott, for advice about conducting a war to reunite the nation. Born a Virginian, but loyal to the Union by virtue of his half-century of military service, Scott proposed a plan to demonstrate to the rebellious South its dependence on the Union for survival. Organize a large army near the capital, he advised, in order to keep the principal southern army pinned in place, then establish "a complete blockade of the Atlantic and Gulf ports" and organize "a powerful movement down the Mississippi to the Ocean." Such actions, Scott insisted, would "envelope the insurgent States and bring them to terms with less bloodshed than by any other plan." Many in the North found Scott's proposals far too passive and, eager for a more active war, they derisively dubbed it the "Anaconda Plan" for the South American reptile that slowly strangles its prey. But while Scott's hopes for a bloodless war would soon be smashed to bits, his strategic blueprint nevertheless remained at the heart of Union strategy. And two of the three elements of that strategy involved the Navy.

The Union Navy was presided over by a Connecticut newspaper publisher named Gideon Welles who served as Lincoln's Secretary of the Navy throughout the war. Despite his lack of naval expertise, Welles's mane of white hair (actually a wig) and long beard suggested to some the image of Neptune himself, and Welles made an effort to learn on the job. For one thing he hired a professional, Gustavus Vasa Fox, a U.S. Navy captain, as his assistant Secretary of the Navy. Though Fox's position was purely administrative, he became, in effect, a kind of prototype Chief of Naval Operations. Welles and Fox made a good team, with Welles providing the political insight and Fox the technical and professional expertise.

The most challenging component of the Navy's strategic assignment was to establish and maintain a blockade of the southern coast. Declared by President

Top, left: *During the Battle of Hampton Roads, CSS* Virginia, *having already rammed and sunk USS* Cumberland, *destroys USS* Congress. *The ironclad* Virginia *promised to lift the Federal blockade. The next day, 9 March 1862, USS* Monitor, *the Union's first ironclad, fought* Virginia *to a tactical draw but a strategic victory—the blockade remained intact. (*"Congress *Burning,"* Tom Freeman)

Upper right: *Gideon Welles was Lincoln's Secretary of the Navy. Welles served as Navy secretary throughout the war and provided a stable hand at the helm. (Naval Historical Center)*

Lower right: *The new position of Assistant Secretary of the Navy was filled by Captain Gustavus Vasa Fox, whose job it was to coordinate orders to the squadron commanders and oversee the operational activities of the Navy—in short, to fulfill the function that is today the role of the Chief of Naval Operations. (Naval Historical Center)*

The Confederate steamer Nashville *is depicted running through the blockade early in the war in this contemporary painting. The frequency with which Confederate vessels safely ran the gauntlet of blockading ships in 1861 and 1862 led some to suggest that the blockade was ineffective, but as the Union naval squadrons added more ships, it also became more effective. By 1863 only specially designed low-freeboard steam ships made regular attempts to run the blockade. ("CSS* Nashville,*" The Mariners' Museum, Newport News)*

Ships attempting the run through the blockade used every sort of device to elude the blockaders, including the use of neutral flags. Here a battered blockade-runner, Teaser, *flies the British flag after running the blockade into Charleston. (Photo: Naval Historical Center)*

Lincoln on 19 April, only a week after Fort Sumter, a completely effective blockade would prove easier to announce than to achieve. For one thing, there were legal difficulties. Declaring a blockade was an act of war, and it implied, at least, de facto recognition of the Confederacy as a belligerent power. Lincoln tried to get around this imputation by declaring that domestic unrest in several of America's southern ports prevented the collection of duties at those ports, and for that reason the ports were being closed to commerce. But this legal subterfuge proved unsatisfactory. Closing the ports did not authorize U.S. Navy ships on patrol to stop and search suspicious vessels at sea, or to seize contraband beyond America's coastal waters. By the mid-nineteenth century, a blockade was best effected not only by establishing vessels off the entrances to harbors, but by actively patrolling over the horizon. To allow this, the Lincoln administration in the end had to accept the word *blockade* after all, along with all that it might imply about the Confederacy's belligerent status.

A second legal problem was that international convention also held that simply declaring a blockade was not enough; a mere declaration—a "paper blockade" as it was known—was not binding on neutrals. To make it so, the declarer had to establish a naval force offshore sufficient to constitute a legitimate barrier to trade. In recognition of that fact, Lincoln announced that "a competent force will be posted so as to prevent entrance and exit of vessels." But this, too, was easier said than done. The U.S. Navy in 1861 consisted of some ninety warships, only about half of which were on active service, and only eight of which were in home waters at the time of Lincoln's declaration. The Confederacy claimed a coastline that stretched from the Chesapeake Bay to the Mexican border—some 3,500 miles including the double coastline of Florida—and which was pierced by 189 harbors, inlets, and navigable rivers. To make a blockade both legal and tangible, the U.S. Navy would have to undergo a dramatic expansion.

What made this expansion possible was the fact that in the mid-nineteenth century, warships did not have to be purpose-built from the keel up. The difference between steam-powered merchant ships and steam-powered warships was often little more than a reinforced deck strong enough to bear the naval guns. Given that, the U.S. government went on a buying spree, snapping up merchant ships that could be converted to naval use. Since their mission would be to stop merchant ships, they did not need a large battery; often two or three guns were adequate. By the end of the calendar year, the U.S. government had purchased nearly 200 such

vessels and by war's end, 418 of the Navy's total of 671 vessels would be converted merchantmen. With this jury-rigged fleet, the Navy's blockade of the Confederate coast, porous at first, gradually improved until the Confederacy began to feel the pinch of scarce resources.

To officer and man this vastly enlarged new Navy, the Union states had to overcome two problems: nearly half of the officers in the "old Navy" were from southern states, and nearly half of them resigned their commissions and "went South" to fight for the Confederacy. It is noteworthy that the percentage of those who were born in the South and yet remained loyal to the old flag was much larger among naval officers than army officers, perhaps because naval officers routinely served the nation on foreign stations where they more closely identified themselves with the national government than did army officers who served in frontier or seacoast forts. Still, with the huge expansion of naval ships, there had to be a commensurate expansion of the officer corps. Lieutenants who had aspired to a position as fifth or sixth in command on a sloop, now found that a frigate command was theirs for the asking. Commanders became commodores; captains became flag officers. Junior officer assignments were assumed by brand new midshipmen whose seagoing experience often consisted of little more than their cruise down the coast to take up their new duties on the blockade.

The Navy also had to enlarge its enlisted force. Although there were many volunteers in the first burst of national patriotism following Fort Sumter, most of those volunteers signed up for the Army. To attract volunteers, Navy recruiters offered unrealistic images of prize money and easy duty. After the summer of 1863, when conscription became the law of the land, Navy recruiting posters touted naval service as a means of avoiding army service. Most of the Navy volunteers, however, were enthusiastic patriots. Sixteen-year-old New Hampshire resident Alvah Hunter tried again and again to convince Navy recruiters to accept him. "I had seen two or three score of my former schoolmates but two or three years older than myself put

Unlike the Army, the Navy had a long tradition of accepting blacks as crew members. Moreover, the very nature of naval service militated against any effort to segregate blacks and whites. Here the mixed-race crew of USS Hunchback *poses for the camera. (Photo: Naval Historical Center)*

A Confederate sentinel stands guard atop the battered ramparts of Fort Sumter in Charleston Harbor. In the right near distance Union batteries on Cummins Point are evident, and in the distance, on the horizon, the ships of the blockading squadron can be seen. Despite constant pressure from sea and shore, Charleston held out against Union offensives until cut off by Sherman's march northward in 1865. (Museum of the Confederacy)

Samuel Francis Du Pont, the scion of a well-known and well-to-do Delaware family, presided over the so-called strategy board that set up the blockading squadrons off the Atlantic and Gulf coasts in 1861. Subsequently, Du Pont received command of the most important of these, the South Atlantic Blockading Squadron that he led until the summer of 1863. (Naval Historical Center)

Du Pont's fleet steams in an elliptical circle in Port Royal Sound firing alternatively at Fort Walker (on the left) and Fort Beauregard (on the right) in November 1861. By keeping his steam warships in motion and firing explosive shells from heavy guns, Du Pont demonstrated the emergence of naval vessels as a match for shore-based artillery, and obtained an important base for his blockading squadron. (Naval Historical Center)

on the blue uniforms and march away to the front," he recalled, "and I, because of being only sixteen years old, and rather small and slender for that age, was told again and again that I wasn't wanted. What could I do? I wanted to go to the war, Oh! So much!" In the end, young Hunter's persistence paid off, and he enrolled as a ship's boy on the new monitor *Nahant*.

When Hunter arrived on board *Nahant*, one of the most helpful of his shipmates was "a colored boy named George Patterson." Unlike the Army, where the idea of allowing blacks to serve as soldiers was accepted only with reluctance—and even then only in segregated units—the Navy encountered few such problems because it had always been a racially integrated service. In part this was simple pragmatism: hungry for manpower, Navy recruiters had never balked at including black sailors in their crews. Then too, the idea of segregating crews by race—so that the Navy might have some all-white crews and some that were all black—struck nearly everyone as absurd. Though blacks did not break into the ranks of the officer corps during the Civil War, they did make up a significant percentage of the men serving before the mast, and they fought with distinction in the war that would liberate their race in America.

Having obtained the ships and the manpower, the U.S. Navy had to sustain its blockading squadrons off the southern coast. For a steam-powered fleet, this meant the establishment of coaling stations along the enemy coast, and to do that U.S. Navy squadrons had to attack and overcome the coastal defenses at several key sites. The advent of naval guns with rifled barrels firing explosive ordnance from steam-powered ships marked a shift in the presumed balance of power between ships and forts. Whereas in the 1840s strategists had considered ships no match for shore-based fortifications, the ordnance revolution of the 1850s had reversed that assumption. As if to demonstrate this new strategic reality, in August 1861, Flag Officer Silas Stringham led a powerful squadron against the forts that guarded the entrance to North Carolina's Pamlico Sound. Stringham's steam-driven warships pounded the makeshift Confederate forts into submission and compelled their surrender. Then in November, Flag Officer Samuel Francis Du Pont led an even larger naval squadron against the forts protecting Port Royal Sound in South Carolina. Once again, naval guns proved more than a match for shore-based artillery. By seizing such protected anchorages for their blockading squadrons, the four Union fleets assigned to blockade duty—the North and South Atlantic, and the East and West Gulf Squadrons—could maintain themselves on station year round.

Blockade duty was tedious for the officers and men of those squadrons. There was little break in monotony as the blockading vessels steamed back and forth off the entrance to one or another of the South's seaports. There were periodic trips back to the coaling stations to refuel and, less often, liberty ashore to pick berries or to explore. Even the occasional storm was almost a relief to the tedium. This tedium was broken by a frenzy of activity whenever a blockade-runner tried to make its way in or out of port, almost always at night. The blockading ships rode out the nights at anchor, blacked out, and they frequently shifted their anchorages after nightfall so that Confederate authorities ashore could not signal to would-be blockade runners which channel was most likely to be unguarded. Even so, when a low, gray-painted, and steam-powered blockade runner dashed through the anchored blockaders in the inky darkness, intercepting one was often a matter of pure luck.

The extent to which the Union blockade was strategically effective is a subject on which historians disagree. Critics note that despite herculean efforts by the U.S. Navy, most ships that tried to run the blockade did so successfully, and they note, too, that the Confederate armies never lost a battle due to a lack of resources. The noted naval historian William N. Still, Jr., concludes, "The blockade absorbed hundreds of ships and thousands of men, and generally had

little effect on the war's outcome." On the other hand, it is impossible to measure how many ships were deterred from trying to run the blockade because of the presence of Union warships, and the blockade did create genuine hardships for the Confederacy. Unable to manufacture or import iron in sufficient quantities, it had to cannibalize its lesser used railroads for the iron necessary to keep its principal rail lines in service, or to build new ones, and the dearth of a wide variety of everyday goods contributed to both rampant inflation and a growing war weariness in the South. Finally, the blockade sealed the Confederacy off from potential European sympathizers who might otherwise have had an opportunity to develop closer economic and diplomatic ties with the Confederacy.

A second mission of the U.S. Navy during the Civil War was its participation in the several riverine campaigns in the western theater. Scott's Anaconda Plan called for a movement down the Mississippi to New Orleans. Such a thrust would divide the Confederacy not quite in half and—in Scott's original conception—demonstrate to southerners just how dependent they were on the Union for their economic well being. In addition, the Tennessee and Cumberland Rivers offered additional opportunities to penetrate the Confederate defensive barrier in Kentucky. But any campaign on the western rivers would necessarily involve both the Navy and the Army, and the country lacked an established protocol for coordinating joint operations. In the past when Army and Navy officers had to work together (as in the landing at Vera Cruz, Mexico), the commanders had met and worked out a mutually acceptable plan. During the Civil War, cooperation varied depending on the ability of the commanders to work together effectively.

At first it appeared that the Army would be in charge of the river campaigns: the first three wooden gunboats built on the Ohio River at Cincinnati in the spring of 1861 were under the Army's command. But as the river squadrons grew, it became clear that a shared command arrangement was more practical. While the Army retained overall strategic control of operations within the theater, Navy officers exercised tactical command of their ships and squadrons and they remained outside the direct chain of Army command. Cooperation, not command unity, was to be the key to successful Union efforts on the western rivers.

The seven "City Class" gunboats of the Mississippi River Flotilla were built by James Eads at Carondelet, Missouri, and Mound City, Illinois. With a draft of six feet they could "navigate on a heavy dew" and were instrumental in the Union campaigns along the Tennessee and Mississippi rivers. (Naval Historical Center)

Flag Officer Andrew Hull Foote commanded the gunboat flotilla on the western rivers in the first year of the war. His cooperation with Ulysses S. Grant helped ensure the capture of Forts Henry and Donelson in February 1862, and his squadron played a crucial role in the capture of Island No. 10 in the Mississippi. Foote's poor health forced him to retire soon afterward. (Photo: Naval Historical Center)

Above: *The gunners in Fort Henry fire back at the ironclads of Flag Officer Andrew H. Foote. Recognizing the difficulty of defending his position, Confederate Brigadier General Lloyd Tilghman sent most of his garrison to Fort Donelson and attempted to defend Fort Henry with his heavy guns alone. The low-lying batteries of Fort Henry proved to be no match for the well-directed fire of Foote's naval guns, and Fort Henry capitulated before the arrival of General Grant's supporting army. (American Antiquarian Society)*

Above, right: *Foote's ironclads bombard the Confederate stronghold of Fort Henry on the Tennessee River in February 1862 in this contemporary print. One shot from Fort Henry penetrated the thin iron plate of USS* Essex *and exploded in the boiler killing ten men and wounding twenty-six, but the other three gunboats soon overwhelmed the fort's defenders. (American Antiquarian Society)*

The first cooperative effort came at Fort Henry on the Tennessee River in February 1862. There Brigadier General Ulysses S. Grant and Flag Officer Andrew H. Foote combined to break through a key to the Confederate western defenses along the Kentucky–Tennessee border. Foote's flotilla escorted Grant's soldiers to a point just above Fort Henry, then took the fort under fire as Grant's soldiers advanced overland. As it happened, the Confederate commander of Fort Henry, Brigadier General Lloyd Tilghman, recognized his vulnerability and evacuated his infantry from the fort, choosing to defend it with his artillerists alone. In the ensuing artillery duel, Foote's four ironclad gunboats overwhelmed the fort's batteries, and Fort Henry capitulated before Grant's troops could arrive. Then Foote's gunboats steamed upriver, past the fort, to destroy the railroad bridge over the Tennessee River thus cutting a critical east-west transportation link for the Confederacy.

If the Navy won the honors at Fort Henry, the Army had its turn at Fort Donelson on the Cumberland River, only a half dozen miles east of Fort Henry and the linchpin of the Confederate defenses in the West. There Foote's gunboats proved much less formidable because Fort Donelson was situated high on a bluff over the river from which place its guns could deter Foote's gunboats with plunging shot. This time it was Grant's army that surrounded the fort from the landward side and compelled its surrender. The timorousness of the Confederate commander, former U.S. Secretary of War John B. Floyd, was instrumental in Grant's success. Floyd lost his nerve at a critical moment and allowed Grant to tighten the noose. Subsequently, Floyd abandoned his command and left Simon B. Buckner behind to ask Grant for terms. Grant responded that, "No terms except unconditional and immediate surrender can be accepted," a response that brought Grant to the attention of the war department and started him on his rise to the eventual command of all Union armies.

Commander Henry Walke boldly offered to run his vessel, USS Carondelet, *past the Confederate batteries on Island No. 10 in the Mississippi. His feat, soon duplicated by others, not only led to the eventual capture of Island No. 10, but also showed that river steamers could by-pass enemy strong points and offered a precedent for David Dixon Porter's run past Vicksburg. (Naval Historical Center)*

A third example of Army–Navy cooperation and success was the capture in April 1862 of the Confederate bastion at Island No. 10 on the Mississippi River— so named because it was the tenth island in the river south of Cairo where the Ohio flowed into the Mississippi. Here on an island in a bend of the river near the Kentucky–Tennessee border, the Confederates had placed major defensive fortifications. Protected by impassable marshland to the east and the river itself to west, U.S. Army troops could not get to the island. Union success could be realized only if the Navy vessels upriver could somehow get past the island to join with the Army soldiers (under Major General John B. Pope) and escort them across the river. It was Commander Henry Walke, captain of the ironclad USS *Carondelet*, who volunteered to try it. Choosing a dark night, he steamed past the Confederate batteries on 4 April, and safely reached Pope's outpost at New Madrid, Missouri. The next night another Union gunboat, USS *Pittsburgh*, duplicated this feat, and on 7 April those two ships successfully escorted Pope's army across the Mississippi to attack the Confederate defenses from the rear. The fall of Island No. 10 was a model of effective combined operations.

That same month, five hundred miles to the south (as the river flows) Flag Officer David Glasgow Farragut ran past the forts guarding New Orleans and the lower Mississippi. Farragut's feat was particularly significant for several reasons. First, the fortifications south of New Orleans were not jury-rigged earth and log forts such as those defending Port Royal or Island No. 10. They were instead masonry forts with heavy guns—forts built in the 1840s by the Army Corps of Engineers to defend the U.S. from foreign invasion. Between them, Fort Jackson and Fort St. Philip boasted a total of 128 heavy guns. Nevertheless, three weeks after Walke ran past Island No. 10, Farragut's squadron, consisting of seventeen oceangoing steam-driven warships, passed through an opening created in a log and chain boom across the Mississippi and took the Confederate forts under fire.

The squadron of Flag Officer David Glasgow Farragut runs past Confederate Forts Jackson and St. Philip in the pre-dawn hours of 24 April 1862. Farragut's maneuver led to the capture of New Orleans the next day. For this feat, Farragut was promoted to rear admiral, the first in American history. (Naval Historical Center)

The Navy's Civil War riverine campaigns are memorialized in the Vicksburg National Battlefield Park. USS Cairo, *a gunboat torpedoed and sunk in the Yazoo River, has been raised and now rests in a shelter near the National Cemetery. At the top of the hill overlooking* Cairo *is the site of Lieutenant Commander Thomas Selfridge's naval battery during the siege. (Photo: National Park Service)*

For sheer drama and spectacle, few Civil War actions can match Porter's run past Vicksburg on the night of 16 April 1863. Porter's decision to undertake this risky maneuver was the key to Grant's strategy for the capture of the Confederate "citadel of the West," and Porter undertook it at great personal and professional risk. ("Admiral Porter's Fleet Running the Blockade," U.S. Naval Academy Museum)

David Dixon Porter was the son of David Porter, a U.S. Navy hero of the War of 1812 and the wars with the Caribbean pirates. Lincoln elevated Porter from commander to acting rear admiral in order to endow him with the command of the Mississippi River Squadron. In that command, Porter cooperated effectively with Grant to ensure the capture of Vicksburg. (Photo: Naval Historical Center)

Successfully running this gauntlet against the river's current, and easily dispatching the small squadron of Confederate warships, Farragut then steamed up to New Orleans and demanded its surrender. Unlike the Union victories on the upper reaches of the Mississippi system, this victory was won by the Navy alone as Major General Benjamin Butler's occupying forces did not arrive until 1 May.

Dramatic as they were, these events were but a preview to the decisive campaigning on the western rivers. By far the most important combined operation in the western theater was the capture of Vicksburg in the summer of 1863. Vicksburg was the citadel of Confederate defenses in the west. Situated on a high bluff on the eastern side of the Mississippi above a hairpin turn of the river, Vicksburg's guns dominated all traffic on the river. Moreover, though there was no bridge over the Mississippi, Vicksburg was the transshipment point for the Vicksburg & Jackson Railroad running east, and the Shreveport & Vicksburg Railroad running west. In short, Vicksburg was the buckle on the strap that held the Confederacy together.

Vicksburg was all but impregnable to an attack from the west. Forces assailing the city from the river delta would have to maneuver beneath those dominating batteries, then somehow ascend the 200-foot bluffs before they could even come to grips with the enemy. The only practical way to threaten the city was from the east, across Mississippi's flat upland plain. Aware of this, Grant first sought to attack Vicksburg by ignoring the river altogether and marching southward from Corinth, Mississippi. But Confederate cavalry attacks on his lines of supply, and concerns about the awkward command situation he left behind on the river, led Grant to give up on that line of approach and return to the river. As a supply line, the Mississippi was more secure than railroads, and on the river, Grant would have the support of the Navy's river flotilla, now under the command of Acting Rear Admiral David Dixon Porter.

Porter was the son of David Porter, a hero of the War of 1812. An ambitious man, the younger Porter had despaired when he received orders in 1862 to a staff job, and he begged Lincoln for an active command. Not long afterward, Porter was jumped over the heads of every captain in the Navy as he rose from commander to acting rear admiral in order to assume the command of the Mississippi River fleet. The appointment would prove to be inspired, for Porter and Grant made an effective team.

At Vicksburg, Grant knew from the beginning that he somehow had to get his soldiers atop the high bluff behind the city, but he had great difficulty in finding a way to do it. He had already tried the overland route. Next he tried ascending the Yazoo River and finding a way through Steele's Bayou. He even set his men to work constructing a canal across the hairpin turn in the Mississippi in an effort to bypass Vicksburg altogether. But in the end, the answer to the puzzle proved once again to be effective interservice cooperation. Early in the spring of 1863, Grant asked Porter if he was willing to run his fleet past the Vicksburg batteries in order to position himself south of the city to transport Grant's soldiers across the river. Porter would have been perfectly within his rights to decline the request. After all, if the gambit failed, Porter could not claim that he had been ordered to make the attempt for he was not subject to Grant's orders. But he agreed to do it anyway.

On 16 April 1863 (almost a year to the day after Walke made a similar run past Island No. 10) Porter's gunboat flotilla and three empty Army transports ran successfully past the Vicksburg gauntlet. One transport and one barge were sunk, and other ships were damaged, but the bulk of the fleet survived intact. Over the next several days, Porter first tried to reduce the Confederate batteries at Grand Gulf. Then deciding that they were too strong, he instead landed Grant's troops at Bruinsburg, south of Grand Gulf, on the eastern side of the Mississippi behind Vicksburg. Grant marched north and east, away from the river, capturing the Mississippi State capital at Jackson on 14 May before turning west to close in on Vicksburg itself. Unable to fight his way into the city, Grant settled down to a siege, sustained in that effort by his ability to rely on the Navy's control of the Mississippi for supply and support. The siege ended on 4 July (the day Lee began his retreat from Gettysburg) when Confederate Lieutenant General John C. Pemberton surrendered both Vicksburg and his 30,000-man army. It was the only time in the war until Appomattox that an entire Confederate army was eliminated from the strategic map, and the victory belonged jointly to both the Union Army and Navy.

For its part, the Confederacy recognized its naval deficiencies from the outset. The nineteenth-century naval historian James Russell Soley wrote that "it would hardly be possible to imagine a great maritime country more destitute of the means for carrying on a naval war than the Confederate States in 1861." Unlike the U.S. Navy, which could build on an existing infrastructure of shipyards, ropewalks, smelting works, ordnance factories, and powder mills, the Confederate Navy had to start literally from scratch. The South did have a cadre of trained officers—126 southern-born U.S. Navy officers resigned to "go South"—but the Confederacy had almost no ships for them to command.

Given that, the Confederacy adopted the traditional naval strategy of the underdog—indeed, the same strategy the U.S. had adopted in its wars with England: defend the coast with fortifications and assail the enemy merchant fleet with a strategy of guerre de course conducted by both privateers and national commerce raiders. As noted above, the coastal fortifications proved less effective than hoped. Only in those locations where geography or long preparation had endowed the defenders with special advantages (e.g. Charleston, Mobile, Wilmington) could the South effectively resist the attack of modern warships. Elsewhere the U.S. Navy could work its will, and did, as was evident at Hatteras Inlet, Port Royal, and elsewhere.

Unable to match the Union Navy ship for ship, the Confederacy sought instead to overcome the Union advantage in numbers with innovation. Among the

Porter used a stern-wheeler, Blackhawk, *as his flagship. Although it was less intimidating as a warship than his ironclads or "tin-clads,"* Blackhawk *offered comfortable quarters, and on its commodious decks Porter met frequently with Grant and Sherman to plan the Vicksburg campaign. (Naval Historical Center)*

Stephen Russell Mallory, former chairman of the Senate Naval Affairs Committee, served throughout the war as the Confederate Secretary of the Navy. Mallory recognized from the beginning that the Confederacy could not hope to match the Union states in industrial production and therefore sought to build cutting-edge naval weapons (such as ironclads) to compensate for inferior numbers. (Naval Historical Center)

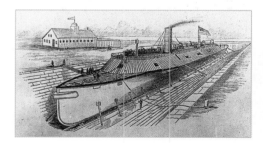

CSS Virginia, *formerly the U.S. steam frigate* Merrimack, *in drydock at Gosport Navy Yard just prior to her launch in February 1862. Although the idea of an armor-clad warship did not originate in the Confederacy,* Virginia*'s duel with the Union* Monitor *in March 1862 was the first confrontation between armored warships. (Naval Historical Center)*

Top: *This is one of several artists' conceptions of the battle between USS* Monitor *and CSS* Virginia *in the Battle of Hampton Roads on 9 March 1862. Although the two vessels slugged it out for hours at close range, the outcome was tactically indecisive. In the end,* Virginia *returned to port, and the Union Navy was able to remain in Hampton Roads. (John Schmidt, Naval Historical Center)*

Above: *John Ericsson, the naval designer who proposed and supervised the construction of a novel type of warship featuring a rotating turret. Built in just 100 days, his curious-looking "cheese box on a raft," named* Monitor, *became a prototype of a whole class. (Photo: Naval Historical Center)*

Below: *The turret of USS* Monitor *showing battle damage from its engagement with CSS* Virginia. *The canvas roof over the turret was erected only when the ship was quietly at anchor in order to provide shade for the crew. (Photo: Naval Historical Center)*

more notable products of this policy were ironclads, submarines, and torpedoes (which the Federal sailors called "infernal machines"). The Confederate Secretary of the Navy, Stephen R. Mallory, explained his policy in a letter to his wife: "Knowing that the enemy could build one hundred ships to one of our own, my policy has been to make such ships so strong and invulnerable as would compensate for the inequality of numbers." The most famous and successful manifestation of this effort was the ironclad ram CSS *Virginia,* converted from the hull of the steam frigate USS *Merrimack*.

The idea of an ironclad warship was not new. France completed *Glorie* in 1860, and England was then building an iron-hulled warship, *Warrior*. In fact, Mallory tried to buy *Glorie* from the French, but they were not selling. Instead, he approved a proposal from naval contractor John Porter and Lieutenant John M. Brooke to raise the partially burned hull of the steam frigate USS *Merrimack,* left behind when Union naval personnel abandoned the Norfolk Navy Yard, and convert it to an ironclad. News of this effort soon reached Washington where Welles contracted with the Swedish-born designer John Ericsson to build an ironclad warship for the Union Navy. Ericsson's design was radically different from that of *Virginia*. While *Virginia* would resemble what one sailor called "a floating mansard roof with guns peeking out the windows," Ericsson's little USS *Monitor,* built in only 100 days, boasted a revolutionary revolving turret housing two heavy guns atop a nearly submerged hull. Resembling a "tin can on a raft" to some, the little *Monitor* headed south to Hampton Roads under the command of Lieutenant John Worden who hoped to arrive in time to neutralize the impact of *Virginia*.

It was very nearly too late. Emerging from the Elizabeth River into Hampton Roads on 8 March, *Virginia,* under Captain Franklin Buchanan, sank the 24-gun sloop USS *Cumberland* with its ram and smashed the 50-gun frigate USS *Congress* into submission. *Monitor* arrived that night and came to anchor only a few miles away near the grounded U.S. frigate *Minnesota*. On 9 March when *Virginia* came out to complete the destruction of the Union fleet, *Monitor* came forward to meet it. In a classic duel, the two iron monsters hammered away at one another for hours, neither gaining a decisive advantage. *Monitor* was more nimble and, with its lesser draft, could retreat into shoal water if necessary. But in the end it was *Virginia* that limped back into port as much because its engines were straining as because of damage from hostile fire. As it turned out, the arrival of *Monitor* effectively neutralized the offensive potential of *Virginia*, and when the Confederate armies retreated up the Virginia peninsula in May, the Confederates had to abandon Norfolk Navy Yard and destroy *Virginia*.

The Confederacy built other ironclads. Two of them, CSS *Palmetto State* and CSS *Chicora,* sortied from Charleston Harbor in early 1863 to chase away the

Union blockading squadron. Charleston's political leaders declared that the blockade had been lifted, but the Union ships were back again the next day, and in the end, despite Confederate attempts to raise the blockade with ironclads, the blockade remained intact. The Confederate ironclad effort was stymied because of the South's weak industrial base. Several ironclad warships were framed up and launched, but failed to get into battle because of a dearth of iron plate and/or engine parts. By contrast, the Union completed a total of fifty-two monitors plus several other ironclads, including the massive USS *New Ironsides* that Du Pont used as the flagship of the South Atlantic Blockading Squadron.

The Confederacy also experimented with submarines and mines. The most famous submarine of the war was *H.L. Hunley* that actually succeeded in sinking a Union warship, USS *Housatonic*, off Charleston, though neither it nor its crew survived the sortie. Underwater mines, or torpedoes, were arguably the most effective of all the Confederacy's experimental naval weapons. Constructed of waterproofed wooden kegs filled with black power and triggered by either a contact mechanism or a remote electric charge, these faceless weapons kept Union blockading squadrons at a distance and claimed several victims, the most spectacular of which was the monitor USS *Tecumseh* during the Battle of Mobile Bay in August 1864.

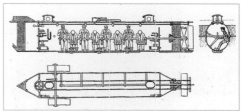

The last moments of the naval battle between USS Kearsarge and CSS Alabama off Cherbourg, France, on 19 June 1864. Semmes has been criticized for accepting the battle with Kearsarge, for Alabama was much in need of a re-fit. For his part, Semmes accused Winslow of behaving unfairly by draping chains over the side of his vessel, thus giving it some "armor" protection. ("USS Kearsarge vs. CSS Alabama," Xanthus Smith, Naval Historical Center)

Opposite, top left: The most famous of all the Confederate commerce raiders was Captain (later Rear Admiral) Raphael Semmes, shown here on the deck of his most famous command, the raider CSS Alabama. Behind him is his first officer, Lieutenant John McIntosh Kell. Semmes captured some sixty-eight Union vessels while in command of Alabama, single-handedly raising maritime insurance rates and prompting a "flight from the flag" that lasted well past the war. (Photo: Naval Historical Center)

Opposite, top right: The crew of one of USS Kearsarge's 11-inch guns celebrates a hit on CSS Alabama. Alabama's executive officer, John Kell, recalled, "The enemy's 11-inch shells [did] severe execution upon our quarterdeck." Within minutes Alabama was listing to starboard, and Semmes ordered abandon ship. ("Kearsarge vs. Alabama," J.O. Davidson, Naval Historical Center)

The final plank of Confederate naval strategy was commerce raiding. From the very outset of hostilities, the Confederacy announced that it would issue letters of marque, documents that authorized private ship owners to capture or destroy enemy merchant ships. The great powers of Europe had outlawed this form of warfare in the Convention of Paris in 1856, but the United States, which had relied heavily on privateering in its own wars, had declined to sign the convention. As a result, the Confederate government saw no difficulty issuing letters of marque to its own citizens. The southern states lacked the raw material that had made privateering effective in those earlier wars and because of that, the Confederacy did not pin its commerce raiding hopes on privateers. Instead Secretary Mallory depended on a few C.S. Navy raiders, most of them built semi-secretly in England. The most famous of these was CSS Alabama commanded by Raphael Semmes who in a two-year cruise took 68 prizes, burning all but four, and using the other four as cartels to rid himself of the prisoners he had accumulated. The exploits of Semmes and others such as John Maffitt in CSS Florida, and James Waddell in CSS Shenandoah, had a disproportionate impact on the conduct of the war. The U.S. Navy had to send literally scores of ships searching for these raiders, and U.S. merchants had to choose between paying exorbitant insurance rates or re-flagging their vessels under foreign registry.

The ship that finally brought Alabama to bay was USS Kearsarge under Captain John A. Winslow. Winslow found Semmes and Alabama in Cherbourg Harbor on France's Atlantic coast and challenged him to a single ship duel. Driven perhaps by his sense of personal honor and perhaps by hubris, Semmes accepted. Winslow carefully prepared his ship for battle by draping chains over the side to protect his engine spaces and magazine. In the ensuing fight on 19 June 1864, the two vessels circled one another firing away until Alabama began taking on water. Unwilling to surrender, Semmes hurled his sword over the side and called for the

Left: *Semmes's nemesis was USS* Kearsarge, *commanded by Captain John A. Winslow, shown here on the deck of* Kearsarge *with his officers. The metal track in the foreground allowed the 11-inch gun amidships to rotate to point either to port or starboard. (Photo: Naval Historical Center)*

men to save themselves. He abandoned ship and was picked up by a private yacht, *Deerhound*, which carried him to England.

By 1864, the cumulative impact of the blockade and the conquest of the western river system had shrunk the Confederacy's logistic base even as the battles on land were sapping its manpower. While Grant in the East and Sherman in the West embarked on the campaigns that would decide the war, Union naval forces concentrated on closing up the last few remaining ports open to blockade runners: Charleston, Mobile, and Wilmington.

Charleston had special significance for both sides. It was the cradle of both slavery and the rebellion, and the rebel flag flying from Fort Sumter was a constant taunt to the blockaders. The U.S. Navy made several attempts to re-capture the city, none of them successful. The most notable of these was Samuel F. Du Pont's attack in April 1863. Du Pont was skeptical about taking his fleet into the cul-de-sac of Charleston Harbor, but Secretary Welles was adamant. Welles believed that the monitors, of which Du Pont had eight (plus *New Ironsides*), would be able to over-come the heavy defenses ringing the harbor. But it proved not to be so. Du Pont's monitors were pummeled by hundreds of rounds of heavy ordnance, and since each monitor had only two guns, they were unable to return an equivalent fire. Du Pont called off the attack, and for his cautiousness he was eventually replaced by John A. Dahlgren. That officer had no better luck. He cooperated with Army forces under Quincy Adams Gilmore to take the city by capturing its forts from the landward side. This led to the controversial sacrifice of the 54th Massachusetts Regiment as it assailed Fort Wagner on Morris Island, but though Wagner was eventually captured, Charleston held out until it was cut off by Sherman's move north in 1865.

Above: *In the spring of 1864, as Grant advanced against Lee in Virginia and Sherman moved against J. E. Johnston in Georgia, Major General Nathaniel Banks and Rear Admiral David Dixon Porter conducted a campaign up the Red River toward Shreveport. It was a poorly managed effort that yielded few results. Moreover, the falling level of water in the river threatened to trap Porter's squadron above Alexandria. In this photo, several of Porter's gunboats are anchored above Alexandria awaiting the rise of the river. An Army engineer, Lieutenant Colonel Joseph Bailey, who built dams to raise the water level, saved the squadron. (Photo: Naval Historical Center)*

Following page, top: *An artist's depiction of the Battle of Mobile Bay on 5 August 1864, at the moment a mine exploded under the Union monitor USS* Tecumseh *(center). Undeterred by the threat of more "torpedoes," Farragut's squadron steams into the bay past Fort Morgan (on the left) while Buchanan's ironclad CSS* Tennessee *(left center) steams to intercept him. ("Battle of Mobile Bay," J.O. Davidson, Library of Congress)*

Below: *Franklin Buchanan was the Confederacy's only full admiral. After a forty-year career as a U.S. naval officer that included service as the founding superintendent of the Naval Academy at Annapolis and as Matthew Perry's flag captain in the expedition to Japan, Buchanan resigned his commission to go South. He commanded both CSS* Virginia *(formerly* Merrimack*) in the Battle of Hampton Roads and CSS* Tennessee *in the Battle of Mobile Bay. (Photo: Naval Historical Center)*

Like Charleston, the city of Mobile, Alabama, had a number of natural and man-made strengths that made it resistant to a naval attack. The city was located at the northern end of a huge arrowhead-shaped bay that was protected by narrow spits of land that seemed designed by Providence to guard the bay against a hostile attack. Only a narrow channel, guarded by masonry forts, allowed access into the bay. Originally, Grant had hoped to include an assault on Mobile as part of his grand offensive in the spring of 1864. But two factors caused a delay until late summer: first, the troops that were to have constituted the Army's contribution to this attack were sidetracked into a profitless expedition up the Red River (along with Porter's gunboats); and second, Farragut was eager to add at least a few ironclads to his fleet before he tackled the Confederate flotilla in Mobile Bay because the rebels had at least one full-size ironclad of their own—CSS *Tennessee*, commanded by the Confederacy's only full admiral, Franklin Buchanan.

Farragut's assault on Mobile Bay is one of the classic tales of U.S. Navy history. A careful planner, Farragut gave detailed instructions to his captains, and he carefully arranged his squadron for the assault (though events soon forced him to improvise). He placed his four monitors in a column to starboard with orders to concentrate their fire on the rebel ironclad. He placed his wooden warships (lashed together in pairs) in a column to port with orders to run past the forts into the lower bay. The fleet got underway at 0530 and steamed toward the channel with Fort Gaines (twenty-six guns) to port and Fort Morgan (forty-five guns) to starboard. Both sides opened fire just before 0700, and then, only moments later, Farragut's lead ironclad, the powerful monitor *Tecumseh*, suddenly rose up out of the water, turned over to starboard, and went down, disappearing in seconds and taking ninety-three men down with her. That, plus the appearance of suspicious-looking buoys in the water, led Captain James Alden in *Brooklyn*, Farragut's leading wooden ship, to order all stop, then half astern. Farragut's column was bunching up like a collapsing accordion.

Farragut reacted instantly and instinctively. He ordered his own ship, *Hartford*, to swing past *Brooklyn*. Alden called out to him that there were

torpedoes in the water ahead to which Farragut replied: "Damn the torpedoes!" Although some sailors later swore that they could hear the primers snapping on several rebel mines, there were no more losses to the dreaded "infernal machines" and Farragut's fleet safely entered Mobile Bay.

There Farragut had to contend with *Tennessee*. Determined to press the issue, Confederate Admiral Franklin Buchanan conned *Tennessee* directly toward the Federal fleet. Accepting this challenge, Farragut ordered *Hartford* directly toward the rebel ironclad. At the last moment, Captain James D. Johnston, who had the deck of *Tennessee*, ordered the helm over so that the two ships struck obliquely. For nearly an hour a dozen U.S. Navy warships pounded *Tennessee* at close range, ramming her three times. Finally at about 0900, a white flag went up on board the rebel ram and the Battle of Mobile Bay was over. Although the city of Mobile held out until the end of the war, Farragut's victory effectively closed the port.

Wilmington, North Carolina, proved tougher than Mobile, and nearly as difficult as Charleston. In a remarkable display of naval dominance, Federal forces assembled a fleet of fifty-nine warships to pummel Fort Fisher that guarded the entrance to the Cape Fear River twenty miles downstream from Wilmington. Even then, it required two attempts and effective joint operations to overcome the Confederate defenses and close the river to blockade runners in January 1865.

By then the Confederacy was collapsing on all fronts. Lee evacuated Richmond on 3 April, and a week later he surrendered his Army at Appomattox Court House. Lee's capitulation was not the last military action of the war, but it was the decisive event and led to other surrenders. James Waddell's CSS *Shenandoah* was cruising off Baja, California, when he heard the news. Rather than lower his flag to U.S. authorities, Waddell took his ship around Cape Horn into the Atlantic and made his way north to Liverpool where he interred his vessel.

Although the Civil War was unquestionably a land war, naval forces on both sides played a significant role in determining how and where it was fought. In addition to the blockade, the U.S. Navy's role on the western rivers, in closing the Confederate ports, and in providing essential logistic support for the U.S. Army was critical. Likewise, the innovative response of Confederate authorities foreshadowed another naval revolution in the ensuing decades.

The dramatic expansion of U.S. naval power during the Civil War is evident in this depiction of the U.S. fleet bombarding Fort Fisher in January 1865. David Dixon Porter committed nearly sixty warships to this bombardment including four monitors (in middle distance). Although the first assault on Fort Fisher failed, a second assault succeeded, and the fall of Fort Fisher effectively closed the last Confederate port connecting Richmond with the outside world. ("Bombardment of Fort Fisher," J.O. Davidson, Naval Historical Center)

In order to be able to see above the smoke of battle, Farragut took a position in the rigging of his flagship, USS Hartford. *According to tradition, it was from this position that he directed his squadron to ignore the torpedo threat and steam into the bay. When a subordinate reminded him of the torpedoes ahead in the water, Farragut is reputed to have responded: "Damn the torpedoes!" (Library of Congress)*

1865-1941

You May Fire When Ready, Gridley 1865-1922

James C. Bradford

At the conclusion of the Civil War, the U.S. Navy's 700 ships and 58,000 battle-tested personnel placed it among the largest and best in the world. Its leaders took pride in the Navy's contribution to Union victory, but many were apprehensive about the future. Within five years their fears were realized. Popular attention turned from war and foreign affairs to domestic developments: reconstruction of the South, urban crowding and immigration in the Northeast, constructing communities in the West, and corruption in government virtually everywhere. The Navy was rapidly reduced to only fifty-two ships in commission (1870) and 8,500 personnel (1873).

Defense policy returned to that of the prewar era: coastal warships and fortifications to protect against foreign invasion, Army troops to garrison those forts and others in the West to defend settlers against Indian attacks, and naval cruisers to protect American commerce around the world. The Navy appeared adequate for these roles. Its monitors seemed able to repel any attack by a transatlantic foe and its sail-steam cruisers more than adequate to ensure American traders access to world markets. When President Ulysses S. Grant ordered the Mediterranean and North Atlantic squadrons to rendezvous off Key West in 1873, reacting to the Spanish impoundment of SS *Virginius*, a blockade runner caught running guns to rebels in Cuba while flying the U.S. flag, the poor quality of the Navy's ships was clear to any observer. But when Spain released *Virginius*, few Americans exhibited any interest in the decrepit state of the Navy and nothing was done to improve it.

Two decades later when the murder of two American sailors from USS *Baltimore* (C 3) and the beating of sixteen others by a mob in Valparaiso almost led to war between the United States and Chile, Americans were chagrined to learn that the South American republic had a superior navy in some ways. The "rebirth" of the U.S. Navy became a matter of public interest for the first time. Its intellectual rejuvenation began in 1873 with the establishment of the Naval Institute as a forum for "the advancement of professional, literary, and scientific knowledge in the Navy," and its publication of *The Papers and Proceedings of the United States Naval Institute* beginning in 1874. Eight years later the Office of Naval Intelligence was formed and sent its first naval attaché, French Ensor Chadwick, abroad to report on technological developments in the European naval arms race.

Finally, in 1885 the Naval War College opened at Newport, Rhode Island, the world's first institution of learning for senior officers. Stephen B. Luce, the first president of the Naval War College, had long been involved in the training of enlisted men and officers. He quickly brought to Newport Captain Alfred Thayer Mahan, whose books on naval history and strategy and journal articles on a wide

The "old" administration building of the Naval War College in 1886, the year Alfred Thayer Mahan arrived to begin teaching naval tactics and strategy. Built during the 1820s on Coaster's Harbor Island as an asylum for the poor of Newport, it remains in use in the twenty-first century. (Photo: Naval Historical Center)

Pages 60–61: Around 1896, the crew of a broadside 8-inch gun of the armored cruiser USS New York *(ACR 2) poses with the entire weapons system. The projectile, center foreground, required two husky sailors to load, and the barrel under the breech collected the debris of the powder bags swept from the weapon after firing. Aimed manually and fired locally, such guns became outmoded by central gun laying pioneered by Admiral Bradley Fiske. (Photo: Library of Congress)*

Opposite and below: USS Chicago *going into commission. In 1881 Secretary of the Navy William H. Hunt informed Congress that the Navy's wooden ships could no longer protect commerce and appointed a committee of naval officers to recommend what type of ships should be built to replace them. After two years of study and consideration, Congress authorized construction of the protected cruisers USS* Atlanta *(below), USS* Boston, *and USS* Chicago *and the dispatch vessel USS* Dolphin. *Though built of steel with watertight compartments and fully electrified, they retained sail rigging. (Photos: Library of Congress, left, and Naval Historical Center, below)*

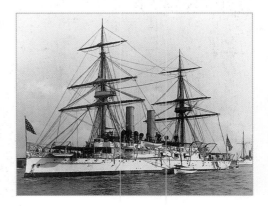

In 1890 Congress authorized construction of USS Indiana *(BB 1)*, USS Massachusetts *(BB 2)*, and USS Oregon *(BB 3)*, the U.S. Navy's first true battleships. When they entered service in 1895 and 1896, they were among the finest warships in the world. Each was 351 feet long, displaced 10,000 tons, and mounted forty guns of various calibers. All fought in the Battle of Santiago. (Photo: Naval Historical Center)

Commander Nathan Sargent, Commanding Officer USS Baltimore *(C 3)* in the ship's flag cabin around 1905. The relative splendor of this cabin, only a few years later than the sparse quarters of the crew shown on the next page, demonstrates the social stratification of the time.

range of topics would earn him worldwide fame as the "Prophet of Sea Power." The philosophical underpinning of the "New Navy" was furthered by civilians such as Theodore Roosevelt, author of *The Naval War of 1812* and the New York attorney James Russell Soley who also wrote naval history and, like Roosevelt, served as Assistant Secretary of the Navy during the 1890s.

The physical rebuilding of the Navy began with the ABCD ships authorized by Congress in 1883. The cruisers USS *Atlanta*, USS *Boston*, and USS *Chicago*, and dispatch vessel USS *Dolphin* were built entirely of steel, had watertight compartments, and were electrified. Plans for the vessels, armor, shafting, and heavy gun mounts had to be purchased abroad, but less than a decade later U. S. Navy vessels were becoming ever more American in both design and materials. The U.S. Navy may not have incorporated all of Europe's innovations in naval architecture and armaments, but at no time was the nation's security at risk nor did American taxpayers waste a great deal of money by constructing ships like those of European navies that were obsolete even before they came off the ways.

The *Indiana*-class battleships laid down in 1891 marked the most significant change in the Navy since the introduction of *Monitor* in 1862. The ABCD ships, USS *New York* (ACR 2), and USS *Olympia* (C 6) all had been designed to execute the traditional roles of commerce protection in time of peace and the raiding of enemy commerce in wartime. Although designated battleships, *Texas* and *Maine* were in fact coastal defense vessels. They could meet the enemy farther from American shores than the monitors still in commission, but they could not cross an ocean without refueling at sea—a difficult task at best during that era. By contrast the *Indiana*-class battleships were designed neither to raid commerce nor as coastal defense ships, but to engage an enemy fleet at long distance and to project American power on a global basis. These were America's first true battleships, and their construction reflected a fundamental shift in American naval strategy.

Left: *The crew was divided into small sections, "messes," each with its own cook. Ingredients were drawn from a central store under the charge of "Jack of the Dust." Individual cooks in each mess then prepared food. Mess cooks live today in the title of sailors assigned unskilled duties in the dining facilities. (Photo: Naval Historical Center)*

Below: *USS* Mahan *(DDG 72) arriving in Tampa, Florida, for liberty call.* Mahan *is the fourth ship to bear the name memorializing the "Father of American Naval Strategy." Her four-letter international call sign flies from the port yardarm, the starboard yardarm carries the signal "Code Hotel," meaning she has a pilot on board. The first* Mahan *was a "four piper" of World War I, DD 102, the second, DD 364, fought in World War II and the third, DLG 11 until redesignated DDG 42, was a veteran of the Cold War.*

Left: *USS* Chicago's *baseball team around 1889 is an example of early morale and welfare activities of the modern Navy. The record of the baseball team is not known, but the pose of the photograph mimics those of professional teams of the times, indicating the seriousness of the endeavor. (Photo: Naval Historical Center)*

Below: *The garrison paraded in front of quarters at Aspinwall, Panama, during an intervention in 1885. As in virtually every short-term intervention of any size before World War II, sailors serving as infantrymen provided the bulk of the forces put ashore. The Landing Party Manual describing the organization and training of sailors in this role existed into the Cold War era, though after expansion of the Marine Corps during World War II use of sailors in this role was only for drill or inspection. (Photo: Naval Historical Center)*

The naval renaissance came none too early. By 1898 the United States and Spain were on a collision course brought on by American sympathy for revolutionaries seeking independence for Cuba. Prior to this time the Navy had successfully fought the "Weekend War" with Korea in 1871, intervened in Panama to keep open transit across the isthmus in 1885, and assisted Americans in establishing an independent republic in Hawaii in 1893. These operations protected American interests, lives, and property, but in Cuba something more was at stake, including the humanitarian desire to assist people. Further, the opponent, Spain, was far more powerful than any foreign power engaged since Great Britain in the War of 1812.

On 25 January 1898, the battleship *Maine* dropped anchor at Havana much to the resentment of Spanish officials. The port visit had been requested by American consul Fitzhugh Lee "to help control the situation," i.e., to protect American citizens and their property during the hostilities between Spain and her rebelling colonists. Tensions heightened when the *New York Journal* published a letter in which Spain's minister to the United States, Dupuy De Lóme, called President William McKinley "weak and a bidder for the admiration of the crowd." On 15 February a mysterious explosion killed 253 of *Maine*'s

William T. Sampson, head of the court of inquiry impaneled to investigate the 15 February 1898 destruction of Maine, *reported that* Maine *was "destroyed by [an] external agency." But in 1976 Admiral Hyman G. Rickover published a more convincing analysis of the disaster, which concluded that the explosion of coal dust in a forward bunker set off ammunition in an adjoining magazine causing the vessel to sink. (Photo: Naval Historical Center)*

The foremast of USS Maine *sits on the waterfront at the Naval Academy. The upperworks of the mast have not been altered since the explosion and the deformation of the platform is evident. The main mast of the ship is also a memorial on a small hill behind the Amphitheater in Arlington National Cemetery. The distance between the two gave rise to the question to Plebes at the Naval Academy, "What is the longest ship in the Navy?"*

358 officers and men, sent the ship to the bottom of Havana harbor, and incensed American public opinion.

While McKinley maneuvered to avoid war, the Navy prepared for combat. On 25 February, Assistant Secretary of the Navy Theodore Roosevelt took advantage of the temporary absence of Secretary of the Navy John D. Long from the office to send a cablegram to Commodore George Dewey, commander of the Asiatic Fleet, ordering Dewey to gather his forces and to "keep full of coal. In the event of [war with Spain] see that the Spanish squadron does not leave the Asiatic coast and then [undertake] offensive operations in the Philippine Islands." Three weeks later a flying squadron was formed to protect the eastern seaboard from Spanish attack. On the next day the battleship USS *Oregon* (BB 3) left California for the Caribbean. "McKinley's Bulldog," as the ship became known, made the 14,700-mile voyage in the record time of only sixty-seven days, but by the time it reached Florida on 24 May, war had been declared.

The Spanish-American War, dubbed a "Splendid Little War" by Secretary of State John Hay, lasted less than four months, but started the United States on the road to world power. By late March American public opinion demanded war and President McKinley sent an ultimatum to Spain demanding its withdrawal from Cuba. When the Spanish government agreed to negotiations with the Cuban rebels but ignored his demand for Cuban independence, McKinley asked Congress for authority to intervene. On 19 April Congress granted his wish, and three days later McKinley proclaimed a blockade of western Cuba. On 25 April Congress declared that a state of war existed with Spain, and Secretary of the Navy Long cabled Dewey: "Proceed at once to Philippine Islands. Commence operations . . . against Spanish fleet."

Dewey responded with alacrity, steamed to the Philippines, and reached Luzon on 30 April. Not finding the Spanish squadron at Subic Bay, he proceeded to Manila Bay. Dewey ran his fleet past Spanish defenses at the mouth of the bay under the cover of darkness, found Rear Admiral Patricio Montojo y Parasón's warships anchored off Cavite, and immediately engaged them. Dewey closed to within 5,000 yards and at 5:40 a.m. told his flag captain on board *Olympia*, "You may fire when ready, Gridley." By noon on 1 May the cruisers *Maria Crislina*,

Castillo, and *Don Antonio de Ulloa* rested on the bottom of Manila Bay, the transport *Isla de Mindanao* was destroyed, and the remaining Spanish gunboats were abandoned. Eight Americans were slightly wounded versus Spanish casualties of ninety-one killed and 280 wounded. Dispatching news of his victory to Washington, Dewey announced that he could occupy Manila at any time, but that he lacked enough men to hold the city. Officials in Washington immediately initiated plans to dispatch an army to take control of the Philippines.

On the day of Dewey's victory, word arrived in Washington that Rear Admiral Pascual Cervera y Topete had sailed from the Cape Verde Islands on 29 April with a Spanish fleet. Hoping to intercept him as he entered the Caribbean, Rear Admiral William T. Sampson positioned his two battleships, an armored cruiser, two cruisers, two monitors, and a torpedo boat along the north coast of Puerto Rico. Cervera stopped at Martinique. Refused coal by the French there, he proceeded to Curaco off the coast of Venezuela, purchased coal at the Dutch colony, then made straight for Cuba's south coast and entered the long narrow harbor at Santiago on 19 May. Ten days later Commodore Winfield Scott Schley's flying squadron located Cervera's fleet and three days later Sampson's fleet arrived off the harbor to engage the Spanish. A stalemate quickly developed: The Spanish would not come out of the harbor and the Americans dared not challenge the forts guarding its entrance.

On 20 June naval transports carrying Army forces under Major General William R. Shafter reached Daiquiri where they were put ashore and quickly

Above: *An electrician adjusts the brushes on a steam driven electric generator on USS* Oregon *(BB 3). New technology not only brought steel hulls but electricity and hydraulics to warships. Engineering officers and enlisted technicians became more than bodies in the crew—they were essential to make the ship go. (Photo: U.S. Naval Institute)*

Top: *Rear Admiral William T. Sampson drew up blockading positions for the North Atlantic Squadron off Santiago. When they did sortie on 3 July, Sampson was en route to a meeting with Army General Shafter. The battle was virtually over before he could join the engagement. When he sent the cable, "The fleet under my command offers the nation as a Fourth of July present the whole of Cervera's fleet," his second in command, Rear Admiral Winfield Scott Schley, believed that Sampson sought to deprive him of the laurels of victory. Animosity between partisans of Sampson and Schley soured relations within the naval officer corps for over a decade. (Alfonso Sanz, Navy Art Collection)*

Above: *Many of President Theodore Roosevelt's foreign policy initiatives depended upon there being a Navy able to enforce them. In addition to his service as the Assistant Secretary of the Navy before the Spanish American War, Roosevelt wrote an authoritative naval history,* The Naval War of 1812. *He had a firm grasp of naval matters and maritime affairs.*

encircled the city of Santiago. Once it became clear that Sampson and Shafter both expected the other to attack the Spanish first, Sampson sought a face-to-face meeting with the general. As he steamed eastward on board *New York* for a meeting on 3 July, the Spanish broke the deadlock between the American commanders for them. Anticipating that the surrender of Santiago was near, Cuban Governor General Ramon Blanco ordered Cervera to sortie. With USS *Massachusetts* (BB 2) coaling at Guantanamo and *New York* steaming away from Santiago, Cervera picked an opportune time to dash for the sea. His flagship, *Maria Teresa* led the cruisers *Vizcaya, Cristobal Colon,* and *Oquendo,* and two destroyers out of the harbor, emerging from its mouth in single file at 9:35 a.m.

Again American victory came swiftly as the Spanish ships were battered by gunfire until their captains beached them along the coast west of Santiago. Every ship was destroyed or surrendered, 160 Spaniards lost their lives, and 1,800 were taken prisoner. Americans suffered only one killed and another wounded. Its fleets devastated, the Spanish government had no choice but to surrender, grant Cuba its independence, and transfer ownership of the Philippines, Guam, and Puerto Rico to the United States.

Thus in the aftermath of the war with Spain the United States became an imperial power. In rapid succession it annexed Hawaii, divided Samoa with Germany, and asserted control over the Wake Islands. In addition to defending this new empire, the Navy would also be charged with enforcing new foreign policies that came with it. In the Open Door Notes, America committed itself to maintaining equal opportunity for all nations to trade and invest in China as well as preserving the territorial and administrative integrity of that nation. Such lofty ideals were beyond enforcement by the United States, but they remained the basis of American foreign policy in the Far East into the 1930s. As a visible sign of

American presence and its determination to uphold these policies, U.S. naval vessels patrolled the coasts of China and some of its rivers .

American Caribbean policy rested on the Monroe Doctrine and Theodore Roosevelt's Corollary, which stated that should intervention be necessary in the affairs of any Western Hemisphere nation, the United States would be the sole executor of such intervention. Roosevelt sought to protect Latin American nations from European interference, but he and succeeding presidents also used their self-assumed power to protect the lives and economic interests of Americans in the region. In the decade between Roosevelt's announcement of his corollary in December 1904 and United States entry into World War I, the Navy and Marines took control of the customs service of the Dominican Republic, intervened in Cuba, Nicaragua, and Panama, and occupied Veracruz, Mexico.

Having become a world rather than a Western Hemispheric power, the United States was drawn into the naval arms race that contributed to the outbreak of World War I. Under Roosevelt's leadership America launched a building program aimed at giving it a navy second only to Great Britain's. Beginning in 1903 the United States began laying down two battleships almost every year. The Naval Academy was rebuilt and expanded to provide officers for the new ships. A recruiting system and a shore-based training infrastructure was established to attract and train young men from throughout the nation, and a general board was established to advise the president on naval policy and strategy. In 1907 Roosevelt sent the Great White Fleet of American battleships on a fourteen-month, 46,000-mile voyage around the world. Designed to reassure citizens of the West Coast that the fleet could steam to their defense in time of danger, and to impress other nations, especially Japan, with the power of the U.S. Navy, this giant training exercise caught the imagination of the American people and increased support for expanding the fleet.

Above, left: Americans played a leading role in the development of submarine warfare. In 1897 John P. Holland and Simon Lake both launched submarines. Lake's Arrogant *was generally judged inferior to the* Holland's *more hydrodynamic design. Holland's invention earned him the title "Father of the Modern Submarine." (Photo: Naval Historical Center)*

Above: The U.S. Navy pioneered aviation at sea. On 14 November 1910 Eugene Ely, a civilian, became the first person to pilot a plane from the deck of a ship when he flew his Curtiss Pusher from a temporary platform erected on the bow of USS Birmingham *(CS 2) in Hampton Roads, Virginia. (Photo: Naval Historical Center)*

Below, left: This photograph taken from USS Georgia *(BB 15) shows the battleships of the Great White Fleet as they entered the Straits of Magellan on their round-the-world cruise, 1907–1908. (Photo: Naval Historical Center)*

Below: The mascot of the battleship USS Connecticut *(BB 18) was a bear, being fed here by Coxswain Deglen. (Photo: Naval Historical Center)*

THEY KEPT THE
SEA LANES
OPEN

INVEST IN THE
VICTORY LIBERTY LOAN

Above: *The incident on which this poster is based occurred on 17 November 1917 when USS* Fanning *(DD 37) forced* U-58 *to surface.* Fanning *closed and took off the German survivors. This was the first successful antisubmarine warfare (ASW) action by the U.S. Navy. (Library of Congress)*

Above, right: *The heavy clothing, gloves, and three men using binoculars indicate that their destroyer is on convoy duty in the North Atlantic. In both world wars, convoy duty meant long hours on open bridges in cold and wet weather for officers and crew of small escort ships. (Photo: Naval Historical Center)*

Secretary of the Navy Josephus Daniels and Chief of Naval Operations Admiral William S. Benson, photographed at the Versailles Peace Conference at the end of World War I, worked together harmoniously. Benson became the first Chief of Naval Operations over thirty-one more senior officers because Daniels believed that he could get along with Benson better than with reformers such as Rear Admiral Bradley A. Fiske, who Daniels believed had a "consuming passion . . . to confer all power on the head of Operations," thereby undercutting civilian control of the Navy. (Photo: Naval Historical Center)

When World War I broke out in Europe in 1914, Americans were determined to remain neutral. The inconclusive Battle of Jutland and the threat of a German victory led President Woodrow Wilson to call for "a Navy second to none," based on a building program that would add ten battleships, six battle cruisers, ten scout cruisers, fifty destroyers, and sixty-seven submarines to the fleet in only three years. Such a navy could secure American interests regardless of the outcome of the war in Europe. In little more than a year Germany's proposed alliance with Mexico, its intrigue with Japan, and its inauguration of unrestricted submarine warfare in early 1917 led America into the war. As in the past, whenever a conflict infringed upon the ability of American ships to navigate freely the North Atlantic, the nation felt compelled to defend its maritime rights and was drawn into war.

When Congress declared war on Germany on 6 April 1917, the United States joined a coalition of powers, and for the first time since the American Revolution had to coordinate strategy and operations with an ally. Rear Admiral William S. Sims reached London with orders to study war at sea and to recommend how the United States should employ its Navy. Sims was shocked to learn that German submarines were sinking British cargo ships faster than they could be replaced, and that the Admiralty feared starvation in Britain by summer if the Germans were not soon countered. When he learned of a report by Royal Navy officers that demonstrated the success of convoys in protecting shipping between Britain, France, and Norway, Sims convinced British Prime Minister David Lloyd George to implement a convoy system that quickly began to reduce losses. To assist in convoy operations, the U.S. Navy dispatched Destroyer Division 8 to Ireland. When the six destroyers reached Queenstown on 4 May and British Vice Admiral Sir Lewis Bayly asked when they would be ready for service, Commander Joseph K. Taussig replied, "We are ready now, sir." Although skeptical that the destroyers could begin operations without major maintenance following their transatlantic voyage, Bayly ordered them to sea and found Taussig was correct. In November the American destroyers USS *Fanning* (DD 37) and USS *Nicholson* (DD 52) forced *U-58* to surface and rescued its crew before the submarine sank: the first to be destroyed by the U.S. Navy.

Meanwhile, in America the Navy organized for war. In May the Cruiser and Transport Service was formed to ferry American troops and supplies to Europe. By war's end it carried almost a million men to France without the loss of a single life to enemy action. Naval aviation was rapidly expanded, and units dispatched to Europe, the first reaching France on 5 and 6 June. These proved the lead elements in what would total 500 planes and 16,000 men stationed at twenty-six naval air stations, sixteen in France, five in Ireland, three in England, and two in Italy. By late 1917 the

five American dreadnoughts of Battleship Division 9, USS *Delaware* (BB 28), USS *Florida* (BB 30), USS *New York* (BB 34), USS *Texas* (BB 35), and USS *Wyoming* (BB 32), began operations with the British Grand Fleet based at Scapa Flow in the Orkney Islands. Back in the United States labor and material were soon reallocated from the construction of battleships to the production of destroyers and patrol craft to counter the U-boat threat. The first of the new 110-foot wooden-hulled subchasers did not reach Europe until May 1918, but the 121 ultimately sent across the Atlantic played an important role in antisubmarine warfare in British, French, and Italian waters.

Naval relations between the United States and Great Britain were not always smooth. Secretary of the Navy Josephus Daniels and Chief of Naval Operations William Benson were reluctant to send to European waters the size fleet the British wished because they calculated that the loss there might leave the United States vulnerable to German attack.

President Wilson questioned relying on convoys to counter the U-boat menace and advocated attacking their bases, preferring to go after "the hornet's nest," rather than "hunting hornets all over the farm." By late 1918 Anglo-American cooperation was close and the friendship of the two nations solid. Working together, their navies developed mutual respect and links that would serve both well when they joined to fight a second world war only two decades later.

When the armistice ending World War I took effect on 11 November 1918, the Navy was only beginning to reach its potential. A second battleship division had reached the war zone in late August. Stationed in Ireland to protect American troop convoys against a breakout by elements of the German High Seas Fleet, its three battleships, the USS *Nevada* (BB 36), USS *Oklahoma* (BB 37), and USS *Utah* (BB 31), had yet to see service. Perhaps most important, work continued on the

Hard-pressed by U-boat attacks, British officials asked Rear Admiral William S. Sims, U.S. naval representative in London, for American assistance on 10 April 1917. Four days later Commander Joseph K. Taussig was ordered to prepare Destroyer Division 8 for "long and distant service." When the six destroyers reached Queenstown, Ireland, on 4 May, they began operations immediately. ("Return of the Mayflower," Bernard Gribble, U.S. Naval Academy Museum)

In March 1917 Congress authorized the enlistment of women in the Navy to perform the clerical duties of the yeoman rate, and by the end of the war, 11,275 women served. These "Yeomanettes," as they were nick-named, are at work here in the offices of the Naval Overseas Transport Service, responsible for getting American soldiers and supplies to Europe. (Photo: Naval Historical Center)

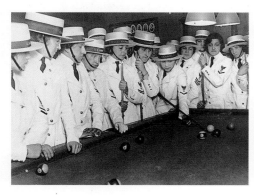

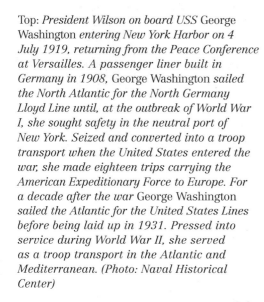

Top: *President Wilson on board USS* George Washington *entering New York Harbor on 4 July 1919, returning from the Peace Conference at Versailles. A passenger liner built in Germany in 1908,* George Washington *sailed the North Atlantic for the North Germany Lloyd Line until, at the outbreak of World War I, she sought safety in the neutral port of New York. Seized and converted into a troop transport when the United States entered the war, she made eighteen trips carrying the American Expeditionary Force to Europe. For a decade after the war* George Washington *sailed the Atlantic for the United States Lines before being laid up in 1931. Pressed into service during World War II, she served as a troop transport in the Atlantic and Mediterranean. (Photo: Naval Historical Center)*

Above: *The stern faces of these "Yeomanettes" indicate that the photograph was probably posed to show that their lives were not all work, though few appear to be enjoying their leisure time and fewer still seem to appreciate the finer points of the game. (Photo: Naval Historical Center)*

Above, right: *Made possible by the American invention of the antennae mine, the North Sea Mine Barrage stretched across 240 miles of open sea between Scotland and Norway. The initial field was laid between 8 June and 20 September 1918, but it was constantly expanded until the end of the war. The Naval Overseas Transport Service carried 82,000 mines to Europe. The crew of this converted merchant ship is laying some of the 56,611 placed in position by U.S. forces; the British laid another 13,652. (Photo: National Archives)*

North Sea Mine Barrage between Scotland and Norway. Over 70,000 mines were in place in a band stretching across 240 miles of open sea, eighty percent placed there by American forces. Six U-boats may have been destroyed attempting to slip through the minefield, but many others made it, usually by hugging the coast of Norway. Avoiding the mines lengthened the time and distance these submarines had to sail to reach the trade routes, thereby limiting the time they could spend on station. Against these accomplishments during the war, the U.S. Navy lost only one major warship, USS *San Diego* (ACR 6), a cruiser sunk by a mine on 19 July 1918 while on convoy duty off Fire Island, New York.

When President Wilson viewed the postwar world he found reason for alarm. During the war Japan had made demands on China that if met would seriously undermine Chinese independence and therefore challenge America's Open Door policy. Maritime issues, especially German unrestricted submarine warfare, had played a major role in Wilson's decision to lead America into war, and the president was angered by the Allies' refusal to accept the principle of "absolute freedom of navigation upon the seas, outside territorial waters, alike in peace and in war," the second of the "Fourteen Points" he laid out as a basis for the peace settlement. Although his motive is not totally clear, this consideration must have influenced Wilson to call not only for completion of his 1916 building program, which would have given the United States the world's most powerful fleet, but also for the construction of thirty-five additional ships.

To avert a renewed naval arms race, diplomats from nine nations gathered in Washington, D.C., in November 1921 to discuss arms limitations and related issues. The result was a series of nine treaties, three of which were of paramount importance. Americans were particularly pleased with the Nine-Power Pact that committed Western nations and Japan to respect the Open Door in China. They also liked the provision of the Four-Power Pact that abrogated the Anglo-Japanese Naval Alliance of 1902, replacing it with a pledge by Japan, France, Britain, and America to respect each other's possessions in the Pacific and to settle disputes in the region through consultation.

Of immediate importance was the Five-Power Pact. It established a ten-year ban on the construction of capital ships, and set a ratio for battleships and aircraft carriers among Britain, the United States, Japan, France, and Italy, at 5:5:3:1.75:1.75 respectively. The pact also limited the size of battleships to 35,000

USS Texas's (BB 35) first action was at Vera Cruz in 1914. She served in the Grand Fleet in World War I, and was part of the bombardment forces at the amphibious landings in North Africa, Normandy, Southern France, Iwo Jima, and Okinawa in World War II. Retired in 1948, she is open to visitors at San Jacinto Battleground Historical Park, LaPorte, Texas. (Photo: David A. Manning)

tons displacement and their main battery to 16-inch guns. Cruisers and aircraft carriers could not exceed 27,000 tons or have guns larger than 8-inch. Britain and Japan objected to extending the ratios to cruisers and other naval vessels, so they were not included. Finally a non-fortification clause banned construction of fortified bases outside Japan's home islands, Hawaii, and Singapore. More warships were stricken from the naval list as a result of the Five Power Pact than were sunk in battle during World War I.

Political and military leaders debated whether the Washington treaties ensured American security or rendered the nation and its possessions indefensible. Regardless of their assessments of the treaties, admirals in the Navy could only look back in wonder. Most had entered the Naval Academy during the 1870s while the Navy continued its decline following the Civil War. As junior officers they had participated in the revival of the 1880s and 1890s, watched as modern steam and steel vessels replaced the wooden vessels of the old sailing Navy, and held their first commands at the turn of the century as the United States took its place among the leading naval powers of the world. By 1922 many naval officers naturally speculated about the future, some with concern, but most felt pride at the role their service had played in making the United States a great power.

One of the railroad guns built and manned by the Navy in World War I in the park outside The Navy Museum, Washington Navy Yard. This gun is among the extensive collection that includes weapons predating the Revolutionary War. The museum is open to the public throughout the year. (Photo: David A. Manning)

A Navy Second to None
1922-1941

Thomas C. Hone

The battleship USS Arizona (BB 39). Spotting for her twelve 14-inch guns was done by her floatplane spotting aircraft and from the top level of her tripod masts. The "clock" on the forward leg of her foremast was in fact a range indicator, so that the ship ahead would know the range of Arizona's target. (Photo: National Archives)

When the governments of the United States, Great Britain, Japan, Italy, and France signed the Five-Power Pact limiting naval armaments in February 1922, the U.S. Navy was at last second to none. The treaty allowed the United States a navy the equal of that of the British Empire and superior to that of the Empire of Japan. Yet the U.S. Navy was like a man caught straddling a fence—not quite out of one world and not entirely safe in a new position. The treaty had frozen much of the Navy in place, cut off much of the massive building program authorized in 1916, and curtailed the planned investment in the ship of the future—the aircraft carrier. The result was a powerful navy, but not powerful enough to gain control of both the Pacific and the Atlantic if the United States were to fight a two-ocean war.

One goal of the Washington Treaty had been to keep any navy a party to it from building up enough strength to overcome its main rival with one major offensive. The treaty therefore left Japan strong in the western Pacific while conceding dominance of the eastern Pacific and the Caribbean to the United States. In the event of a conflict between them, neither navy could be sure of defeating the other with just its treaty strength. The treaty also constrained the advance of naval technology. The three major naval technologies that showed great promise in World War I were the radio, the airplane, and the submarine. Though the treaty's authors could do nothing about radio communications and could not agree to eliminate the submarine, they did place limits on both the size and number of aircraft carriers. Aircraft carriers could be as large as 27,000 tons standard displacement, but the total carrier tonnage allowed the major navies was restricted to 135,000 tons for the United States and Great Britain, and 81,000 tons for Japan. This limited the number of carriers that these navies could build.

Until Japan withdrew from "the treaty system" in 1936, the U.S. Navy struggled to increase its actual fighting power within the tonnage and technological constraints agreed to in Washington in 1922. Denied new battleships by treaty, the U.S. Navy modernized the ones it had. Denied a fleet of carriers, it searched for

The fourteen battleships of the U.S. Fleet in line ahead formation in 1936, led by fleet flagship Pennsylvania. *The battleships have deployed to fire at an imaginary enemy force to starboard, and three floatplanes are flying out to relieve aircraft already spotting the fire of the battleships' big guns. The painting portrays the fleet engagement that the Navy anticipated in the early 1930s—lines of battleships slugging it out at over-the-horizon range. ("Pacific Bulwark," James Flood)*

USS Lexington's *(CV 2) air group ranged on her flight deck prior to flight operations in 1934. One of her escorting destroyers is off her port quarter, serving as a plane guard. Plane guard destroyers rescued pilots whose aircraft accidentally pitched into the water during landings and takeoffs. (Photo: National Archives)*

The huge airship Macon with two of her specially designed scout aircraft. Macon and her sister Akron each carried five of these Sparrowhawks in an internal hangar. One of the planes is on display in the Smithsonian Institution's Air and Space Museum in Washington, D.C. Macon and Akron were designed as very long-range scouts. Both airships were lost in storms. (Photo: National Archives)

World War I destroyer USS Perry (DD 340) refuels from the battleship USS Pennsylvania (BB 38) while underway in 1932. Destroyers carried less fuel than larger ships, and so the Navy, under the leadership of future Admiral Chester W. Nimitz, pioneered the transfer of oil at sea, eventually including delivery from battleships and carriers to their escorting destroyers. (Photo: Naval Historical Center)

alternative means of projecting its aviation striking power through the use of long-range seaplanes and huge aircraft-carrying airships. Denied funds during the decade after the Washington Treaty was signed, the U.S. Navy nevertheless pursued new technologies—in electronics and in gunnery fire control—and new tactics, particularly attack from the air. The period between the wars was therefore both exciting and frustrating—a time of revolutionary developments in aviation and electronics and yet also a time when naval tradition made a last stand by focusing on the central tactical role of the battleship in a daylight fleet versus fleet engagement.

The strategic problem facing the U.S. Navy was daunting. Army and Navy planners assumed that Japan would attack the Philippines in the beginning of any war with the United States. The defenses of the Philippines, which could not be modernized because of the Washington Treaty, were assumed adequate to hold Manila Bay and perhaps the Bataan Peninsula for no more than six months. In that time, the Navy, accompanied by a relief force of Army divisions, would have to fight its way across the Pacific in the teeth of Japanese opposition. How the Navy could break through Japanese defenses and rescue the Philippines was the question that preoccupied Navy war planners and tacticians. Little thought was given to a two-ocean war.

Navy planners had been thinking about a Pacific campaign since the United States had annexed the Philippines, but the restrictions imposed by the Washington Treaty, combined with the high cost of new naval technologies, especially aviation, posed a serious problem for Navy leaders. They could not procure and maintain both existing (gunnery) and new (aviation) forces at a level sufficient to overwhelm the Imperial Japanese Navy. Indeed, the growth in the reliability and striking power of airplanes, for example, gave Japan a new and potentially very potent weapon that it could shift quickly from base to base to counter an American move

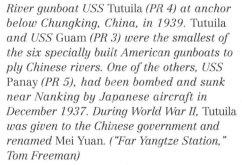

across the Pacific. Similarly, the increased range of submarines meant that Japan might be able to impose a blockade on Pearl Harbor, bottling up U.S. Navy forces there and forestalling an American offensive.

The admirals sitting on the General Board, who served as advisors to the Secretary of the Navy, had recognized as early as 1919 that the fleet would have to carry its own aviation as it went west. They had recommended a vigorous program of aviation development, one that would provide the fleet with one carrier for every three battleships. Unfortunately for this plan, the Washington Treaty made this goal unattainable, and by 1923 the service still had only one experimental carrier—USS *Langley* (CV 1), converted from a modern collier. Progress in aviation was necessarily slower than desired. Yet progress—at times spectacular—there was, and by the summer of 1941 the U.S. Navy was on the verge of a revolution in carrier striking power.

High-frequency radio communications allowed widely separated fleet units to coordinate their movements, but over-the-horizon radio communications had to be

River gunboat USS Tutuila *(PR 4) at anchor below Chungking, China, in 1939. Tutuila and USS* Guam *(PR 3) were the smallest of the six specially built American gunboats to ply Chinese rivers. One of the others, USS* Panay *(PR 5), had been bombed and sunk near Nanking by Japanese aircraft in December 1937. During World War II, Tutuila was given to the Chinese government and renamed* Mei Yuan. *("Far Yangtze Station," Tom Freeman)*

The former collier Jupiter *was converted into USS* Langley *(CV 1), the U.S. Navy's first aircraft carrier. Though described by Admiral William A. Moffett as "entirely inadequate,"* Langley *served as a carrier until 1936, when she became a seaplane tender in which capacity she served until sunk by Japanese bombers in February 1942. On her, the rudiments of carrier aviation were created. (Photo: National Archives)*

Above: *USS* Ranger*'s (CV 4) aircraft, shielded temporarily from the wind by hinged palisades, are spotted for takeoff. (Photo: National Archives)*

Above, right: *USS* Ranger *(CV 4) entering Hampton Roads in 1937.* Ranger *was the first ship designed and built as a carrier for the Navy. This photograph shows her funnels rigged at the horizontal and her very small island. (Photo: National Archives)*

Vindicator dive-bomber taking off from carrier USS Saratoga *(CV 3) in 1938.* Saratoga*'s high speed created a strong "wind over deck," enabling most aircraft of this period to get airborne after a short flight deck run. (Photo: Naval Historical Center)*

sent in code in case they were intercepted. The Navy had experimented with radio direction finding receivers in World War I, and in 1918 the Royal Navy had shared with selected Americans the secret of its successful interception and decoding of German naval communications. In 1921, the Office of Naval Intelligence stole a copy of the Imperial Japanese Navy's code book. The next year, the Office of the Chief of Naval Operations (OPNAV) began development of an electric cipher machine for use by the fleet. In 1924, the Office of Naval Communications within OPNAV set up a fledgling communications intelligence branch. It was just a start—there were only seven personnel—but it was the germ of one of the most important Navy programs to be established in the years before World War II.

The submarine was an altogether different matter. One of the primary reasons the United States declared war against Germany and her allies in 1917 was to stop unrestricted submarine warfare. Throughout the 1920s and 1930s, the government of the United States pledged to adhere to the legal prohibitions on unrestricted submarine warfare that had been endorsed by a number of international conferences. At the same time, the Navy worked hard to construct a submarine with long range, adequate facilities such as air conditioning, and a heavy torpedo load. As Captain (later Admiral) Thomas Hart told senior admirals in 1919, Japan was the Great Britain of the Pacific—vulnerable to a submarine blockade.

Before and during World War I, the U.S. Navy fielded only coast defense submarines. The 1916 congressional Navy authorization led to the construction of a larger type, but these S-class boats proved to lack the necessary endurance for Pacific warfare when Captain Hart led a force of them from New London, Connecticut, to Manila in 1921. The problem was propulsion. U.S. diesel engine manufacturers could not produce equipment that met German standards for World War I duty, let alone what was required for a transpacific campaign against Japan.

In 1922, the military characteristics a submarine should have or how it could be built in the United States were not known. Submarine officers wanted a "fleet boat" with which to experiment, but the Navy's Bureau of Construction and Repair could not get them to agree on a clear set of characteristics. The result was a series of essentially experimental submarines. The first, three B types, were, at 2,100 tons displacement, more than twice the size of the preceding S-class boats. The next class, three "cruiser" submarines, carried two 6-inch deck guns apiece (for shelling

merchantmen), approached 3,000 tons in displacement, and finally had the range (8,000 nautical miles at ten knots speed) to patrol the Pacific. Unfortunately, they were slow to submerge (a fatal flaw if attacked by a fast-diving airplane), ungainly and slow submerged and therefore vulnerable to depth charging by surface ships, and could not—because of the London Treaty of 1930—be built in enough numbers to do the job of cutting off Japanese seagoing commerce.

The London Treaty of 1930 halted the construction of large cruiser submarines and limited the total tonnage of submarines to just 52,700 tons. Displacement of each had to be less than 2,000 tons. Under these restrictions, only twenty-six large, long-range submarines could be deployed and that was not enough to meet the requirements for scouting, fleet support, and commerce raiding. Submarine officers and the naval architects in the Bureau of Construction and Repair worked to develop a submarine of high endurance, relatively high sustained surface speed, a powerful torpedo armament, and a healthy environment for the crew—and they eventually got it, just in time for the great building program of 1940.

The organization of the Navy in this period reflected the focus on the Pacific. Most of the fighting ships were based in California, at San Diego and

Seven submarines moored alongside tender USS Holland (AS 3) in 1937. From left to right they are USS Nautilus (SS 168) and USS Narwhal (SS 167); beyond them are USS Shark (SS 174), USS Dolphin (SS 169), USS Porpoise (SS 172), USS Pike (SS 173), and USS Tarpon (SS 175). The forward 6-inch gun of Narwhal is visible. She and Nautilus were designed as very long-range scouts and commerce raiders. Early submarines were given letter-number names. During the 1930s submarines were named for sea creatures. For consistency, these later ships were still painted with a letter-number designation despite the ships being assigned SS series hull numbers. In 1941, SS series hull numbers were painted on the ships. (Photo: Naval Historical Center)

Underway off Portsmouth, New Hampshire, where she commissioned in March 1941, USS Grayling (SS 209) typified the end of years of development and several classes of submarines; each improved over the last. By 1939 the parameters were set for the "fleet boats" so successful in the Pacific campaigns. Just over 300 feet long and displacing 2,400 tons submerged, these ships had the range, endurance, and speed that would make them the scourge of the Japanese merchant marine. (Photo: Naval Historical Center)

Above: *The destroyers USS* Monaghan *(DD 354), USS* Dale *(DD 353), and USS* Worden *(DD 352) dash through a smoke screen laid by Navy patrol planes in a demonstration staged for Movietone newsreel cameras in 1936. Attacks through such smoke screens were an essential part of destroyer tactics. (Photo: Naval Historical Center)*

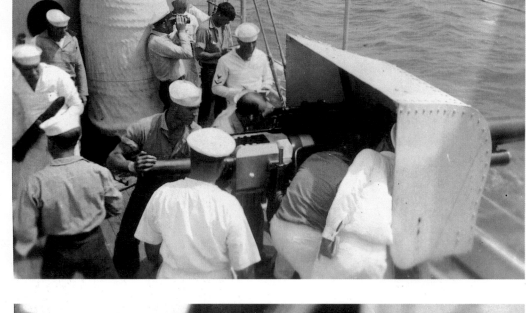

Above: *Outrigger canoes alongside the heavy cruiser USS* Augusta *(CA 31) in the Philippines, 1936. This was just the sort of scene that inspired young men from farms and small towns in the Midwest to "join the Navy and see the world." (Photo: Naval Historical Center)*

Upper right: *The crew of one of the 3-inch guns of converted yacht USS* Isabel *(PY 10) drilling in 1933.* Isabel*, purchased by the Navy during World War I, was still in active service "on the China station" in 1939. (Photo: Naval Historical Center)*

Lower right: *Machinist's Mate Paul Schaefer from light cruiser USS* Memphis *(CL 13) with two visiting Japanese sailors in Manila in 1931. Relations between the Japanese and American navies were not always so cordial, especially after Japan went to war with China in July 1937. (Photo: Naval Historical Center)*

San Pedro. The heart of the fleet was the Battle Force—the twelve most modern battleships, plus accompanying light cruiser divisions and destroyer flotillas, and the fleet's aircraft carriers.

By the mid-1930s, the newer heavy cruisers of 10,000 tons displacement with 8-inch guns were grouped with the fleet's seaplane wings to form the Scouting Force, which was also based on the West Coast. The Submarine Force was there, too, as was the Base Force, the collection of auxiliaries (e.g. oilers, tugs, minesweepers that supported the fleet with supplies, repairs, and other essential services). These forces were under the immediate command of the commander in chief, United States Fleet, who commanded the fleet from his flagship, the battleship USS *Pennsylvania* (BB 38) through most of this period. Much smaller forces, under other commanders, were stationed in the Atlantic, the Philippines, the Panama Canal Zone, the Caribbean, and even on the Yangtze River in China.

The Navy's bureaus provided shore support and developed and acquired weapons. Commanded by a senior officer trained as a naval architect, the Bureau of Construction and Repair's uniformed and civilian naval architects, engineers, and draftsmen were responsible for the preliminary and contract designs of Navy ships and for major ship alterations or modernizations. The Bureau of Navigation, run by a line officer, was in fact the Navy's personnel and recruiting agency, though it also published maps and charts as aids to navigation. Ordnance, likewise commanded by a line rear admiral, designed, procured, and tested the service's

weapons and ammunition. Engineering was in charge of ships' boilers and engines, electrical wiring on ships, and radio equipment. Aeronautics designed, procured, tested, and repaired Navy aircraft—and also supervised the training and assignment of pilots and aviation mechanics. Yards and Docks was the Navy's civil engineering corps, responsible for construction and maintenance of piers, drydocks, power plants, repair yards, and other facilities. The functions of the bureaus of Supplies and Accounts and Medicine and Surgery are manifest in their names.

There were also a number of joint Army–Navy agencies. The most important were the flag-level Joint Board where Army–Navy policy disputes were discussed; the Aeronautical Board to coordinate Army and Navy aviation policy; and the Munitions Board, which coordinated plans and schedules for industrial mobilization in the event of war.

As important in the Navy's development between wars were the education and training institutions. The Naval Academy at Annapolis turned midshipmen into officers. Those with strong academic credentials returned to Annapolis seven or eight years later to attend the postgraduate school, or entered graduate programs at prestigious universities. A few young officers studied overseas, in France and in Germany. Selected commanders and captains were assigned to the year's course at the Naval War College in Newport, Rhode Island, where they studied tactical and strategic problems through the use of simulations and war games. Rear Admiral William S. Sims, president of the Naval War College after World War I, had argued forcefully that no officer should be promoted to flag rank who had not attended the War College. For that reason, the best officers sought the War College, especially in the 1920s. Consequently the college became a center of innovation until the expansion of the Navy in the mid- and late 1930s drained highly talented officers away to man new ships.

Secretary Josephus Daniels had left the Navy with a wonderful heritage, the policy of making deliberate training the core of an enlisted man's years in the service. By the mid-1930s, that training began in earnest once a young man was formally accepted into the Navy. Basic instruction took twelve weeks. Then, as apprentice seamen, new recruits were sent aboard ship, where they began the process literally of learning a trade—as firemen maintaining and operating boilers and engines, signalmen, gunners, machinists, electricians, clerks, or deck hands. To advance beyond the status of apprentices, enlisted personnel had to demonstrate ability, reliability, and basic leadership skills. To encourage further training, the Navy rewarded successful trainees with increased pay and responsibility.

Above, left: *The battleship USS* California *(BB 44) being commissioned in 1921 at Mare Island Naval Shipyard. Her Marine detachment has just come aboard, and her sailors are coming up the gangway with their gear packed inside their rolled-up hammocks. (Photo: San Francisco Maritime Museum)*

Above: *Enlisted men's lockers and wash buckets on the light cruiser USS* Brooklyn *(CL 40) in 1938. The small locker held all a sailor's possessions—mostly his uniforms and shoes. His personal bucket was a holdover from the nineteenth century, when sailors had to do all their own washing. The use of the buckets survived until the introduction of centralized laundries. (Photo: Naval Historical Center)*

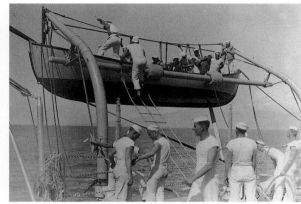

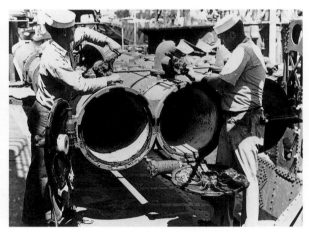

Above: *The galley of a new light cruiser in 1938. By the late 1930s, cafeteria-style meals had replaced the older and more traditional practice of carrying the cooked food from the galley to the crew's living spaces. (Photo: Naval Historical Center)*

Upper right: *Sailors drill with battleship USS* New York's *(BB 34) whaleboat during an exercise in 1932. Rowing contests between ships' boats—a common form of ship-to-ship competition carried over from the days of sail—continued through the 1930s. Contests among ships' crews were often keen. In the case of rowing, it also had a practical side— training sailors for "man overboard" drills. (Photo: Naval Historical Center)*

Above, lower right: *Destroyermen J. Wilkerson (left) and J. W. Linkletter (right) clean the 21-inch torpedo tubes of an old destroyer being reconditioned in 1939. (Photo: Naval Historical Center)*

A seaman's goal was to work his way up the ladder, from apprentice to seaman and then through petty officer grades and finally chief petty officer. Enlisted personnel could prepare for examinations on board ship using instruction books written by the Bureau of Navigation. Trainees worked through their instruction books, took written examinations, and demonstrated their mastery of certain skills. To qualify for gunner's mate third class in 1939, for instance, the trainee had to know how ammunition was marked and stored on board ship; how ammunition magazines were ventilated, lighted, flooded in case of emergency, and cooled, and how ammunition hoists and gun recoil mechanisms worked. The trainee also had to disassemble and reassemble the breech mechanism of a 3-inch or a 5-inch gun, rig a gun for bore sighting, and disassemble and reassemble a .30-caliber rifle and a .45-caliber pistol. And that was just for starters.

Through the 1920s and 1930s, the service's continued pursuit of Secretary Daniels' goal to increase the training and education opportunities open to enlisted personnel turned ships into informal schools. Other leaders of the Navy followed by creating formal schools ashore that taught cooking and baking as well as photography, hard hat diving, optics and fire control, and stenography. Petty officers wore the badges of their acquired proficiencies on the sleeves of their uniforms, on the right arm for the "seaman" rates and on the left arm for all others. Seamen who had not yet advanced to petty officer wore their white or blue "watch" mark on their right shoulders. Firemen wore theirs (in red) on their left shoulder. Badges of skill and achievement were the mark of proud sailors.

This training and study were necessary as the Navy became more technological. Even during World War I, a lot of the skilled work, such as handling a whaleboat in surf, or freeing an anchor fouled on the bottom of an anchorage, could be learned by watching and doing. Sailors could gain promotions even if they were only marginally literate. This changed in the 1920s and 1930s.

The difference is made clear, for instance, by comparing Marcus Goodrich's *Delilah,* a tale of the 1914 Navy, with Richard McKenna's *The Sand Pebbles,* an equally powerful depiction of the 1925 Navy. Although both books are novels, both are rich and sympathetic portraits of enlisted life with the feel of memoirs.

Sailor Jake Holman, the protagonist of *The Sand Pebbles*, is a fireman, thoroughly at home with steam engines: "Jake Holman loved machinery in the way some other men loved God, women and their country." Holman also despises ceremony, what he calls "battleship stuff." He gives his loyalty to machinery first, "because machinery was never taken in by pretense and ignorance." This is an extraordinary point of view—technology as more important than the ceremonial routine that was then thought so important in maintaining discipline. Holman is a craftsman. He wants respect for his skill and relief from what he sees as the unnecessarily paternalistic supervision that to him characterizes the "battleship Navy." His story compresses into one episode the revolution that technology forced on the Navy. If victory in naval warfare is dependent upon mastering technology, then authority within the Navy should derive from the same mastery. But if that were the case, then what distinguishes officers from enlisted sailors?

In the earlier *Delilah*, by contrast, the Navy is composed of two sharply defined classes: officers and enlisted. Officers are educated gentlemen; sailors are laborers, though sometimes quite skilled at the essentially manual tasks associated with operating a reciprocating steam-driven warship at sea. The gulf between officers and enlisted is huge; the educated enlisted man is an anomaly. This class consciousness began to change in the 1920s and especially in the 1930s, when the joblessness of the Great Depression brought the Navy intelligent young men with high school diplomas and an eagerness to learn.

Secretary Daniels knew his effort to promote the training and education of enlisted sailors implied that the education of officers would also have to grow

President Herbert Hoover being shown around the heavy cruiser USS Salt Lake City *(CA 25) in 1930. The two aircraft are O2U float seaplanes. Launched from a catapult, a seaplane returned to its ship by landing in the water alongside the moving vessel taxiing onto a floating mat. The plane was then hoisted aboard by the large crane. (Photo: Naval Historical Center)*

Opposite, bottom: *Sailors chipping old paint and applying a new coat to carrier USS* Saratoga's *(CV 3) huge stack. Like any large structures, they required constant and careful maintenance. (Photo: National Archives)*

Above: *Rear Admiral William A. Moffett, pictured in 1932 with his two sons—both of whom were Navy ensigns—was the pioneering leader of the Navy's Bureau of Aeronautics from 1921 until his death in the crash of the giant airship Akron in April 1933. Under his stewardship, the Navy developed one of the largest and best naval air arms in the world. (Photo: Naval Historical Center)*

Above, right: *The Martin T4M torpedo bombers land on USS* Saratoga *(CV 3) in the late 1930s. In the early 1920s and early 1930s, this aircraft, its predecessor the T3M, and another variant, the TG2, were the primary striking arm of the Navy's carriers. Unfortunately, the performance of these aircraft at sea was comparatively poor. As a result, USS* Ranger *(CV 4) was designed not to carry any torpedo bombers, relying on dive-bombers as her strike force.*

A senior officer's stateroom on a new cruiser in 1938 shows the luxury of space, privacy, and a porthole (for fresh air)—all precious commodities on a warship crammed with guns, engines, and sailors. (Photo: Naval Historical Center)

more sophisticated, if only to protect the authority those officers needed to have in order to exercise command. As a result, the faculty and courses at the Naval Academy were improved and the academy was academically accredited as a real college in the 1930s. It also accepted qualified enlisted sailors as midshipmen. Moreover, like the sailors they commanded, officers had to pass examinations. By the 1930s, those able to progress in their profession were selected and promoted. "Acceptable performance" was no longer a sufficient justification for advancement. The Navy's stress on knowledge and training paid dividends, especially among younger officers who would be the senior officers of World War II and the decade thereafter.

Nowhere was this clearer than in the field of naval aviation. But technical progress in aviation was intertwined with a dispute over whether all military aviation should be organized into a separate air service along the lines of Britain's Royal Air Force, which had absorbed the Royal Navy's air service in 1918. Senior U.S. Navy officers did not want to lose their fledgling aviation arm. Experience in World War I and experiments after the conflict had suggested that aviation was a critical naval arm. But Army General William ("Billy") Mitchell, leader of many military aviation enthusiasts, was a popular, charismatic figure, and he and his supporters in Congress worked for years to amalgamate the air arms of the Army and Navy and to form them into an independent service.

Mitchell forced dramatic confrontations with the Navy twice. The first time was in June and July 1921, during the bombing tests conducted against veteran German warships ceded to the United States after World War I. With destroyers guiding them to the target, Mitchell's land-based Army bombers sank the stationary German dreadnought battleship *Ostfriesland*, and Mitchell proclaimed that the day of the battleship and the surface Navy in general was over. But the real victory went to the Navy's aviators on 12 July 1921, when Congress authorized the Navy to create a separate bureau for aviation, the Bureau of Aeronautics, or BuAer. The first chief was an inspired choice, Rear Admiral William A. Moffett, a former battleship skipper. Under his leadership, BuAer harnessed aviation technology to the Navy's military needs.

In August 1921, the Joint Board of the Army and Navy, chaired by Army General John J. Pershing, rejected General Mitchell's interpretation of the summer's bombing tests. That decision temporarily put off a confrontation between Mitchell

and the Navy over the future of the Navy's air arm, and Moffett and his talented staff went to work developing aviation technology, pilot and aircrew training, and naval aviation doctrine. They also teamed up with the Naval War College and the fleet to chart a course for the future of naval aviation development.

BuAer supplied the War College with projections of what both carrier planes and seaplanes would be able to do five and ten years in the future. The War College used that information in its simulations and games. The results of the War College exercises were then communicated to the fleet and tested in the annual fleet problems, force-on-force maneuvers, which began in 1923. The lessons learned from these major maneuvers were then presented to both BuAer and the War College staff, and the cycle repeated.

This cycle was the key to the Navy's development of carrier aviation. In the 1923–1924 academic year at the Naval War College, Captain Joseph M. Reeves was an outstanding student. The following year he headed the tactics department at the War College, and in 1925 he completed the aviation observer's course at Pensacola, a catch-up course on flying for older officers. In September 1925, Reeves became commander of the fleet's air squadrons, then operating from San Diego and from the experimental carrier *Langley*. He carried what he had learned in war games at Newport with him to his new command.

It was just in time. That same month, the Navy airship *Shenandoah* was torn apart in the air in a violent thunderstorm over Ohio. Incensed, General Mitchell charged both the Army and the Navy with "incompetency, criminal negligence and almost treasonable administration of the national defense." In response, President Calvin Coolidge appointed a special board to study all aspects of aviation; Congress had already begun its own hearings. Mitchell, brought before a court-martial, claimed that the only way to foster effective military aviation was to follow the British model and create a unified air force as a separate military service. Rear Admiral Moffett claimed otherwise. But he and other senior Navy spokesmen needed evidence to support their position.

Reeves, *Langley*'s flight deck crew, and the fleet's aviators gave it to them. At the War College, Reeves had discovered that a carrier's military power was a function of the number of aircraft the carrier could launch in a single strike. The more planes a carrier could put up, the greater the chance that its aviators would control the air and go on to wreck any opposing carrier. But British practice, in force on *Langley* when Reeves took command of the fleet's air squadrons, was to stow each plane below the flight deck after it had landed in order to clear the flight deck for the next approaching aircraft. This took so much time that *Langley* could only operate about a dozen aircraft safely. Reeves knew that this number was too low. He challenged the aviators and flight deck crew of *Langley* to shorten the intervals between plane launchings and landings so that *Langley* could cease being an experiment and become an operational unit of the fleet.

Top, left: *USS* Enterprise *(CV 6) and her sister USS* Yorktown *(CV 5) were the first truly satisfactory aircraft carriers built for the Navy. Fast (34 knots), and large enough to carry eighty planes, these ships were the finest American carriers on hand when the country entered World War II. This illustration shows* Enterprise *as the beautiful ship she was.* Yorktown, *lost at Midway in 1942, has since been discovered on the seafloor.* Enterprise, *the most decorated Navy warship of World War II, was scrapped in 1958. (Collection of Author)*

Top, right: *Admiral William V. Pratt in 1928. As president of the Naval War College and a participant in the naval arms limitation conferences of 1922 and 1930, Pratt brought fresh thinking and new policies to the Navy. He became Chief of Naval Operations in the fall of 1930. (Photo: Naval Historical Center)*

Above: *The world-renowned pilot Charles A. Lindbergh with Admiral Joseph M. Reeves. Reeves was directly responsible for converting the experimental carrier USS* Langley *(CV 1) into an operational unit of the fleet. Reeves was also an early advocate of the carrier task force and of the use of signals intelligence in war at sea. (Photo: National Archives)*

Above: *A PBY Catalina patrol bomber flies along the Golden Strand south of the Naval Air Station North Island, San Diego, in 1940. Designed for high-level bombing, a role in which they were never used, the graceful but slow Catalinas were very successful scout and surveillance vehicles. (Photo: Naval Historical Center)*

Above, right: *A P2Y (right) with a PBY-1 (left) flying over USS* Dale *(DD 353) of Destroyer Squadron 20, during an exhibition for Movietone News, off San Diego. The coordination of patrol bombers and destroyers proved too difficult to execute in combat.*

November 1925 was the crisis. General Mitchell's court-martial was the center of national attention. Out of the limelight, however, *Langley*, her flight deck crew, and her aviators were beginning a revolution. Their ability to launch planes faster, though recovery was still slow, gave senior Navy leaders the evidence needed to rebut General Mitchell's charge that the Navy was ignoring the full military potential of aviation. By mid-June 1926, British practice was abandoned completely. When a plane landed safely at the after end of the flight deck, it disengaged from the ship's arresting gear wires and taxied forward. As it did so, the next plane landed. When all the planes in a flight were on board, the flight deck crew pushed them aft, where they were refueled and rearmed for the next flight. This technique allowed *Langley* to operate thirty-six aircraft routinely and forty-two in a pinch.

But *Langley* was small and slow. The real test came when the converted battle cruisers USS *Lexington* (CV 2) and USS *Saratoga* (CV 3) joined the fleet. Capable of regularly carrying seventy-two aircraft (four squadrons), both ships were fast (over 33 knots), large (888 feet in length, over 33,000 tons displacement), and possessed great endurance (over 10,000 nautical miles at 15 knots). Their performance in Fleet Problem IX in January 1929 was the first real test of large carriers operating under simulated wartime conditions. Under the command of now Rear Admiral Reeves both the ships and their air squadrons performed well, fully justifying all that so many individuals and organizations had invested in carrier operations. After Fleet Problem IX, carriers were accepted as mainstream fleet units.

Why, then, didn't the Navy build a whole fleet of carriers? First were the limits set by the Washington Treaty and reaffirmed at the London naval disarmament conference in 1930. Those restrictions held until 1936, when Japan refused to renew the naval arms limitation agreements. Second, carriers seemed to be extremely vulnerable to attack. In the annual fleet problems held through the 1930s, carriers were always being "sunk" in surprise attacks, usually in the opening phase of any fleet versus fleet engagement. U.S. carriers did not have armored flight decks that could deflect heavy bombs because only by reducing the complement of planes could armor be fitted—and the fleet problems demonstrated that the number of planes launched by a carrier was the key factor in a carrier versus carrier showdown. Third, it wasn't until the late 1930s that carrier dive bombers really became ship killers. Developing a dive bomber that could withstand the stresses of a high-speed dive and carry a 1,000-pound bomb over two hundred nautical miles took years. The first such heavily armed dive bomber was the BT-1, delivered to fleet squadrons in 1938. Its successor, the SBD Dauntless, replaced it in 1941. Along with the TBD Devastator torpedo bomber, which first flew from a

carrier in October 1937, the Dauntless was the core of the Navy's carrier attack aviation when Japanese carrier aircraft attacked Pearl Harbor.

But there was more to Navy aviation than carriers and their embarked squadrons. In the 1920s, the Navy designed two huge (785 feet long) airships—USS *Akron* (ZRS 4) and USS *Macon* (ZRS 5)—for long-range scouting. Each could carry five small aircraft in an interior hangar. Both were designed to give the fleet advanced warning of the approach of Japanese forces. Both were destroyed in storms before they could demonstrate their potential. Also judged a failure was BuAer's effort to equip a submarine with a small airplane.

Large seaplanes, by contrast, were a success. The first models of the twin engine PBY Catalina flying boat were delivered to the Navy in 1936. That year, the Navy fielded 218 seaplane patrol bombers. The successful performance of the Catalina as a scout and as a high-altitude level bomber led BuAer to purchase enough of the new planes to give the Navy over four hundred seaplane patrol bombers in 1941. By the middle of 1938, fourteen squadrons of Catalinas were deployed, five at Pearl Harbor. They carried four 1,000-pound bombs out as far as 1,000 nautical miles. A follow-on seaplane, the four-engine PB2Y Coronado, carrying eight 1,000-pound bombs, first flew as a prototype at the end of 1937.

But the mainstay of the fleet throughout the 1920s and 1930s continued to be the battle line composed of the twelve most modern battleships. The newest and most powerful of these were the three ships of the *Maryland* class. In 1927, catapulting their own small seaplanes to spot their gunfire, these ships shot 16-inch shells accurately to ranges greater than seventeen miles. Each 2,100-pound 16-inch shell was a potential shipkiller. The only weapon with comparable power was the torpedo, carried by both submarines and aircraft. To fire a torpedo accurately, however, submarines had to get within a thousand yards of their target. The Navy's T3M and T4M torpedo bombers operated from *Langley* in 1927, and later from *Lexington* and *Saratoga*, but they were slow (top speed just over 100 mph), and therefore vulnerable both to ship's gunfire and opposing fighters.

The ability of the battleships to fire a huge number of concentrated shells in a few moments, coupled with their armor and antitorpedo protection, kept them in the forefront. Senior Navy officers looked forward eagerly to the new battleships that the Washington Treaty would allow them to build after 1936. However, new battleships faced the same problem as the older models—striking moving targets

The battleship USS Maryland *(BB 46) and her sisters USS* Colorado *(BB 45) and USS* West Virginia *(BB 48) were the most powerful battleships in the fleet in the 1920s and 1930s. Each carried eight 16-inch guns, twelve 5-inch guns to ward off destroyer attacks, and eight 5-inch antiaircraft guns. Though slower than their Japanese contemporaries, these three ships were heavily armed and protected.* Maryland *and* Colorado *served through World War II.* West Virginia, *sunk at Pearl Harbor after being hit by six torpedoes, was raised and reconstructed in time to bombard Japanese forces in the Pacific in 1944 and 1945. (Collection of Author)*

The Navy first purchased Grumman F3F-2s in 1937, and the stumpy but maneuverable fighters served in Marine Corps squadrons and in Fighting Squadron 6 on aircraft carrier USS Enterprise (CV 6) *until 1940. This photograph shows a restored F3F-2 with markings for a section leader of Fighting Squadron 6, but with a black tail for aircraft assigned to carrier* Wasp (CV 7). *Her "Fighting Wasp" insignia was carried in 1940 by Fighting Squadron 7. Her upper wing is a bright peacetime yellow, and the star just behind the engine cowling was worn by Navy aircraft that participated in the neutrality patrol of 1940. (Air Classics)*

at very long range. Though the 16-inch shells traveled to their target at over twice the speed of sound, the shells had to be fired at the *expected* location of the target, which was not always where the target actually was. The greater the range or the speed of the target, the more complex the mathematics required to solve the problem of where the target would be when the shells arrived. To handle this problem, the Bureau of Ordnance sent some of its brightest officers to the Massachusetts Institute of Technology to participate in the development of servomechanisms to link guns with analog computers. Their work bore fruit: by the end of the 1930s, the U.S. Navy had developed excellent gunfire control systems.

The interwar Navy was often referred to as a balanced fleet, a force balanced among different types of weapons—battleships, cruisers, destroyers, submarines, aircraft carriers, and seaplanes. The nature of this force was shaped by arms control agreements, constrained budgets, public opposition to large military forces, and technology. For example, the Washington Treaty had allowed the signatories to construct forces composed of heavy cruisers—cruisers of 10,000 tons and armed with 8-inch guns. When a miniature arms race developed in this type of ship, the nations that had signed the agreement in Washington tried to constrain it. When navies considered building combined cruiser-carriers to get around the treaty restrictions on carrier tonnage, new negotiations thwarted that gambit. But the influence of the arms control negotiations created navies that were in some sense artificial. The shape of the major navies was the result of political factors as much as military assessments of likely future campaigns.

There was also a great deal of uncertainty about the future of naval technology. Would carriers remain vulnerable? Would sound ranging equipment blunt the threat of submarines? Would radar make it possible to control whole formations of ships in night engagements? Uncertainty, coupled with insufficient money, forced the Navy to invest in all the major warship types, but only in likely

technological improvements. The leaders did not believe they could risk a gamble on a technology or a tactic that might lead to catastrophic failure.

The changing composition of the fleet reflected this conservative approach. In 1923, the fleet had eighteen battleships; in 1938, it had just twelve first-line units. In 1923, it had no heavy cruisers like USS *Houston* (CA 30); in 1938, it had seventeen. In 1923, it had five light cruisers; in 1938, it had seventeen. There were no aircraft carriers in 1923 except the experimental *Langley*. By 1938, there were five larger carriers, and *Langley* had been converted to a seaplane tender. In 1923, the Navy had a huge stock—over 250—of destroyers built during World War I. By the early 1930s, these ships were obsolete, so there were only fifty new destroyers in commission in 1938. There were only twenty-five modern submarines. The naval authorizations of 1938, however, provided for three new battleships (two others were already under construction), two aircraft carriers, eight heavy and light cruisers, eighteen destroyers, and ten submarines. A new, more modern fleet was gradually taking shape.

Above: *Sailors hoist aboard the teak gangway on fleet flagship USS* Pennsylvania *(BB 38). The admiral's barge is to the left. Both the barge and his seaplane were painted Navy dark blue with gold and silver trim. (Photo: National Archives)*

Above left: *The destroyer USS* Dewey *(DD 349) in 1936. Armed with 5-inch guns and eight torpedo tubes, such fast, maneuverable ships were the logical successors to the "four-stacker" destroyers that had been produced in such large numbers during World War I. (Photo: Naval Historical Center)*

This striking portrait of heavy cruiser USS Portland *(CA 33) shows her slicing through heavy seas at dusk. Designed to the 10,000-ton limit set by the Washington naval agreements, and armed with nine 8-inch guns,* Portland, *her sister USS* Indianapolis *(CA 35), and the six cruisers of the* Northampton *class were graceful, fast, and heavily armed, but lacked much armor protection. (Collection of Author)*

Above: *For nearly a generation, USS Lexington (CV 4) and her sister USS Saratoga (CV 3) were the longest (888 feet) and fastest (almost 35 knots) ships in the Navy. Leaving San Diego in October 1941, Lexington is bound for Pearl Harbor; her flight deck contains F2A Buffaloes forward and SBD Dauntless dive-bombers and TBD Devastator torpedo planes aft. The camouflage paint on the bow makes it difficult for a submarine captain observing through a monocular periscope to determine exactly what course the ship is steering. (Photo: Naval Historical Center)*

Marines debark from an experimental landing barge at Quantico, Virginia, in the mid-1930s. Through the 1930s, the Navy experimented with ways of landing Marines on a hostile shore. In this case, the barge is lightly armored, but it can't put its human cargo directly on the shore. The landing craft made in such great numbers during World War II had yet to be designed. (Photo: National Archives)

Not all the news was good, however. For example, the annual fleet problems had shown that the fleet's surface forces were vulnerable to night torpedo attack by opposing cruisers and destroyers; no remedy had been found for this vulnerability by the time war came in 1941. The fleet remained short of fast tankers, tenders, amphibious transports, and many other auxiliaries. The solution to this problem was to draw on civilian construction—to convert merchant ship designs to military standards. The Merchant Marine Act of 1936 laid the foundation for this step, and the new auxiliaries, especially fast oilers, were reaching the fleet in 1941. But there were no specially designed amphibious warfare ships. In the last summer of peace (1941), exercises finally demonstrated that carriers, using radar and careful control of fighters, could protect themselves from enemy air attack. But the onset of war delayed the development of effective carrier air defenses until 1943.

Finally, the Navy remained socially conservative. Black sailors, for instance, were restricted to being cooks, bakers, and kitchen help. They could advance in pay grade, but they had to accept a rigidly segregated life, where they were excluded from most organized social activities and athletic events, and denied entry into specialties that would give them authority over white sailors. The "battleship Navy" also held onto the trappings of the past—the social class distinction between officers and enlisted, the dominance of the officer corps by graduates of the Naval Academy, inspections that put more stress on how clean a ship was than on how well its crew could fight, and ceremonies and customs that were anachronisms.

Despite its social conservatism, the Navy was eager to grasp the latest technology and do the thinking that was the key to victory in wartime. By 1941, its leaders had created or fostered the elements necessary for victory in World War II: a generation of officers capable of planning and then directing the operations of a huge fleet spread across the sweeping theater of war that was the Pacific Ocean; code breaking and high-frequency direction finding; a more efficient shipbuilding industry; carrier aviation; modern ships, from submarines to oceangoing tugs; an efficient, effective set of training and educational institutions; and radar and sonar.

Sailors "man the rail" of a battleship during a presidential fleet review in San Francisco Bay in July 1939 as their ship passes the heavy cruiser USS Houston *(CA 30). (Photo: Naval Historical Center)*

The Naval Gun Factory, now the Washington Navy Yard, Washington, D.C., manufactured large caliber guns for battleship main batteries. (Photo: Library of Congress)

1941-1945

Attack. Repeat. Attack. Winning a Two-Ocean War 1941-1945

Paul Stillwell

Boot camp provided the initial indoctrination and training after sailors enlisted or were drafted into the naval service. These recruits, outfitted in dungarees, white hats, and leggings, pay rapt attention as a chief petty officer calls on one of them for an answer. (Photo: U.S. Naval Institute)

The Navy that won World War II was very much the product of the two decades that preceded the war. Though Herman Wouk's novel *The Caine Mutiny* is officially fiction, it overflows with large dollops of truth, and perhaps none is more fundamental than the author's flippant observation, "The Navy is a master plan designed by geniuses for execution by idiots." He wasn't speaking literally, but his meaning was clear nonetheless. The officers and petty officers of the prewar Navy brought with them ideas and ways of doing things that were then replicated thousands and thousands of times as each new Navy man or woman took the oath, went through training, and developed into a productive sailor or junior officer. Willie Keith, Wouk's imaginary protagonist, had thousands of counterparts in the real Navy.

As Keith discovered, the explanation of how to do virtually everything, from loading a gun to filling out a pay receipt, was "in the book." It was a matter of

Above: *Hundreds of thousands of young men emerged from the Great Depression of the 1930s to serve in the Navy in World War II. Television anchorman Tom Brokaw refers to them and their contemporaries as "the greatest generation." (Photo: U.S. Naval Institute)*

Pages 92–93: *Task Force 38 maneuvering off the coast of Japan on 17 August 1945. The aircraft carrier USS* Wasp *(CV 18) is at lower right. Four other Essex-class carriers, two light carriers, and Iowa- and South* Dakota-*class battleships can be identified in this fleet. (Photo: Naval Historical Center)*

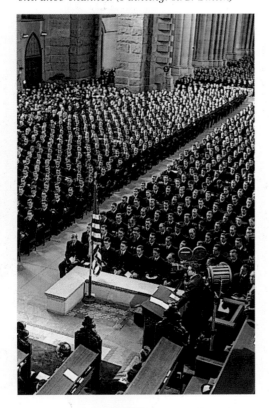

learning "the book" and then repeating actions so often that they became second nature. For the old-timers who served in the decades before the war, newer was not necessarily better, so change was often met begrudgingly. But change was inevitable as the small prewar Navy exploded in size to embrace some thirty-six hundred named ships, more than a hundred thousand unnamed craft, and more than three million men and women in uniform.

When France fell to the Nazis in the spring of 1940, the isolationists in the U.S. population still held considerable influence, but alarm bells were ringing nonetheless. Representative Carl Vinson, a sage congressman from Georgia, wielded a combination of political savvy and naval knowledge to bring into being the new armada of ships and planes that eventually led to victory. At the other end of Washington's Pennsylvania Avenue, Franklin D. Roosevelt himself drew upon a fund of naval experience to help gird the nation for war. He was Josephus Daniels's assistant Secretary of the Navy in World War I and had taken an almost fatherly interest in the Navy after becoming president in 1933.

From mid-1940 onward, the Navy was essentially on a war footing. The national strategy was to consider Germany as the primary threat and Japan a lesser one. U.S. warships became ever bolder in the Atlantic as they conducted a "Neutrality Patrol" that heavily favored British interests. In the Pacific, Roosevelt sent the Battle Force, comprising the Navy's principal combatant ships, to be based at Pearl Harbor in Hawaii. Ironically, the intended deterrent acted as a magnet. Japan's Admiral Isoroku Yamamoto realized that the existence of an undamaged U.S. fleet on his flank could seriously interfere with his nation's plan to seize and occupy resource-rich areas in southern Asia. The events of Sunday, 7 December 1941, emblazoned the words "Pearl Harbor" indelibly into the consciousness of both the United States and Japan.

Ted Mason was a young man who entered the Navy in 1940 as a reservist. As a radioman in the battleship USS *California* (BB 44) in December 1941, he planned to take flying lessons Sunday morning. Instead, the urgent summons of the general alarm sent him to his battle station atop the ship's mainmast. There he had a panoramic view of the death and destruction inflicted by some

350 Japanese fighters, torpedo planes, and bombers during their surprise attack. Amidst the experience of being shot at, Mason vowed never again to kill an animal.

As news of the attack began to settle in, Lieutenant Jim Ogden of Patrol Squadron 23 rushed to the squadron's hangar on Pearl Harbor's Ford Island and prepared to take off in the first patrol-plane search for the attackers. The squadron's skipper, Lieutenant Commander Massie Hughes, was there with his uniform pants pulled on over pajamas. They manned a twin-engine PBY flying boat with a makeshift crew. As soon as the plane was in the water and beaching gear off, Ogden revved the engines and began preparing for takeoff. He had to maneuver around debris on the surface of the harbor, then got airborne and headed out at such a low altitude that his tail gunner could almost reach out and chop cane from the fields they passed over.

As Ogden flew the lumbering PBY, it was with the knowledge that with more such planes before the attack the approaching enemy might have been detected. Thus Commander Hughes issued a running string of obscenities, most of them directed at U.S. congressmen, rather than at the Japanese. And Ogden had a few uncomfortable thoughts of his own to ponder during the flight, particularly, wondering what was happening back on Oahu. Many of the Navy families had Japanese maids, and that caused them to wonder where loyalties really lay. The story around town was that someone asked a maid, "If we have a war with Japan, do you kill us?"

"Oh, no, you my master. I kill Mr. Jones, and Mrs. Jones's maid kill you." Somehow, the joke didn't seem quite so funny to Ogden now that the war had started and he had a young bride and year-old child at home.

Then he wondered just exactly what he might do if he did find the Japanese, who were obviously far superior in both numbers and firepower. More thoughts went through his head, including, "I guess we'll be able to get off the

Seen against the rugged backdrop of the snow-covered Aleutians is a PBY-5A Catalina. The ubiquitous PBYs were seldom used in their intended mission as bombers during the war, but provided great service nonetheless as scouts, rescue aircraft, and transports. (Photo: U.S. Naval Institute)

Though she was commissioned in September 1919, less than a year after the conclusion of World War I, the old four-stack destroyer USS Gillis *(AVD 12) still performed usefully a generation later. Converted to a seaplane tender destroyer, she is shown here in the Aleutian Islands in June 1943 with motor torpedo boats alongside and a PBY flying boat astern. (Photo: U.S. Naval Institute)*

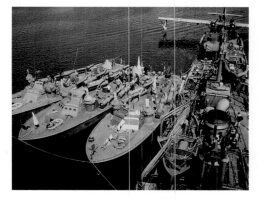

Top: *The N3N "Yellow Peril" floatplane was a staple of naval aviation training during World War II. This plane is at Pensacola Naval Air Station. (Photo: U.S. Naval Institute)*

Above: *The last "Yellow Peril" hangs in the overhead of Dahlgren Hall at the Naval Academy where thousands of midshipmen flew indoctrination lessons in them. (Photo: U.S. Naval Institute)*

plain-language dispatch before we get shot down. But if we do, is anybody going to hear it?" As it happened, the Japanese were more interested in making good their escape than hanging around to do additional damage. Ogden and his PBY crew survived to fight another day.

Earlier that same morning, Ensign Joe Taussig was standing watch on the quarterdeck of USS *Nevada* (BB 36), which was moored last in line in Battleship Row. His immediate concern as 0800 approached was to find out what size flag should be raised at morning colors. Before that could happen, though, he saw a Japanese plane approach one of the battleships ahead and launch a torpedo. War had come, and that meant the junior officer, less than a year out of the Naval Academy, was soon climbing six ladders to reach his battle station in the starboard antiaircraft director. Shortly after he got there, a projectile passed completely through his thigh, and he found his left foot under his left armpit. For young Taussig, the son of an admiral, the war ended almost as abruptly as it had begun.

Years later, a surgeon amputated the damaged leg, and still later, Taussig, by then a retired captain, expressed no complaints over that day's turn of events. He had opted to become a warrior, and he took what went with it. Moreover, he observed that if the ships in Pearl Harbor had been alerted and at sea, their inferior antiaircraft guns would have provided scant protection against attacking Japanese planes. On that Sunday morning, the Navy lost more than 2,000 men, including 1,177 in the battleship USS *Arizona* (BB 39). Though the toll was substantial, all but a handful of the ships were salvaged and returned to duty. Had they been at sea, they and their trained crews

would have gone to the bottom. As it was, the attack on the fleet in harbor aroused the American populace as little else could have. Isolationism evaporated instantly.

The trauma extended far beyond the Hawaiian outpost. American war planners generally conceded that the Philippines could hold out for only a short time and would have to be recaptured later. Army General Douglas MacArthur, in command in the Philippines, was more optimistic, but his hope was crushed. In fact, the initial damage was exacerbated by his sluggish reaction when the war started. The Philippines were doomed, with Army and Navy forces there having to engage in a fighting retreat. The fates of two Navy enlisted men illustrate the alternative possibilities.

For decades the U.S. Navy had maintained a small Asiatic Fleet in the Western Pacific as a means of establishing presence and looking after the nation's interests. For years the heavy cruiser USS *Augusta* (CA 31) served as the fleet flagship until relieved in November 1940 by the USS *Houston* (CA 30). Two of the sailors who made the switch from one cruiser to the other were Radioman Dick Harralson and Yeoman Cecil King. They were members of the flag allowance, that is, enlisted members of the staff of Admiral Thomas C. Hart. In 1941, as war approached, Admiral Hart and his people moved into more commodious spaces ashore.

Japanese bombers, faced with only token opposition, unleashed a heavy bombing attack on the Cavite Navy Yard on 10 December. Explosions and fires were soon everywhere. Harralson grabbed a laundry bag, carefully stripped down to his skivvies, put his possessions into the bag, and dove into the water to escape

Top left: *As the island fortress of Corregidor became ever more vulnerable to the Japanese in the spring of 1942, submarines provided the primary vehicle for escape. Here the crew of USS* Trout *(SS 202) loads a valuable cargo so it can be rescued from capture. All told, the treasure comprised twenty tons of gold bars and silver pesos. (Photo: U.S. Naval Institute)*

Upper right: *This was the typical shipboard berthing arrangement for enlisted men. These men, on board a tank landing ship (LST), are stacked in three-high tiers held up by chains. Privacy is not part of the arrangement. (Photo: U.S. Naval Institute)*

Lower right: *Sailors relax in a berthing compartment of USS* Chandeleur *(AV 10). This space is relatively commodious compared to similar arrangements in smaller ships, but the pipe rack bunks that could be triced up to clear space for relaxation or cleaning and the cable run through the overhead were typical of all ships. (Photo: Library of Congress)*

Above: *The combined forces of American, British, Dutch, and Australian were no match for the Japanese in the Dutch East Indies, now Indonesia. In the last battle in this area, the cruisers USS* Houston *(CA 30), HMS* Exeter, *and HMAS* Perth *stumbled onto a Japanese invasion force as they entered Sundra Strait. Both* Houston *and* Perth *were lost in the battle against great odds.* Exeter *escaped severely damaged but was sunk the next day. (Painting: "Battle of the Sunda Strait," John Hamilton, Navy Art Collection)*

Sailors in the old Asiatic Fleet held the superstition that a tattoo of a rooster on one foot and a pig on the other would save one from drowning. Here is Yeoman Cecil King, who escaped from the Philippines in late 1941; he left three different ships shortly before they sank.

the flames. He had no real likelihood of returning to reclaim his gear, but the ingrained Navy habits of neatness took over. He later caught a ride to Corregidor, an island fortress in Manila Bay. The situation went steadily downhill, and by the spring of 1942 the Japanese landed. Near the end, Harralson emerged from one of the tunnels that honeycombed the island and observed fires that reminded him of scenes depicted in Dante's *Inferno*. Though they were prisoners of war, a number of the Americans were executed on the spot. Harralson escaped being shot by virtue of being picked for a detail to tend to Japanese corpses. Subsequently he rode a prison ship to Japan, where he spent the rest of the war in captivity, gradually growing thinner, but engaging in small acts of sabotage as his contribution to the U.S. war effort.

Yeoman King also made it to Corregidor, but he was more fortunate. The old destroyer USS *Peary* (DD 226) was about to make a run for it, and King went aboard by the luck of the draw. The ride south was harrowing; the ship steamed at night and hid next to islands in the daytime. She cautiously made her way to the Dutch East Indies, and King subsequently rode on board the submarine USS *Sturgeon* (SS 187) to Australia. There King briefly went aboard the seaplane tender USS *Langley* (AV 3), which two decades earlier had been the U.S. Navy's first aircraft carrier. In early 1942 the remnants of the Asiatic Fleet had been merged with British, Australian, and Dutch ships to form a combined command. The odds were heavily against it, and only a few ships escaped.

During *Peary's* stop in Java, one of the intermediate points in King's long odyssey, he stood in line outside a telephone office so he could make a call to his parents in Texas. By that time the Kings had been informed that their son was missing and presumed dead, because an outdated roster still showed him on board *Houston*. His parents had gone to Mexico for a change of scenery, and finally some local officials there tracked them down and told them their son was still alive. In

his classic novel of the Asiatic Fleet, *The Sand Pebbles*, Richard McKenna wrote of a character who had a pig tattooed on one foot and a rooster on the other, keeping with an old sailor superstition that they would prevent him from drowning. King had the same tattoos on his feet. For whatever reason, luck was with him, because he managed to leave three different ships—*Houston*, *Peary*, and *Langley*—before they sank. When he later got home to Texas on leave, he found that the town had held a nice memorial service for him.

In the years just before the war, American submarine designers perfected a long-range weapon known as the fleet boat. It became most useful because Japan had gone to war to plunder the rich natural resources of the Dutch East Indies and Southeast Asia. As an island nation, Japan needed oil and raw materials brought in by sea in order to feed its people and its war machine. American submarines went primarily after those cargo ships and tankers; enemy warships were secondary targets.

During the early part of the war, however, U.S. submarine successes were fewer than expected. Torpedoes often ran deeper than they were set, and they frequently failed to go off because of faulty exploders and malfunctioning depth mechanisms. Moreover, a number of the early skippers failed to get hits because they were overly cautious. Gradually the Navy selected younger and younger officers to command submarines. One of the older skippers who had the characteristics of the young tigers was Lieutenant Commander Lew Parks of the submarine *Pompano* (SS 181).

One of the *Pompano*'s early wartime assignments was to reconnoiter the island of Wotje in the Marshalls and prepare for a raid by carrier plane. The aggressive Parks moved in so close to the beach that he almost made a nervous wreck of Slade Cutter, his executive officer. The difficulty of the mission was increased by the presence of two Japanese destroyers. Parks maneuvered for hours to get into position to shoot. When he did, the torpedoes exploded prematurely, alerting the Japanese to the submarine's presence. Parks was so excited that he posed a question through the boat's general announcing system, "Slade, did you ever have so much fun before with your clothes on?" Both the submarine and the Japanese survived the encounter.

This is one of thousands of pictures taken by noted Hawaiian photographer Tai Sing Loo, who worked at the Pearl Harbor Navy Yard from 1919 to 1949. This is the crew of the submarine USS Pompano *(SS 181). Front and center is her aggressive skipper, Lieutenant Commander Lew Parks. Second from left in the front row is Lieutenant (junior grade) Slade Cutter, who went on to become an outstanding wartime skipper in his own right. (Photo: U.S. Naval Institute)*

Submarines lined up in a row at Pearl Harbor at war's end are, left to right, USS Flying Fish *(SS 229), USS* Spadefish *(SS 411), USS* Tinosa *(SS 283), USS* Bowfin *(SS 287), and USS* Skate *(SS 305).* Bowfin *is now a memorial at Pearl Harbor. (Photo: U.S. Naval Institute)*

101

The Battle of Coral Sea was the first naval engagement in which ships of the opposing sides never saw each other. Offensive fire was delivered entirely by aircraft. The first carrier air battle in history resulted in the first serious defeat of the Japanese in World War II. ("Battle of Coral Sea," R.G. Smith, U.S. Naval Institute)

Looking like a college professor in uniform, Thomas H. Dyer used mental prowess as his main weapon in the war against Japan. He and his fellow code breakers worked in secrecy as a combat intelligence unit in a Pearl Harbor basement. Led by Commander Joe Rochefort, the code breakers were able to divine Japanese intentions, leading to strategic victories against the Japanese in the battles of Coral Sea and Midway.

After that, *Pompano* patrolled in the South China Sea and then went to Pearl Harbor. Parks was in an expansive mood and bought his officers a couple of cases of beer at the local club. Once they had that fuel pumping through their systems, they went to the Royal Hawaiian Hotel, which was set up for the recreation of submariners. They ran into some ribbing from young Army officers, who pointed out that they had a command car at their disposal. So a group of *Pompano* officers, including Parks and Cutter, "commandeered" the car when the Army men were in the club. In the car the submariners found a rifle and bandoleer of ammunition. Out of professional curiosity, of course, they wondered about the capability of the Army's small arms. So they began shooting at streetlights and a large Dole water tower painted to look like a giant pineapple. Alas, the car ran up over a curb and into a palm tree. Marine Military Policemen arrested the officers and took them to the local police station. Fortunately for the submarine service, the federal prosecutor in the area was Parks's brother, who managed to get the miscreants released. Cutter later took command of USS *Seahorse* (SS 304) and became one of the most successful skippers of the war. His nineteen ship sinkings, four Navy Crosses, two Silver Stars, and one Bronze Star provided bold evidence of his courage and skill.

While the Navy was making small steps to rebound from the Japanese blows, a small group of men labored in secrecy in the basement of a building at Pearl Harbor. This was the Combat Intelligence Unit under the direction of Commander Joe Rochefort. The mission of these men was to break Japanese codes and thus try to divine the intentions of the enemy. They formed an eccentric group, given to long periods of intense mental activity, storing and correlating hundreds of pieces of information, and often relying on hunches. The unofficial motto was, "You don't have to be crazy to work here, but it helps a hell of a lot."

For years after the war, the code breakers were constrained by an oath of silence not to discuss their work. In the 1970s and 1980s, information leaked out, and the code breakers were freer to talk. One of those who did was Captain Tommy Dyer. When he sat for oral history interviews not long before his death in 1985, Dyer wore glasses, a white goatee, and a twinkle in his eye. Quietly, and with a considerable amount of pride, he told of the accomplishments of the subterranean group and of Joe Rochefort in particular. Dyer said that he himself

was tops as a pure code breaker; Rochefort complemented him with a seemingly intuitive ability to figure out what should go into the blank spaces when messages could not be completely broken. In his interviews, Dyer addressed the thrill he felt when he was able to crack a particular code after months and months of frustration: "Almost in sexual terms. Physiologically, it's not the same, but the emotional feeling is pretty much the same." Other individuals made their contributions to the war—and got satisfaction—by launching bullets, bombs, and torpedoes. These men did it solely with their minds.

In early 1942 the code breakers discovered that the Japanese intended to invade Port Moresby on the island of New Guinea to establish a base from which to attack Australia. Admiral Chester Nimitz, who had become commander in chief of the Pacific Fleet in the wake of the Pearl Harbor debacle, responded. He directed a force of warships to the Coral Sea, which was the site of a momentous battle in early May 1942.

Beyond its strategic significance, the battle completed the symbolic shift of power from battleships to aircraft carriers. This was the first naval battle in which the attacks were made entirely by carrier planes. The opposing fleets never came in sight of each other. The carrier USS *Lexington* (CV 2) was sunk and USS *Yorktown* (CV 5) damaged. The Japanese lost a small carrier, the *Shoho*, leading Lieutenant Commander Bob Dixon of a *Lexington* bombing squadron to add a new term to the lexicon with his message, "Scratch one flattop!" In spite of the disparity in losses, Coral Sea was a strategic victory for the Allies, because the Japanese thrust toward Port Moresby was defeated.

The crew of the cruiser in the foreground looks on as men abandon ship from USS Lexington (CV 2) in the background. The "Lex," first of the Navy's big flattops, was sunk in the aftermath of the Battle of the Coral Sea in May 1942; before the year was over, the U.S. Navy also lost Yorktown *(CV 5),* Wasp *(CV 7), and* Hornet *(CV 8).*

A mural in the main rotunda of Bancroft Hall at the Naval Academy memorializes the performance of USS South Dakota *(BB 57) at the Battle of Santa Cruz in October 1942. With introduction of the proximity fuze, the ships' antiaircraft fire was extremely effective. The Japanese lost a large number of pilots and withdrew their carriers from supporting the Guadalcanal campaign.*

103

Gunner's Mate Charles Hansen works on a 40-millimeter gun mount. The tattoos on his shoulders commemorate the battles in which he has fought and the loss of his shipmates in the cruiser USS Vincennes *(CA 44), which was sunk off Guadalcanal in August 1942. (Photo: U.S. Naval Institute)*

Here on the bridge of the battleship USS Washington *(BB 56) are the skipper, Captain Glenn Davis, at right, and Rear Admiral Willis Lee, the flag officer who commanded the victorious task force in a battle off Guadalcanal the night of 14–15 November 1942. Admiral Lee continued to command battleship formations throughout the war. (Photo: U.S. Naval Institute)*

A pattern developed as the Japanese fed reinforcements piecemeal onto Guadalcanal and unleashed heavy surface bombardments. In addition, aircraft carrier planes dueled, and submarines were sometimes part of the mix. The bombardments by Japanese naval gunfire made life hellish ashore. The Americans commanded the seas in the daytime, and the Japanese frequently did so at night. The situation came to a climax in mid-November when a force of U.S. cruisers and destroyers kept a Tokyo Express task group from fulfilling its bombardment mission, but at heavy cost in lives and ships.

Two nights later, 14–15 November, it fell to Task Force 64, under the command of Rear Admiral Willis A. Lee, Jr., to fend off yet another bombardment. Lee had a team of four destroyers and two new fast battleships, USS *Washington* (BB 56) and USS *South Dakota* (BB 57). The Japanese mounted a complex, multi-pronged attack around Savo Island, near Guadalcanal. The narrow waters in the area were not well suited for battleship actions, but the situation was desperate. The ensuing action was one of only two occasions during the entire war that U.S. and Japanese battleships engaged in a surface duel at sea. It was the only one decided entirely by major-caliber gunfire.

The American ships traced a boxlike pattern around Savo Island, using their radars to track the movements of the oncoming Japanese ships. Shortly after midnight on the morning of 15 November, Lee's flagship, the *Washington*, opened up with her 16-inch guns, the first time a U.S. Navy battleship fired her main battery in anger during the Pacific War. Admiral Lee was on the starboard wing of the bridge when the opening salvo of gunfire erupted and sent bright flashes against the night sky. The concussion knocked his thick glasses to the deck followed by he and Lieutenant Al Church, the ship's radar officer, groping for them.

Above: *On the night of November 14–15 1942, the battleships USS* Washington *(BB 56), foreground, and USS* South Dakota *(BB 57) were the key elements of an American task force that turned back an intended bombardment of Guadalcanal. In the encounter the Japanese lost the battleship* Kirishima *and destroyer* Ayanami. *("Night Action off Savo," Dwight C. Shepler, Navy Art Collection)*

Crewmen on board the battleship USS Alabama *(BB 60) load a powder charge into a passing scuttle during part of its trip from a storage magazine below decks to one of the 16-inch guns in a topside turret. Powder for the big guns of the main battery is encased in silk bags. Great care is taken to prevent a path for flame to reach into the magazines where the ammunition is stored. (Photo: U.S. Naval Institute)*

107

Above: *Marines and sailors take in sunny weather topside as the attack transport USS* Monrovia *(APA 31) steams as part of a convoy bound for Tarawa in the Gilbert Islands. In the background is a battleship that provides part of the convoy's protection. (Photo: U.S. Naval Institute)*

Above, right: *The sophisticated equipment of World War II demanded an array of technical skills on the part of enlisted men. These three sailors are working on a submarine high frequency radio transmitter at the Submarine Base, New London, Connecticut. (Photo: U.S. Naval Institute)*

enough to grab Parker by the earlobe, lead him to the right valve, and proclaim that he must be serving with the dumbest individual he'd ever encountered. "This is the valve," he said. "Close it." Thus did Jackson Parker learn one more thing.

Generally *Mervine* escorted merchant ship convoys from the East Coast of the United States to the Mediterranean, Ireland, North Russia, or some other overseas port, and then made the return trip. If the ship needed repairs, such as the replacement of damaged hull plating, she got it between trips. The sailors were renewed as well. Parker went to the USO and the Navy YMCA in Brooklyn, the Paramount Theater in Manhattan, and often to a place called the Tango Palace, where the going rate was a dime a dance. The dancing was really secondary. The main thing was just to have, if only for a brief time, the companionship of an attractive young lady.

Ed Logue entered the Navy even before the onset of war, and he was fortunate enough to get more formalized training as a machinist's mate than did Parker. What's more, he found a welcome home in the Navy after surviving through the Kansas dust bowl of the Depression-wracked 1930s. After he finished boot camp at Great Lakes, Illinois, Logue went to Dearborn, Michigan, where the Ford Motor Company turned part of its facility into a training station for fledgling machinist's mates. Top-quality Ford machinists served as the instructors, and if a Navy man ruined a piece of metal stock as a result of a mistake on a lathe, it was not a problem. Henry Ford, the company's patriarch, concerned himself with the welfare of the sailors. He went around to talk to the Navy men, asking where they were from and what their interests were. When he was talking to Logue and a friend, he said, "Now, boys, if you ever see me anywhere, I don't care if I'm talking to the president of the United States, I want you to come up and interrupt me. Tell me who you are, where we met, and shake hands with me. I want you to promise that you'll do that. Will you?'

Both of them solemnly promised they would. Once Ford was out of earshot, Logue said to his sidekick, "I don't think I'll interrupt the president. You can suit yourself."

Another who had a humble background was Kent Lee, from a two-horse family farm in Florence County, South Carolina. He was entranced with aviation from the time a barnstormer brought a Ford Tri-Motor to a local fair in the late 1930s. After joining the Navy, Lee encountered culture shock. He was accustomed

to southern courtesy, but soon his head was shaved, he was given a series of shots, issued a seabag full of ill-fitting clothes, quartered in a crowded barracks, and placed at the not-so-tender mercies of a chief petty officer in charge of training. Soon enough he went to a training school to become an aviation machinist's mate. Then he was assigned to the Naval Air Station, Miami, Florida, to work on aircraft. Some Navy airplanes still had metal frameworks covered with fabric for wings, sometimes even for fuselages. Whenever the cloth tore, Lee and his mates sewed up the rips with a two-needle, V-shaped baseball stitch.

While stationed at Miami, Lee talked to some of the young aviation cadets coming through for training, and he concluded he had as much to offer as they did. Moreover, he had wanted to fly ever since the fairground experience. The Navy had an enormous training pipeline, because it was buying hundreds of planes. His first stop was preflight training at St. Mary's College in California. After indoctrination and heavy doses of physical conditioning, cadets went on to flight training. Lee began flying at Los Alamitos, California, flying in a Stearman N2S biplane. Later he went to Corpus Christi, Texas, for operational training and then to Jacksonville, Florida, and finally made eight practice landings on the training carrier USS *Sable* (IX 81) on Lake Michigan. By mid-1944, now wearing a pair of shiny gold wings, he reported to Air Group 15, commanded by Commander David McCampbell, on board the carrier USS *Essex* (CV 9). Lee flew an SB2C Helldiver, which he considered "the worst dive-bomber ever built." When the opportunity came to switch to an F6F Hellcat, he leaped at it, and soon bagged a Japanese Betty bomber while his carrier was operating near Formosa. Lee had come a long way from the fairgrounds in Florence County.

The Allies adopted a Europe-first strategy, and because the Soviet Union needed help dealing with the Germans on the eastern front, the United States felt pressure to get actively involved against Germany as early as possible. But 1942 was too soon for a major invasion of the continent. Instead, the United States settled for landings in North Africa, which had been the site of considerable fighting between the Axis and the British. French Morocco was the target for the invasion. One of the ships involved was the destroyer USS *Ludlow* (DD 438), which steamed out of Norfolk, Virginia, in late October as part of the large invasion force. Rear Admiral Kent Hewitt's Task Force 34 comprised more than one hundred ships.

Above, left: *The battleship USS* Washington *(BB 56) refuels a* Porter-*class destroyer at sea in 1942. The ability to replenish at sea was a key to the island-hopping campaign because the fleet did not need sheltered waters in the objective area. ("Fueling at Sea," Dwight C. Shepler, Navy Art Collection)*

Above: *An American invasion convoy of transports crosses the Atlantic en route to the invasion of North Africa in November 1942. In the foreground is the old battleship USS* New York *(BB 34). She was present at the British naval base at Scapa Flow in the Orkney Islands when the German High Seas Fleet surrendered in the wake of World War I. (Photo: U.S. Naval Institute)*

During the invasion of Sicily, German air raids were an intermittent but steady activity. A space in which to stretch out on board a warship or troop transport is always a rare commodity. In such circumstances, sleep is prized. Anywhere will do, as these sailors demonstrate. (Photo: National Archives)

Left: *A tank landing ship's (LST) bow doors are flung wide open to receive men and equipment destined for North Africa and eventually the invasion of Sicily. LSTs were high-priority equipment and their allocation to various theaters and operations was the subject of discussion at the highest levels of government. (Photo: U.S. Naval Institute)*

Above: *Troops and trucks cram the deck of a Coast Guard–manned tank landing ship (LST) as she and the ships ahead of her proceed en route the invasion at Hollandia, New Guinea, in April 1944. In wartime, the Coast Guard operates as part of the Navy. (Photo: U.S. Naval Institute)*

Below: *In addition to various other resources, the Navy used land-based bombers in its hunt for submarines. The Army Air Forces called its Liberators B-24s; the Navy designation for the same aircraft was PB4Y. Here a waist gunner is intent on doing harm to someone. (Photo: U.S. Naval Institute)*

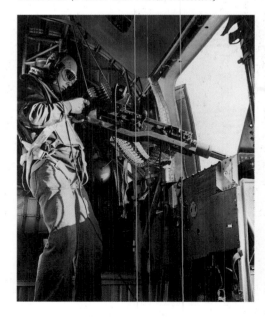

Opposite: *During the island-hopping campaign, Navy Seabees carved landing strips out of the jungle. Most Seabees were experienced construction workers in civil life. Their ability to construct military works in short periods was prodigious. (Photo: U.S. Naval Institute)*

In the darkness on the early morning of 8 November, American transports loaded troops into their landing craft. On board the destroyer *Ludlow*, Apprentice Seaman Arvid Sahlin joined his shipmates listening to a radio broadcast from President Roosevelt. The president addressed his remarks to the French Moroccans, asking them to let the landings be peaceful rather than offering resistance. To acknowledge their agreement in the scheme, he asked the Moroccans to shine searchlights upward into the night sky. As landing craft approached the beaches, the American soldiers felt a sense of relief when they saw shafts of light beam upward. But as they went ashore at Cape Fedala, a searchlight swept down onto the landing beaches, and gunfire fell upon the troops. The landings were not to be unopposed after all.

Shortly before dawn, a projectile exploded near *Ludlow*'s starboard side; she was under fire from shore batteries. She reacted by shooting back, weighing anchor, and moving farther away. Shortly she was one of several ships conducting shore bombardment in response to the prearranged signal, "Play ball." At one point she was in a column of destroyers that came under fire from Vichy French cruisers. A 6.1-inch projectile exploded in *Ludlow*'s starboard bow, doing heavy damage inside the ship and starting fires. When Seaman Sahlin entered a passageway filled with smoke, a thought went through his mind, "This is a hell of a place for a little ol' farm boy from Vermont." Fortunately, the destroyer got assistance from ships with bigger guns, the battleship USS *Massachusetts* (BB 59) and the cruisers USS *Brooklyn* (CL 40) and *Augusta*. Elsewhere planes from the carrier USS *Ranger* (CV 4) provided support. The toehold of the invaders from across the Atlantic would continue to grow on the African continent.

In the coming year the Allies continued to expand their presence in the Mediterranean, moving along the coast of North Africa and using it as a base for further operations. The next major step was the invasion of the island of Sicily in July 1943, because it cut the Mediterranean in half. The operation was a good deal more dangerous than hitting Casablanca because now the enemies were Germans, rather than the supposedly friendly French. Among the support ships

Top: *Tracer rounds of antiaircraft fire from American warships at Salerno, Italy, produced dramatic patterns in the night sky when German aircraft appeared overhead to contest the Allied invasion in September 1943. (Photo: U.S. Naval Institute)*

Above: *Booms of a transport swing a loaded Army truck into an LCT—tank landing craft—as part of the invasion of Salerno, Italy, in September 1943 (Photo: U.S. Naval Institute).*

was the destroyer USS *Mayrant* (DD 402). Damaged considerably when a German Ju-88 aircraft dropped a bomb that exploded underwater and blew in the side of the ship, the casualties included the skipper, Commander Edward Walker, and his executive officer, Lieutenant Franklin D. Roosevelt, Jr.

From Sicily the Allies ventured onto the Italian mainland, mounting amphibious landings at Salerno south of Naples and across the Straits of Messina in the fall of 1943. In January of 1944, in an attempt to bypass the German defenses in the mountains south of Rome, the Allies conducted an amphibious landing at Anzio. In all these amphibious assaults, the initial landings were lightly opposed, but as the beaches filled with troops and equipment before the beachhead was secured, the Germans counterattacked ferociously. At Anzio, tank landing ships (LSTs) were pressed into service as a shuttle to ferry men and equipment from the port of Naples. The port was so cluttered by debris from Allied bombing that only LSTs could enter, and when they did, they were under frequent attacks from German bombing and shelling. The shelling came from a large gun that was able to fire into the harbor from a great distance. Enemy frogmen were also a threat at the beachhead. This last amphibious landing on the Italian coast was clearly not a milk run.

Though much of the attention during the war went, understandably, to the fighting forces, the vast amount of support they got from the shore establishment enabled them to confront and then overwhelm the enemy. Career personnel eagerly sought sea duty assignments, both for the sake of the war effort and as a means of enhancing promotion prospects. But they also recognized the need for the work ashore. One shore-bound individual was Lieutenant Commander Fred Edwards, an engineering duty officer who had been chief engineer of the battleship USS *North Carolina* (BB 55) when she joined the fleet in 1941. He reported to the Bureau of Ships in Washington the following year and spent the remainder of the war there.

Edwards served on a Type Desk, caring for the destroyers and the destroyer escorts of the fleet. The demands were staggering, often keeping him in his office for ten hours a day followed by a couple more hours of work at home after dinner. His only day off in the calendar year of 1943 was Christmas, and he puckishly observed years later that he did so much reading on the job that occasionally he had to take his reading glasses to a water fountain to cool them off.

One of Edwards's chores was to oversee delivery of propulsion machinery. Propulsion plants involved high priority, long time-of-manufacture items, whether steam systems or diesel. Getting them delivered to shipyards on time required continual juggling and a great deal of contact with the manufacturers. One of Edwards's feats was to get the machinery from the destroyers USS *Cassin* (DD 372) and USS *Downes* (DD 375), both badly damaged at Pearl Harbor, shipped to the West Coast so new ships could be built around the salvaged portions. Repairs to damaged ships often required air transport of replacement parts to minimize the down time. Such air transport was by no means routine in the 1940s. In the years before the war Edwards served in destroyers as a line officer. Now he had an opportunity to observe the trials of the first of a new class, the *Fletchers*. Years later, with the benefit of hindsight and perspective, he said, "I always felt it was the *Fletcher* class that won the war. . . . They were the heart and soul of the small-ship Navy."

Before the attack on Pearl Harbor, battleships symbolized the power of the U.S. Navy. The newest one through the interwar decades was the USS *West Virginia* (BB 48), which was commissioned in 1923, shortly after international arms limitation agreements went into effect. On 7 December she had been the most heavily damaged of the battleships that survived the attack. By the spring of 1943 she had received enough patches to be seaworthy and was ready to steam to the Puget Sound Navy Yard for repair and rebuilding. Assigned to

A Navy band plays for hundreds of shipyard workers at a war band rally held in the Puget Sound Navy Yard, Bremerton, Washington, in mid-1943. To the right is the battleship USS West Virginia *(BB 48) minus her old superstructure. She has just been brought to the Pacific Northwest to be repaired and rebuilt following the heavy damage sustained at Pearl Harbor. Eventually, she will be the only battleship to be both at Pearl Harbor in December 1941 and in Tokyo Bay in September 1945. (Photo: U.S. Naval Institute)*

In the summer of 1943 this subchaser, USS PC-565, battled and sank a German U-boat in the Atlantic. The insignia on the bridge conveys the crew's feelings about Nazis. (Photo: U.S. Naval Institute)

provide antisubmarine protection during the voyage was the four-stack destroyer USS *Chew* (DD 106) originally commissioned in December 1918, the month after World War I ended.

Fire Controlman Jesse Pond was on board *Chew* as she escorted the old battleship to safety. On the third day out, a lookout spotted a periscope (or so he thought), sonar picked up a sound contact, and the old greyhound fired eleven depth charges at the target. It may have been a whale, but *Chew* had taken action—better to be safe than sorry. After both ships reached their destinations, Pond and three shipmates went into a bar to slake their thirst. They encountered some *West Virginia* sailors who expressed their gratitude for the role the old destroyer had played in saving their defenseless battleship during the eastward transit. Pond and his fellow destroyermen accepted the hospitality graciously, kept to themselves their thoughts concerning the suspected aggressor, and observed that free drinks are particularly tasty.

A four-stacker that carried out the antisubmarine mission in the Atlantic was the old *Borie*. Early in the war, the preferred tactic was to use escort ships to protect the transatlantic convoys. Now, aided by radio direction-finding and code breaking, some ASW forces formed hunter-killer groups and went on the offensive.

One such was Task Group 21.14, which was built around the new escort aircraft carrier USS *Card* (CVE 11) and had a screen that included *Borie*, USS *Barry* (DD 248), and USS *Goff* (DD 247), three World War I–vintage four-stack destroyers.

A particularly noteworthy duel occurred between the *Borie* and *U-405* on 1 November 1943. The destroyer's skipper, then Lieutenant Charles Hutchins, had graduated from the Naval Academy in 1936. However, after some escapades while in the crew of the battleship *Nevada*, the Navy sent him back to civilian life in 1938. Returned to active duty as a naval reservist in 1942, he had much more training and experience than the vast majority of reserve officers who entered the fleet upon the outbreak of war. Given command at age twenty-nine—much earlier than he probably would have by following a regular Navy career path—circumstance put him on the bridge of the old ship as she peppered the surfaced U-boat with gunfire during that November night.

Hutchins ordered his crew to stand by to ram, and he headed directly for the German craft. Fire Controlman Bob Maher watched in fascination as the Germans fired sporadically at the approaching ship. As the destroyer closed in, a wave picked up her bow. It came crashing down on the submarine and ripped holes into both of *Borie*'s engine rooms. The ships separated and continued fighting. The aggressive four-stacker attacked with depth charges, torpedoes, and gunfire—finally compelling a surrender. The U-boat sank soon thereafter.

Borie rejoined her task group, but her engine room wounds were fatal. Hutchins ordered his victorious crew to abandon ship, and so Bob Maher and his shipmates went into the Atlantic. The lifeboats had already been jettisoned in a vain attempt to save the destroyer. The men clung to rafts until rescued by *Barry*, but even that was fraught with peril. Maher grabbed hold of a propeller guard and hung on, even when the guard rolled underwater. A thought passed through his head, "Married only three months and I'm going to die." But a *Barry* man went out on the propeller guard and grabbed him. Maher didn't want to let go, but finally he was convinced that doing so was his only chance for survival, and he was pulled safely aboard. Years afterward Maher took the lead in forming a reunion group for the men who had fought the war on board *Borie*. As he observed, "Friends come and go, but shipmates are forever."

The tide in the Battle of the Atlantic turned in favor of the Allies in mid-1943. For the most part, it had been confined to the North Atlantic as the Navy moved men and equipment to the British Isles and the Mediterranean.

In the Pacific, U.S. submarines were potent. By mid-1943, thanks to the efforts of Rear Admiral Charles Lockwood as Commander Submarine Force Pacific, torpedoes were much more reliable than earlier. Moreover, the prewar skippers went to other duty, so that those who took command later had already proved themselves in combat. New skippers, such as Bub Ward, Slade Cutter, and Dusty Dornin, were from the Naval Academy's class of 1935.

As commanding officer of the USS *Guardfish* (SS 217), Norvell G. Ward commanded a team whose mission was sinking ships. During attacks he manned the periscope; his executive officer manipulated a little plastic calculator known as the "is-was" that solved for course and speed of enemy ships; the operator of the target data computer provided recommended courses and speeds to intercept the target and sent mechanical inputs to the torpedo guidance systems. In June 1943 he felt a sense of exhilaration with his first sinking as a skipper. Submerged, he torpedoed the *Suzuya Maru*, a mother ship for fishing boats. Part of the purpose of the submarine campaign was to impose an economic blockade on Japan and its island possessions. Denying food to a warring country contributed to that mission

Much attention has been paid to notable skippers such as Mush Morton,

Commander Richard O'Kane was the most successful American submarine skipper of the war. As commanding officer of USS Tang *(SS 305), he was credited with sinking twenty-four Japanese ships. At that, his operations were cut short when a circular run by one of* Tang's *own torpedoes sank the submarine in October 1944. O'Kane—along with the handful of shipmates who escaped—spent the rest of the war as prisoners of the Japanese. (Photo: U.S. Naval Institute)*

USS O'Kane *(DDG 77) is commissioned at Naval Station, Pearl Harbor. Astern, across the water, is the Submarine Base, Pearl Harbor, where Commander Richard O'Kane started war patrols. Submarines were able to begin offensive operations in enemy controlled waters immediately after Pearl Harbor.*

Mealtime on board a submarine didn't leave much elbowroom. At right is the ship's library; at left are records to be played during off-duty hours. (Photo: U.S. Naval Institute)

Sam Dealey, and Dick O'Kane, who were bold and successful. They went hours without sleep, judged the zigzag tracks of their intended targets, and used periscopes so skillfully that they could scan the entire horizon in a few seconds and thus minimize detection. History has paid far less attention to the enlisted crews of those submarines, fifty-two of which did not survive the war. They were a select group, volunteers who had gone through a rigorous training program that included both the technical aspects of the job and also a judgment of the psychological factors, including the ability to operate for long periods in the confined, claustrophobic spaces where daylight did not penetrate. Their view of battle was a vicarious one, brought by words of what officers saw through periscopes or gunner's mates saw topside when operating deck guns during surface actions. Above all, they shared a common sense of peril.

One such individual was Jim Dickinson. After growing up in the 1930s, Dickinson went to the University of Georgia so he could distance himself from his demanding father in New York. In 1942, the son enlisted in the Navy and volunteered for submarine duty. He was a plank owner in the submarine USS *Puffer* (SS 268). He enjoyed the camaraderie with the crew and the liberty opportunities in Australia.

Eight war patrols—"runs," as the submarine veterans call them—were the result of his choice of duty. During the first run, in October 1943, *Puffer* had been in the Makassar Strait near Borneo. She attacked a tanker and then underwent a merciless depth-charging by a Japanese torpedo boat that held her down for nearly forty hours. Dickinson, then a fireman second class, recorded in a diary the fear that

engulfed him and his shipmates during their ordeal. They could hear the splashes as depth charges hit the water, the click of detonators, and the explosions that rocked the boat. The air grew foul. Shutting off the air-conditioning let the temperature rise to 125 degrees. Bodies were drenched with sweat, and some men urinated in their uniforms because the terror was so intense. Some resorted to prayer, some to anger and swearing. Some essentially went berserk as their self-discipline broke down. At last *Puffer* surfaced, and Dickinson was able to breathe clean air again. Everything else in his wartime experience was easier by comparison.

In late 1943, the Navy–Marine Corps team geared up for the Central Pacific campaign, the strategy of which involved amphibious assaults on some Japanese-held islands and the bypassing of others that would be left to die on the vine. The campaign began with the seizure of the Gilbert Islands, where bloody Tarawa proved a difficult test. One of the victims was an early hero of the war, Lieutenant Commander Edward H. "Butch" O'Hare, a fighter pilot who dispatched five Japanese bombers on one mission in early 1942, thereby saving the carrier *Lexington* and earning himself a Medal of Honor.

In late November 1943, Japanese Betty bombers posed a substantial threat to American naval forces when they operated at night. Up to then, carrier aviation operations were almost exclusively daylight affairs. O'Hare sought to challenge the bombers with a three-plane team composed of one TBF torpedo plane equipped with radar and two F6F fighters that would use the TBF as a guide. As O'Hare left *Enterprise*, he took off into the dark night, planning to join up with the TBF flown by Lieutenant Commander John Phillips.

The fleet boat's long range and lethal torpedoes made her an ideal weapon for attacking Japanese commerce during the Pacific War. (Photo: U.S. Naval Institute)

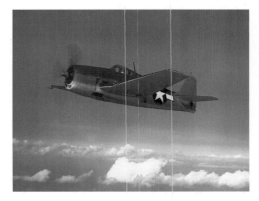

From late 1943 onward, the fast carrier forces had the benefit of a superb fighter plane in the Grumman-built F6F Hellcat. (Photo: U.S. Naval Institute)

Aviation Ordnanceman Alvin Kernan sat in the TBF's rear seat. Like hundreds of petty officers during the war he rode backward in his carrier plane, using his machine guns to fend off enemy aircraft. On this night, Kernan reacted when the Bettys came near. As he wrote later in his memoir *Crossing the Line*, "It all developed so fast that training took over from thinking." And that was the point, after all, of the training program—that actions would take place by reflex in an emergency. Kernan's bullets hit and blew up the Japanese plane. But this night fighter experiment was something for which there was not much experience or training. The fighters and torpedo planes turned on their running lights to effect a rendezvous and thus gave themselves away to other Japanese in the area. A cigar-shaped outline appeared against the night sky; it was a Betty that hurled bursts of machine-gun fire into O'Hare's Hellcat and sent it tumbling into the sea.

Liberty ships were mass-produced cargo ships that carried the load in getting the tools of war to the combat theaters. They were crewed by merchant mariners and also carried a complement of Navy men known as the armed guard. John W. Brown, *shown, is now preserved in Baltimore as one of the last surviving Liberty ships.*

Ships of the merchant marine, manned mostly by civilians, bore a vital part of the maritime portion of fighting. Hundreds of new ships, principally Liberties and Victories, that were turned out in shipyards around the country supplemented old tonnage. Their cargoes included soldiers, tanks, fuel, aircraft, ammunition, food, and thousands of other commodities. In addition to the merchant mariners, small contingents of Navy men known as armed guards were on board. They manned each ship's weapons and served as specialists for radio and visual communication.

Cornelius Aloysius Burke, a signalman who much preferred to be called Pete, entered the Navy in September 1941 and during the course of the war was on board more than twenty merchant ships as they made their convoy runs to and from U.S. ports. The destinations included places such as Trinidad, Sicily, and North Africa. In the spring of 1944 Burke was in New York City to catch a Liberty ship named *William Tyler Page*. The officer in charge of the ship's armed guard detail was a reserve officer, Lieutenant Gordon Webber. They first met when they shared a cab on their way to join the ship. As they rode together, Burke spun out a tale about his exploits to date. He told of the ships that he had ridden, colorful shipmates, the perils of the sea, and so forth. As sailors sometimes will, he exaggerated somewhat in the process. To his surprise, Webber wasn't buying any of it. Later, he found out why. In civilian life the officer had been a scriptwriter for NBC radio. Burke concluded somewhat ruefully to himself, "Christ, he's been bullshitted by experts!"

The two new shipmates soon joined efforts as the ship crossed the Atlantic, pulled into Liverpool, England, and discharged her cargo. While there, Lieutenant Webber called in some of his signalmen and gunner's mates for a meeting and

Opposite: Aviation Ordnanceman N. F. Nitishin carries belts of .50-caliber machine-gun ammunition as he prepares to arms the guns of a Vought F4U Corsair fighter at a Pacific base. The red-nosed tracers are mixed in with the black-nosed armor-piercing projectiles. (Photo: U.S. Naval Institute)

Members of the Navy armed guard on board the merchant ship William J. Worth *fire the installed 4-inch deck gun. In the foreground are two 20-millimeter antiaircraft guns. (Photo: U.S. Naval Institute)*

Top: *This is one sector of a breakwater created by a line of Liberty ships deliberately sunk off Colleville, France. A major role of this line was to provide a mooring place for small craft. These shelters were in place just four days after D-Day. (Photo: U.S. Naval Institute)*

Above: *U.S. soldiers emerge from a Coast Guard-manned landing craft, vehicle, personnel (LCVP) and move toward the Allied beachhead at Normandy. Coxswains of these small craft were young men with little experience in boats until trained for this assignment; many were in their first combat situation at Normandy (Photo: U.S. Naval Institute).*

offered them drinks. That was normally not done by Navy men on board ship, so it amounted to a pleasant surprise. It was also a going-away party, as Webber announced he was leaving for other duty. Burke immediately piped up and asked, "Do you need a good signalman? How about letting me come along?"

Webber responded, "I wouldn't wish this assignment on my worst enemy." The group then had a few more drinks, and Webber left. Burke subsequently found out that Webber was assigned to the skeleton crew on board one of the merchantmen that were to be deliberately scuttled off the invasion beaches at Normandy, France, in order to form an artificial breakwater. Because the landings in German-occupied France would be over beaches with open roadsteads, rather than in harbors, the Americans had to create artificial harbors by scuttling ships, some of them old, some relatively new Liberty ships.

The preparations for that D-Day assault included Exercise Tiger, a practice invasion of Slapton Sands in southern England, because the beach topography resembled that which would be encountered at Utah Beach on the French coast. Unfortunately, the arrangements for the escorts for the amphibious convoy broke down, and a group of German E-boats—similar to the American motor torpedo boats—attacked the practice convoy. The ensuing fight resembled a group of foxes laying waste to an unguarded chicken house. Torpedoes whizzed through the night, sinking two tank landing ships (LSTs) and damaging a third. All told, 750 Americans died as a result.

One result of the tragedy of Slapton Sands was that General Dwight Eisenhower, supreme commander for the upcoming invasion, sent for Commander John Bulkeley, a naval officer who had earned the Medal of Honor early in the war for commanding a squadron of PT boats around the Philippines and for safely evacuating General Douglas MacArthur from Corregidor. Eisenhower remembered being present for a briefing Bulkeley had given the Secretary of War in 1942, so he sent for him to bring in a contingent of PT boats to support the upcoming invasion and provide protection against German E-boats. As the boats arrived and were based in England, the British King, George VI, came aboard for an inspection. He made small talk with the crew of Bulkeley's *PT-504*, telling crew members he had taken part in the momentous Battle of Jutland in 1916 when he was a

Top: *The English Channel is awash with landing craft off Normandy's Omaha Beach on 6 June 1944, the beginning of the liberation of France. Destroyers, such as the USS* Emmons *(DD 457), moved in close to the beach to provide much-needed gunfire support to soldiers trying to claw their way inland. ("The Battle for Fox Green Beach," Dwight C. Shepler, Navy Art Collection)*

Left: *American troops crowd into landing craft in an English port as they prepare for the D-Day invasion of Normandy in June 1944. The trans-Channel invasion fleet was the largest in history. (Photo: U.S. Naval Institute)*

Above: *Tank landing ships (LSTs) were invaluable during World War II because of their ability to carry tanks and other rolling stock across the seas and then deposit the cargo directly onto a beachhead or onto a pontoon causeway connected to the shore. These LSTs are shown during the Lingayen Gulf operation in early 1945, part of the reconquest of the Philippines. (Photo: U.S. Naval Institute)*

midshipman. While he was visiting, he had a cup of coffee, which brought great satisfaction to the PT boat's cook. After that, the cook brooked no complaints about his coffee from his shipmates, telling them that if it was good enough for the King of England, it should be good enough for them.

The armada for the greatest amphibious assault in history set out from ports in southern England on the night of 4 June 1944, in order to carry out the planned invasion the following morning. As the *LST-282* pushed her bow through the waves of the English Channel, the assistant gunnery officer was Ensign Hans Bergner, a reserve officer who was the son of a preacher in the Texas hill country. Young Bergner was less concerned with making history than with just surviving. As he lay in his bunk that night, he said a few more prayers than usual. But the weather was too rough, and so the invasion ships returned to port. Then they set out again on the night of the fifth, preparing once more for a landing on the morrow. When it was time to pray that night, the tired Bergner told the Lord that everything he had mentioned the night before still applied. On the morning of 6 June, the *LST-282* sent her load of troops into landing craft for the assault on Utah Beach.

Paul Fauks, a signalman from South Dakota, was on board the *LST-372* that morning. During the voyage across the channel, he saw an amazing array of vessels, ranging from a World War I British battleship to small craft the size of fishing boats. When German bombs fell near his ship, the vibration below decks was enough to rattle teeth. He and his shipmates had the feeling of being in a metal

The threat from large caliber naval guns influenced German General Rommel to keep his armored forces well back from the beaches in France. Rommel experienced the damage inflicted on massed armor by naval gunfire support in Sicily. USS Texas (BB 35) and the other old battleships played important parts in the bombardment supporting the Normandy invasion. (C.G. Evers, U.S. Naval Institute)

Crew members of the old battleship USS Texas (BB 35) vie for spots from which to watch as Army Rangers come aboard in June 1944 for treatment of wounds sustained in the invasion of Normandy. With the Navy's newest battleships away in the Pacific, it was left to World War I–era battleships—Texas, USS Arkansas (BB 33), and USS Nevada (BB 36)—to provide gunfire support during the invasion of France. (Photo: U.S. Naval Institute)

coffin. The young men's fears were reinforced when they saw how others reacted. As they approached Omaha Beach, they saw bodies in the water.

Fauks went down the side of the ship on a rope ladder and into an LCVP landing craft for the trip to bloody Omaha, where his job was to serve as a signalman. When he got there, he realized it would mean near-certain death to stand and signal as Germans poured down a murderous fire from machine guns on the heights beyond the beach. He then concluded that his only job that day was to stay alive, so he and his buddies dug a hole in the sand and stayed there until it was safe to emerge. He and some soldiers then occupied a former German pillbox that had been an emplacement for an 88-millimeter gun. He later concluded that he and those with him were good signalmen, but not that great as soldiers. He did survive the battering experience on Omaha Beach and later returned to England to resume his interest in Barbara Clare, an English sales clerk whom he had met in a London department store. She became one of hundreds of war brides. The couple was married in 1946.

The steel-hulled minesweeper USS *Tide* (AM 125) was operating off Utah Beach on D-Day plus one, 7 June. Motor Machinist's Mate Bill Branstrator took a break from his duty in the ship's engine room so he could go topside and watch some Army C-47 transport planes. While he was there, Branstrator took a seat and joined others sharing a snack from a box of K rations. Just as he reached for a piece of cheese, *Tide* detonated a German magnetic influence mine. Those on ships nearby said *Tide* came completely out of the water, rising perhaps five feet. Branstrator went up like a rocket; when he landed he was grievously injured. The minesweeper was sinking, and *PT-504*, commanded by John Bulkeley, came alongside to take off survivors. Branstrator was dragged across and left to lie on deck. He asked for a cigarette. Bulkeley took from his mouth the one he had just lighted and put it in Branstrator's. The boat went to the *LST-282*, Hans Bergner's ship, and from there

the wounded man was evacuated to England for medical care. In the years to come, Branstrator lost a leg, endured more than fifty operations, and spent thirteen years in hospitals—all because of what happened on the morning of 7 June 1944. He had paid a high price to help liberate the people of France.

Above: *Army infantrymen rush ashore from medium landing ships (LSMs) during the invasion of Southern France in August 1944. This landing came two months after the assault on Normandy. ("Hitting the Beach," Albert K. Murray, Navy Art Collection)*

The war had a transforming effect on much of the nation. Some of the changes would depart with the end of the war; others would remain from then on. In filling the jobs throughout the fleet and the shore establishment, the prewar Navy had been virtually all male and all white. In the spring of 1942, the service began accepting black enlisted personnel for general service ratings, meaning they would no longer be restricted to servant-type jobs. The following year—because of social and political pressures—the Navy decided to institute a hurry-up program to commission black officers. So in January of 1944 sixteen black enlisted men gathered at Great Lakes, Illinois, for a cram course in subjects such as naval history, gunnery, navigation, airplane recognition, and communications. In mid-March twelve were commissioned as Naval Reserve ensigns and one as a warrant officer. Subsequently they came to be known as the Golden Thirteen, the Jackie Robinsons of the naval profession.

As was the case of baseball's Robinson, progress was often slow. Graham Martin, one of the new officers, took his wife Alma out for a meal in Chicago. Because of civil rights laws, the restaurant couldn't refuse service, but did put laxative in the couple's food. Another member of the group was George Cooper. Soon after he became an ensign and donned his new uniform, he went to the railroad station in Chicago so he could catch a ride home to his see his wife, Peg, in Ohio. Wherever he went in the station, people came to a stop—arrested by the hitherto-impossible sight of a black man in a naval officer's uniform. He soon reported for

In March 1944 the Navy commissioned its first black officers as reservists following a short course at Great Lakes, Illinois. They have subsequently come to be known as the Golden Thirteen—twelve ensigns and a warrant officer. FRONT ROW, LEFT TO RIGHT: James E. Hair, Samuel E. Barnes, George C. Cooper, William Sylvester White, Dennis D. Nelson. MIDDLE ROW: Graham E. Martin, Charles B. Lear, Phillip G. Barnes, Reginald E. Goodwin. TOP ROW: John W. Reagan, Jesse W. Arbor, Dalton L. Baugh, Frank E. Sublett.

Above: *A WAVE operates the control tower at Brooklyn's Floyd Bennett Field, a naval air station, in November 1943. Assigning women to such positions freed the men who would otherwise be doing these jobs for combat duty. (Photo: U.S. Naval Institute)*

Above, right: *Yeoman Marjorie Adams, a member of the WAVES (Women Accepted for Voluntary Emergency Service) delivers mail to a Postal Clerk Wilbur Harrison from an attack transport. The fleet post office in San Francisco was a key facility in providing morale support to those serving on board ships and distant shore stations. (Photo: U.S. Naval Institute)*

duty in Hampton, Virginia. There he went out of his way to cultivate white sailors, explaining that he wanted them to see him "as a human being and not as a black son of a bitch wearing officer shoulder boards."

Women were also moving into largely uncharted waters. A few women had served as "yeomanettes," essentially secretaries in uniform, during World War I, but they were sent on their way after the war's end. A quarter century later, a newer generation suited up with the idea that each woman could "free a man to fight." Mildred McAfee, president of Wellesley College, became the first director of the WAVES, as Navy women were nicknamed. They moved into a variety of jobs ashore and demonstrated aptitude in many capacities.

Among the first women to be commissioned as a Naval Reserve officer was Ensign Winifred Quick, who took her training in the summer of 1942. Before the war, she was a groundbreaker as well, being among the first five women to get management training from professors of the Harvard Business School. Her talents and training would serve her well in the Navy, helping to administer the WAVES as essentially a new and separate branch of the service. In 1944 Congress passed a law that enabled Navy women to serve, for the first time, outside the limits of the continental United States. Admiral Nimitz, as Commander in Chief of the Pacific Fleet, objected to having women in Hawaii, saying he had enough problems already. But when the Bureau of Naval Personnel issued orders for thousands of women to go overseas, he graciously invited Lieutenant Quick to lunch at his quarters and put her at ease, recognizing that she was nervous in the presence of many of his staff officers. A week later, she met him again at a reception. Nimitz, who had a keen recall for names, greeted her by name saying, "Oh, Lieutenant Quick, you certainly made history." He then recounted something she did subconsciously on leaving his luncheon, adding, "I must tell you, you're the first lieutenant in the history of the Navy who blew a kiss to the Commander in Chief and hasn't been court-martialed." Nimitz's sense of humor was legendary, as was his kindness.

In early 1944 the Central Pacific campaign included a successful invasion of the Marshall Islands, and in the summer came the conquest of the Marianas—

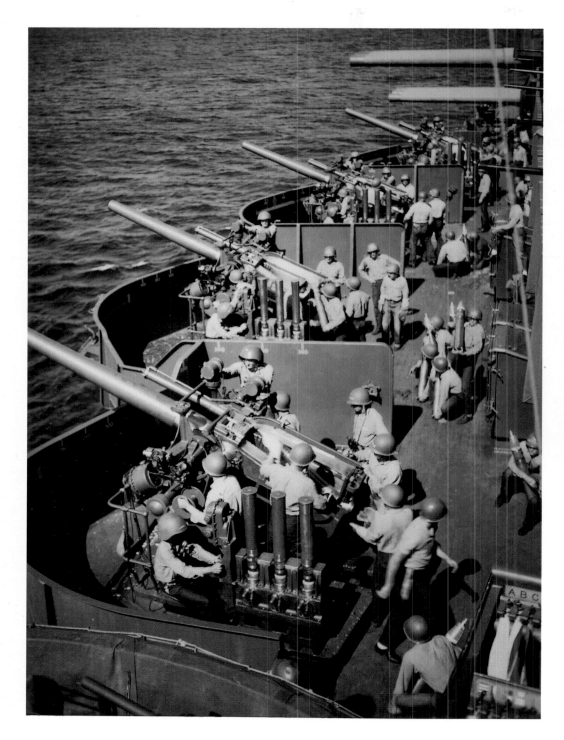

Saipan, Tinian, and Guam. The operation was marked by a great air battle, known as the "Marianas Turkey Shoot," in which Navy fighters shot down more than three hundred Japanese aircraft in one day. Admiral Spruance sparked controversy by failing to steam west in pursuit of the Japanese fleet, choosing instead to fulfill his mission of protecting the invasion beachheads.

Getting troops and their equipment to those beaches benefited from the work of a new organization of underwater demolition teams—the forerunners of today's SEALs. Lieutenant Commander Draper Kauffman was stationed in Britain at the outset of the war and had been trained in bomb disposal techniques to defuse unexploded ordnance. He later brought his knowledge to the U.S. Navy, both to teach it and then to start the process of creating explosions rather than preventing them. He set up a training school at Fort Pierce, Florida, to teach demolition techniques. The hazards presented by the offshore reefs at Tarawa dramatically underscored the need to discover such obstacles before the assault forces had to cross them and to get rid of them. The planning for the invasion of Saipan called for Kauffman's men to conduct a preliminary reconnaissance and then blow up coral to make way for tanks and other equipment to get ashore. The men would swim in from a mile offshore, considerably farther than they had before. Some of his men groused about the one-mile training swims before breakfast. When the ship carrying the teams was en route to Saipan, one of the men pointed out to Kauffman

Above: *A column of water shoots skyward to mark the site of an explosion set by an underwater demolition team at Guam in the Marianas. The geyser contains water, smoke, and debris as the Navy swimmers set off an explosive charge to clear away beach obstacles and thus permit entry by landing craft and amphibious vehicles. (Photo: U.S. Naval Institute)*

Above, right: *Men of the 1st Marine Division head for the beach as their landing vehicles tracked (LVTs) churn past the offshore line of gunboats converted from amphibious assault craft at Peleliu on 15 September 1944. These amphibious tracked vehicles could maneuver over obstacles in the water and climb up beach slopes. (Photo: U.S. Naval Institute)*

that it would actually amount to a two-mile swim in order to get in and then back out. Kauffman responded, "Well, I assumed that if you could swim the mile in, there would be a sense of urgency that would enable you to swim the mile out."

And so they swam in to the beach, having conducted training by having ships fire their big guns overhead to accustom them to the experience. As the swimmers went in, they discovered that shells were splashing around them. Kauffman got on his little radio and said in an excited voice to his executive officer, "For God's sake, tell the support ships they're firing shorts."

The exec replied very calmly, "Skipper, those aren't shorts; they're overs. They're not ours."

To which Kauffman replied, "Oh."

But few of the swimmers were hit. In the excitement and tension, they had not realized how difficult it was for the Japanese to hit the heads of swimmers bobbing in the water. More than one hundred thousand pounds of explosive in twenty-pound packages were planted. Each package had to be attached securely to the coral reef and connected with explosive cord as a fuse. Only ten minutes' fuse time was allowed for their escape. When the explosives went off, they sent a cloud of debris soaring into the sky, raining down black water onto nearby ships, including the transport USS *Cambria* (APA 36), flagship of an amphibious group commander, Rear Admiral Harry Hill. Kauffman was summoned to Hill's cabin for an explanation. He dripped black water onto the admiral's carpet and agreed that it would be a good idea to let the task group commander know the next time he was going to set off an explosion like that.

Among the most controversial operations of the Pacific War was the U.S. invasion of the island of Peleliu in the Palau Islands in September 1944. It proved to be costly in casualties, especially in terms of going after well-entrenched Japanese in the island's rugged terrain. The island was seen as a

base for Japanese air operations that might threaten the forthcoming landings in the Philippines

At that time, these arguments were well above the pay grade of the men who made up the crew of USS *PC-1129*, a 170-foot-long, 280-ton craft intended originally as a submarine chaser. She had a distinctly different role at Peleliu, where she was assigned to anchor near the beach to serve as a guide for landing craft as they made their way shoreward from the transports that were their mother ships. Chief Quartermaster Herb O'Quin was assigned to the bridge as the small ship performed her task just offshore. From there, he witnessed an illustration of the Japanese approach to war—the idea that death was far preferable to the dishonor of surrender. He saw a Japanese officer and two of his men trapped on a small beach at the base of a low cliff. Marines, by then ashore in force, were likely to find the three soldiers. To avoid being captured, the officer deliberately executed his two subordinates and then shot himself.

In the autumn of 1944, the Navy transported General MacArthur's amphibious forces to the island of Leyte, where he was able to fulfill his previous pledge to the Filipinos, "I shall return." But the Japanese were not willing to give up the islands without a fight. They sent a multi-pronged naval force toward the Philippines, setting the stage for the naval action they had avoided with their long-distance air attacks in the Marianas in June. In terms of numbers of ships and men, it proved to be the largest naval battle in history and one of the most complex as well, comprising a number of independent actions.

Battle was joined on 23 October as the submarines USS *Darter* (SS 227) and USS *Dace* (SS 247) sank two Japanese heavy cruisers and badly damaged a third. USS *Bream* (SS 243) crippled still another heavy cruiser. The following day came heavy attacks against the U.S. ships from Japanese airplanes based on the

By the end of 1944, shore bombardment in preparation for an amphibious landing had developed techniques of saturation as well as directed fire. Some medium landing ships (LSMs) were converted to this purpose by the installation of rocket launchers. At the landing in Balikapan, Borneo, the Seventh Fleet fired 20,000 rockets in preparation for a landing of Australian forces. (Photo: Library of Congress)

Transports and landing craft operated by the Navy and Coast Guard present this remarkable tableau as American forces consolidate their hold on the Okinawa beachhead in the wake of the April 1945 invasion. (Photo: U.S. Naval Institute)

129

Top: *Commander David McCampbell and his wingman, Lieutenant (junior grade) Roy Rushing splash fifteen Japanese aircraft on 24 October 1944 during the Battle of Leyte Gulf. The F6F Hellcat replaced the Wildcat as the primary carrier based fighter in 1944. ("High Side Attack over Leyte Gulf," Ted Wilbur, U.S. Naval Institute)*

Above: *The Navy's top fighter ace in World War II was Commander David McCampbell, who shot down thirty-four Japanese aircraft during a remarkable deployment on board the carrier USS* Essex *(CV 9) in 1944. He bagged nine planes during one mission in the October Battle of Leyte Gulf. (Photo: U.S. Naval Institute)*

island of Luzon. Among the carriers targeted was *Essex*, lead ship of the class that contributed mightily to victory during the last two years of the war. Her air group commander was Commander David McCampbell, who was more intent on being a fighter pilot than commanding the group as a whole. As the Japanese planes approached, McCampbell and his wingman, Lieutenant (junior grade) Roy Rushing, were among those who went to meet them. Using the .50-caliber machine guns of the F6F Hellcats to great advantage, McCampbell shot down nine planes and Rushing added six. McCampbell's one-mission total earned him a Medal of Honor and contributed to his eventual total of thirty-four planes shot down, the most by any U.S. Navy fighter pilot during the war.

Also on the 24th, carrier planes pounced on a force of Japanese surface ships in the Battle of the Sibuyan Sea. The battleship *Musashi* was hit by a combination of bombs and torpedoes. She and her sister *Yamato* were the largest battleships in the world, each armed with 18.1-inch guns. On the night of 24–25 October, another Japanese surface force sought to approach the invasion beachheads through the Surigao Strait, which separates Leyte and Mindanao. There the Japanese were slaughtered by Rear Admiral Jesse Oldendorf's combination of battleships, cruisers, destroyers, and PT boats. Marking the end of an epoch, this action was the last time during the war that ships engaged each other with big guns.

On board a small ship during the action was Lieutenant (junior grade) Jim Holloway. In 1944 he was the gunnery officer of the destroyer USS *Bennion* (DD 662); three decades later he became Chief of Naval Operations. In *Bennion*, his general quarters station was a Mark 37 director that controlled the aiming of the ship's battery of 5-inch guns. At times he could see all of the action unfolding; when he wanted a close-up, he looked through the high-powered lens of the director's optical range finder and found it filled by the towering pagoda-like mast of a Japanese battleship. The thought went through his mind that it matched the images he'd seen in training courses at the Naval Academy not long before. As the ships of the two

Above, left: *A carrier plane takes off from the deck of an Essex-class carrier and heads into the setting sun. At the lower part of the picture are the raised barrels of two 5-inch gun mounts located forward of the island superstructure on the starboard side. (Photo: U.S. Naval Institute)*

Above: *Officers gather to confer on the island superstructure of an Essex-class aircraft carrier in the Pacific. Parked forward are TBF Avenger torpedo planes; wings folded. The bulletin board in the lower part of the picture is for the information of pilots taking off so they will know where to look for the ship when it is time to return and land. (Photo: U.S. Naval Institute)*

Left: *A flock of SB2C Helldivers sits on the stern of an Essex-class carrier. The wings are folded so the planes will take up less deck space. The SB2C was the standard carrier-based dive-bomber during the latter part of the war, but some veterans lamented the passing of the SBD that had been so effective in the Battle of Midway. (Photo: U.S. Naval Institute)*

Tom Freeman
©1998

Twenty-year-old Lieutenant (junior grade) Don Engen flies his SB2C Helldiver close to the hybrid Japanese battleship-carrier Hyuga on 25 October 1944, during the Battle of Leyte Gulf. Burning behind him is the carrier Zuikaku. Engen planted a bomb on the carrier's deck and contributed to her sinking. She was then the last surviving aircraft carrier of the six that launched the attack on Pearl Harbor. Engen later became a vice admiral and eventually served as director of the Smithsonian's National Air and Space Museum until his death in 1999. (Too Close for Comfort," Tom Freeman)

navies sped toward each other at a relative speed of fifty knots, projectiles from Japanese battleships created towering splashes as they dropped near the *Bennion*. As Holloway's ship and other destroyers were making their final torpedo runs, the Japanese steamed forward into the massed firepower of Oldendorf's battle line, which sent armor-piercing shells arcing toward them. Holloway watched with fascination as the projectiles found their mark and started fires that gradually enveloped the enemy ships.

Still another tentacle of the Japanese octopus approached Leyte from the north. This arm included aircraft carriers and battleships, though the former were largely denuded of planes. Impotent, this force was a decoy to lure Admiral William Halsey, Commander Third Fleet, away from San Bernardino Strait, to allow the damaged but still potent central force in the Sibuyan Sea to get through and attack the invasion transports.

One of the young aviators in the strike was twenty-year-old Lieutenant (junior grade) Don Engen, who was typical of the hundreds of young men who became officers and completed flight training when they were barely out of high school. (One of his classmates in flight training had been George Bush.) On 25 October he was flying an SB2C dive-bomber. He and his rear seat man flew in and dumped an armor-piercing bomb on the flight deck of the carrier *Zuikaku*, contributing to her sinking. She was one of the carriers that launched the strike against Pearl Harbor three years earlier. As he made his escape amidst thousands of rounds of antiaircraft fire, Engen flew toward the hybrid battleship-carrier *Hyuga*, so low that he was about level with one of the anchors on her bow and so close that he could pick out the Japanese officers and enlisted men on deck.

The destruction of the northern force was not as total as it might have been, because the work of Halsey's aviators was interrupted by urgent calls for help from the mouth of San Bernardino Strait. The Japanese surface ships managed to shake off earlier damage and again steam eastward to menace the American transports. The Japanese ran into a valiant group of destroyers and escort carriers that put up as tenacious a fight as would have the larger ships of Halsey's force.

Mike Bak was a quartermaster on board the destroyer USS *Franks* (DD 554) that October morning. Shortly after breakfast an urgent call from the ship's announcing system sent him to his battle station on the bridge. As he looked out toward the horizon, he saw what looked like toothpicks poking up in the distance. In reality there were the tops of the masts of Japanese ships, and they were coming ever closer. Planes from the small jeep carriers began taking off to commence their strikes. *Franks* and other destroyers fishtailed back and forth in their courses as they sought to provide cover for the carriers.

Other destroyers were on the offensive. One of them was USS *Johnston* (DD 557), commanded by Commander Ernest E. Evans, a man seemingly without fear. His ship steamed in close against the enemy issuing torpedoes and 5-inch projectiles. The ship's action report later told of her encounter with a battleship: "As far as accomplishing anything decisive, it was like bouncing paper wads off a steel helmet; but we did kill some Japs and knock out a few small guns." Neither Evans nor *Johnston* survived the action. A sailor swimming in the water saw a Japanese destroyer skipper salute *Johnston* as she went down. The small boys had made a large contribution to victory as the Japanese, severely mauled, withdrew before closing on the transports in Leyte Gulf.

Logistic support of the combatant ships was vitally important to keep them running for extended periods. The Navy experimented with underway replenishment before the war and perfected it once hostilities began. Conning officers on combatants developed the skill of guiding a ship into a parallel position less than one hundred feet off the beam of a supply ship and then taking on the "beans, bullets, and black oil" that kept them going. One of the organizations that supplied this support was Service Squadron 10, based at Manus in the Admiralty Islands.

The long at-sea periods during the war required ships to keep steaming until they could be pulled off the line and sent back for repairs and maintenance. Navy yards in the United States performed the larger jobs, but it was also useful to have repair facilities in the forward areas so that ships would not be taken away from the combat areas for extended periods. One of these repair facilities was at Manus; included in the facilities was a floating drydock. Commander Ralph James, the maintenance officer on the squadron staff, ran the facility. Commander James particularly praised the damage control work accomplished on board the torpedoed cruiser USS *Houston* (CL 81); it was directed by Commander George Miller, the ship's first lieutenant, and was instrumental in saving the ship. The repair crews had the grisly job of removing the bodies of dead crew members after they had dewatered flooded compartments.

In dealing with these various ships, the repair facility personnel sought to get them back into action as quickly as possible, though not everyone approved. One skipper spoke in jest, though he probably expressed the true feelings of a number of his crew when he said, "Gol darn you naval constructors. We thought we were going home for a Navy yard repair and a rest. Now you bastards have put us back on the line, and we don't love you for it." Stateside liberty, and the chance to visit families while on leave, was undoubtedly a good deal more desirable than the attractions offered in the Admiralty Islands.

Crew members of a new submarine tender go about their business topside as the ship undergoes shakedown training. Tenders of several varieties were essentially floating machine shops that could perform wonders of maintenance and repair to enable smaller ships to operate from remote locations. (Photo: U.S. Naval Institute)

The battleship USS Wisconsin *(BB 64) nears completion in this picture taken at the Philadelphia Navy Yard. Behind her is one the world's largest hammerhead cranes. With the capacity to lift several hundred tons, these cranes could lift the battleship turret and the associated barbettes and lower them into place in the hull. (Photo: U.S. Naval Institute)*

Above: *The battleship USS* Massachusetts *(BB 59) takes a drink of fuel from a fleet oiler. The ships are connected by wires hooked up for the operation; the heavy fuel hoses hang from these span wires. Larger ships, such as battleships and carriers, used some of their very large capacity to refuel destroyers and other small ships. (Photo: U.S. Naval Institute)*

Above, right: *The Marine Corps War Memorial in Arlington, Virginia, commemorates all the campaigns of the Marine Corps. The model for the statue derives from a photo of the flagraising at Iwo Jima—one of the most hard fought battles in World War II. Appropriately, one of the men raising the colors was a Navy corpsman. (Photo: Eric Long)*

By mid-December 1944, with the Japanese fleet almost nonexistent, the carrier planes of Task Force 38 were launching strike after strike against the Philippines. Then they encountered an enemy even more potent than the Japanese—the weather. Admiral Halsey was determined to get his ships fueled from the oilers of the mobile support force and inadvertently took the fleet into the path of a violent typhoon. Radioman Bill Buckner was riding USS *Patuxent* (AO 44), a replenishment oiler whose load of oil gave her a deep draft and thus made her roll less than the destroyers. The carriers, with their large above-water structures that acted as sails in the teeth of the fierce winds and flying spume, were also vulnerable to storm damage.

On the bridge of *Patuxent*, the captain and the chief quartermaster didn't leave things to chance. Hour after hour, they handled the helm themselves. The one who wasn't steering often went out on the wings of the bridge to observe the frightening conditions and to avoid other ships, including a helpless destroyer escort that wallowed nearby. Visual sighting was the only way to do it—and in terribly limited visibility at that— because the sea spray made the radar almost useless. Buckner stepped out from the radio shack, a deck below the bridge, and got facefuls of salt spray. As the waves plunged and rose, *Patuxent* at times went into the trough. As Buckner looked out and saw the crest of a wave, it was sometimes forty or more feet above him—a wall of water alongside. Some waves broke over the ship's bridge.

The anemometer registered winds of more than 100 knots before it was blown away and registered no more. As the storm sent the ship twisting, turning, bouncing, and bucking, Radioman Buckner was "scared to death at the power of the thing." Problems reverberated throughout the fleet. Three destroyers capsized and sank during the storm; many ships were damaged. The typhoon—the "other enemy"—was formidable indeed.

In February 1945, the Americans carried the war ever closer to Japan by invading the island of Iwo Jima. It was a bitter struggle for Marines as they walked on the treacherous footing of the island's volcanic soil and faced fanatic resistance from Japanese defenders. Captain Harold B. "Min" Miller, Pacific Fleet public information officer, was charged by Secretary of the Navy James Forrestal

to see that the service improved telling its story to the public. He arranged for transportation of reporters and photographers to the site and then provided darkroom facilities for the development of film. One of the pictures that emerged from the process was taken by Joseph Rosenthal of the Associated Press. It depicted the memorable scene in which a group of Marines and a Navy pharmacist's mate raised the American flag over the island's Mount Suribachi. The image has become one of the icons of the American culture, celebrated with a large sculpture in Arlington, Virginia.

Later in February aircraft carrier task forces began bombing the Japanese capital of Tokyo, supplementing the heavy strikes inflicted by the Army's B-29s. On 1 April, the campaign moved almost to the doorstep of Japan with the invasion of Okinawa, only a few hundred miles from the home islands. It was a campaign that wearied the Navy as it defended against hundreds of Japanese kamikazes, young pilots who deliberately went on suicide missions to crash their aircraft into American ships.

During the late afternoon of 6 April, less than a week after the invasion, the destroyer USS *Newcomb* (DD 586) was screening minesweepers to the west of Okinawa. Captain Roland Smoot, the embarked destroyer squadron commander, stood on the port wing of the bridge when the suicide planes began targeting the ship. Three hit within about fifteen minutes and knocked out both smokestacks. With the ship dead in the water, without power, Smoot saw yet another plane heading right toward ship. Crewmen fled from the center part of the ship, which was already a mass of flames. As the plane approached, Smoot looked through his binoculars and saw the pilot's white scarf and clenched teeth. The kamikaze seemed headed straight toward him, and the commodore wondered if he would share the pilot's fate.

Fortunately, the gunner's mates in the ship's forward 5-inch mount were able to train it around and shoot at the threatening aircraft. A projectile exploded under the right wing of the kamikaze, tipping it sideways, and sending the plane skidding across into the destroyer USS *Leutze* (DD 481) which was alongside the *Newcomb* to fight her fires. That was the fifth kamikaze attack against the *Newcomb* that terrible day. She was one of dozens of destroyers and destroyer escorts damaged in the fearful suicide assault that accompanied the Okinawa operation.

Top, left: *The battleship* Tennessee *(BB 43), a veteran of the attack on Pearl Harbor, provides fire support as landing vehicles tracked (LVTs) grind ashore during the invasion of Okinawa on 1 April 1945. (Photo: U.S. Naval Institute)*

Top, right: *Japanese suicide attacks were a surprise to the Americans. The ultimate in guided missiles, these aircraft took a heavy toll on the ships supporting the Okinawa landings. Carriers and destroyers took the brunt of the damage. The heavy armor on the battleships, in this case USS* Missouri *(BB 63), generally limited the damage to topside equipment and exposed personnel. (Photo: Library of Congress)*

Above: *After her kamikaze ordeal of 6 April 1945, off Okinawa, the destroyer USS* Newcomb *(DD 586) was a blazing inferno amidships. Much of the superstructure has been swallowed into the center part of the ship, falling on top of a boiler. (Photo: U.S. Naval Institute)*

OS2U Kingfishers sit on catapults on the stern of the heavy cruiser USS Quincy *(CA 71). Floatplanes such as these were typically used on board battleships and cruisers during the war to observe the fall of shot of gunfire and to perform search and rescue missions. The cranes were used to pick up the aircraft after the returned to the ship and landed alongside in the water. (Photo: U.S. Naval Institute)*

This picture, showing the Remagen railroad bridge collapsed into the Rhine River, demonstrates the reason Navy landing craft were transported overland to Germany. Here an LCVP landing craft carries a Jeep upstream. (Photo: U.S. Naval Institute)

Two of the security precautions during the war were censorship of outgoing mail and the prohibition against keeping personal diaries. The chance that either diaries or mail would fall into enemy hands was small, but better to be cautious. Any number of individuals evaded the proscription on diaries, and history has been the beneficiary. Probably the most noted example is that of James Fahey, who enlisted in the Navy in Boston in October 1942 and reported to the crew of the new light cruiser USS *Montpelier* (CL 57), in which he served in a 40-millimeter gun crew. His notes were published in 1963 as a best-selling book titled *Pacific War Diary*, hailed for its depiction of the life of an enlisted man. In that sense, Fahey was Everyman, conveying in simple prose what it was like to live in the cramped quarters of a berthing compartment, to go without sleep, to react quickly in moments of alarm, and to cope with the tedium that is so often a part of shipboard life.

The censorship of mail deleted references to what a ship had been doing, what she would be doing, where she was—in short, the sort of things people back home would like to know. Though there was a legitimate reason for the censorship, it could and did have unintended consequences, as demonstrated by an incident in April, when the light cruiser USS *Mobile* (CL 63) was operating off Okinawa. One night a defective powder charge for a 6-inch gun exploded in a turret, where it killed an officer and five enlisted men. The officer was Ensign Bill Stephens. The ship's main battery officer, Lieutenant Jerry King, was a close friend of Stephens and wanted to tell the dead man's parents what had happened, but could not because of censorship. The explosion and resulting casualties were considered classified.

In 1947, long after King had left *Mobile*, he and his wife were traveling cross country as he headed for a new duty assignment. They made it a point to stop in the small crossroads town in west Texas that had been the home of his shipmate. King went to the local post office and said he was looking for the family of a naval officer named Bill Stephens. The man at the window said nothing, but he acted as if he had seen a ghost. Finally, he put his window down, left the

Left: *The submarine U-858 flies American colors as her U.S. crew brings the boat to anchor at Cape Henlopen, Delaware, in May 1945 after the Germans surrendered that month. Overhead are a Navy blimp and a Sikorsky helicopter. (Photo: U.S. Naval Institute)*

Above: *Those kamikazes that managed to get through the antiaircraft defenses of combat air patrol and escorting ship antiaircraft gunfire, aimed for the biggest targets, the aircraft carriers. Lightly armored and loaded with aviation gasoline and bombs, the fires that resulted were spectacular and deadly. Several carriers were out of action but none was sunk. Heroic action and skilled damage control kept all afloat and minimized casualties. (Photo: U.S. Naval Institute)*

building, and motioned for King to follow. He drove several miles in his pickup truck with the Kings close behind in their car. When they came to a ranch house, both vehicles stopped. The Kings got out and watched as the man approached the porch and said to a woman sitting there, "Ma, this man wants to talk about Billy." And then they listened as King told the story of how their son had died and what a fine officer he had been. Since they heard no details during the war, they assumed that their boy died in disgrace. Now they knew differently. Two years after the war, they finally received closure.

The Navy made an enormous contribution in Europe by its tremendous sealift effort, by carrying assault troops to invasion sites in Normandy and the Mediterranean, and by providing naval gunfire support. But geography meant that the bulk of the fighting would be ashore once the troops were landed and moving inland. But the Navy still had a role as the fight moved on to Germany itself. The Rhine River stood as a barrier or a passageway, depending on modes of transportation available.

Lieutenant Commander William Leide headed a Navy unit whose mission was ferrying the men and equipment of the Army across the Rhine. Trained first in France, they then hauled Navy landing craft, LCVPs and LCMs, overland on trucks. Normally gray, the craft were painted olive drab, and their Navy crewmen wore khaki-colored Army uniforms. Hauled overland in convoys of Army trucks, sometimes they knocked corners off buildings that were too close to streets that were intended for cars rather than high-riding landing craft. Other times stone road markers had to be pulled up to enable the trucks to pass, but pass they did facilitating the Army's trip into the heart of Germany. In the first twenty-four hours of operation, the craft ferried fifteen thousand soldiers and more than a thousand vehicles across. That was in late March; in early May the Germans capitulated.

The savage fighting between U.S. and Japanese forces was a life-and-death

Mail call is one of the most enjoyable parts of shipboard life. Here a sailor pauses to read a Christmas greeting on board an aircraft carrier. A sister ship can be seen in the distance, through the open hatch. (Photo: U.S. Naval Institute)

struggle, but occasionally humanitarian exceptions took place. One such instance occurred in early July 1945, when Navy patrol planes spotted what appeared to be a Japanese hospital ship approaching Wake Island, apparently to evacuate members of the garrison that had been there since the island fell in December 1941. Pacific Fleet headquarters directed the destroyer USS *Murray* (DD 576) to intercept the Japanese ship to make sure it was legitimate and that it was not carrying weapons to the island. The destroyer caught up with the ship, which was painted white and bearing an illuminated red cross on her smokestack. The skipper of *Murray* directed two crews to board motor whaleboats and inspect the hospital ship.

Lieutenant Bill Beinecke, the destroyer's gunnery officer, was amused by what happened next. As the first boat was about the leave, the ship's captain handed a signaling pistol to the boat officer, telling him, "If they try any monkey business, shoot this thing, and I'll blow them out of the water."

This order prompted one of the enlisted men in the boat crew to turn to the man with the pistol and ask, "Sir, are you really going to shoot that thing?"

"Do you think I'm crazy?"

"I'm not sure. You're an officer."

As it happened, the inspection determined that the hospital ship, *Takasago Maru*, was in accordance with international conventions and on a legitimate mission to take starving Japanese off the long-bypassed island. Few supply ships had made it to Wake, so the men there were living on rats and gooney birds. The ship took aboard nearly one thousand patients, and as she headed toward home, a party from *Murray* again went aboard for inspection. The destroyer's doctor examined a number of the patients and found that many had tuberculosis and even more were malnourished. He concluded that 15 to 20 percent would not live to see Japan again.

On 6 August 1945, the Army Air Forces B-29 bomber *Enola Gay* delivered an atomic bomb on the city of Hiroshima, Japan, wreaking instant and widespread devastation. The weaponeer on board was Navy Captain William S. "Deak" Parsons, who was involved with the bomb's development as part of the Manhattan Project in the New Mexico desert. Three days later, it was the turn of another B-29 to drop an atomic bomb. This time the bomb expert was Commander Dick Ashworth. It was he who, amidst the great secrecy surrounding the Manhattan Project, first informed Admiral Nimitz of the existence of these super weapons. He had carried a letter about the bomb, written by Fleet Admiral Ernest King, the Chief of Naval Operations, in a sweat-stained money belt that he took out from inside his khaki shirt to present to Nimitz.

On the mission itself, cloud cover obscured the intended target of Kokura, Japan, and sent the B-29, nicknamed Bock's Car, toward the port city of Nagasaki. Thus did the latter go down in history rather than Kokura. During the time it took to get overhead, the skies over Nagasaki clouded up, but those on board the plane knew they had to do something with the bomb. Ashworth watched in admiration as the Army bombardier took advantage of a brief twenty-second break in the clouds. He lined up his bombsight and dropped the powerful weapon toward its target. Then the plane banked sixty degrees and turned away to escape. The mushroom cloud erupted, leveling the city and sending shock waves back toward the American plane. Ashworth likened the experience to being in a metal trashcan beaten upon by a baseball bat—more noise than anything else.

At a time when the Americans were making plans to invade Japan's home islands in November and the Japanese were preparing to defend them, the atomic bombs provided a shock that upset previous calculations. These new weapons were well beyond anything that had been used in warfare. In the years since then, some

Above: *Steward's Mate Second Class Miles Davis King carries a loaded magazine for a 20-millimeter machine gun in August 1944, as the escort carrier USS* Tulagi *(CVE 72) steams through the Mediterranean en route to the amphibious landing area in southern France. (Photo: Naval Historical Center)*

Opposite, top: *U.S. Navy SB2C-3 Helldivers bank over the aircraft carrier USS* Hornet *(CV 12) before landing, following strikes on Japanese shipping, January 1945. Dive bombing was pioneered by Navy pilots in the middle and late 1930s. Development depended on building airplanes that could stand the strain of pullout at the bottom of the dive. (Photo: Naval Historical Center)*

Opposite, bottom: *40-millimeter antiaircraft guns firing on board a Task Force 58 aircraft carrier operating off Japan in February 1945. Though there were attacks by kamikazes after Okinawa, the Japanese hoarded what remained of their planes to attack at the invasion of Japan. (Photo: Naval Historical Center)*

historians have questioned the morality of the atomic weapons and whether they were really necessary in order to get a weakened Japan to capitulate. To Americans who would have been involved in the invasion, and to American prisoners of war who might well have been slaughtered by their captors, the issue is not worth debating. Aviation Ordnanceman Al Kernan, who was present during Butch O'Hare's last fight, put it eloquently when he wrote, "Each of us felt that those bombs had saved our lives, not lives in general, but our own felt, breathing lives. No one who was not there will ever understand how fatalistically we viewed the invasion of Japan. It had to be done, and would be, but each of us felt that survival was unlikely."

Finally, on 15 August, the Japanese agreed to capitulate, and hostilities ceased. The news of the cease-fire reached the new submarine USS *Requin* (SS 481) at Pearl Harbor. Her crew had completed shakedown training and was heading for what it presumed was combat duty. The skipper, Commander Slade Cutter, was on board *Pompano* near Pearl when the war began. Now he went back to the crew's mess to have a cup of coffee and discuss the electrifying news. One of the youngest men on board had tears streaming down his face. Cutter asked, "For God's sake, what's the matter?"

"I can't get a submarine combat pin. It's been two-and-a-half years since I enlisted to get into a submarine to make a war patrol, and now the war is over."

Cutter replied, "Boy, you are lucky. You are alive."

For the boat's captain there had been many days and nights when he wondered whether he would make it. He had seen the enemy close up. He had endured the violence of depth charging. He had reflected on the fact that one in five U.S. submarines sent into combat was lost on patrol. At many a dawn, as the morning stars faded, he had prepared to submerge for the day to avoid detection. As he did so, he wondered whether he would be alive that evening to surface again and see the evening stars. Being a survivor at war's end was a gift to be treasured.

On board the battleship USS *Missouri* (BB 63), flagship of Admiral Halsey's triumphant Third Fleet, the ship's whistle was blown in celebration of the news of peace. It got stuck for a time and drowned the conversations of those on board.

Missouri, which had entered combat for the first time in early 1945, had one more role to play in the great Pacific drama. Harry S. Truman became president

in April when Franklin Roosevelt died. He decreed that the formal surrender ceremony would be held on the deck of *Missouri*. If the decision had been to hold it on board the ship that contributed most to the naval victory, that likely would have been the carrier *Enterprise*, which was Halsey's flagship in December 1941 and fought in battle after battle throughout the war. But Truman selected Halsey's last wartime flagship instead, because it was named for his home state, and because his daughter Margaret had christened the ship.

The morning of Sunday, 2 September 1945, was quiet and overcast. The flagship was anchored in Tokyo Bay, within sight of the Japanese mainland. Ringed around her were dozens of other combatants, though many were elsewhere to ensure the fleet wouldn't be devastated by some last-minute suicide act. A somber delegation of eleven Japanese came aboard and trudged up to the 01 deck, just outside the captain's cabin. To begin the proceedings, General of the Army Douglas MacArthur read a short speech, and then the Japanese foreign minister came forward and sat down at a table from the enlisted men's mess. At 0904 Mamoru Shigemitsu signed, and the war officially ended.

As the Japanese delegation turned away and began leaving *Missouri*, the sun for the first time broke through the low-hanging layer of clouds. The visual scene was complemented by the roar of hundreds of engines as Navy planes from the Third Fleet carriers and bombers of the Army Air Forces flew over, seemingly so low that they would clip the tops of the masts of the anchored American warships.

As Gunner's Mate Walt Yucka, a member of *Missouri*'s crew, looked up at the spectacle of sun and planes, he was overcome with emotion. Nearly fifty years later, as he described the scene, Yucka felt chills as the memory sent a flood of images through his brain. He summed up his feelings by saying, "That was the greatest thrill of my life. The war was over."

The crew of USS Missouri *(BB 63) provides a watchful audience as Americans and Japanese gather on the captain's 01 veranda deck to sign the surrender that marks the end of the most far-reaching war in human history. (Photo: U.S. Naval Institute)*

Admiral Chester W. Nimitz, Commander in Chief, U.S. Pacific Fleet and Pacific Ocean Areas, was as respected and revered as any senior officer in World War II. On commissioning USS Nimitz *(CVN 68), President Gerald Ford eulogized him as "a keen strategist who never forgot he was dealing with human beings . . . aggressive in war without hate, audacious while never failing to weigh the risks." His bust decorates the court outside the library at the Naval Academy.*

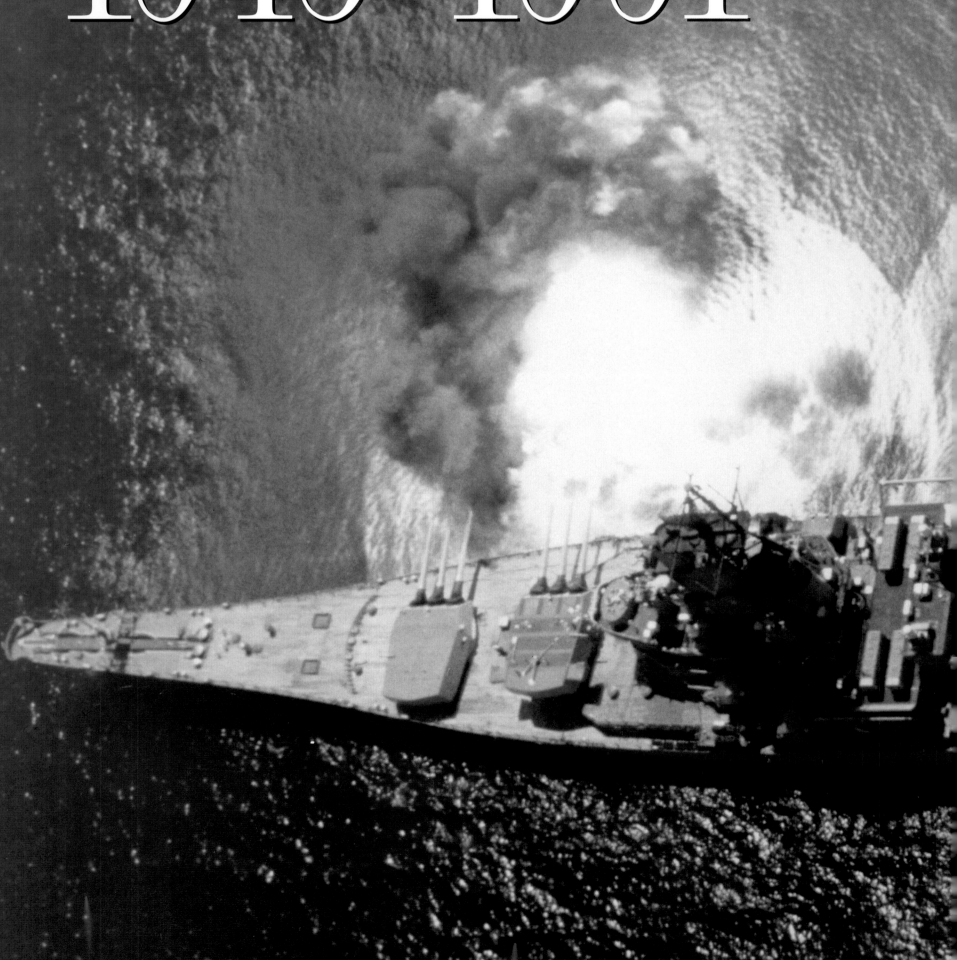

1945 -1991

Cold War to Violent Peace
1945-1991

Edward J. Marolda

USS Renshaw *(DD 499) in right center, with President Harry S. Truman embarked, steams up the Hudson River past USS* Orion *(AS 18) and USS* Howard W. Gilmore *(AS 16) during his review of the fleet on 27 October 1945. After celebrating the end of the greatest maritime war in history, the Navy would experience only a short-lived stand down from sustained operations. At the time few expected a return to a world of confrontation. (Photo: Naval Historical Center)*

Dawning of the Cold War

Soon after helping defeat Fascist tyranny in World War II, American sailors faced a new global threat to the United States and the values for which their nation had long been a standard bearer: democracy, basic human rights, and freedom. The USSR, under a murderous dictator, Joseph Stalin, acted to solidify the wartime conquests of the Soviet Red Army and advance the cause worldwide of Marxism-Leninism, an ideology that subverted the very ideals most Americans held sacred.

Working with local Communist leaders and movements in the years after the war, Stalin eliminated the political and economic independence of Poland, Czechoslovakia, and other nations in Eastern Europe. He put diplomatic and military pressure on Turkey and Iran in the Middle East and supplied war material to Communists fighting to overthrow the government of Greece. In 1948, the Soviets sparked a confrontation with the United States and its European allies over control of Berlin, the occupied and divided capital of the defeated German nation.

In the Far East, regional Communist movements took the lead, but received military assistance from Moscow in efforts to eliminate opposing movements and governments. Ho Chi Minh led Vietnamese Communists and other nationalists against the French colonial government in Indochina. Kim Il Sung and his Korean Communist supporters engaged in a vicious struggle for political control of the Korean people with Syngman Rhee and his anti-Communist adherents. In 1949, Mao Tse-tung and his Chinese Communist armies pushed the forces of the Chiang Kai-shek government off the mainland of Asia and established the People's Republic of China.

The United States, under the leadership of President Harry S. Truman, had already taken economic, political, and military steps to deal with the new threat posed by the Soviet Union and its allies. American taxpayers provided billions of dollars to restore the war-ravaged economies of Western Europe under the Marshall Plan, and the similarly devastated Japanese economy. The U.S. government strengthened political ties with many like-minded anti-Communist governments around the globe. Finally, the Truman administration adopted a broad "Containment Strategy," in simplest terms a major effort to build a wall around the Communist world that would be defended by the armed might of the United States and its allies.

The battleship USS Missouri *(BB 63), a potent symbol of U.S. military might, lies at anchor off Istanbul, Turkey, with an American destroyer and a Turkish cruiser in April 1946. President Truman dispatched the warship to those waters to signal his opposition to Stalin's aggressive activities in the region. In spite of the effectiveness of this demonstration, Truman was not a supporter of maintaining a Navy capable of worldwide deployments. (Photo: National Archives)*

The Big Three wartime leaders seated left to right: British Prime Minister Winston Churchill, American President Franklin D. Roosevelt, and Soviet Generalissimo and Premier Joseph V. Stalin at the Yalta Conference in February 1945. Stalin's aggressive behavior would soon end the wartime alliance and lead to the Cold War. Standing behind Roosevelt is Fleet Admiral William D. Leahy, USN, Chief of Staff to the President who was the senior member of the Joint Chiefs of Staff during World War II. (Photo: Naval Historical Center)

Pages 142–143: *The battleship USS* Iowa *(BB 61) fires a broadside with her 16-inch naval rifles. The integration into the fleet of the new Tomahawk land attack missiles in the 1980s gave a new lease on life to* Iowa *and her powerful sisters USS* New Jersey *(BB 62), USS* Missouri *(BB 63), and USS* Wisconsin *(BB 64). (Photo: Naval Historical Center)*

145

USS Valley Forge *(CV 45), USS* Leyte *(CV 32), and USS* Hector *(AR 7) moored in Sasebo, Japan, in December 1950. The "Happy Valley" was deployed to the Western Pacific when the North Koreans invaded South Korea on 25 June 1950. Planes from her air group struck at enemy supply lines to slow the North Korean drive against Pusan. Naval jet aircraft flew into combat for the first time from this carrier. (Photo: Naval Historical Center)*

Calm before the storm. Accompanied by a Republic of Korea Army interpreter, sailors from aircraft carrier USS Boxer *(CV 21) enjoy liberty in Seoul, South Korea, during the spring of 1950. (Photo: Naval Historical Center)*

The United States Navy, its warships and aircraft—and above all its sailors—guarded the ramparts of the containment wall from the beginning of the so-called Cold War to its end. Soon after Stalin pressed Turkey and Iran for territorial and other concessions in 1946, Truman dispatched battleship USS *Missouri* (BB 63), an unmistakable symbol of American military power, to the Eastern Mediterranean to make clear his determination that the United States would oppose aggressive Soviet actions. With establishment of the U.S. Sixth Task Fleet (later simply the U.S. Sixth Fleet) and creation of the North Atlantic Treaty Organization in 1949, it became clear to most observers that the United States meant to stand by its friends in the region.

Hot War in a Cold Place

President Truman moved decisively to defend American and allied interests in the Far East when Kim Il Sung's North Korean armed forces, equipped with Soviet tanks, artillery, and combat aircraft, invaded the Republic of (South) Korea on 25 June 1950. The commander in chief ordered U.S. air, ground, and naval forces to help South Korean and other United Nations forces resist the Communist attack. He also directed the U.S. Seventh Fleet based at Subic Bay in the Philippines to prevent the war from spreading to the waters and islands off China, where Chiang Kai-shek continued his fight against the Communist mainland government. The aircraft carrier USS *Valley Forge* (CV 45), the heavy cruiser USS *Rochester* (CA 124), and eight destroyers sortied from Subic Bay in the Philippines and made a show of force along the China coast. The presence of these Seventh Fleet forces off China

deterred the Communists from launching a long-planned amphibious assault on Chiang's stronghold on the island of Taiwan. Truman's bold actions can also be credited with influencing Stalin to take back an earlier pledge to Mao of Soviet air support in Korea. For the rest of the Korean War, Seventh Fleet submarines, land-based patrol aircraft, and carrier task forces kept watch on the seas around Asia to discourage the Soviet Union and the People's Republic of China from intervening in Korea with their naval forces.

The U.S. Navy took full advantage of its control of the sea and the air above it. On 2 July, little more than a week after the outbreak of war, the cruiser USS *Juneau* (CL 119), the British cruiser HMS *Jamaica*, and the British frigate HMS *Black Swan* intercepted North Korean torpedo boats and motor gunboats off the east coast of South Korea and destroyed five of the Communist naval vessels. The following day, aircraft from *Valley Forge* and the British carrier HMS *Triumph* bombed Pyongyang, the capital and war-making heart of North Korea.

The Republic of Korea Navy (ROKN), with the key assistance of the U.S. Navy, added its firepower to the fight. The South Korean navy had only been created a few years before the war and had little operational experience. Another problem was the absence from Korea at the start of the war of Admiral Sohn Won Il, the Korean chief of naval operations. He was in the United States accepting the transfer of three former U.S. submarine chasers. With the agreement of South Korean authorities, the U.S. naval command provided an American officer to help direct the allied service for the short term. Commander Michael J. Luosey took operational control of the ROKN. During the next month, Luosey set up inshore patrol sectors on the coast, managed the redeployment by sea of South Korean marine forces, and helped stiffen allied maritime defenses around the southern and

Top: *Royal Canadian Navy destroyer HMCS* Athabascan *bucks heavy seas off Korea. The United Nations effort to defend South Korea from Communist aggression involved not only the navies of Canada, the United States, and the Republic of Korea, but the United Kingdom, Australia, France, New Zealand, Colombia, Netherlands, and Thailand as well. (Photo: Naval Historical Center)*

Above: *Commander Michael J. Luosey, USN, acted as the operational commander of the Republic of Korea Navy shortly after the outbreak of the Korean War. He served in this capacity for a month until relieved by Admiral Sohn Won II, who had been in the United States for ship transfers. During his month in command, Luosey set up patrol sectors, redeployed South Korean naval forces, and stiffened the defenses on the western and southern coast. (Photo: National Archives)*

Right: *A sailor stands by as U.S. Marines board an attack transport at San Diego, California, in July 1950. The ability of the Navy's Military Sea Transportation Service to rush reinforcements and supplies to Korea helped the UN command preserve a toehold on the peninsula at Pusan. (Photo: Naval Historical Center)*

Below: *Navy Skyraiders fire 5-inch rockets at North Korean forces. Navy and Marine Corps aircraft carried out the majority of the UN command's close air support sorties in the Korean War. (Photo: National Archives)*

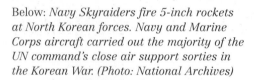

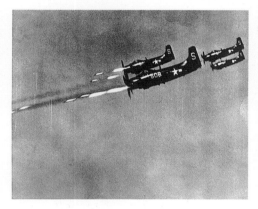

General Douglas MacArthur and several key subordinates share a laugh on the bridge of USS Mount McKinley *(AGC 7) as Marine forces strengthen their beachhead ashore. MacArthur was the driving force behind the decision to launch an amphibious assault at Inchon. (Photo: Naval Historical Center)*

western coastlines. With the return to Korea of Admiral Sohn and his three ships, South Korean naval forces became even more effective at destroying Communist junks, motorized sailboats, and sampans trying to deliver reinforcements, ammunition, and supplies to the swiftly advancing North Korean ground troops.

U.S. naval aircraft and warships added their firepower to the United Nations campaign to halt the North Korean invading forces before they overran the entire peninsula. U.S. and allied cruisers and destroyers bombarded enemy units moving along coastal roads as Navy and Marine air units pummeled Communist troops and supply convoys heading south on inland roads. Simultaneously, the ships of the Navy's Military Sea Transportation Service reinforced and resupplied UN troops holding a small toehold on the peninsula near the key port of Pusan. Without fleet support, the UN forces in South Korea would have been forced to make a costly withdrawal, like the British and French had at Dunkirk in World War II.

The Navy's mobility and command of the sea enabled General Douglas MacArthur and his UN command to reverse the tide of battle in Korea. In mid-September 1950, Vice Admiral Arthur Struble, Commander Seventh Fleet, led 230 amphibious and other ships into the Yellow Sea and toward the North Korean–occupied port of Inchon. As this armada approached the narrow channel leading to Inchon in the early morning hours of 15 September, a beacon suddenly shined from the top of a lighthouse that had been out of operation for some time. Inside the lighthouse was Lieutenant Eugene F. Clark, who had been executing a daring

intelligence mission behind enemy lines since the beginning of the month. The brave and resourceful naval officer had been landed on a nearby island, Yonghung Do, with a small party of South Koreans and another American to learn about local tides, currents, and other information that would be valuable to allied amphibious planners. Clark and his men gathered their intelligence, fought a small naval action with the Communists in which the enemy lost two boats to accurate machine-gun fire, and repaired the light. The enemy overran Yonghung Do, and caught and executed fifty villagers who had helped the Americans and South Koreans. But the "Blackbeard of Yonghung Do," as Clark would soon be called, avenged them by accomplishing his very important mission.

For days, naval gunfire support ships and carrier aircraft attacked enemy defensive positions ashore at Inchon. Then, at 0633 on 15 September, fleet amphibious landing craft disembarked the 5th Marine Regiment of the 1st Marine Division on Wolmi Do, an island in Inchon Harbor. After several days of hard

"Hitting Home," a colored pencil drawing by combat artist Herbert Hahn, shows Navy AD-4 Skyraiders dropping aerial torpedoes at the Hwachon Reservoir Dam. (Navy Art Collection)

fighting and reinforcement by other Marines, South Korean troops, and elements of the Army's 7th Infantry Division, the allies seized the port and nearby Kimpo airfield. On the 21st, U.S. Army units that had broken out of the Pusan Perimeter linked up with the Inchon forces. One week later, after bloody, street-to-street fighting, the 1st Marine Division captured Seoul. The amphibious units at Inchon suffered 3,500 killed, wounded, and missing, but inflicted 20,000 casualties on the enemy. More importantly, the Inchon assault led to the disintegration of the North Korean People's Army and the liberation of South Korea.

General MacArthur hoped to destroy the enemy army completely and to occupy northeast Korea with another amphibious assault, at Wonsan on the Sea of Japan. He intended that the Navy would land the X Corps at Wonsan. This corps would then advance overland to the Yalu River and the North Korean border

Navy tank landing ships (LST) are emptied of critical supplies at Inchon's Red Beach soon after the men of the 1st Marine Division secured a lodgment ashore. The shallow draft and beaching ability of these vessels made them essential to the landing operation. (Photo: Naval Historical Center)

with the People's Republic of China and the Soviet Union. Fast-moving South Korean troops, however, got to Wonsan on 10 October, a week before the planned landing. In addition, the Navy discovered—the hard way—that the Communists had placed between 2,000 and 4,000 Soviet-made magnetic and contact mines in the approaches to the harbor. A number of American and South Korean mine clearing vessels were sunk before the task force opened a safe passage into the port. Finally, on 25 October 1950, the 1st Marine Division began moving ashore and advancing into the forbidding mountains of North Korea.

The mobility that resulted from the fleet's control of the waters off Korea also enabled MacArthur to withdraw his forces to the safety of the sea when the battle ashore turned against the UN command. This occurred when the "volunteers" of the Communist Chinese People's Liberation Army emerged from the snow-covered mountains of North Korea in November 1950 and fell upon over-extended Army, Marine, and South Korean units. The X Corps, which included the 1st Marine Division, the Army's 3rd and 7th Infantry Divisions, and three South Korean divisions of the I and II Corps had to fight their way back to the coast in bitter cold and howling winds. Marine and Navy attack squadrons operating from fleet carriers USS *Philippine Sea* (CV 47), USS *Valley Forge* (CV 45), USS *Princeton* (CV 37), and USS *Leyte* (CV 32), and several escort carriers hit Chinese troops trying to surround UN units inland. In only one week of operations, naval aviators carried out 1,700 sorties against the enemy.

During these air operations to support the beleaguered men on the ground, Lieutenant (jg) Thomas Hudner, Ensign Jesse Brown, and two other F4U Corsair pilots from *Leyte*'s air group flew north of the Chosin Reservoir on the lookout for Chinese troops. Once there, Brown reported that his plane was losing oil pressure, perhaps after being hit by enemy ground fire, and that he had to crash land in the frigid, snow-covered mountains. The force of the crash was so severe that it separated the engine from the fuselage and badly twisted the latter. Brown survived the crash, but was injured and trapped in the cockpit. Fearing that fire would soon engulf the plane, Hudner called for a rescue helicopter (which he knew would take thirty minutes to arrive at the site) and decided to crash land his own Corsair next to Brown's to help rescue his squadron mate and friend. Hudner safely put his plane down in the snow not far from Brown's and rushed over to help him. Since Brown was already suffering from the extreme cold, Hudner covered the man's head with his spare wool cap and his hands with a scarf. Try

As men of the 1st Marine Division advance along the road from the Chosin Reservoir to Hungnam in North Korea, bombs dropped by naval aircraft explode on enemy positions ahead. The fleet's close air support was critical to the survival of the UN troops under assault from all directions by the Chinese army. (Photo: U.S. Marine Corps)

Ensign Jesse L. Brown, a pilot of USS Leyte's (CV 22) Fighter Squadron 32, poses in the cockpit of his F4U Corsair. Brown would become the first African-American naval aviator to die in combat when his plane went down in the snow-covered mountains of North Korea. (Photo: Naval Historical Center)

Sailors clear snow from the flight deck of an aircraft carrier steaming in the frigid seas off Korea. Sailors of the Seventh Fleet endured heavy snow, fierce winds, and bitterly cold weather during Korean winters. (Photo: Naval Historical Center)

as he might, however, Hudner could not free the pilot from the mangled cockpit. When Brown lapsed into unconsciousness from his injuries and the cold, and the pilot of the rescue helicopter told Hudner that they had to fly out of the mountains before nightfall or risk another crash, the lieutenant realized that they had to leave his friend behind. They had done all they could for Jesse Brown, the first African-American naval aviator to die in combat.

Meanwhile, most of the UN ground troops had fought their way to the coast, where battleship USS *Missouri* (BB 63), cruisers USS *Rochester* (CA 124) and USS *St. Paul* (CA 73), and numerous destroyers and rocket vessels put a wall of fire between the infantrymen and the enemy. Navy and allied surface ships fired over 23,000 16-inch, 8-inch, 5-inch, and 3-inch rounds and rockets at the Communist units trying to capture the port of Hungnam.

By Christmas Eve day, the Navy's Amphibious Task Force (Task Force 90) had completed the withdrawal by sea of 105,000 troops, 91,000 civilian refugees, 350,000 tons of cargo, and 17,500 military vehicles. Air Force and Marine planes airlifted out another 3,600 troops, 1,300 tons of cargo, and 196 vehicles. That day, 24 December 1950, Navy explosive demolition teams leveled the port facilities at Hungnam to deny them to the enemy, and the fleet steamed south. Within a few weeks, the units withdrawn from North Korea were back in the fight to preserve the independence of the Republic of Korea.

Throughout the Korean War, U.S. and allied naval forces maintained a tight blockade of North Korean waters so the enemy could not use the sea to transport troops and supplies. Control of the sea also allowed the UN command to threaten other amphibious landings in the rear of the Chinese and North Korean armies arrayed along the 38th parallel. The enemy took the threat seriously and positioned sizable troop units along both coasts and far from the front lines where they were badly needed. To keep the enemy's attention focused on the sea, the fleet executed a number of naval feints and demonstrations. In Operation Decoy during October 1952, Navy aircraft carriers, battleships, cruisers, and destroyers attacked Communist defenses around Kojo, and Task Force 90 maneuvered as if to land elements of the Army's 1st Cavalry Division near Wonsan. The enemy rushed forces to the coast to defeat amphibious assaults that never came.

The Navy also put special operations forces ashore on the east and west coasts of North Korea and on many of the thousands of islands that stud those waters. U.S. Navy underwater demolition teams, U.S. Marines, and British and South Korean naval commandos frequently destroyed highway bridges, supply dumps, railroad tracks, and railroad tunnels behind enemy lines. The blockade of

The men of a Navy underwater demolition team pull a rubber boat ashore on the east coast of Korea. American, British, and South Korean special operations forces carried out numerous such missions, often behind enemy lines. (Photo: Naval Historical Center)

The whaleboat of destroyer USS Douglas H. Fox (DD 779) prepares to get underway with North Korean prisoners captured during one of the small craft's forays along the enemy-held coast. These daring and imaginative operations by the Seventh Fleet sailors kept Communist eyes focused on their seaward flanks throughout the war. (Photo: Naval Historical Center)

As American sailors watch, North Korean fishermen captured by the ship's whaleboat team proceed along the deck of Douglas H. Fox. From men such as these, allied intelligence often learned the location of enemy coastal guns, troop barracks, and supply depots. (Photo: Naval Historical Center)

Wonsan from 16 February 1951 until the end of the war prevented the Communists from using that potentially important port.

A number of American warships operating in the waters off North Korea used their ship's whaleboat to carry the action to the enemy. Commander James A. Dare, the enterprising commanding officer of destroyer USS *Douglas H. Fox* (DD 779), manned his whaleboat with his most resourceful officers and daring blue-jackets and equipped them with a 75-millimeter recoilless rifle, small arms, demolition charges, grenades, a radio, and tools for destroying fishing nets. Every night, the boat would sortie five to seven miles from the ship, the range of the destroyer's radios and surface search radar, to seize fishing boats and their crews and return both to the ship. By destroying North Korean nets, impounding their boats, and otherwise disrupting the local fishing activity, the U.S. naval force denied enemy

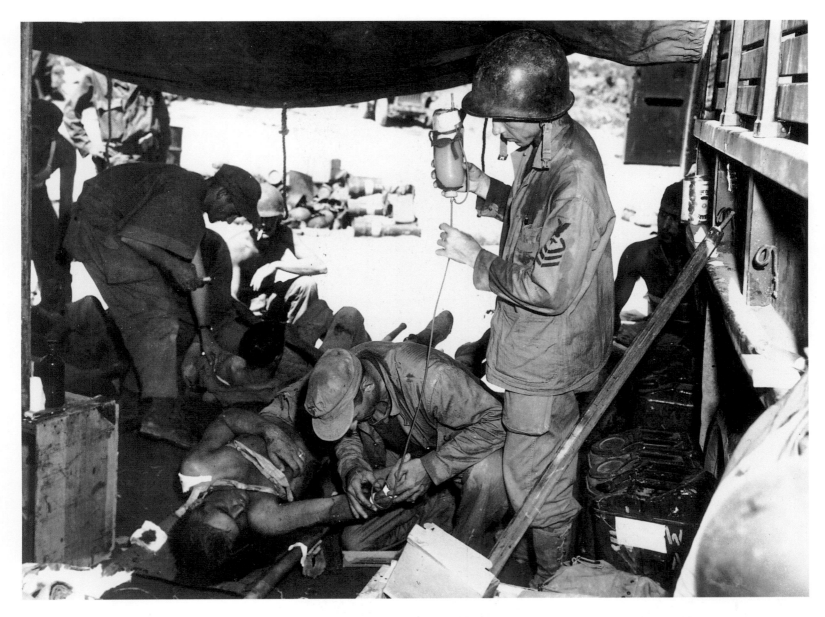

Navy hospital corpsmen tend to wounded Marines in an aid station during the advance north after the North Korean army was shattered by the invasion at Inchon. Their reputation for bravery under fire is legendary, the word "corpsman" itself carrying strong connotations for all Marines. (Photo: Naval Historical Center)

Navy flight deck crewmen of the carrier USS Bataan *(CV 29) prepare Marine F4U Corsairs for another bombing operation. The Corsair's high speed and extreme maneuverability combined to give these airplanes a longer operational life than their World War II counterparts. (Photo: Naval Historical Center)*

troops ashore the bounty of the sea. In addition, quite often the prisoners provided information on where the Communists had positioned their coastal artillery and the daily routines of the guns' crews. The sailors also practiced a little psychological warfare on the enemy. The night before May Day 1952 (1 May was an especially important date in the Communist world) *Douglas H. Fox*'s whaleboat sailors planted an American flag on an island at the mouth of Hungnam Harbor. As the sun rose at dawn in the east on the big day, the enemy's first sight was Old Glory flapping in the sea breeze.

On the carrier USS Antietam *(CV 36) naval air crewmen discuss the results of a just-completed strike operation in Korea. Most American sailors did their duty in the Korean War, but their morale suffered when they recognized that victory was not the goal of U.S. or UN policy after the start of armistice negotiations in July 1951. (Photo: Naval Historical Center)*

F9F Panther jets are launched from the carrier USS Valley Forge *(CV 45) for strikes behind Communist lines in Korea. The war marked the combat debut of American jet aircraft. (Photo: Naval Historical Center)*

In a general sense, the battleships, cruisers, and destroyers of the Blockade and Escort Force (Task Force 95) and the naval air units operating from carriers and from shore airfields provided essential support to the U.S. and allied troops fighting this first limited war of the Cold War period. The U.S. Navy did not lose a single major warship in the Korean War. Over 1,177,000 Navy personnel served in Korea. Of these, 458 sailors were killed in action, 1,576 suffered wounds, and 4,043 succumbed to injury or disease. Without the dedicated service and sacrifices made by Navy men and women, ashore and afloat, the UN would not have been able to preserve the independence of the Republic of Korea or achieve the armistice agreement with the Communist belligerents that ended the conflict on 27 July 1953.

Global Confrontation

Even before the Korean War and throughout the 1950s, sailors died during missions to gather military intelligence on the enigmatic and belligerent Union of Soviet Socialist Republics and People's Republic of China. In August 1949, the submarines USS *Cochino* (SS 345) and USS *Tusk* (SS 426) were deployed to the frigid waters off

Above: *USS* Cochino *(SS 345) prepares to get underway from the United Kingdom in July 1949, one month before battery explosions and fire sent her to the bottom in waters north of Norway while she was gathering intelligence on Soviet military activities. Throughout the Cold War, ships and aircraft were lost and sailors killed in the effort to keep close watch over America's Communist adversaries. (Photo: Naval Historical Center)*

Right: *A P2V Neptune flies over the coast of Japan near Atsugi to begin a long patrol in the Sea of Japan. The P2V was the first land based aircraft designed for maritime patrol. Throughout the Korean War, Navy seaplanes, land-based aircraft, submarines, destroyers, and on occasion carrier task forces, operated in international waters off the Soviet Union and the People's Republic of China to assert U.S. control of the sea. (Photo: Naval Historical Center)*

Vietnamese refugees in the Tonkin region of Vietnam prepare to board attack cargo ship USS Montague *(AKA 98) for a journey south to Saigon. In Operation Passage to Freedom, Seventh Fleet ships transported from northern to southern Vietnam over 310,000 Vietnamese who preferred not to live under the repressive regime of the Communist leader Ho Chi Minh. (Photo: National Archives)*

Norway and a little more than 100 miles from the Soviet Northern Fleet's bases at Murmansk and Polyarnyy to learn what they could about Soviet missile testing and other military activities. Without warning, batteries in *Cochino* exploded and badly burned one officer. Fire and noxious gases released by this and subsequent blasts spread throughout the submarine, endangering the entire crew. Two brave *Cochino* men, trying to bring help from nearby *Tusk,* were pitched into the bitterly cold water when their rubber boat overturned. Without hesitation, bluejackets from *Tusk* jumped in to help rescue their fellow sailors. Several men drowned in the valiant attempt and their bodies drifted silently off into the unforgiving northern waters. Finally, after herculean efforts, the surviving crewmen of both submarines gathered safely on board *Tusk.* The men watched helplessly as *Cochino,* gutted by fire and explosion, finally slipped beneath the waves.

Thousands of miles away off Siberia in September 1954, Soviet MiG fighters shot down a P2V Neptune patrol plane, killing one of its crewmen. Two years later the Chinese Communists shot down a Navy P4M Mercator reconnaissance plane flying over the sea along their coast. Many more sailors suffered death or injury due to heavy seas, fierce winds, or Arctic cold and ice as they carried out their duty to keep watch over potential enemy nations. Americans did not want a repeat of the surprise Pearl Harbor attack on the United States and its allies, especially in the dangerous nuclear age.

Tensions remained high in the Far East after the Korean War, as Ho Chi Minh's army defeated French forces at the climactic battle at Dien Bien Phu and established the Democratic Republic of Vietnam in the region of Indochina around Hanoi. Tens of thousands of northern Vietnamese decided they would rather live under a separate non-Communist Vietnamese government in southern Indochina than under the harsh, anti-religious regime of Ho Chi Minh and his Communist followers. To facilitate this major population transfer, the U.S. Navy mounted Operation Passage to Freedom. The Pacific Fleet concentrated 113 tank landing ships, transports, and other vessels in the South China Sea. Between August 1954 and May 1955, these ships carried over 310,000 Vietnamese civilians, many of them Catholics, from north to south Vietnam. This group of immigrants soon became the core of support for the anti-Communist government of the Republic of Vietnam.

Meanwhile, Mao Tse-tung's Chinese Communists intensified their efforts to eliminate the opposition to their government posed by Chiang Kai-shek and his Nationalist supporters, who still held many islands, including the large island of Taiwan off the coast of China. In September 1954 the Communists began shelling Quemoy Island and announced their intention to seize Taiwan. Truman had ordered Seventh Fleet aircraft, destroyers, and submarines to patrol coastal waters to prevent a Communist invasion of Taiwan at the start of the Korean War, and his successor, Dwight D. Eisenhower, was even more determined to support Chiang Kai-shek's anti-Communist Republic of China government. As a result, the president proposed and Congress approved a resolution in January 1955 pledging U.S. military assistance for the defense of Quemoy and Matsu Island, if doing so helped protect Taiwan itself. The two nations also put into force a mutual defense treaty.

The growing U.S. interest in the security of Japan and the anti-Communist governments in South Korea, South Vietnam, and Taiwan required the continuous presence of the U.S. Seventh Fleet in Far Eastern waters throughout the Cold War. The Navy's repair and supply bases at Yokosuka in Japan and on Okinawa, at Subic Bay in the Philippines, and on Guam supported this powerful commitment to the defense of America's Asian allies.

As landing craft from ships of the Seventh Fleet stand by in the harbor, the inhabitants of the Tachens off China prepare to evacuate their islands in February 1955. When the government of Chiang Kai-shek's Republic of China concluded that the islands could not be defended against Communist attacks, the United States helped transport the anti-Communist islanders to Taiwan. Throughout the 1950s, the Navy was involved in crises between the Chinese antagonists over the offshore islands. (Photo: National Archives)

Below: *Sailors of the attack transport USS* Lenawee *(APA 195) help soldiers of the Chinese Nationalist garrison on the Tachen Islands to come aboard after evacuation of the islands. In 1955, the U.S. Senate ratified a mutual defense treaty between the United States and the Republic of China. (Photo: National Archives)*

USS Forrestal *(CVA 59) was the lead ship of the first class of post–World War II carriers. This ship steams behind USS* Caloosahatchee *(AO 98) awaiting her turn to fuel during the Jordanian crisis in 1957. Ahead refueling are USS* Lake Champlain *(CVA 39) and USS* Salem *(CA 139), then Sixth Fleet flagship. The air group on deck contains F3H, FJ, F2H, F9F-8, A3D, AD, and S2F aircraft. (Photo: National Archives)*

Above: *Admiral Hyman G. Rickover, the "father of nuclear propulsion" in the U.S. Navy, emerges from a hatch on board* Nautilus, *the world's first nuclear-powered warship. The no-nonsense naval pioneer, a brilliant engineer and an inveterate perfectionist, was the most important figure in the development of America's Cold War submarine fleet. (Photo: Naval Historical Center)*

Above, right: *"Start of Able Bomb," by Charles Bittinger, depicts the test explosion in 1946 of a nuclear device among excess naval vessels positioned in the lagoon of the Marshall Islands' Bikini Atoll. While these tests demonstrated the toughness of warships, the advent of nuclear weapons had a profound impact on the Navy in the late 1950s and 1960s. The impact was not on warship design or naval operations, but on roles and missions, development of aircraft to carry nuclear weapons, positioning of carriers along the Communist periphery for strategic warfare missions, development of the fleet ballistic missile and submarines, and a neglect of conventional readiness to prepare for nuclear war in the late 1950s and 1960s. (Navy Art Collection)*

Below: *The huge A3J Vigilante attack plane was one of a number of carrier aircraft designed by the Navy during the 1950s to drop nuclear weapons on distant targets. The airplane was large because the nuclear weapons at this time were still very large. (Photo: Naval Historical Center)*

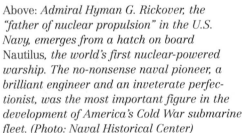

The Naval-Industrial-Scientific Partnership

Back home in the United States, the Navy strengthened its partnership with industry and the scientific establishment to meet the military demands of the Cold War. That partnership had served the nation well during World War II. The nuclear age, dramatically ushered in with the explosion of an atomic bomb over Hiroshima, Japan, in August 1945, took on special meaning for the Navy when it tested the impact of nuclear weapons on its warships at Bikini Atoll in the Marshall Islands during the summer of 1946. The two detonations, one at low altitude and the other in shallow water, sank only a few ships, but demonstrated that nuclear weapons and their radioactive fallout could wreak great havoc on man and machine.

Under the strong guiding hand of Rear Admiral Hyman G. Rickover, a determined and persuasive advocate of nuclear propulsion, the Navy commissioned USS *Nautilus* (SSN 571), the world's first nuclear-powered warship, on 30 September 1954. The following year, the service commissioned the 59,630-ton *Forrestal* (CVA 59), the lead ship of a class of "super carriers" designed to handle the new AJ-1 Savage and other jet-powered naval aircraft. Within a few years the Navy was operating carrier squadrons that were equipped to drop nuclear bombs.

Crises in the Mediterranean and the Far East

In addition to symbolizing the U.S. commitment to NATO and the defense of Western Europe against Soviet aggression, the Sixth Fleet in the Mediterranean reflected the American interest in helping to resolve the bitter Arab-Israeli conflict that so troubled the region during the 1950s. In 1956, during the Suez Crisis, President Eisenhower ordered carrier forces deployed in strength to the Eastern Mediterranean and in 1958 directed the landing of U.S. Marines in Lebanon to support friendly governments in the volatile Middle East.

Conflict in the Far East during the late 1950s once again demanded the Navy's attention. In August 1958, the Chinese Communists began shelling Quemoy and Matsu islands in the Strait of Taiwan, attempting to cut off 100,000 Nationalist Chinese defenders from outside logistic support. At the president's direction, the Navy deployed six carrier task groups to the waters off China and began escorting Nationalist ships on their runs to resupply the islands. Eisenhower also entertained diplomatic action to resolve the crisis peacefully. Faced with American resolve, and lack of Soviet support, Mao Tse-tung's government in Beijing did not take additional incendiary actions and the crisis abated.

From 1959 to 1962, Laotian Communists, with the military assistance of Ho Chi Minh's government in Hanoi, launched guerrilla attacks intended to overthrow the generally pro-Western Laotian governments in the capital of Vientiane. On several occasions, Washington ordered Seventh Fleet carrier task forces into the South China Sea to demonstrate U.S. opposition to the Communists' actions. In 1962, President John F. Kennedy took the additional step of deploying U.S. Marines and U.S. Army troops into Thailand, an American ally to the west of Laos. In each crisis, the possibility that U.S. troops, backed by nuclear-armed American sea and air power, would move into Laos to protect the national government persuaded the Communists to limit their aggressive activity. But Southeast Asia remained an international hot spot.

Sixth Fleet landing craft disembark U.S. Marines on the beach at Beirut, Lebanon, in July 1958. The Eisenhower administration took the action—which did not result in hostilities—to demonstrate support for the local government and to discourage aggressive behavior by Lebanon's anti-American neighbors. (Photo: U.S. Naval Institute)

USS Nautilus's (SSN 571) message "Underway on nuclear power" heralded a new era in maritime warfare. Reactor plants gave submarines unlimited endurance and the ability to operate virtually without detection. Marriage of that endurance and stealth with the ballistic missile eventually shifted most of the country's strategic deterrence force to the Navy. (Photo: Nautilus Museum, Groton, Connecticut)

159

New Frontiers

As trouble brewed in Asia, the Navy redoubled its efforts to provide the country with powerful tools to discourage or, failing that, defeat a Soviet nuclear attack on the United States itself. Admiral Arleigh Burke, the first Chief of Naval Operations to serve for three tours, from 1955 to 1961, had a profound impact on the Cold War navy. The veteran warrior, known to many as "31-knot Burke" for his World War II exploits as a destroyerman, argued successfully that Navy-controlled, ballistic-missile launching submarines should be added to the nation's strategic defense force of land-based missiles and bombers. As a keen judge of leaders, Burke called on Rear Admiral William "Red" Raborn to oversee the development of America's first submarine-launched intercontinental ballistic missile. In only a few years, Raborn could report to Burke that he had accomplished his mission. On the penultimate day of 1959, the Navy commissioned USS *George Washington* (SSBN 598), and in July 1960 the submarine made the first submerged launch of the Navy's new Polaris missile.

For the remainder of the Cold War, the Navy's ballistic submarine force served as one of the nation's most powerful deterrents to nuclear attack. The "boomers" routinely spent months away from their bases at Holy Loch, Scotland, Rota, Spain, and on the U.S. east and west coasts as they carried out their vital missions. The highly trained and professional sailors who operated these naval vessels had to endure a cramped, male-only existence at hull-crushing depths for long periods of time. That they did so willingly was a testament to their dedication to protecting the United States and its people.

Admiral Arleigh Burke, a renowned World War II combat leader and forceful Chief of Naval Operations from 1955 to 1961, addresses the sailors of destroyer USS Waller *(DD 466) during one of his frequent visits to the fleet. Burke's advocacy and leadership were instrumental in the initiation and the funding of the Navy's Polaris and follow-on Poseidon ballistic missile submarine programs. (Photo: Naval Historical Center)*

160

Only a few months before the first launch of a Polaris missile the Navy demonstrated what its undersea warships could do when the nuclear-powered submarine USS *Triton* (SSN 586), under Captain Edward L. Beach, completed a 41,519-mile circumnavigation of the globe—submerged. Complementing the naval arsenal, in November 1961 USS *Enterprise* (CVAN 65), the world's first nuclear-powered aircraft carrier, joined the fleet, and nuclear-powered cruisers and destroyers followed.

During this period, the Navy Department was starring in another environment—space. In May 1961 Commander Alan Shepard became the first American to pass beyond earth's atmosphere when his Mercury capsule, *Freedom 7*, blasted off from Cape Canaveral, Florida, and reached an altitude of 116.5 miles. When his craft descended from space and safely splashed into the Atlantic Ocean, helicopters from the aircraft carrier USS *Lake Champlain* (CVS 39) were on hand to recover him from the sea. The following February Marine Lieutenant Colonel John H. Glenn, Jr., traveled 81,000 miles in space when he made three orbits of the earth in his Project Mercury capsule, *Friendship 7*. The destroyer USS *Noa* (DD 841) retrieved the now-famous officer when he and his capsule touched down in the Atlantic.

Cuban Missile Crisis

Many Americans were exhilarated in February 1962 about the potential benefits to humankind of technology and space travel. But this euphoria turned to anxiety in October when U-2 reconnaissance planes operated by the Central Intelligence Agency discovered work underway in Communist Fidel Castro's Cuba, only ninety miles from Florida, to construct launch sites for Soviet nuclear-armed ballistic missiles. As President John F. Kennedy gathered additional information on Soviet activities in Cuba, he ordered the concentration of naval and other forces in the Atlantic and Caribbean and preparation for likely contingencies. *Enterprise* and *Independence* carrier task groups put to sea as did six Polaris submarines based in Holy Loch, Scotland. The American armed forces went to a heightened state of alert worldwide.

Along with U.S. intelligence organizations, the Navy's aerial reconnaissance units joined the effort to investigate the goings-on in Cuba. In one such operation, Commander William B. Ecker, a combat veteran of World War II and commanding officer of Light Photographic Squadron (VFP) 62, nicknamed "Fightin Photo," led six aircraft on a mission over the island from the airfield at Key West, Florida. At a speed of 350 knots and an altitude of 400 feet, the advanced F8U-1P Crusaders filmed a targeted site. Even though the Cubans would later shoot down the plane of Air Force Major Rudolph Anderson, killing him, they did not fire on Ecker's planes. The unit returned to Florida, where the film was quickly removed from the aircraft, processed, and dispatched on the highest priority to Washington. Under orders, Ecker jumped back in his plane and flew to the nation's capital. The tired, sweaty naval officer raced over to the Pentagon to provide his personal analysis of the mission to the Joint Chiefs of Staff. Ecker, his men, and other brave Americans brought home conclusive evidence that Soviet Premier Nikita Khrushchev and Castro were building a nuclear-armed redoubt in Cuba.

On the evening of 22 October, President Kennedy informed the world what American intelligence had discovered in Cuba and announced that he had ordered a naval quarantine, a blockade, to prevent further transportation of Soviet offensive weapons to the island. To discourage rash Soviet behavior at sea, the Navy established Task Force 135 and Task Force 136, consisting of antisubmarine carriers, cruisers, and close to thirty destroyers and guided missile frigates, and deployed them into the Atlantic and the eastern Caribbean. Navy shore-based patrol planes

A Navy P2V Neptune patrol plane and destroyer USS Vesole *(DDR 878) operate off the port side of the Soviet freighter* Volgoles *to make a close visual inspection of her cargo on deck, later determined to be dismantled missiles. By this and other means, American intelligence confirmed the removal of Soviet missiles and long-range bombers from Cuba. (Photo: Naval Historical Center)*

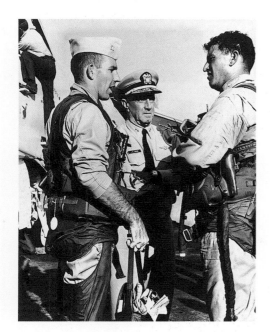

Lieutenants Gerald L. Coffee and Arthur R. Day, two naval aviators from Light Photographic Squadron (VFP) 62, discuss operations as Rear Admiral Joseph M. Carson, Commander Fleet Air Force, Jacksonville, listens. Because of its skilled personnel, excellent airplanes, and advanced cameras, military leaders considered the squadron first rate. The squadron's pictures played a vital role in convincing the national command authorities of the situation in Cuba, and then in providing evidence to present to the United Nations Security Council. (Photo: Naval Historical Center)

kept a close watch over Soviet submarines and merchant ships steaming toward Cuba. To demonstrate American resolve, on 26 October a party of sailors from destroyers USS *John R. Pierce* (DD 753) and USS *Joseph P. Kennedy, Jr.,* (DD 850) stopped and searched the Lebanese-flagged merchantman *Marucla,* which carried Soviet goods destined for Cuba. Since the vessel held no military cargo, she was allowed to proceed. Other Soviet vessels reversed course before they reached the American quarantine line. Finally, Khrushchev communicated to Kennedy that he would withdraw Soviet offensive weapons from Cuba if the United States promised not to invade the island and to remove its own missiles deployed in Turkey, a NATO ally. Kennedy agreed.

By the end of November, Navy carrier- and shore-based aerial reconnaissance units reported the dismantling of Soviet missile batteries ashore. Surface ships and other air patrol units then verified the presence of missile tubes and long-range bombers on Soviet merchantmen as the ships left Cuban ports and headed for the USSR. The crisis was over. By employing U.S. naval forces, the president had been able to achieve his strategic objectives and deal with a dangerous and well-armed adversary without starting a war.

The Naval War in Vietnam

The U.S. Navy was faced with another challenge in the early 1960s in faraway Southeast Asia, where the Vietnamese Communists under Ho Chi Minh pursued their goal of unifying Vietnam. Beginning in 1959, the North Vietnamese began constructing the Ho Chi Minh Trail through southern Laos and into the mountains of South Vietnam. They transported arms and other supplies via this land route and by sea to the Communist Viet Cong guerrillas in South Vietnam, and initiated an armed struggle to overthrow the government of the Republic of Vietnam.

The Navy's unmatched capability to project its power ashore, maintain control of the sea, and logistically support a major overseas commitment of the American armed forces enabled America's involvement in the Vietnam War. Furthermore, Vietnam's long coastline, thousands of islands, and many miles of inland waterway demanded the use of naval forces.

For the Vietnam War, the Navy operated under different chains of command. Commander Seventh Fleet took his orders from the Commander in Chief, U.S. Pacific Fleet (CINCPACFLT), who in turn followed the direction of the Commander in Chief, Pacific Command (CINCPAC). The latter, always a Navy admiral who is headquartered in Hawaii, oversaw the air campaigns waged against the enemy in North Vietnam, Laos, and later in the war, Cambodia. Though CINCPAC theoretically commanded the subordinate Commander, U.S. Military Assistance Command, Vietnam (COMUSMACV), that officer, General William C. Westmoreland and then General Creighton Abrams, operated virtually autonomously. These generals directed the actions of III Marine Amphibious Force and the U.S. Naval Forces, Vietnam, (NAVFORV), which was in charge of Navy river, coastal, advisory, special operations, and logistical commands in South Vietnam. Far down the chain of command, U.S. naval forces routinely executed policies and operations engineered in Saigon or even more distant Hawaii and Washington.

Such was the case with the famous Tonkin Gulf incidents of August 1964. Dissatisfied with the course of the South Vietnamese government's fight against the Communists, President Lyndon B. Johnson and Robert S. McNamara, Secretary of Defense, decided to put military pressure on the North Vietnamese, who directed and largely fueled the conflict in the south. The U.S. leaders believed that naval force could be used to make Ho Chi Minh cease his support for the Viet Cong. The U.S. Navy supplied the Republic of Vietnam Navy with Norwegian-built fast patrol boats (PTF), trained their crews, and maintained the vessels at a small base in Danang. In a covert operation code named 34A, these patrol boats shelled radar stations along the coast of North Vietnam and landed saboteurs to destroy bridges and other military targets inland. Lack of accurate intelligence about the enemy, however, hampered the effectiveness of these operations.

As a result, U.S. leaders in Washington ordered the Navy to put greater

"Operation Pierce Arrow" by R. G. Smith depicts the first American strike on North Vietnam. Commander James B. Stockdale's squadron of F-8 Crusaders attack the oil facilities at Vinh on 5 August 1964. Stockdale was later shot down and became a prisoner. Awarded the Medal of Honor for his bravery, exemplary conduct, and inspirational leadership as a prisoner, he returned to serve as a vice admiral and Naval War College president.

Admiral Thomas H. Moorer observing a review as part of a graduation ceremony at Recruit Training Center Orlando, Florida. Moorer served with distinction as Commander Seventh Fleet, Commander in Chief Pacific, Commander in Chief Atlantic, Chief of Naval Operations, and Chairman of the Joint Chiefs of Staff. As chairman he was instrumental in persuading President Richard Nixon to mine the harbors of North Vietnam during the Linebacker campaign of 1972. (Photo: Naval Historical Center)

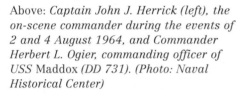

Above: *Captain John J. Herrick (left), the on-scene commander during the events of 2 and 4 August 1964, and Commander Herbert L. Ogier, commanding officer of USS* Maddox *(DD 731). (Photo: Naval Historical Center)*

Above, right: *The American destroyer USS* Maddox *(DD 731), which was attacked by North Vietnamese naval forces on 2 August 1964. Spurred by what was believed at the time to be a second attack two nights later, the U.S. Congress overwhelmingly passed the Tonkin Gulf Resolution. (Photo: Naval Historical Center)*

Below: *A Norwegian-built "Nasty"-class fast patrol boat proceeds at high speed. These boats, repaired by U.S. naval personnel and crewed by South Vietnamese sailors, operated from Danang in South Vietnam against targets on the coast of North Vietnam in the clandestine Operation 34A. (Photo: Naval Historical Center)*

Below, right: *Bombs from a diving Skyhawk destroy a Communist barracks in Dong Hoi, North Vietnam. A-4 Skyhawks were the backbone of the carrier attack force until the increasing lethality of enemy air defenses in North Vietnam allowed their use only in the less hostile skies of South Vietnam. (Photo: Naval Historical Center)*

emphasis in its long-standing Desoto Patrol on North Vietnam. The Desoto Patrol involved destroyers in intelligence-gathering missions outside the territorial waters and along the coasts of Communist countries, including the Soviet Union, China, and North Korea. As a result, in early August 1964, the destroyer USS *Maddox* (DD 731), under the direction of Captain John J. Herrick, conducted an intelligence cruise along the littoral of the Democratic Republic of Vietnam in the Gulf of Tonkin. Shortly before, the South Vietnamese patrol force had bombarded targets further to the south.

The North Vietnamese were frustrated by their inability to catch the South Vietnamese boat force. And, knowing of the American connection to Operation 34A, on 2 August the Communists dispatched three Soviet-built P-4 motor torpedo boats to attack *Maddox*. The torpedoes they fired missed their target, but one round from a Communist deck gun hit the American destroyer. Planes sent from the aircraft carrier USS *Ticonderoga* (CVA 14) to support *Maddox* shot up the trio of attackers and left one boat dead in the water. The destroyer steamed safely out of the area.

The Johnson administration was surprised that Hanoi not only failed to back down to U.S. pressure, but responded to it in such a hostile manner. Washington, and naval leaders in the Pacific, however, decided that they could not retreat from this open Communist challenge to the Seventh Fleet. *Maddox* was reinforced with destroyer USS *Turner Joy* (DD 951), and both were sent back into the Gulf of Tonkin to continue the intelligence mission. On the night of 4 August the two warships reported making contact and then being attacked by several fast craft far out to sea. Officers in the naval chain of command and U.S. leaders in Washington were persuaded by signals intelligence and other information that North Vietnamese

naval forces had fired torpedoes at the two destroyers, although most analysts now believe that an attack never occurred. Acting swiftly, the president ordered Seventh Fleet carrier forces to execute a strike mission against North Vietnam, which took place on 5 August. Planes from carriers *Ticonderoga* and USS *Constellation* (CVA 64) hit an oil storage site at Vinh and damaged or destroyed about thirty enemy naval vessels in port or along the coast. More importantly, on 7 August the U.S. Congress overwhelmingly passed the Tonkin Gulf Resolution, which allowed Johnson to employ military force as he saw fit against the Vietnamese Communists. The Communists did not relent. In late 1964, guerrillas destroyed American combat planes at Bien Hoa airfield north of Saigon, and on Christmas Eve set off a bomb at a bachelor officers' quarters in the South Vietnamese capital, killing two Americans and wounding over 100 Americans, Australians, and Vietnamese.

The enemy followed up these bombings in early 1965 with attacks on the U.S. embassy in Saigon and American military facilities in Pleiku and Qui Nhon, during which more Americans died. As a result of these Communist outrages, the Johnson administration ordered a full-scale bombing campaign against North Vietnam.

The aircraft carriers of the Seventh Fleet's Task Force 77 played a major role in U.S. bombing operations when the war began in earnest during March 1965. The carriers and their cruiser and destroyer escorts steamed at Yankee Station in the Gulf of Tonkin and, for over a year, at Dixie Station southeast of

"Enterprise on Yankee Station," by R. G. Smith. The nuclear-powered carrier and the A-4 Skyhawk attack planes launching from her flight deck were mainstays of the air war in Southeast Asia. Yankee Station was one of the carrier operating areas in the South China Sea. (Navy Art Collection)

Above: *An SA-2 missile explodes beneath a U.S. F-4 Phantom, instantaneously setting the plane on fire. The Navy lost 881 pilots and crewmen and 900 aircraft to enemy action during the Vietnam War. (Photo: Courtesy of Dino Brugioni)*

Right and below: *Fire and smoke envelop carrier USS* Oriskany *(CVA 34) in October 1966. The following year, USS* Forrestal *(CVA 59) suffered an even more deadly conflagration. The two fires claimed the lives of 178 officers and bluejackets, many of them aviators. But from these tragic experiences the Navy gained valuable insights about firefighting that served the service well in later years. Firefighting training is critical to the survival of sailors and ships. (Photo, right: Naval Historical Center)*

Cam Ranh Bay. The Rolling Thunder, Linebacker, and other campaigns involved the bombing of enemy power plants, fuel and supply facilities, highway and railroad bridges, and rail lines in North Vietnam and Laos.

Early in the war, massive, multi-carrier "Alpha Strikes" were typical. In one such action, the air wings from USS *Coral Sea* (CVA 43) and USS *Hancock* (CVA 19) went after North Vietnamese radar sites on the coast and on Bach Long Vi, Nightingale Island, in the Gulf of Tonkin. The seventy-plane operation knocked out the mainland facilities, but had to return to finish the job on the island. During this strike, enemy antiaircraft guns blackened the sky with shell bursts as *Coral Sea*'s attack aircraft dove through the cloud ceiling. The Communists focused their fire on lead aircraft, soon hitting the planes of three American squadron commanders. Commander Jack Harris, commanding officer of Attack Squadron 155, ejected

from his stricken plane, parachuted safely into the sea, and floated around for a while contemplating his unhappy situation. To his surprise, the periscope of an American submarine broke the surface and he was soon safely on board for the vessel's return to the depths of the Gulf of Tonkin. The leader of Attack Squadron 153, Commander Pete Mongilardi, used his years of flying naval aircraft and professional skill to nurse his plane home. Commander William N. Donnelly, who led Fighter Squadron 154, had an even more dramatic experience. He ejected from his shot-up F-8 Crusader fighter moments before it hit the water, and he sustained severe injuries in the process. Despite a dislocated shoulder and six cracked vertebrae, Donnelly inflated a life raft and with great effort climbed in. For the rest of the day and into the night, the naval aviator floated just off the island, bathed in flame and smoke from the American air strike. Searchlight beams played across the water as the enemy tried in vain to find the downed American flyer. Forty-five hours after Donnelly hit the water, planes from *Hancock* spotted him. Soon an HU-16 amphibian aircraft landed close by and an Air Force paramedic jumped into the water. As circling sharks closed to investigate, the airman eased the injured pilot into the plane and safety.

The Americans were more successful a few months later when a group of Fighter Squadron 21 F-4 Phantom II jets flying a combat air patrol over Thanh Hoa were pounced upon by four North Vietnamese MiG-21s. As the enemy planes closed on the American formation, Commander Louis C. Page and his radar intercept officer, Lieutenant Commander John C. Smith, fired off a Sparrow air-to-air missile that seconds later hit and destroyed one of the attackers. Almost at the same time, Lieutenant Jack E. Batson and his radar intercept officer, Lieutenant Commander Robert B. Doremus, launched another Sparrow, which also flamed a MiG. The remaining pair of assailants immediately turned tail and headed home.

During this period, the Navy's carrier squadrons were destroying two enemy fighters for every one they lost, an unacceptable win-to-loss ratio. As a

F-4B Phantom II jets jettison fuel as they lower their tail hooks and prepare for recovery on board their carrier. Phantom variants served the Navy and the Air Force in fighter, attack, and reconnaissance roles, making them the most recognizable aircraft of the air war in Southeast Asia. (Photo: National Archives)

Naval aviator Lieutenant Randall H. Cunningham describes how he and his radar intercept officer, Lieutenant (jg) William P. Driscoll, shot down three enemy fighters in one day (complementing two earlier kills) to become the Navy's two Vietnam War "Aces." Both men were graduates of the Top Gun School, established to provide realistic air combat training. In fighter pilot language, the bullet holes are always in the left hand. (Photo: Naval Historical Center)

Heavy cruiser USS St. Paul's (CA 73) 8-inch guns open up against enemy positions ashore in North Vietnam. In Operation Sea Dragon, the battleship USS New Jersey (BB 62), U.S. cruisers, and American and Australian destroyers bombarded enemy bridges, radar sites, and coastal defenses. (Photo: Naval Historical Center)

USS Chicago's (CG 11) Senior Chief Radarman Larry Nowell at his radar console during the Linebacker campaign of 1972. He was awarded the Navy Distinguished Service Medal for directing Navy and Air Force fighters against North Vietnamese MiGs, twelve of which the Americans shot down. (Photo: U.S. Naval Institute)

result of intensive air-to-air combat training at California's Miramar Naval Air Station, the "Top Gun School," the ratio improved to 12-to-1 during air operations in 1972 and early 1973. Lieutenant Randy Cunningham and Lieutenant Willie Driscoll, graduates of the Top Gun School, demonstrated they had paid attention in class. During the early days of the Linebacker campaign, the F-4J Phantom crewmen shot down two MiGs. Then, on one momentous day, 10 May 1972, these men of *Constellation*'s Fighter Squadron 96 bagged three "bandits."

Surface ship sailors also helped reduce the enemy's fleet of MiG interceptors. From the first year of the war to the last, the Navy positioned a cruiser equipped with advanced radars and communications between the enemy coast and Task Force 77. The warship, with the call sign "Red Crown," was responsible for keeping track of aircraft, friend or foe, flying over eastern North Vietnam and the Gulf of Tonkin. The ship often warned U.S. strike aircraft of approaching MiGs and directed escorting fighters toward the threat. In August 1972, guided missile cruiser USS *Chicago*'s (CG 11) Senior Chief Radioman Larry Nowell was awarded the Navy Distinguished Service Medal for helping American air units destroy twelve North Vietnamese MiGs.

Despite the earnest efforts of American aviators and fleet sailors, the multi-year Rolling Thunder, Linebacker, and other major operations did not achieve their objective of cutting Communist supply lines. In addition, the campaign resulted in the death or capture of 881 Navy pilots and other aircrewmen and the loss of 900 aircraft. But, the campaigns inflicted substantially higher personnel losses on the enemy, destroyed an enormous amount of war material, and delayed and weakened Communist ground offensives throughout Indochina.

A landing craft, mechanized (LCM) and an amphibian tractor (LVT) inch their way into the well deck of dock landing ship USS Catamount *(LSD 17). Amphibious ships enabled the fleet to deploy Marine infantry battalions and helicopter squadrons anywhere along the 1,200-mile coast of South Vietnam. (Photo: National Archives)*

Carrier-based planes also provided essential close air support to U.S. and allied ground forces fighting North Vietnamese Army and Viet Cong forces in South Vietnam. Helicopters and fixed-wing aircraft operating from Seventh Fleet destroyers and carriers executed search and rescue missions that saved hundreds of U.S. aviators whose aircraft went down in North Vietnam and Laos or at sea.

As in Korea and World War II, Navy warships were on hand in the Vietnam War to project their firepower ashore. Battleship USS *New Jersey* (BB 62), 8-inch and 6-inch gun cruisers, and destroyers bombarded bridges, radar sites, rail lines, and coastal artillery positions in North Vietnam. The enemy's coastal batteries fought back, hitting a number of U.S. ships and killing and wounding sailors. The North Vietnamese, however, failed to sink even one U.S. combatant. Joined by Vietnam Navy, Royal Australian Navy, and U.S. amphibious and patrol vessels, the Seventh Fleet's major warships also ranged along the 1,200-mile coast of South Vietnam to strike Viet Cong troop concentrations, supply caches, and fortifications. During the enemy's Easter Offensive of 1972, the fleet's bombardment force took a huge toll of North Vietnamese tanks and troops advancing south on the coast against the city of Hue.

Naval amphibious forces exploited the sea to hit the enemy at different locations along the length of the coast of South Vietnam, from the Demilitarized Zone (DMZ) in the north to the Gulf of Siam in the south. These landings included large-scale assaults involving many ships, aircraft, and troops; combat raids; and intelligence-gathering missions. In Operation Starlite during August 1965, the

Rounds from a North Vietnamese coastal battery bracket USS St. Paul *(CA 73). Enemy counterbattery fire hit nineteen allied ships through 1970, killing six sailors and wounding at least thirty. Communist gunfire, however, did not sink a single warship during the long war. (Photo: Naval Historical Center)*

Above: *Amidst the destruction of war, Navy Lieutenant Commander Frederick E. Whitaker (CHC) delivers a sermon. Navy personnel serve as hospital corpsmen, doctors, dentists, and chaplains with Marine combat units. (Photo: U.S. Marine Corps)*

Above, right: *A Marine races up a ladder on amphibious assault ship USS* Okinawa *(LPH 3) before boarding an assault helicopter for a combat operation ashore. (Photo: Naval Historical Center)*

war's most successful amphibious assault, Navy amphibious vessels deployed Marine units ashore, which then linked up with Army of Vietnam forces to encircle and destroy the 1st Viet Cong Regiment. Afterward, large enemy units avoided the coastal areas and employed only booby traps and snipers to oppose most allied amphibious operations. The naval command then used the Navy–Marine Corps Amphibious Ready Group/Special Landing Force as a floating reserve, especially during the climactic ground battles along the DMZ in 1967 and 1968. Rested, rearmed, and resupplied, Marines could be deployed ashore quickly to reinforce their comrades.

Navy chaplains, doctors, and hospital corpsmen served in every large Marine unit, both afloat and ashore. They shared the dangers of an infantryman's life in the hot, overgrown jungle, in the shell-pocked hills along the Demilitarized Zone, and in the lethal streets of Hue during the Tet Offensive of 1968. Casualties were especially high among hospital corpsmen. As one of many examples of courage and self-sacrifice, on 19 March 1969 Hospital Corpsman Second Class David R. Ray was serving with a Marine artillery battery near the town of An Hoa. Before dawn the enemy launched a rocket, mortar, and ground attack on the American position, immediately wounding many Marines. Petty Officer Ray moved from position to position giving medical help and in the process was hit by enemy fire. Despite his serious wounds, Ray killed an attacker and wounded another while continuing to bandage downed Marines. When the sailor ran out of ammunition, the Communists wounded him again and threw a grenade into the position. Before he died, Ray threw his body across that of a wounded Marine, saving the man's life. Petty Officer Ray was awarded the Medal of Honor. Such courage was not uncommon among the sailors who served ashore in Vietnam.

The U.S. Navy was charged with establishing and then maintaining control of the sea off Vietnam and the air above it. The North Vietnamese operated close to 100 combat aircraft and forty motor gunboats and fast attack craft, but only on a few occasions did they challenge the American fleet in the Gulf of Tonkin. In August 1964 and July 1966, the Communists dispatched P-4 torpedo boats against the Seventh Fleet. The attackers were either sunk or forced to beat a hasty retreat back to North Vietnam. As they had in Korea, Chinese "volunteers" entered the combat arena to fight alongside their Communist allies. At various times, 50,000 Chinese soldiers operated antiaircraft guns, built coastal fortifications, or repaired

A Navy nurse cares for a wounded American. A total of 425 female nurses served in hospital ships USS Sanctuary *(AH 17) and USS* Repose *(AH 16), the naval hospitals in Danang and Saigon, and in other naval medical facilities ashore in South Vietnam during the war. (Photo: Naval Historical Center)*

The fifty-foot Swift fast patrol craft, here PCF-38, was one of the Navy's most versatile vessels in Vietnam, serving along the coast in Operation Market Time and far upriver in the Mekong Delta during the SEALORDS campaign. (Photo: Naval Historical Center)

Below, left: *U.S. and Vietnamese sailors prepare to board and search a fishing junk. Normally, the men found only fish, but every so often discovered munitions or Viet Cong intelligence agents. (Photo: Naval Historical Center)*

damaged bridges, railroads, and roads. Because of the U.S. power at sea, however, the Chinese did not interfere with naval operations.

In Operation Market Time, the U.S. Navy, Vietnam Navy, and U.S. Coast Guard largely shut down the seaborne infiltration effort started by the Communists during the early 1960s. Destroyers, mine warfare ships, Coast Guard cutters, gunboats, patrol craft, shore-based patrol planes, and high-powered coastal radars made it almost impossible for the North Vietnamese to slip one of their munitions-laden, 100-ton supply ships past the Market Time patrol. Allied naval forces destroyed or forced back to North Vietnam all but two of the fifty steel-hulled trawlers that tried to run the blockade between 1965 and 1972. Hanoi did manage to get supplies through to its forces fighting in South Vietnam, via the port of Sihanoukville in neutral Cambodia and the Ho Chi Minh Trail, but it took much longer and cost the Communists untold lives and military resources.

While denying the enemy free use of the sea, the U.S. Navy exploited its control of the vast Pacific Ocean to maintain an expeditionary force of a half-million men and women on the Asian continent, far from the sources of supply

Above: *The U.S. Coast Guard high endurance cutter USCGS* Rush *(WHEC 723) on the Market Time patrol off South Vietnam. The Coast Guard participated in Vietnam and the Gulf War, where the service's experience in maritime control, inshore operations, and civil law enforcement were particularly valuable. In such operations, the Coast Guard forces assigned served as an integral part of the Navy operations. (Photo: National Archives)*

173

A bluejacket prepares to drop a round down the tube of an 81-mm mortar as his shipmate stands by to receive communications via earphones from the vessel's commander. The dual-mounted mortar and .50-caliber machine gun was a standard weapon on board Swift boats of the coastal/river patrol force. (Photo: Naval Historical Center)

Below: A P-2 Neptune patrol plane flies low over a junk in the South China Sea. If such contacts looked suspicious, the naval aviators directed surface ships to investigate. (Photo: Naval Historical Center)

Bottom: "Firefight—Swift on Soi-Rap," by John Steel, shows the other component of the dual-mounted weapon in action. (Navy Art Collection)

in the United States. Military Sealift Command ships transported 95 percent of the ammunition, fuel, vehicles, supplies, and other war materials that reached U.S. forces in South Vietnam. Navy Seabee construction units built thousands of bridges, fortifications, and encampments, paved thousands of miles of road, and developed the huge Navy–Marine Corps logistics bases at Danang and Saigon.

The U.S. Navy was as vital to the war effort ashore as it was afloat. Commander U.S. Naval Forces, Vietnam, was responsible for securing the many rivers and canals that wound their way through the lush, tropical landscape of South Vietnam. In Operation Game Warden, Navy river patrol boats moved along the major rivers of the Mekong Delta and farther north near Hue. These units' mission was to deny the enemy use of the waterways for transporting guerrillas and supplies. Every day, the young warriors of the Navy's River Patrol Force stopped and searched sampans and similar small craft for hidden munitions and other contraband. The discovery of Viet Cong guerrillas operating on the river, which occurred often, led to fierce gun battles at close quarters.

One action that stands out involved Boatswain's Mate First Class James E. Williams, who received the Medal of Honor for his extraordinary bravery and leadership on 31 October 1966. That day Williams, patrol commander for his boat, River Patrol Boat 105, and another patrol boat were searching for Viet Cong guerrillas operating on the Mekong River. Suddenly, Communists manning two sampans

Upper left: Fast combat support ship USS Sacramento (AOE 1) refuels the carrier USS Hancock (CV 19) via hose lines as the logistic ship's UH-46 helicopter delivers dry cargo. Underway replenishment, perfected by the Navy during World War II, enables the fleet to remain on station anywhere in the world's seas. (Photo: Naval Historical Center)

Lower left: A lighter moment during the war as Bob Hope, renowned comedian and patriot, performs with fellow entertainers Vic Damone, Anita Bryant, and Joey Heatherton for the appreciative crew of the carrier USS Bennington (CVS 20). (Photo: Naval Historical Center)

Above: A Seabee naval constructionman moves a heavy load of concrete in South Vietnam. The Navy's construction battalions built bridges, airfield runways, fortifications, cantonments, and storage facilities, continuing to live up to their motto, "Can Do." (Photo: Naval Historical Center)

175

opened fire on the Americans. When Williams and his comrades wiped out one boat
crew, the other one escaped into a nearby waterway. The sailors followed and soon
found themselves in a hornet's nest of enemy activity as Viet Cong soldiers fired
rocket-propelled grenades and other weapons from fortified river bank positions.
Despite overwhelming odds, Williams repeatedly led his unit against several concentrations of enemy junks and sampans and called for support from the heavily armed
UH-1B Huey helicopters of Navy Helicopter Attack (Light) Squadron 3, the "Sea-
wolves." When that help arrived, he resumed the attack in the failing light, boldly
turning on his boats' searchlights to illuminate enemy forces and positions. As a
result of the three-hour battle, the American naval force killed numerous Viet Cong
guerrillas, destroyed over fifty vessels, and disrupted a major enemy logistic operation.

Equally important to the war on the rivers were the service's highly trained,
motivated, and courageous SEAL (Sea, Air, and Land) naval special forces. Small
detachments of SEALs operated routinely in Viet Cong–controlled areas gathering

intelligence and killing or capturing key enemy personnel. Navy mine counter-measures units, despite losing a number of minesweeping boats to the enemy's rocket-propelled grenades and command-detonated mines, kept the tortuous, forty-five-mile channel from the sea to Saigon, a major logistics hub in southern South Vietnam, open throughout the war.

Sharing these inland operating areas was the joint Army-Navy Mobile River-ine Force, which consisted of heavily armed and armored monitors, troop carriers, assault support patrol boats, and combat troops from the U.S. Army's 9th Infantry Division. Much like the soldiers of General Ulysses S. Grant and the sailors of Admiral David Dixon Porter, who fought together on the Mississippi River in the Civil War, the American fighting men of the Mobile Riverine Force often closed with the enemy. In battle after battle, the naval force deployed troops on the flanks and rear of Communist combat units, and with American helicopter teams decimated the foe.

After several years of war, however, the enemy had begun to find ways of countering the allied river patrol and river assault operations. The guerrillas shifted their resupply activities to small rivers and canals, and the main force North Vietnamese Army and Viet Cong combat units either avoided contact with the Mobile Riverine Force or waited for the right opportunity to spring deadly ambushes.

In order to regain the initiative, Vice Admiral Elmo R. Zumwalt, Jr., a dynamic officer who took charge as COMNAVFORV in the fall of 1968, followed a new strategic approach, which he named SEALORDS (Southeast Asia Lake, Ocean, River, Delta Strategy). The thrust of the SEALORDS campaign was to establish closely patrolled sectors along the Cambodian border (where the enemy brought most of his munitions and supplies into South Vietnam) and penetrate Viet Cong strongholds in the almost impenetrable marsh and swampland areas of the Mekong Delta. The enemy resistance to this new strategy was fierce and sustained during 1969 and 1970, but the allies established increasing control of the targeted areas. Coupled with the U.S. and South Vietnamese incursion into Cambodia in the

Top: *American and Vietnamese river patrol force sailors fire at enemy troops concealed in thick vegetation ashore during a SEALORDS operation. A major feature of the campaign was the integration of allied naval operations. (Photo: Naval Historical Center)*

Above: *A monitor of River Assault Squadron 9 moves cautiously along a waterway prepared to open up on the Viet Cong with its 40- and 20-millimeter guns and 81-millimeter mortars. Since most Mekong Delta water-ways were narrow and bordered by dense foliage, sailors had to be especially vigilant. (Photo: Naval Historical Center)*

Engineman First Class Carl L. Scott, an advisor to the Vietnamese Coastal Force (often referred to as the Junk Force), pauses during a mission along the coast south of Danang early in the war. By the end of the conflict, the Vietnam Navy had become a sizable component of the Republic of Vietnam's armed forces. (Photo: Naval Historical Center)

Opposite: USS Will Rogers (SSBN 659) proceeds south on the River Clyde leaving Holy Loch, Scotland, en route to a strategic deterrent patrol. As the range of the missiles grew, the need for the forward bases diminished. When Trident replaced Poseidon missiles, the need for foreign bases for the ballistic missile submarines ended. (Photo: Yogi Kaufman)

A sailor embarked in USS Harold E. Holt (DE 1074) provides cover to Marines who just stormed aboard SS Mayaguez, an American merchantman seized in the Gulf of Thailand by Khymer Rouge guerrillas. Once the Marines secured the ship, sailors boarded her to inspect and attach a tow line to the ship. (Photo: Naval Historical Center)

latter year, the SEALORDS campaign severely hindered enemy operations in the Mekong Delta. An indication of the allies' success was the ability of the South Vietnamese to deploy an Army of Vietnam infantry division out of the Mekong Delta to fight elsewhere during the Communist Easter Offensive of 1972.

Another important aspect of the SEALORDS campaign was the emphasis on improving the combat performance of the Vietnam Navy. Since 1950, thousands of American naval advisors had worked especially hard to prepare their Vietnamese counterparts for operating the ships, coastal and river craft, planes, weapons, and equipment that the Vietnam Navy received in U.S. military assistance programs. The objective of this effort was to enable Vietnamese sailors to carry on the fight with the Communists largely on their own. The mission became especially important after 1968, when the new administration of President Richard M. Nixon began withdrawing U.S. military forces from the war in Southeast Asia. Eventually, the Vietnam Navy was ranked the fifth largest in the world with 42,000 men and women and 1,500 naval vessels. While the Vietnam Navy had the weaknesses of the other South Vietnamese armed forces, its sailors often fought with courage and self-sacrifice.

The powerful Pacific Fleet could have stopped the enemy from using neutral merchant ships to transport war materials into Cambodia or North Vietnam, but President Johnson did not want to provoke open Soviet or Chinese intervention in the war, so he prohibited a blockade. In 1972, however, President Nixon was confident there would be no opposition from Moscow or Beijing, so he ordered the Seventh Fleet to mine the waters of North Vietnam. Navy and Marine attack aircraft from aircraft carrier *Coral Sea* (CVA 43) dropped thousands of mines in the approaches to Haiphong and North Vietnam's other major ports. With no merchant ships bringing in supplies of surface-to-air missiles or other munitions, the Communist war effort quickly lost steam. The Seventh Fleet's mining of North Vietnam's ports in 1972 and 1973, in conjunction with the Air Force Navy Linebacker bombing campaign, helped end America's involvement in the long, frustrating war by inducing the enemy to agree to reasonable cease-fire terms and to release all American prisoners of war.

Despite the best efforts of American, South Vietnamese, and Cambodian fighting men, however, in April 1975 Communist forces seized Phnom Penh, the capital of Cambodia, and Saigon, the capital of South Vietnam. That month the Seventh Fleet evacuated thousands of American and allied personnel from Cambodia and South Vietnam. The following month, Communist Khmer Rouge guerrillas seized the U.S. merchant ship *Mayaguez* and her crew off Cambodia. A boarding party of sailors and Marines from frigate USS *Harold E. Holt* (DE 1074) retook the ship, which had been abandoned by the Cambodians earlier that day. Suspecting that the crewmen were being held on nearby Koh Tang Island (actually they were held elsewhere and subsequently released by their captors), the U.S. command in Thailand dispatched a strong force of Marines in Air Force helicopters and the guided missile destroyer USS *Henry B. Wilson* (DDG 7) to investigate the site. The operation to land on Koh Tang resulted in the death of eighteen servicemen, wounding of another fifty, and combat loss of three helicopters, but demonstrated that the United States would not tolerate the seizure of its ships on the open sea.

In contrast to the Khmer Rouge guerrillas, the sailors of the Seventh Fleet came to the aid of seafarers during the next several years as U.S. naval vessels rescued thousands of Vietnamese "boat people" fleeing political and religious persecution and economic deprivation in the new Socialist Republic of Vietnam.

Over 1,842,000 men and women of the U.S. Navy served in Southeast Asia; 2,555 sailors died in the conflict and 10,000 suffered from wounds, disease, and injury. This was service for which America's sailors could be proud: their sacrifice and dedication to duty helped the United States win the Cold War, of which the conflict in Vietnam was a significant part.

Above: *Captain William McGonagle, the commanding officer of USS* Liberty *(AGTR 5), demonstrated leadership of the highest order during and after the devastating Israeli air and sea attack on his ship. Even though wounded, the courageous officer refused to leave* Liberty's *bridge until he was sure his sailors and his ship were no longer under attack. (Photo: Naval Historical Center)*

Above, right: *Sixth Fleet intelligence-collection ship USS* Liberty *(AGTR 5) after the attack by Israeli combat aircraft and naval vessels in the Eastern Mediterranean. The ship was badly damaged and many sailors were killed or wounded. The incident highlighted the fact that even when the United States was not directly involved in hostilities, its Cold War global responsibilities called for sacrifice. (Photo: Naval Historical Center)*

Seaman Daniel J. Lewis stands a lonely, cold watch on the bridge of ballistic missile submarine USS John Adams *(SSBN 625) during the 1960s. Because the Navy's "boomers" could vanish into the world's oceans and were thus invulnerable to attack, they became the cornerstone of the nation's strategic deterrent forces. (Photo: Naval Historical Center)*

Global Responsibilities and a Changing Navy

Despite its heavy commitment to the war in Southeast Asia, the U.S. Navy was responsible for other security missions around the globe during the 1960s and 1970s. The Seventh Fleet kept watch over northeast Asia, while the Sixth Fleet asserted a powerful presence in the Mediterranean. In both theaters, hostile forces attacked U.S. warships.

In June 1967, Israeli planes and motor torpedo boats unexpectedly attacked USS *Liberty* (AGTR 5), an intelligence ship gathering information on the Arab-Israeli war that had just broken out. After the first attack, the Israelis struck again. In both instances hostile fire killed and wounded many *Liberty* officers and bluejackets. In the emergency, the commanding officer, Commander William L. McGonagle, displayed extraordinary courage and professionalism. Despite being seriously wounded and under fire, he stayed at his post on the shot-up bridge to coordinate defense of the ship, the work of damage control parties, and medical treatment for the many wounded sailors. As a result of his steady and skillful leadership, *Liberty*'s crewmen efficiently extinguished fires that were ravaging the ship and prevented further flooding. Commander McGonagle was instrumental in saving the ship. Not until a U.S. destroyer reached the scene, seventeen hours after the start of the attack, did the bleeding and injured officer relinquish his post on the bridge so that his wounds could be treated. Even then, he insisted that the more grievously wounded get medical care first. Commander McGonagle received the Medal of Honor for his worthy leadership and valor under fire.

As demonstrated in the *Liberty* incident, America's Cold War sailors often risked life and limb to do their duty, even during periods of "peace." This point was reemphasized the following February, when North Korean naval forces fired on and seized USS *Pueblo* (AGER 2), another intelligence-collection vessel that was operating in international waters in the Sea of Japan. For the next year, the North Korean Communists imprisoned and tortured her crewmen, coercing some to sign "confessions" of guilt and to make political radio broadcasts.

Other American sailors died to help the Navy meet the serious threat posed by an increasingly capable and globe-ranging Soviet navy. Like their fellow submariners in USS *Thresher* (SSN 593), which went down in 1,400 fathoms of water

east of Boston in April 1963, the men of USS *Scorpion* (SSN 589) paid the ultimate price for their country when the ship imploded on the bottom of the Atlantic in the spring of 1968. The loss of these submarines and their crews re-energized the Navy's efforts to make America's submarine fleet the safest and most capable in the world. Throughout the Cold War, the U.S. attack submarine fleets operating in all the world's oceans, but especially in the Atlantic, became more and more effective at finding and trailing Soviet submarines, often without the knowledge of the latter. Both U.S. and Soviet submariners knew that if war broke out between their nations, the Americans had a decided advantage with their technologically superior warships and professional skills.

The 1970s marked a watershed in the social history of the U.S. Navy. Under the spirited stewardship of Admiral Zumwalt, who served as Chief of Naval Operations from 1970 to 1974, the Navy Department worked to accomplish the full integration into the naval service of African Americans and women. In April 1971, Samuel L. Gravely became the first black American to be selected to flag rank, and the following April, Alene B. Duerk became the first female to do so when she took charge of the Navy Nurse Corps. Zumwalt, however, was dissatisfied with the status of blacks and women in the Navy. He initiated measures to increase their recruitment and retention, better their chances for promotion, and eliminate everyday discrimination. To shake up the personnel bureaucracy and eliminate needless regulations for all sailors, Zumwalt issued a series of Navy-wide directives, labeled "Z Grams." He also took steps to improve communication between officers and enlisted personnel. Not all of Zumwalt's actions succeeded, and his unconventional approach angered many traditionalists, but the Navy was long overdue for changes that Americans expected to see in the armed forces.

Zumwalt's successors continued his work; the first women entered the U.S. Naval Academy in July 1976. Two years later other Navy women began serving on board naval vessels other than the traditional hospital ships and transports. One unique Navy woman was Rear Admiral Grace Murray Hopper, who dedicated her life to improving the Navy's information technologies and systems. Early in her career, she helped develop the Navy's first computers, including the Mark I, II, III, and UNIVAC systems. Perhaps her greatest achievement was to pioneer the development of COBOL, a computer language that non-mathematicians could understand and employ. When Hopper retired from the service in 1966, the Navy realized it could not lose her unique skills and brought her back on active duty for an indefinite time. During this period, she served as director of Navy Programming

Admiral Zumwalt has a "rap session" with Seventh Fleet bluejackets to relate his policies and address first-hand the causes for racial discord during the turbulent early 1970s. (Photo: Naval Historical Center)

Petty officers review the current "Z Gram," a method used by Admiral Zumwalt to communicate directly with the sailors of the fleet. Few were neutral in their views about the advantages or disadvantages of this form of communication. (Photo: Naval Historical Center)

Top, left: *As his wife snaps on his new insignia, Rear Admiral Samuel L. Gravely is congratulated on his promotion. During the 1980s an increasing number of African Americans completed careers in the naval service as senior officers and senior petty officers. (Photo: Naval Historical Center)*

Top, right: *Women recruits in formation at the Naval Training Center in Orlando, Florida, in November 1975. Throughout the 1970s and 1980s, Navy women were assigned to an increasing number of billets ashore and afloat. By the end of the Cold War, female sailors served in fleet oilers, ammunition ships, and tenders, flew helicopters and patrol aircraft, and commanded Seabee and other shore-based units. (Photo: Naval Historical Center)*

Above: *Admiral James L. Holloway III inspecting a submarine torpedo room during his tenure as the Chief of Naval Operations. A destroyer gunnery officer who fought at the Battle of Leyte Gulf, Holloway switched to naval aviation and flew strikes in Korea. He commanded USS* Enterprise *(CVAN 65) during her first combat cruise to Vietnam and later the Seventh Fleet during that conflict. As CNO, Holloway put the Navy on an even keel after the post-Vietnam force reductions and switch to an all-volunteer force. (Photo: Naval Historical Center)*

Right: *"USS* Lloyd Thomas *Departing Jiddah, Saudi Arabia," by Gene Klebe. As the Royal Navy gave up some security responsibilities "east of Suez," the U.S. Navy increasingly operated in the volatile region. The Navy established the Middle East Force to protect U.S. interests in the Persian Gulf in 1949. (Photo: National Archives)*

Languages Group (OP 90) in the Office of the Chief of Naval Operations. Grace Hopper served in the Navy for two more decades. When she finally retired, Rear Admiral Hopper was awarded the National Medal of Technology and many other distinctions. But she considered her highest award to have been "the privilege and honor of serving very proudly in the United States Navy."

The Middle East remained a troubled region during the 1970s. In the Arab–Israeli Yom Kippur War of October 1973, the Sixth Fleet protected U.S. transport planes that flew emergency supplies of weapons and ammunition from the United States to the Israelis, who were fighting desperately to survive the Arab onslaught. Soon, however, the Israelis launched devastating counterattacks that threatened to overwhelm the Egyptian army. The Soviet Union moved strong naval forces into the Eastern Mediterranean and prepared to fly paratroopers into Egypt to prevent the Israeli military from completely crushing the Egyptians. The Nixon administration put U.S. forces on alert worldwide and ordered the reinforced Sixth Fleet into waters off Egypt to signal the opposition of the United States to the proposed Soviet measures.

At the same time, Washington helped arrange a cease-fire between the belligerents, and redoubled efforts to bring lasting peace to the region. In this vein, in 1974 the Navy deployed mine countermeasure forces, which had recently opened the mined waters off North Vietnam to merchant traffic, into the Eastern Mediterranean. Between April and December, Task Force 65 cleared mines from the Suez Canal and assisted in the removal of numerous ships sunk there during the war. Guided missile cruiser USS *Little Rock* (CLG 4) was among the first ships to transit the newly opened canal.

A Navy RH-53D Sea Stallion mine counter-measures helicopter tows a Mark 105 mine sled past a merchant ship in the Suez Canal during mine-clearing operations in 1974 after a Middle East war. (Photo: Naval Historical Center)

The Maritime Strategy and a 600-Ship Navy

By the mid-1970s, a muscle-flexing Soviet Union began to cause serious concern in Washington. The USSR spent enormous resources on its war-making establishment, hoping to take advantage of America's post-Vietnam retrenchment. The Soviets deployed thousands of mobile, intercontinental ballistic missiles and other nuclear-armed weapons, built up large ground and air forces in Eastern Europe and the Far East, and aided Communist guerrilla movements in Africa, Asia, and Latin America. Of greatest concern to the U.S. Navy, Soviet naval forces increased their presence around the world, challenging America's overseas interests and control of the sea. A 1975 Soviet naval exercise, Okean 75, involved 220 ships and new, long-range bombers in mock strikes against the continental United States. Soviet warships steamed brazenly in all the world's oceans, and even in the Gulf of Mexico. As a symbol of the changing naval balance of power, Soviet surface combatants and patrol planes began operating from the American-built base at Cam Ranh Bay in Vietnam. Just before he retired as Chief of Naval Operations in June 1978, Admiral James L. Holloway III concluded that the U.S. Navy then had only a "slim margin of superiority" over the Soviet navy.

President Ronald Reagan was elected partly on his pledge to restore America's military superiority. In addition to strengthening the nation's strategic retaliatory arm with advanced B-1B bombers, deploying Pershing II theater missiles to Europe, and producing sophisticated Abrams main battle tanks and

A key in the Reagan buildup was improvement and enlargement of the nation's strategic forces. Trident-class submarines and a new highly accurate long-range ballistic missile (D 4) went to sea replacing the older Polaris and Poseidon submarines. Because the weapons had longer range, overseas basing was abandoned and all strategic submarines operated out of bases at Bangor, Washington (top), or Kings Bay, Georgia (bottom).

Admiral Thomas B. Hayward, being briefed before a check flight, came to be Chief of Naval Operations after serving as Commander in Chief, U.S. Pacific Fleet, where he developed plans for offensive operations in the event of war. Those plans became the foundation of the Maritime Strategy, a doctrine that rejuvenated the offensive spirit of the whole Navy and served as the intellectual basis for planning, operations, and procurement during the Reagan administration.

As Chief of Naval Operations, Admiral James D. Watkins played a key role in aligning America's strategic forces in the Reagan buildup by leading the Joint Chiefs to reject land basing missile schemes. In publishing the Maritime Strategy, he energized the service in a common strategic concept while explaining to Congress and the country the role of the Navy in the Cold War. (Photo: Naval Historical Center)

Bradley armored fighting vehicles, his administration dramatically increased the size and capability of the U.S. Navy. In 1981 USS *Ohio* (SSBN 726), the largest submarine ever built and the first of her class, was commissioned. The ship carried twenty-four Trident I nuclear missiles, each one capable of hitting targets 4,000 miles distant. Construction of the 90,000-ton, nuclear-powered *Nimitz*-class carriers, *Los Angeles*-class nuclear attack submarines, and the *Ticonderoga*-class guided missile cruisers equipped with the revolutionary Aegis antiair warfare system was stepped up. Also joining the fleet during the 1980s were Tomahawk land attack, Harpoon antiship, and high-speed, anti-radiation (HARM) missiles; improved versions of the F-14 Tomcat fighter, A-6 Intruder attack, and EA-6B Prowler electronic countermeasures aircraft; and the new F/A-18 Hornet strike fighter. The venerable battleships USS *Iowa* (BB 61), USS *New Jersey* (BB 62), USS *Missouri* (BB 63), and USS *Wisconsin* (BB 64) once again put to sea with their awesome 16-inch guns and new Tomahawk surface-to-surface missile batteries.

With these advanced instruments of sea power, naval leaders concluded that if it came to war with the USSR, the country should follow a new strategy—a Maritime Strategy. Admiral Thomas B. Hayward and his successor as Chief of Naval Operations, Admiral James D. Watkins, argued that the Navy should use its inherent flexibility and mobility by hitting the enemy when and where he was most vulnerable. Rather than passively guarding America's sea lines of communication to Europe, the fleet should mount offensive operations in northern Europe and the Far East and force the Soviet Union into a disadvantageous two-front war.

Watkins and John Lehman, an outspoken, forceful, and media-wise Secretary of the Navy, persuaded Congress and many citizens that the Maritime Strategy was the right approach, and that the nation needed a "600-ship Navy" to carry it out. By 1990, the Navy had not reached the 600-ship number, but did operate the most powerful fleet on earth, with fifteen carrier battle groups, four battleship surface action groups, 100 attack submarines, and scores more cruisers, destroyers, frigates, amphibious ships, and auxiliaries. The Navy received additional resources to recruit, retain, and train the professional sailors who were so essential to modern operations.

Hostilities in the Middle East and the Caribbean

As it had throughout its 200-year history, the U.S. Navy responded to a number of international crises during the 1980s. The decade began with Colonel Muammar Qaddafi, the mercurial and belligerent leader of Libya, announcing that the territorial waters of his nation extended far out into the international waters of the Mediterranean. He announced that if any U.S. ships or aircraft proceeded south of 32°30' north latitude, a demarcation he labeled the "line of death," his forces would attack them.

To back up his outrageous claim, on 19 August 1981 Qaddafi dispatched two Soviet-built SU-22 Fitter ground attack planes toward the American fleet. First contact was made by Commander Henry M. "Hank" Kleemann and his radar intercept officer, Lieutenant David J. Venlet, who were flying a combat air patrol in their F-14 Tomcat fighter. On their wing was the F-14 of Lieutenant Lawrence M. Muczynski and Lieutenant (jg) James P. Anderson. The Libyans were challenging one of the most lethal combat aircraft then in service. The F-14s were

184

Secretary of the Navy John F. Lehman, Jr., on the deck of the carrier USS John F. Kennedy (CV 67). He was the Reagan administration's strongest advocate of the "600-ship Navy." (Photo: Naval Historical Center)

USS Nimitz (CVN 68), the first ship in the class of nuclear-powered aircraft carriers, steams with her escorts in the Mediterranean, where trouble with Libya and its unpredictable leader, Muammar Quaddafi, occurred frequently in the 1980s. (Photo: Naval Historical Center)

equipped with a radar that could detect another plane 200 miles away and could track as many as twenty-four targets at the same time. The Tomcats were armed with short-range AIM-9L Sidewinder heat-seeking missiles and medium-range AIM-7F Sparrow radar-guided missiles. The two missile types had taken a huge toll of Communist aircraft in Southeast Asia.

Venlet and a carrier-based E-2C Hawkeye early warning plane picked up the approaching "bogeys," or unidentified contacts, about eighty miles from the F-14s and approaching fast. The Libyans increased their speed to 550 knots. Fearing that the contacts might have hostile intent, the two F-14s got into a "loose deuce" formation that had served naval aviators well in Korea and Vietnam. Muczynski moved his fighter, with the call sign of "Fast Eagle 107," 4,000 feet above and slightly forward of Kleemann in "Fast Eagle 102." Whenever the Americans changed the direction of their flight, Libyan ground controllers directed the Fitters to do the same. The Americans upped their speed to 550 knots and soon made visual contact with the Fitters. In a standard "eyeball/shooter intercept" tactic, Kleeman kept his jet flying straight toward the Fitters as Muczynski maneuvered his aircraft to get to the "six" or vulnerable rear of the fast-approaching jets. As Kleeman changed course to fly parallel with the Libyans, one of the Fitters suddenly fired an Atoll heat-seeking missile at him at a distance of 1,000 feet. The Libyan missed, but Kleeman did not. He worked his fighter behind the Fitter, now clearly a "bandit," and destroyed the plane with one Sidewinder missile. Meanwhile

A command and control system in the sky, the E-2C Hawkeye became an integral part of the carrier air wing in the 1960s. Featuring a radar that can survey over six million square miles, large computers, and displays, the system allows the air controllers to detect intruders and guide interceptors to favorable positions. In operations off Libya they alerted F-14 Tomcats to the presence of potentially unfriendly aircraft and kept them informed of their movements

At a press conference, Commander Hank Kleemann, one of four F-14 crewmen involved in the shoot-down of two Libyan jets in August 1981, describes how he and his fellow aviators out-fought their attackers. (Photo: Naval Historical Center)

A crewman on the flight deck of the aircraft carrier USS Independence (CV 62) surrounded by steam from one of the ship's catapults, prepares an F-14 Tomcat for launch during operations in the Mediterranean in the early 1980s. The Tomcat, equipped with advanced radars and armed with Sidewinder and Sparrow air-to-air missiles, was then one of the most capable fighter aircraft in the world. It would remain so for over twenty years. (Photo: Naval Historical Center)

Muczynski had outmaneuvered his opponent and launched a Sidewinder that tore the second Fitter apart in a bright explosion. Both Libyans managed to eject from their flaming aircraft and parachute safely to the sea for later rescue. In this first American air-to-air victory since the Vietnam War, the Navy dramatically under-scored President Reagan's determination to meet Qaddafi's challenge head-on.

The Middle East continued to draw U.S. attention in 1982, when President Reagan ordered the Sixth Fleet to deploy U.S. Marines into Lebanon as part of a multinational peace-keeping force whose mission was to separate the Israeli army and its chief foe, the Palestine Liberation Organization. The U.S. fleet then over-saw the evacuation by sea of the PLO. As American Marines increasingly came under fire from hostile militia groups in Lebanon, U.S. cruisers and destroyers provided gunfire support. Matters came to a head on 23 October 1983, when a militiaman bent on martyrdom crashed a truck packed with 2,000 pounds of high explosive into the Marine barracks in Beirut, killing 241 Marines and other Americans. The situation worsened that December, when Syrian antiaircraft fire downed two Sixth Fleet aircraft, resulting in the death of one naval aviator and the capture of Lieutenant Robert O. Goodman. For the first time since the Vietnam War, battleship USS New Jersey (BB 62) fired her 16-inch guns in combat,

The battleship USS New Jersey (BB 62) fires a salvo from her main battery of 16-inch guns off Beirut, Lebanon. The twenty-mile range of these big guns could dominate any firefight in the vicinity. The limits of naval power to influence events ashore were demonstrated during this frustrating campaign. (Photo: Naval Historical Center)

bombarding hostile militia positions ashore. Finally, deciding early in the new year that the United States had nothing to gain by retaining forces in the war-torn country, the president ordered their withdrawal.

Meanwhile, another crisis had developed in the Caribbean when Marxists on the island of Grenada seized control of the government. With evidence that the Cuban Communists intended to develop a military presence in Grenada, and fearful for the safety of American students there, Reagan directed that American forces led by Vice Admiral Joseph Metcalf III occupy the island. On 25 October 1982 Navy SEALs secured Government House in the capital of St. George's, while Marine helicopters operating from the amphibious assault ship USS *Guam* (LPH 9) landed troops at Pearls Airport and later in the day at Grand Mal Bay. Simultaneously, Army paratroopers of the 82d Airborne Division dropped onto an unfinished airstrip at Point Salinas. Aircraft and ships of the *Independence* task group ensured that there would be no external interference with the operation. By the 27th, American forces had overcome spirited resistance by some 1,000 Cuban and Grenadian Marxist troops, rescued the American students, and liberated the island. The operation cost the lives of eighteen Americans, but resulted in elimination of the Cuban presence and restoration of democratic government on the island.

The Middle East continued to command attention as various radical terrorist groups and the Libyan government preyed on American citizens and U.S. interests in the region. In December 1984, radical Shiite Muslims hijacked a Kuwaiti airliner and killed two American passengers. The following June, other

"Moment of Impact, Operation Prairie Fire," by Morgan I. Wilbur, depicts the dramatic nighttime destruction of the Libyan combatant Waheed *by two air-launched Harpoon antiship missiles. (Navy Art Collection)*

CH 53D Helicopters lift off the flight deck of USS Guam *(LPH 9) carrying the 22d Marine Amphibious Unit to Grenada in October 1983. The mobility of amphibious forces enabled Vice Admiral Joseph Metcalf III, the U.S. commander, to bring over-whelming forces to bear against the enemy at points of his choosing. (Photo: Naval Historical Center)*

187

A-6E Intruder attack planes of the carrier USS America's *(CV 66) Attack Squadron 34, the "Blue Blasters," that took part in the April 1986 strike against Qaddafi's military installations in Libya. The success of the operation depended not only on the fleet's aviation units, but surface ships and attack submarines as well. (Photo: Naval Historical Center)*

Vice Admiral Frank B. Kelso II, USN, Commander, U.S. Sixth Fleet, on the flag bridge of USS Saratoga *(CV 60), organized and commanded the joint operation of Navy and Air Force bombing of Libya. Kelso later served as Commander in Chief, U.S. Atlantic Fleet, and then Chief of Naval Operations.*

terrorists in the Hezbollah organization seized an American passenger plane and ruthlessly murdered U.S. Navy Petty Officer Robert D. Stethem, who died with great courage and dignity. In October 1985, four terrorists seized the Italian cruise ship *Achille Lauro*, killed wheelchair-bound Leon Klinghofer, an American citizen, and threw his body into the sea. The perpetrators of this grisly murder were captured shortly afterward when F-14s from USS *Saratoga* (CV 60) intercepted an airliner bearing the men and forced the plane to land in Sicily, where they were turned over to Italian authorities.

Qaddafi trumpeted Libya's support for these and other anti-American outrages. Determined not to stand idly by in the face of these provocations, the president ordered the 27,000-man Battle Force Zulu, composed of aircraft carriers USS *Coral Sea* (CV 43), USS *America* (CV 66), and *Saratoga*, twenty-three other warships, and 250 aircraft into waters north of Libya. When U.S. ships and aircraft crossed Qaddafi's "line of death" on 24 March 1986, the Libyans fired shore-based surface-to-air missiles at the planes and sent three fast missile attack craft toward the fleet. During the next two days, American air-launched missiles and bombs knocked out the missile site on shore, sank two of the vessels, and damaged the third.

Apparently, Qaddafi was not chastened by the experience, because in early April U.S. and British intelligence organizations intercepted communications that proved Libyan agents had exploded a bomb in the La Belle Discotheque in West Berlin, Germany, killing two Americans and injuring many more.

The president ordered execution of El Dorado Canyon, a one-time Navy–Air Force strike on military and terrorist-associated targets in Libya to punish Qaddafi for his actions. The French and Spanish governments did not allow U.S. military aircraft to fly over their countries on this mission. As a result, the United Kingdom-based U.S. Air Force units had to follow a course over the Atlantic and Mediterranean that required four in-flight refuelings to reach Libya and four more to return to Great Britain. In contrast, the Sixth Fleet deployed the *Coral Sea* and *America*

THE NAVY IN SPACE: *The then Chief of Naval Operations Admiral James D. Watkins, USN, on commissioning the Naval Space Command in 1983, remarked that "Sailors have always looked to the stars." That ceremony confirmed but did not mark the entry of the Navy into space. Not only was the first astronaut a naval officer, Captain Scott Carpenter, but also long before initiation of any operational space command, the Navy was the largest user of space systems for tactical purposes. Now a component of the U.S. Space Command, the Navy Space Command continues to provide services and support worldwide.*

The two earliest space related missions for maritime purposes were long-range communications to ships and the tracking of objects in space to alert ships of overflights by unfriendly spy satellites. Components of the Navy Space Command continue to execute both of these missions.

Tactical radio communications using satellites were originally built only for the Navy, the FLEETSAT system. FLEETSAT's successor, UHF Follow On satellites now carry all of the Department of Defense's long-range tactical communi-cations. The ten satellites are controlled by the Navy Satellite Operations Center, headquartered at Point Mugu, California. This center, originally established in April 1962 as the Navy Astronautics Group, operated TRANSIT, the first electronic navigation system based in space. That mission ended in 1996 with the advent of NAVSTAR, the Global Positioning System.

As the service that operates all over the world every day, the Navy has need for and uses space-based assets to an extent unappreciated by others and even by many of its own members. But there is a reason naval ranks were used in the crews on Star Trek.

Below, left: Navy Commander Alan B. Shepard, Jr., smiles after he becomes the first American to travel beyond earth's atmosphere. Shepard and other naval officers made solid contributions to the nation's space program during the 1960s and afterward. (Photo: U.S. Naval Institute)

Below, right: The satellite antennae at Naval Computer and Telecommunications Master Station, Pacific are the nodes of a major earth terminal for communications for deployed units of all the servides in the Pacific and the Middle East. Real time, all the time contact between theater commanders and the national command authorities has been made possible by these systems.

carrier battle groups within easy striking range of the Libyan coast. In the early morning hours of 15 April 1986, in a surprise attack, Navy and Air Force combat aircraft crossed the Libyan coast, quickly neutralized the enemy air defenses, and dropped their ordnance on aircraft on the ground, barracks, and other military targets near Tripoli and Benghazi. All but one Air Force plane and its two crewmen, who were killed, returned to base. The operations against Libya during 1986 clearly demonstrated that Qaddafi's rogue behavior could have serious consequences for him and his country. They also showed once again that the U.S. government could employ naval power to achieve short-term political objectives without putting troops on shore or going to war.

The Tanker War

The guided missile frigate USS Stark *(FFG 31) lists to port after being hit by two Iraqi-fired Exocet air-to-surface missiles. The ongoing hostilities between Iran and Iraq made the Persian Gulf a dangerous place in which to operate, but America's friends depended on the protection provided by the U.S. Navy. Courageous action and good damage control saved the ship. (Photo: Naval Historical Center)*

The U.S. Navy had little respite from crises in the Middle East during the turbulent 1980s. In 1987, Iran, led by the virulently anti-American government of Ayatollah Khomeini, and at war for seven years with nearby Iraq, employed surface-to-surface missiles, fast-attack vessels, and mines to curtail oil traffic in the Persian Gulf. The Iranians hoped to cut off this source of revenue for its enemy Iraq by attacking the oil tankers owned by Kuwait, a country from which the Iraqis got financial support. Since the economic well-being of the world depended on the

Iranian frigate Sahand *burns from stem to stern in the Strait of Hormuz. U.S. carrier aircraft sank the vessel with Harpoon anti-ship missiles in retaliation for Iranian mining of American frigate USS* Samuel B. Roberts *(FFG 58). (Photo: Naval Historical Center)*

190

ready availability of Persian Gulf oil, President Reagan agreed to a Kuwaiti request that their tankers be allowed to fly the American flag and thus receive the protection of the U.S. Navy. By the end of the year, there were thirteen American cruisers, destroyers, frigates, and minesweepers steaming in the gulf and escorting U.S.-flagged Kuwaiti tankers. Close at hand east of the Strait of Hormuz were an aircraft carrier, battleship USS *Missouri* (BB 63), and their escorts.

Dangers abounded in the volatile Persian Gulf. At night on 17 May 1987, for instance, an Iraqi F-1 Mirage mistakenly launched two Exocet air-to-surface missiles against USS *Stark* (FFG 31), killing thirty-seven sailors and coming close to sinking the frigate. The surviving crewmen, however, applied training they had received in damage control to save the ship. A few months later, *Bridgeton,* one of the re-flagged tankers, struck a sea mine laid by the Iranians. U.S. Army AH-6 Sea Bat helicopters, operating from the deck of USS *Jarrett* (FFG 33), a guided missile frigate, discovered the Iranian vessel *Iran Ajr* putting mines in the water one night. U.S. naval forces captured and then sank her. Iranian-inflicted damage to another re-flagged tanker and to American frigate USS *Samuel B. Roberts* (FFG 58) in April 1988 sparked more U.S. retaliation. On the 18th, warships, Navy carrier aircraft, and Marine helicopters destroyed two Iranian platforms in the Gulf and sank or severely damaged three Iranian naval vessels. In contrast to these positive actions, on 3 July the guided missile cruiser USS *Vincennes* (CG 49) mistakenly shot down an Iranian airliner, killing all aboard the plane. Finally, Iran, recognizing the futility of the antishipping campaign and exhausted after eight years of war, agreed to a cease-fire with Iraq. The U.S. Navy's operations during the so-called Tanker War not only kept the oil flowing to a thirsty global economy, but persuaded America's friends in the region that the United States could be counted on to oppose aggression. The importance of this perception would be clear a few years later.

An Iranian oil platform that served as a command and control site burns after being shelled by destroyers in April 1988. The destruction followed an Iranian attack on a Kuwaiti super tanker that was sailing under American colors. (Photo: Naval Historical Center)

War in the Persian Gulf

The U.S. Navy's dominance of the waters around the Arabian Peninsula and its capacity for launching naval power against the enemy ashore were vital to the UN coalition's victory over Saddam Hussein's armed forces in the Gulf War.

When Iraqi forces stormed into Kuwait on 2 August 1990, warships of the U.S. Middle East Force were in the Persian Gulf defending U.S. interests, as they had been since 1949. In short order, the *Independence* carrier battle group changed course in the Indian Ocean and headed toward the gulf. USS *Dwight D. Eisenhower* (CVN 69) and her escorts deployed from the Eastern Mediterranean through the Suez Canal and into the Red Sea. Within five days, the air wings of both carriers were in range to attack advancing Iraqi armored vehicles and supply convoys, had Saddam decided to invade Saudi Arabia,

As these forces steamed in harm's way, President George Bush began forging an international coalition to oppose the Iraqi aggression and ordered the deployment of powerful American forces to the troubled region. On 7 August three carrier battle groups, a battleship surface action group, a Marine expeditionary force, and various U.S. Army and U.S. Air Force units began deploying into the region. This was the operational theater of the U.S. Central Command, headed by Army General Norman H. Schwarzkopf, Jr. The Air Force Military Airlift Command carried most American soldiers, Marines, airmen, and coastguardsmen to Saudi Arabia. Sailors deployed to the region in their ships. The Navy's Military Sealift Command transported almost everything else needed by the American armed forces to fight a war half way around the globe. This included their tanks, armored

The guided missile cruiser USS Bunker Hill *(CG 52), equipped with the advanced Aegis electronic battle management system, steams past a carrier of Battle Force Zulu in the Persian Gulf. Aegis provided the American air defense commander with a sophisticated system for coordinating the protection of UN naval vessels, merchant ships, and the ports on the south shore of the Gulf from Iraqi air attack. (Photo: Naval Historical Center)*

Battle Force Yankee, with three aircraft carriers and seven escorts, moves in formation through the Red Sea. The U.S. Navy deployed powerful battle forces to the Central Command theater during the Persian Gulf War. (Photo: Naval Historical Center)

Patrol aircraft were critical to the effectiveness of the maritime intercept operations mounted against Iraq. During the Gulf War, the antisubmarine warfare (ASW) mission for which these planes had been designed was much less significant than surface surveillance. American forces were augmented by planes from the Royal Navy and the French Navy. (Photo: Naval Historical Center)

fighting vehicles, artillery pieces, fuel, ammunition, supplies, and a mountain of other essential material.

Protecting the planes and ships that began streaming from U.S. airfields and ports across the Atlantic and Pacific, through the Mediterranean Sea and Indian Ocean, and into the theater were the warships of the U.S. Navy and its allies. For political reasons, some countries like Germany could not take part in the Persian Gulf effort. But German naval vessels operating in the Eastern Mediterranean in keeping with their NATO responsibilities helped guard the Military Sealift Command's unarmed merchantmen as they steamed along the coasts of Libya and other potentially hostile nations.

As U.S. and allied ground and air forces grew in strength on the Arabian Peninsula during August, naval forces put up a strong shield to protect the country's airfields and three critical gulf ports: al Jubayl and ad Dammam in Saudi Arabia and Mina Sulman in Bahrain. An attack on these ports by Saddam's seven-hundred-plane air force, 165-vessel navy, or saboteurs could have been devastating to the allied buildup. On hand to counter air or surface vessel threats were cruisers equipped with the advanced Aegis battle management system, and carriers, battleships, destroyers, frigates, and other combatants operating a lethal array of aircraft, missiles, and guns. SEALs and Coast Guard and Navy port security/harbor defense units guarded the ports. By 1 September, the naval contingent in the region was formidable and included three U.S. carriers, one battleship, six cruisers, five destroyers, and eight frigates, and numerous warships from other coalition navies. Other important units, including Seabee construction battalions and the hospital ships USS *Mercy* (T-AH 19) and USS *Comfort* (T-AH 20), whose staffs included Naval Reserve doctors, nurses, and other medical support personnel in addition to active duty officers and enlisted, had arrived in the region or were en route.

One of the first ground combat formations to reach Saudi Arabia was the 7th Marine Expeditionary Brigade (MEB). The unit's equipment and supplies were

delivered by the ships of Maritime Prepositioning Squadron 2, anchored year-round at Diego Garcia in the Indian Ocean for just such a contingency in the Persian Gulf. The arrival of a second MEB enabled the formation of the I Marine Expeditionary Force, under Marine Lieutenant General Walter Boomer. These Marines and the soldiers of the Army's 82d Airborne Division soon stood ready to defend Saudi Arabia. To provide these troops with armored muscle, eight special Fast Sealift Ships of the Military Sealift Command were dispatched from the United States with hundreds of Abrams main battle tanks and Bradley armored fighting vehicles on board. By early November 1990, the 173 ships involved in the sealift operation and the transport planes of the Military Airlift Command had deployed such strong forces to Saudi Arabia that fears for the defense of the country largely evaporated.

While taking full advantage of the sea, naval forces of the UN coalition denied the Iraqis access to it. In August, the United Nations Security Council adopted resolutions that authorized coalition naval vessels to embargo Iraqi overseas trade, with armed force if necessary. The resolutions' advocates hoped that the embargo would induce Saddam to withdraw his forces from Kuwait, but at the least prevent him from importing tanks, guns, and planes. On 17 August, a Maritime Interception Force, established under Vice Admiral Henry H. Mauz, Jr., Commander U.S. Naval Forces, Central Command (COMUSNAVCENT), began operating in the waters around Saudi Arabia. Eventually, warships from Argentina, Australia, Belgium, Canada, Denmark, France, Greece, Italy, Netherlands, Norway, Spain, and the United Kingdom joined the effort. American P-3 Orion, British Nimrod, and French Atlantique patrol planes also took part in the operation. With the greatest resources in the area, the U.S. Navy was recognized as "first among equals" and in that capacity coordinated periodic meetings to decide matters such as patrol sectors and search procedures.

Normally, the patrol planes would spot a merchantman and direct coalition surface units to her. Once contact was made, the commanding officer of a warship would communicate with the master of the merchant vessel by radio and gather information about her identity, point of origin, destination, and cargo. Boarding parties that routinely included American sailors and coast guardsmen, the latter members of law enforcement detachments, were dispatched to suspicious ships to investigate their manifests and cargo. Those ships found carrying prohibited cargo were ordered to the ports of the coalition's Arab members for impoundment.

If a master refused to stop for inspection, the allies used helicopters to drop armed teams onto the ship. These men then secured the bridge and took control of

Above: *In a vertical insertion operation, British Royal Marines "fast rope" from a Royal Navy helicopter onto the deck of an Iraqi merchant ship suspected of transporting cargo prohibited by UN resolutions. In this tactic, UN patrol units could stop a ship without having to disable her by gunfire. (Photo: Naval Historical Center)*

Right: *A Tomahawk cruise missile, as seen through the periscope of attack submarine USS Pittsburgh (SSN 720) operating in the Eastern Mediterranean, breaks the surface of the sea en route to a target in Iraq. Cruise missiles enhanced the ability of the Navy to project power hundreds of miles inland. (Photo: Naval Historical Center)*

Below: *A Tomahawk cruise missile leaves USS Missouri (BB 63) on the first day of the Gulf War. The Navy successfully fired 282 such missiles, which were used to suppress antiaircraft defenses and to hit targets in highly defended areas. (Photo: Naval Historical Center)*

the vessel. An example of one such operation occurred on 28 October 1990 when the master of the Iraqi oil tanker *Amuriyah* would not speak by radio to the on-scene naval commander or stop his vessel for inspection. Even though an F-14 Tomcat and an F/A-18 Hornet from *Independence* made low passes over the ship and USS *Reasoner* (FF 1063) and Australian guided missile frigate HMAS *Darwin* fired warning shots across her bow, the vessel's master still refused to heave to. Eventually, helicopters lowered U.S. Marines onto the ship and with the reinforcement of Navy SEALs, coastguardsmen, and British and American sailors the allies took control. Saddam must have been testing the coalition's resolve, for the ship carried no prohibited cargo. She was allowed to proceed.

Navy aircraft take on fuel from an Air Force aerial tanker over Saudi Arabia. In the Gulf War, each of the armed services depended on the others for some kind of support; no one service could perform its mission alone. (Photo: Naval Historical Center)

The embargo patrol did not force the Iraqis to quit Kuwait, but it did prevent Saddam from acquiring more arms, ammunition, and spare parts or sell oil to finance his war effort. The operation also strengthened the international coalition, because it showed the governments and peoples of many countries that UN military measures could be executed without heavy casualties or indiscriminate use of force.

This consensus was valuable in the fall of 1990, when President Bush decided to launch a campaign to oust the Iraqi army from Kuwait and restore the country to its people. General Schwarzkopf developed a four-phase air, land, and sea campaign plan that would require the deployment to the theater of 200,000 more American service men and women. Additional units included three more carrier battle groups, another battleship, a Marine expeditionary force, a Marine expeditionary brigade, over 400 Air Force planes, and the Army's VII Corps.

As these new forces headed for the Persian Gulf, Vice Admiral Stanley R. Arthur replaced Vice Admiral Mauz and took additional measures to prepare U.S. naval forces for war. He established Battle Force Zulu in the Persian Gulf and Battle Force Yankee in the Red Sea. Carrier air squadrons practiced operating with Air Force units, the amphibious components carried out landing exercises, and the fleet's battleships, destroyers, and frigates prepared for naval gunfire support and antiaircraft operations.

Vice Admiral Stanley R. Arthur, who led U.S. Naval Forces, Central Command, and the Western Pacific-based U.S. Seventh Fleet during Desert Storm. The frank and forthright admiral proved to be an able combat leader. (Photo: Naval Historical Center)

195

Above: *In a routine flight-deck operation, repeated thousands of times during hostilities, red-shirted carrier ordnancemen prepare to load bombs on A-6 Intruder attack aircraft. (Photo: Naval Historical Center)*

Above, right: *Lieutenant Commander Mark Fox, the first coalition pilot to shoot down an Iraqi MiG, sits in the cockpit of the F/A-18C he flew during the mission (another pilot's plane). Each plane has more than one crew; the name painted on the side of the aircraft is that of the senior pilot or plane commander. (Photo: Naval Historical Center)*

In the early morning hours of 17 January 1991, the UN coalition launched Operation Desert Storm. Tomahawk land attack missiles fired by ships in the Red Sea and the Persian Gulf (and later by a submarine in the Eastern Mediterranean) began hitting targets throughout Baghdad, the capital of Iraq. That day or soon afterward, attack, fighter, electronic countermeasures, and other aircraft from carriers USS *John F. Kennedy* (CV 67), USS *Saratoga* (CV 60), USS *America* (CV 66), USS *Ranger* (CV 61), USS *Midway* (CV 41), and USS *Theodore Roosevelt* (CVN 71) struck other enemy sites in Iraq. In the next few weeks Navy cruise missiles and the bombs and missiles of Navy, Air Force, and coalition aircraft destroyed leadership and communications sites, air defense radars, military depots, airfields, bridges, naval bases, and facilities connected with nuclear, biological, or chemical weapons throughout Iraq and Kuwait.

Simultaneously, allied fighters established air superiority, shooting down almost all of the Iraqi MiGs and Mirages that rose into the sky to challenge them. The Navy's two kills occurred on the first day of the war when Lieutenant Commander Mark I. Fox and Lieutenant Nick Mongillo, flying F/A-18 Hornets from the Red Sea-based carrier *Saratoga*, each destroyed a MiG-21 with Sidewinder and Sparrow air-to-air missiles.

Even as coalition air forces concentrated on the destruction of enemy resources in Iraq and establishment of air superiority in the theater, they began a campaign to weaken Saddam's field army in Kuwait. The latter campaign reached a crescendo in mid-February as Navy carrier planes, shore-based Marine aircraft, and other coalition units eliminated tanks, artillery pieces, armored personnel carriers, surface-to-air missile sites, headquarters, and fortified positions facing the coalition's combat divisions in northern Saudi Arabia. Schwarzkopf was determined not to start the ground campaign until the enemy army had been badly hurt and its soldiers demoralized. He especially wanted to reduce the effectiveness of the multi-division Republican Guard Forces Command, Saddam's elite corps and the mainstay of his regime. During Desert Storm, Navy and Marine Corps aviation squadrons operated 600 aircraft, roughly a third of the overall coalition air force, and executed approximately one-third of the combat sorties. The Navy lost six air crewmen and six aircraft in the Persian Gulf War. Their contribution and that of their fellow sailors on, over, and under the sea was vital to allied success.

In addition to taking part in the air campaign, the Navy was responsible for eliminating enemy naval forces in the northern Persian Gulf and convincing Saddam that the coalition intended to execute a major amphibious assault on the coast of Kuwait or Iraq. As this was underway, the Army's powerful VII Corps and XVIII Airborne Corps prepared for a massive, surprise attack on the enemy's desert flank.

Workhorse A-6E Intruder, loaded with bombs, has been checked for safety by a flight-deck crewman who hustles away from the jet signaling thumbs up to the catapult officer just prior to catapult launch. A large fuel tank is mounted on the centerline station of the aircraft.

Soon after the start of Desert Storm, U.S. and British naval forces launched an effort to neutralize the Iraqi navy, especially its thirteen fast craft armed with antiship missiles, and eliminate oil platforms occupied by enemy troops. U.S. Navy SH-60B LAMPS III, Royal Navy Lynx, and U.S. Army OH-58D Kiowa Warrior armed helicopters operating from the decks of allied surface ships coordinated with Navy SEALs, U.S. and Canadian fixed-wing aircraft, and American, British, and Kuwaiti warships in the sea control operation.

Two days after the start of the air campaign, Commander Dennis G. Morral, the commanding officer of guided missile frigate USS *Nicholas* (FFG 47), led his ship and the Kuwaiti guided missile patrol boats *Istiqlal* and *al-Sanbouk* into the northern gulf near the platforms of the ad-Dorra oil field. On board the flotilla were SEALs, a Coast Guard law enforcement detachment, two LAMPS helicopters, and a pair of Army Kiowa Warrior helicopters. The Army helicopters discovered the presence on the platforms of Iraqi radars, guns, and armed troops. The Kuwaitis also reported seeing tracer fire come from the site. Morral's group retired from the scene to assess the information, but returned the following evening to take out the enemy forces. The Army helicopters, equipped with quiet engines, night vision devices, and Hellfire laser guided missiles, glided unseen toward two occupied platforms. When the Kiowa Warriors were in range, Morral gave them order to open fire. Then *Nicholas* and *Istiqlal* moved close and opened up on seven other enemy positions with their guns and rockets. The devastating surprise attack killed five Iraqi soldiers and quickly convinced the survivors to surrender. That night and the next day the allied naval force collected enemy weapons and twenty-three Iraqis, Desert Storm's first enemy prisoners of war. In later weeks, coalition naval units, including U.S. Marine forces, liberated Kuwaiti islands that had been occupied by the enemy.

Coalition air forces also neutralized the Iraqi navy. One noteworthy action occurred on the night of 29 January, when a pair of *Ranger* A-6 Intruders flying near Bubiyan Island discovered an enemy presence below them. Commander Richard Cassara, a bombardier/navigator in one of the attack jets, notified the pilot, Commander Richard Noble, that he had picked up a big blip on his radar. On closer inspection, the blip turned into four naval vessels proceeding with lights out from Iraqi to Iranian waters at 15 to 18 knots. Once the aviators confirmed the identity of the contacts as Iraqi missile boats and received permission to open fire, they and the other Intruder launched 500-pound laser guided bombs that stopped three of the boats dead in the water and set them afire. A Canadian CF-18 joined the American planes and then strafed the fourth boat, which managed to limp to safety in Iran. This attack was the opening salvo of what became known as the "Bubiyan Turkey Shoot," in which UN naval air forces destroyed or severely damaged numerous other Iraqi combatants and ended the surface threat.

Free from this worry, Admiral Arthur deployed the *Midway, Ranger, Theodore Roosevelt,* and *America* carrier battle groups further north in the gulf and nearer to Kuwait. Battleships USS *Missouri* (BB 63) and USS *Wisconsin* (BB 64), a thirty-one-ship amphibious task force carrying two Marine expeditionary brigades and a smaller unit, and a flotilla of U.S. and allied mine countermeasures ships also closed with the enemy-held coast.

These mine countermeasures ships were critical to the success of the naval operation because the Iraqis had established a minefield with almost 1,300 magnetic, acoustic, and other mines. The ships and ship-based mine countermeasures helicopters cleared lanes through what they believed were the minefields. USS *Tripoli* (LPH 10) and USS *Princeton* (CG 59), however, while operating nearby, struck mines. No crewmen died, but damage was massive. These ships would have gone to the bottom if not for their sturdy construction, the professional skill of the damage control parties, and the crews' determination not to lose the ships.

An Iraqi fast patrol boat, one of more than 100 enemy vessels of all types destroyed by coalition naval forces during the Gulf War, sits on the bottom of the Persian Gulf. (Photo: Naval Historical Center)

Crewmen on the carrier USS Saratoga *(CV 60) wearing protective masks monitor flight deck operations during a chemical warfare drill. Such precautions were necessary to ensure the safety of sailors, even though the enemy's ability to effectively employ chemical weapons against ships at sea was limited. (Photo: Naval Historical Center)*

Following page, top: *Dutch heavy lift ship* Super Servant III *partially submerges to float mine countermeasures ship USS* Avenger *(MCM 1) and ocean minesweeper USS* Adroit *(MSO 509) after a long passage from the U.S. While limited in resources, the allied mine-clearing forces eventually eliminated 1,288 sea mines from the waters of the Gulf. (Photo: Naval Historical Center)*

Below: A member of Explosive Ordnance Disposal (EOD) Mobile Detachment 6 rinses his gear in clean water after diving in Ash Shuaybah Harbor, Kuwait, where the waters were polluted by oil released by Iraqi forces before their retreat and surrender in the Gulf War. EOD teams from Australia, France, and the United Kingdom assisted in clearing these waters of ordnance left by the retreating Iraqis.

Despite the danger, coalition naval forces pressed on toward Kuwait. The two battleships shelled targets on the mainland and on the large island of Faylaka to soften up the enemy's defenses. Another important goal was to help persuade Saddam that the accompanying amphibious task force was about to assault his army from the sea.

For that same reason, after dark on the evening of 23 February 1991, four fast boats carrying SEALs from Task Force Mike of Captain Ray Smith's Naval Special Warfare Group One deployed to a point off the coast of Iraqi-occupied Kuwait. Lieutenant Thomas Dietz and fourteen of his men put three Zodiac rubber assault craft overboard and filled them with explosives and floating marker buoys. The group then silently pulled the craft to within 500 yards of the shore. At that point, six SEALs swam toward the beach, placed the buoys precisely as they had been trained to do for amphibious assaults, and set the charges for the explosive packages. When the entire party was safely recovered on board the speedboats, all waited for the appointed hour. Exactly at 0100, on 24 February 1991, the charges exploded and the SEALs opened up with machine guns and grenade launchers against Iraqi positions ashore. Soon afterward, air strikes called in by the naval commandos hit the enemy defenders. Even as the special warfare warriors retired from the area, satisfied with their night's work, other allied forces prepared to launch the long-awaited ground offensive into Kuwait.

Early on 24 February 1991, coalition ground forces, including the 1st and 2d Marine Divisions of General Boomer's I Marine Expeditionary Force, smashed into the Iraqi army in Kuwait and southern Iraq. That day, the battleships increased the volume of their fire and Marine ship-based helicopters flew directly toward the coast; each of these actions designed to focus enemy eyes on the sea. To counter the expected landing, the Iraqis fired two Silkworm missiles at *Missouri*; one fell harmlessly into the sea and the other was destroyed by two surface-to-air missiles fired by British destroyer HMS *Gloucester*. Meanwhile, the seven enemy divisions positioned on the coast aimed their artillery out to sea and braced themselves for the U.S. Marine assault. It never came.

By the early hours of 28 February 1991, when the allies declared a cease-fire, General Schwarzkopf's 500,000-man armored/infantry force had destroyed the Iraqi army on the Saudi Arabia–Kuwait border, liberated Kuwait City, and soundly defeated Saddam's vaunted Republican Guard armored divisions. The United States and the other nations of the UN coalition had accomplished the mission of restoring Kuwait to its rightful government. By maintaining a powerful presence in the region, continuing the seagoing embargo operation, and flying combat air patrols over Iraq in the years after the Gulf War, the U.S. Navy helped discourage the Iraqi dictator from launching other attacks on his neighbors.

The U.S. Navy was vital to the accomplishment of American objectives in the Persian Gulf War, as it had been throughout the long and often bloody Cold War. Millions of Navy men and women braved the hazards of raging seas and tempestuous skies and endured years of service far from home and loved ones to serve their country in a time of real peril. Thousands of sailors paid with their lives to ensure that powerful adversaries dared not attack the United States; that other peoples and nations around the globe would have a chance to survive the onslaught of an ideology that respected neither life nor the most basic human rights; and that the world would be a better place for future generations of Americans.

The battleship USS Wisconsin *(BB 64) fires on targets in Kuwait. The explosive power, range, and accuracy of the powerful 16-inch naval rifles enabled the venerable warship to make a lasting impression on Iraqi troops dug in on the coast of Kuwait. The threat of an amphibious assault kept seven Iraqi divisions deployed along the coast while the coalition forces turned their flank inland. (Photo: Naval Historical Center)*

Bluejackets march proudly through the streets of Manhattan and accept the cheers of their fellow Americans for a job well done in the Persian Gulf War. The victory parade was a fitting symbol not just of the U.S. Navy's role in Desert Storm, but of its vital contribution to the nation in the long, difficult Cold War. (Photo: Naval Historical Center)

The Fleet Today

Today's Fleet—
Forward from the Sea

Vice Admiral Robert F. Dunn, USN (Ret)
President, Naval Historical Foundation

Pages 200–201: *The Navy is on station, at sea, and ready for whatever the nation may call on it to do. USS* John F. Kennedy *(CV 67) and her battle group, shown here, are ready to answer the question asked by America's national leaders in every foreign crisis, "Where are the carriers?"*

Above: *Carrier aircraft are key to maintaining dominance and projecting power ashore. Able to steam anywhere on the seas of the world without political interference or permission, carriers bring their aircraft from one crisis to the next—at times without pause. This F/A-18 Hornet is being brought to the catapult on USS* Saratoga *(CV 60) for launching in the dawn's early light. (Photo: © Greg E. Mathieson/MAI)*

At the dawn of the twenty-first century the United States Navy is second to none in size, quality, readiness, and in the professionalism of its sailors and officers. It trains in, visits, and patrols all the oceans and seas of the world. This ability to maintain a capable worldwide naval presence is what separates the United States Navy from all other navies of the world and is its major contribution to world peace. History has proven that there is no substitute for being on station, ready to reassure friends, deter potential troublemakers, or be immediately available with a credible force when the nation or an ally calls.

Should there be a call, the forward-deployed Navy can at a moment's notice dominate a section of the sea—above, on, and below—and it can project naval power, guns, missiles, aircraft, and Marines or other ground forces over the land. It can supplement the efforts of other services and allies without extraordinary support from overseas bases and depots. It can provide humanitarian relief and evacuate those in peril around the world. All of this the Navy does with the ships, aircraft, submarines, weapons, and organizations described in the chapters to follow, but none of it could happen without the dedicated people, many with specialized skills, who operate, maintain, and build this formidable and ready force.

Top: *Submarines maintain a stealthy watch while ready to fight from under the sea or to launch missiles far ashore. Invisible and invulnerable, submarines operate independently and with battle groups, dominating the ocean in which they operate. This is the diving party of USS* Seawolf *(SSN 21).*

Above, left: *Silhouetted against the superstructure of the carrier USS* Stennis *(CVN 74), this attack aircraft pilot represents the front edge of a powerful and mobile weapon, the carrier battle group. (Photo: Sandy Schaeffer/MAI)*

Above: *Destroyers are the utility infielders of the Navy, influencing events on, over, and under the sea, close inshore and far inland as well. Destroyermen take great pride in being heirs to Admiral Arleigh Burke, ready to go anywhere "at 31 knots." These fire controlmen are loading ammunition into a Close-In Weapons System.*

Top: *A petty officer from Beachmaster Unit One directs a U.S. light armored vehicle onto a beach near Vladivostok, Russia, from a utility landing craft of USS* Dubuque *(LPD 8) as part of a combined American–Russian disaster relief exercise.*

Above and above, right: *The Navy–Marine Corps team is equally ready to evacuate those in peril ashore or to engage those who challenge them from "The Halls of Montezuma to the Shores of Tripoli." On the left, Marines of the 22d Marine Expeditionary Unit from USS* Nassau *(LHA 4) escort State Department personnel and dependents to helicopters evacuating the Embassy in Tirana, Albania. On the right, a landing craft, air cushion (LCAC) brings part of the 24th Marine Expeditionary Unit to shore in Egypt in a combined exercise with Egypt, the United Arab Emirates, Kuwait, the United Kingdom, France, and Italy.*

It is the people of the Navy at sea, and those who back them up ashore—uniformed, active and reserve, navy civilian and family alike—who make it all go. These selfless citizens follow in the great naval traditions and contribute daily to the traditions of tomorrow as they perform their duties in exemplary fashion, often going far beyond what is expected. By and large these men and women are young; the average age of the sailors in an aircraft carrier, for example, is between nineteen and twenty. They are among the best their generation has to offer, and they make all generations proud by what they do.

This youth brings to the Navy an innovative spirit, which, while capitalizing on tradition, continually discovers and develops new ideas for getting the job done better. Today, the Navy has ships, aircraft, and weapons designed for an earlier era that have been evolved into systems that are wonderfully capable today. It is the Navy's readiness to adopt new ideas and technology that keeps it at the forefront of military preparedness. The Navy has moved into the information age with vigor and leads all the services with such concepts as network-centric warfare, cooperative engagement, and the use of electronic warfare. At the same time, the Navy pioneers the development and use of space, missiles, precision weapons of all kinds, advanced undersea technologies, and post-modern logistics support.

Today, the emphasis in the Navy is forward from the sea, the ability to project American presence, power, and support from ships afloat in international waters, while concurrently working arm-in-arm with the other American armed services and our allies. As it does so, the Navy continues to practice and prepare for the more traditional Navy missions at sea. All of this put together is an essential ingredient for American success in foreign affairs, economics, and the general welfare of people around the world, and for Americans in particular.

As the Navy moves into the twenty-first century there will be ever-increasing numbers of advances in technology, many affecting the conduct of naval operations at sea. Yet, the constants will remain. Tradition will be a guide, naval presence will be the hallmark, and it will be the young people of America who keep our nation strong on, over, and under the ocean waters.

Sailor power sustains the fleet around the world. The ability to replenish food, fuel, and ammunition on the sea allows the American Navy to go anywhere there is salt water and stay there for as long as there is a need. In the information age, some things still need muscle: here the deck hands of USS Moosbrugger (DD 980) heave in the fuel line from USNS Kanawha (T-AO 196) off the coast of Venezuela.

The great adventure that is the Navy begins for most at the Recruit Training Command, "Boot Camp." The young people transformed there from adolescent to eager volunteer go on in the Fleet as trained sailors, and in an incredibly short time become experienced veterans.

Surface Action Starboard!

Captain Bruce R. Linder, USN (Ret)

USS Carney *(DDG 64), anchored in a port in the Middle East, represents the first flight of the* Arleigh Burke *destroyer class built with a wide of beam for stability and a modest, slanting superstructure to reduce the ship's radar signature. Guided missile destroyers are designed for antiair, antisubmarine, antisurface, and strike warfare.*

At Sea-0530 (local)

The first gray-yellow of twilight greeted USS *Benfold* (DDG 65) as her sharp bow sliced comfortably through long rollers at a crisp twenty-five knots. A dying breeze from the southwest barely rippled the leaden-blue surface of the long, easy southerly swell. Flying fish darted out of her path, and an albatross, surprised by the gray bulk of the sleek destroyer, fled across the face of a rising wave.

There was no horizon, as is frequently the rule of early morning in these climes. Sea and sky blended imperceptibly into a distant fuzz of dirty tans and gunmetal blues. Far to starboard lay the low hump of a small island, treeless and sterile, more like the back of a great whale sunning in the first light of day than land. To port at 10,000 yards raced the slowly sharpening silhouette of a *Spruance*-class destroyer with a splendid bow wave that stood in vivid contrast to the blue-gray dullness of dawn.

Benfold's officer of the deck, sandy-haired and tanned after four months of near-constant at-sea operations, squinted through a pelorus sight to confirm her station on USS *Elliot* (DD 967). The air, invigorated by the night, swirled into the bridge through open hatches, mixing with an aroma of fresh-perked coffee.

"GPS shows nine miles to PLP," sang out a report from the quartermaster's table.

"We're there. Sound General Quarters," was the curt reply.

The shrill call of a boatswain's pipe joined the jarring peal of the gong, shattering the peace of the morning watch. Cries down passageways, sharp clangs from closing hatches, and thumps of hurrying feet took but three minutes to die down. A gripping quietness added an electric tension to the air that had not been present ten minutes before. Nine miles to the Preferred Launch Position or "launch basket" meant that a deadly salvo of the ship's Tomahawk missiles could be launched in as little as twenty minutes.

The Tomahawk Launch Sequence Plan had been received hours before. *Benfold*'s Strike Team had completed their meticulous planning of missile flight

USS Cole *(DDG 67) demonstrating a Flank III port turn. Early* Arleigh Burke*-class ships are equipped with a helicopter deck aft for operations primarily devoted to logistics. Later flights of the class will have full support capabilities for Seahawk helicopters, including a hangar.*

Highly automated gas turbine engineering controls in modern cruisers and destroyers provide a distinctly different watchstanding environment for the Navy's engineering rates that are experienced in oil-fired steam plants, as pictured on pages 236 and 270. This trend will continue as the Navy begins experimenting with electric drive for warship propulsion systems that will allow naval architects to disperse engineering spaces throughout the ship instead of their traditional locations either low in the hull or near the stern.

A daytime Tomahawk launch from an Arleigh Burke-class guided missile destroyer. Pieces of plastic from the missile cell cover join the clouds of exhaust smoke from the booster ignition as the missile streaks skyward.

The Aegis Combat System of USS Gettysburg *(CG 64) and her sister cruisers and* Arleigh Burke-*class destroyers is an integrated search, track, and weapons system centered on an electronically steered phased array radar. The information displayed in the combat information centers is an electronic visualization of the world out to 100 miles or more from the ship. Management and maintenance of the system depends upon highly skilled and well-trained personnel functioning as a well-drilled team.*

paths, waypoints, and warhead parameters. An INDIGO message had authorized launch. Within the past hour *Benfold*'s launch control operators and engagement planners had rebooted the Tomahawk weapon system, reentered mission data, and aligned three primary and two spare missiles so that each could fly across a thousand miles and explode within a few feet of their target.

The captain slipped quietly into a darkened Combat Information Center and received a crisp "thumbs-up" salute from the Tactical Action Officer. CIC was strangely quiet; the muffled chatter of equipment status, contact reporting, and weapons readiness checks was confined to internal communications circuits. Ventilation blowers further stifled static and syncing beeps from radio speakers. Colored computer displays competed with radar displays for their operators' attention, while the oversized slabs of the large screen displays provided a point of convergence for a swirling symphony of information centered on the captain and TAO. The large screen displays pulsed a constantly changing parade of geography: the coastlines of bordering countries, nearby oil tankers, merchantmen, fishing vessels, traffic separation lanes, patrol boats, Tomahawk ingress paths, the figure-8 bow tie of an airborne early warning aircraft station, the "AWACS."

"All missiles Mode 7."

"Aye."

"Two minutes to Execute Plan THREE."

The Launch Controller called up Plan THREE on his console, rechecked his status indicators, and glanced toward the dominating displays and then back toward the captain.

"Missiles released. Execute Plan THREE," came the order.

SURFACE WARFARE MOSAIC: Puffy white clouds of a mid-Pacific sunrise catching the first rays at their creamy peaks . . . night Tomahawk launches . . . fantail cookouts . . . batteries released . . . haggling with a rug dealer in Abu Dhabi . . . full power . . . planeguard . . . the vibrancy of Hong Kong harbor . . . "Flight quarters, flight quarters" . . . a humid softball game in GITMO . . . sliders . . . "Close up ROMEO" . . . hurricane evasion in thirty-foot seas . . . turning & burning . . . breakaway songs . . . pride . . . high-speed turns . . . on station . . . snipes . . . CORPEN NINER . . . Reveille . . . Main Brace . . . "Birds away" . . . "Now go to your stations all the Special Sea and Anchor Detail" . . . PMS . . . hitting your pit . . . up-doppler . . . SITREPS . . . night orders . . . mid-watches . . . skunks . . . quarterdeck . . . goat locker . . . eight o'clock reports . . . zone inspections . . . lookouts . . . shift colors . . . "You are approaching a United States naval warship" . . . POD . . . the smell of fresh coffee brewing and bacon frying on the morning watch . . . deck crawlers . . . "Stand by for shot lines fore and aft" . . . "Moored. Shift Colors" . . . wheelbooks . . . the conn . . . BRAVO ZULU.

The Launch Controller flipped the cover of the lighted "Execute" button on his console, paused for a deep breath, and firmly pressed the button. As he did, the button turned from a dull pink to a bright red. A tidal wave of electrical energy surged through the ship's weapons circuitry, finally terminating at the firing squibs for Tomahawk missile number 18052 sitting comfortably in *Benfold*'s forward missile cell F26.

The missile's booster engine jumped to life. The entire 9,000-ton bulk of the ship shuddered with the pure power of thousands of pounds of thrust. A thunderous roar, a stabbing white-hot propellant flame buried deep within a smoke cloud, a low throaty whoosh—all riveted the attention of every member of the bridge watch.

Thick clouds of noxious smoke, ash, and flecks of plastic from the missile's protective covers rained down on the forecastle. The officer of the deck rushed to a side window to watch the white and gray missile contrail that rose from the ship as straight as a ruler's edge.

"Bird away," came the report of the obvious.

A dozen pairs of binoculars now sought the bright pinpoint of light at the tip of the contrail. To the shock of the sudden launch, the surge of excitement, and the boost of adrenaline were now added a sharp edge of anticipation, an ounce of doubt, and a collectively held breath.

A split second later the booster flame winked out, the booster fell away, and the missile leveled and continued steadily in flight.

"Transition to cruise," came the next report, hardly heard above the sudden crescendo of cheers sweeping those topside.

Within eight minutes the drama was replayed twice more on board *Benfold* and four additional smoky arrows rose skyward in tandem from *Elliot*—to those watching from *Benfold*, their flashes of light and accompanying rumbles were like that of a midwestern thunderstorm mystically relocated to an Arabian seascape.

Minutes later the scene was again quiet. The ships had reversed course back into the long rolling swells, their speed boosted to Flank III. *Benfold*'s bow again rose and dipped to match nature's seafaring rhythms. It would be almost two hours before the seven Tomahawks would unleash their pinpoint destruction on an enemy unaware even of their approach; an enemy, even to last instant, probably still blindly confident of a desert dictator's empty promises of invincibility.

Seven messengers of power volleyed from a thousand miles distant. Seven arrows that could scale any fortress walls or trump billions of dollars invested in a nation's defenses arrayed against an older threat. This day's mission called for seven launches, but *Benfold* and *Elliot* could just as easily have launched 150

Conning the ship is among the most satisfying evolutions for seamen and is especially thrilling in close quarters. This midshipman is getting her taste of the emotional high involved under the direction of the commanding officer of USS Mahan *(DDG 72) and his executive officer.*

The Officer of the Deck on board the guided missile cruiser USS Normandy *(CG 60) keeps a watchful eye off the port side of the cruiser.*

209

During the Cold War, American and Soviet ships often steamed in close proximity and not, as here, in situations where honors were rendered. After the fall of the Berlin Wall, the meeting of Russian and American ships called for rendering honors as these Spruance and Soveremenny destroyers are doing. Before that, encounters were less formal and less friendly.

The guided missile frigate USS John L. Hall (FFG 32) moored during the Christmas holiday season. These lighted "up and overs" can be seen for miles and are a festive reminder of the Navy's presence in each of its major homeports.

missiles on this hazy morning—two surface ships capable of raining 150 missiles down on any target within a thousand miles.

No naval force in the world today can boast such pinpoint power harnessed to meet a nation's will—no force, that is, except for the power projection forces of the U.S. Navy.

Walk along the piers in San Diego, Norfolk, or Pearl Harbor today and you see our naval forces hitting a comfortable stride after years of purposeful transition. They are leaning forward and rapidly adapting to change. The United States Navy's force of cruisers, destroyers, and frigates has realigned to new geo-strategic circumstances and to major technological and operational changes. Aging platforms, obsolete weapons, and outmoded sensors have been retired to successfully recapitalize and modernize for the demands of tomorrow.

Today, lightning-quick communications, space-based systems, precision weapons, and advanced engineering systems are no longer the rare exception or the sole purview of the lab technician. They are everywhere.

Rarely in our naval history has a force been transformed so completely in a decade's span. Ten years ago the piers of our naval bases were spotted with aging cruisers, single-mission escorts, and ships with high-maintenance engineering plants. Crews were large, shipboard tasks were labor intensive, sailors waited for "mail call." Obsolete tactical nuclear weapons harking back to a different mission and time still dotted ships' magazines. Navigators still plotted positions drawn from LORAN lines and celestial fixes. Officers sweated the arrival of the 1,200-pound Propulsion Examining Board. Message traffic was photocopied.

The average age of the Navy's guided missile destroyers was reaching a quarter-century, and a decided technology gap separated "high-mix" Aegis cruisers from the other escorts in a carrier's antisubmarine screen.

Today, the Navy's surface combatants have been streamlined along four distinct ship families, each carefully balanced to mesh with the others. Leading this modern surface warship force are the twenty-seven ships of the *Ticonderoga* class of guided missile cruisers. These versatile cruisers have a powerful integrated combat system centered on the Aegis weapon system and the SPY-1 multi-function, phased array radar. The *Ticonderoga* combat system includes the Standard Missile-2, unmatched air warfare systems, advanced antisubmarine warfare systems, sea-control Seahawk helicopters, and a robust command-control-and-communications suite. Twenty-two members of the class are equipped with the Mk 41 Vertical Launching System, giving them a long-range, precision strike capability with the Tomahawk Land Attack Cruise Missile.

The state-of-the-art *Arleigh Burke* class of guided missile destroyer is entering the fleet at a constant pace of three or four ships per year. Its combat systems center on the Aegis weapons system and the SPY-1D multi-function, phased array radar. *Arleigh Burke*'s combat system includes the Mk 41 Vertical Launching System, an antisubmarine capability, advanced antiair warfare missiles, and Tomahawk cruise missiles. Incorporating all-steel construction and gas-turbine propulsion, these destroyers provide multi-mission offensive and defensive capabilities and are specifically designed to operate independently or as part of a carrier battle group, surface action groups, amphibious ready groups, or underway

Bunker Hill *(CG 52) makes a before-breakfast approach on USS* Cimarron *(AO 177) in Hawaiian waters during RIMPAC, an exercise involving the U.S. Pacific Fleet and ships and aircraft representing a number of allied nations. (Photo: Surface Navy Association)*

Every sailor can remember days when whitecaps and towering waves made the simplest watch a challenge, and when bridge watchstanders, clothed in oil skins or raingear, would wedge themselves in between bulkhead and table to find the best position to ride out the gyrations of the ship.

replenishment groups. A follow-on variant of the class, led by USS *Oscar Austin* (DDG 79), incorporates facilities to support two embarked SH-60 Seahawk helicopters to enhance the ship's sea control and antisubmarine capabilities.

The mainstay of the destroyer force for over twenty years has been the *Spruance* destroyer. Originally built with enormous margin for modernization and mission conversion to antiair warfare, these relatively roomy ships have aged gracefully, keeping step with the changing missions of the modern Navy. Over the years, the *Spruance*'s reliable engineering plant, conspicuous automation, and modular design have allowed the class to easily absorb warfighting upgrades, including a reengineered sonar, various towed arrays, the Harpoon antiship

USS Fife *(DD 991) shows that the crews of U.S. Navy warships still see the world. Here she enters Port Jackson, Sydney Harbor, to moor alongside the Royal Australian Navy's downtown wharf. The "E" symbols are yearly awards recognizing a ship's excellence over-all and in individual areas. The hash marks indicate repeated awards.*

missile, and entire suites of new communications and intelligence gathering equipment. The class could even have traded its forward 5-inch gun for an 8-inch major caliber gunnery system. In the 1990s, the class continued to stay abreast of the times by replacing the ASROC system with a vertical launching system (holding over sixty Tomahawk missiles) and upgrading the originally configured SH-2 Seasprite helicopter to the modern SH-60 Seahawk sea control helicopter. The inherent versatility of the basic *Spruance* design can also be seen in the lines of the *Kidd* class of guided missile destroyer and the *Ticonderoga* cruiser.

Today's fourth primary surface combatant class is the versatile, successful, and thrifty *Oliver Hazard Perry* guided missile frigate. These ships carry out a host of tasks, from battle group escort to lone patrol and open-ocean ASW. They feature a balanced combat systems suite with towed array and active sonars, a medium-range surface-to-air missile system, a lightweight 76mm gun, and, most importantly, two SH-60 Seahawk helicopters. Every cubic foot on this modestly sized combatant has been carefully designed to allow an optimal mix of combat capability, agility, and accommodation.

Surface combatants are highly dependent on the helicopter to fulfill true multi-mission goals. Helicopters extend the eyes and ears of the warship's commanding officer beyond the horizon, an indispensable advantage for missions that may include enforcing embargoes, tracking smugglers, or responding to a long-range submarine contact. Shipboard helos can also extend the reach of shipboard armament by performing strikes against distant surface targets, engaging them with either Penguin or Hellfire missiles. Mainline SH-60B and SH-60F Seahawk helicopters are undergoing conversion to the SH-60R variant, which emphasizes the aircraft's multi-mission capacities. This upgrade involves a Service Life Extension Program for the airframe, the incorporation of advanced multi-mode inverse synthetic aperture radar and infrared sensors, the airborne low frequency (dipping) sonar, and an upgraded computer suite. Thus equipped, these helicopters will enhance the sea control and littoral capabilities of the *Ticonderoga*, *Oscar Austin*, *Spruance*, and *Oliver Hazard Perry* surface combatants.

Navy surface combatants have declined in numbers by about a third during the 1990s, from the mid-1980s plan for 224 surface warships to about 108 ships in the active forces and another ten ships in the Naval Reserve. The current number is expected to stay relatively stable in aggregate terms, but should evolve into a richer Aegis force as *Perry* frigates and *Spruance* destroyers are slowly replaced by new guided missile destroyers. While the number of the surface

USS Stethem *(DDG 63) was named for a Seabee, Steelworker Second Class Robert Stethem, the victim of a 1985 terrorist hijacking of an airliner in the Middle East. Navy destroyers and frigates are generally named for notable members of the naval service who have inspired others by their sense of duty, courage, or selflessness.*

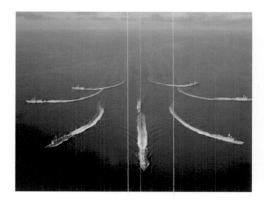

Above: *Destroyer Squadron One, a squadron of Naval Reserve ships, during fleet exercises in the Pacific. The Naval Reserve has provided many ready ships for a variety of operational assignments, including maritime interception operations and short-term deployments.*

Left: *Ships of the Constellation Battle Group steam west across the Pacific en route the Persian Gulf to enforce United Nations sanctions in the region. From foreground back, the ships are the cruisers USS* Lake Erie *(CG 70) and USS* Chosin *(CG 65), the ammunition ship USS* Mount Hood *(AE 29), and the fleet oiler USS* Cimarron *(AO 177). No carrier proceeds into an area where action may take place without surface warships to provide antiaircraft defense and logistic ships to support the group. An oiler is required for a transoceanic voyage of cruisers and smaller ships*

Right: *An SH-60 Seahawk helicopter fires an AGM-114B Hellfire missile while on a training evolution off the coast of San Clemente Island, California. With the advent of the Hellfire and Penguin missiles, the LAMPS helicopter provides surface combatant commanding officers with a pinpoint over-the-horizon attack capability.*

Below: *Flight deck personnel watch as flight operations are in progress. Nearly every surface ship in the Navy has the capability of receiving and operating helicopters, and the brightly colored vests worn by flight deck crews are a common sight.*

In spite of much mechanization, some tasks remain to be performed by "Norwegian steam"—muscle. Transferring people between ships by high line is one of those tasks where people are trusted over machinery. Passengers in the transfer rig are eager to complete the trip as quickly as possible and so appreciate the enthusiasm demonstrated here.

combatants have declined during the 1990s, three other indicators have shown increasing trends during this same period, each telling a different story of evolving and expanding capabilities.

During the 1990s, the number of vertical launch cells capable of firing Tomahawk cruise missiles or advanced surface-to-air missiles skyrocketed. Despite a one-third reduction in the number of surface combatants during this period, the number of vertical launch cells increased by a factor of four, providing a tremendous increase in flexibility that allows for future improvements in Tomahawk missiles and theater ballistic missile defense.

The average displacement of surface combatants also steadily increased during the decade by a factor of almost twenty percent. This is testimony to the Navy's move away from a fleet mix of large and small escorts favored during the Cold War and toward a clearer dependence on fewer numbers of larger multi-mission combatants for its littoral missions.

Finally, but troublingly, the average age of surface warships has also steadily increased since 1994 and is projected to increase still further. Already this aging trend has added over three years onto the Navy warship's average age as the decommissioning of relatively large numbers of older ships has slowed and the rate of introduction of new combatants has been held to modest levels. The trend of increasing missions versus a decreasing force structure is a clear indication that the challenges of today and tomorrow will be neither static nor easy to solve.

The Missions

The characteristics of today's surface combatants resonate to the dramatic change in missions the Navy has undertaken since the end of the Cold War. With the dawn of the 1990s, the United States Navy began to shift its orientation away from the Soviet Union and toward multi-mission forces. During these years, a host of strategies came forward to define the Navy's new place in a changing world, but a common theme stood out across all these concepts, white papers, and strategies—the overwhelming importance of long-range, pinpoint power projection from the sea. And as the importance of power projection increased during the decade, so too has the importance of surface combatants.

The changing dynamics of the threat throughout the forty years of the Cold War played its inevitable role in shaping the fleet. By the 1980s, antisubmarine warfare priorities called for a relatively large number of smaller escorts in the

fleet—primarily frigates—to deploy antisubmarine helicopters and towed array sonars across wide ocean areas. But the new naval missions of the post–Cold War era changed everything. By 1991, the annual *Naval Review* could report: "Although not stated officially, power projection clearly has replaced ASW as the Navy's top warfighting priority."

In this environment of change, traditional surface combatant missions involving aircraft carrier escort, heavy gunfire against defended beachheads, or open-ocean antisubmarine screens fell by the wayside. Replacing them were missions ranging from new wrinkles on the timeless tasks of maritime interdiction and blockade—even convoying—to the untried missions of long-range Tomahawk strikes and ballistic missile defense. As the fleet moved closer to the littoral, missions of mine avoidance or neutralization became ever more important, as did the need to combat quiet diesel submarines operating in shallow water, to extend air defenses over rugged terrain, and to react more quickly to stealthy sea-skimming missiles launched from land. As the Gulf War demonstrated, the fleet also found itself operating as never before in close association with the Army and Air Force in a tightly networked tactical environment.

In 1992, the director of surface warfare was one of several voices setting the stage: "Most of the world's populations live within fifty miles of a coast and most of the commerce transits within fifty miles of a coastline: that is the battle space we have to control as the enabling force." More succinctly, Admiral William A. Owens added in 1995, "Naval forces would maneuver from the sea, not on the sea." The shift from the open ocean to the global littoral was on.

The Navy's metamorphosis from a Cold War force to one able to meet the new operational demands of the global littoral has focused attention on an entirely new mission set: maritime dominance, land attack, and theater air dominance. To practice maritime dominance, the Navy must still preserve significant offensive capabilities in antisubmarine warfare and the ability to

Crewmen of USS Mitscher *(DDG 57) calmly fight the elements safely above the rush of water during an underway replenishment in heavy weather. Through years of best practices engineering, naval architects have learned to design ship systems so that warships are able to continue operations in nearly every weather condition.*

USS Philippine Sea *(CG 58) steams alongside USS* Detroit *(AOE 4) during replenishment operations in the Adriatic Sea. Replenishment underway is key to allowing surface ships and aircraft to operate for long periods far from ports of supply.*

215

USS Nicholson *(DD 982) is silhouetted in the glare of a night Tomahawk launch.* Spruance-*class destroyers were prized cruise missile launch platforms because they could maximize their Tomahawk loads in combat areas and did not have to surrender vertical launch cells in their magazines to surface-to-air missiles as did* Aegis *cruisers and destroyers.*

The Engineering Officer of the Watch is the person on watch in charge of the propulsion plant, the equipment that makes the ship's electricity and fresh water, and the hydraulics, plumbing, and other auxiliary systems that operate the ship's control surfaces and make her habitable. In the complex machinery of a warship, there is almost always something demanding this officer's attention.

neutralize other maritime foes in both the open ocean and in the global littoral. To these missions has been added the requirement to be fully interoperable with all other forces on the joint battlefield.

A land attack emphasis requires precision strike and surface fires from the sea to enable freedom of maneuver by joint and combined forces and successful prosecution of the land battle. New gun technologies will enable warships to provide gunnery support up to sixty miles inland in planned calls-for-fire. Medium-range interdiction will extend naval fires out to almost 200 miles using tactical missiles for suppression of enemy air defenses and to attack choke points, missile launching sites, command and control nodes, troops, and logistics sites. Long-range strike will employ Tomahawk cruise missiles to attack targets up to 1,600 miles away with tactical precision.

Theater air dominance is the naval capability that allows joint and combined forces freedom of action in the littoral by commanding the air battlespace. In many crises, naval forces are the first to arrive on the scene and must be able to establish a multi-tiered air defense umbrella to protect both maritime and land forces against aircraft, low-flying cruise missiles, or hypersonic theater ballistic missiles. To counter the air threat in a challenging environment of short reaction times, terrain masking, and low-level stealthy missiles, an array of new missiles and sensors will enrich the effectiveness of the powerful Aegis weapon system.

Sweeping change does not come overnight, but the intense heat of changing geopolitical realities has provided the impetus for change within the Navy's forces. During the Cold War, the Navy and Marine Corps responded to an average of about one crisis operation every eleven weeks. But since 1990, the Navy and Marine Corps have been called upon to respond to crises and combat approximately every four weeks.

The template for the post–Cold War engagement of naval forces was established early in the decade of the 1990s. In many instances naval forces were the

NAVY SALVORS—UNDISPUTED WORLD LEADERS

Navy salvage operations have blossomed from harbor clearance and emergency towing assignments of World War II to operations that employ today's cutting-edge technology in wresting all nature of lost material from the clutches of an unforgiving sea. Navy salvors can deploy on board state-of-the-art dedicated salvage vessels such as the Navy's newest, USS Grapple (ARS 53), or can operate from a wide variety of ships of opportunity. Their skills cross the entire gamut of underwater operations: ship salvage, underwater search and recovery, underwater ship husbandry, diving equipment evaluation, archeological salvage, criminal evidence recovery, humanitarian relief, and saturation diving.

Increasingly, emphasis is being placed on rapid response, with designated flyaway detachments with containerized portable diving and salvage equipment. This equipment may include highly specialized deep-ocean search and salvage systems designed to work as deep as 20,000 feet. These systems can locate items as small as an aircraft propeller or as large as a sunken ship. Once a target is located by wide-area debris surveys, sophisticated remotely operated vehicles, such

as Deep Drone 7200, can deploy to closely inspect and, if necessary, pick up items. In operations as diverse as the recovery of data flight recorders from stricken airliners to the recovery of historic artifacts from the sunken USS Monitor, Navy salvage successes have commanded many a world's headline.

Top: After completing forty minutes of work on the ocean floor, Navy divers from Mobile Diving Salvage Unit Two are raised to the deck of USS *Grapple* (ARS 53) at the crash site of Swissair Flight 111 off Peggy's Cove, Nova Scotia. *Grapple* is the newest rescue and salvage ship and can deploy the Mobile Underwater Debris Survey System, synthetic aperture sonar, and the Laser Electro-Optics Identification Systems to provide detailed images of the ocean floor.

Above: USS *Grasp* (ARS 51) anchored over the site of the crash of TWA Flight 800 off Moriches Inlet, Long Island, New York, conducts salvage operations to recover debris. Modern salvage ships can perform manned diving operations, de-beach stranded vessels, tow large disabled ships of almost any size, lift heavy objects from the oceans depths, or fight maritime fires.

Left: The Deep Drone is a remotely operated vehicle (ROV) that the Navy has used in many deep-ocean recovery operations, including searches for cockpit voice recorders from airliners. The system is air transportable, and can operate down to 7,200 feet and from various Navy salvage ships.

first to be assigned to the scene for peacekeeping and humanitarian missions, peace enforcement, and combat actions—and were the last to leave. Early in the decade, warships operated for over fifteen months in Operations Restore Hope and Sustaining Hope off Somalia and in Operations Uphold Democracy and Support Democracy that enforced United Nations sanctions and ultimately military actions against Haitian military regimes. They were busy with evacuations and refugee assistance in Africa and the Caribbean. They participated with a multi-national team of minesweepers to sweep the waters of the northern Persian Gulf. They began the first in a series of naval exercises with navies of the former Soviet Union and Warsaw Pact. They responded to regional dangers initiated by North Korea, Iraq, Iran, the former Yugoslavia, Pakistan, and India and participated in the first of a long series of punitive Tomahawk strikes against Iraq.

An early morning launch of a Tomahawk missile against a target in Serbia catches the national ensign in the light of its afterburner. USS Gonzalez *(DDG 66) patrolling in the Adriatic Sea provided the on-scene commanders with a balanced and flexible choice of weapons to use in coordinated attacks against air defense and command systems.*

Amber lights illuminate the deck of the fast combat support ship USS Detroit *(AOE 4) during an early morning underway replenishment. The deck lighting is designed to illuminate the working areas without creating a beacon or even a wide glow. Replenishment is carried out day or night, but is never treated as a routine affair—danger waits for the unwary in every move.*

A decade-long emphasis on operations in the Adriatic began in 1992 and U.S. warships participated in multinational operations including those of NATO Standing Naval Forces, Mediterranean. They helped enforce economic sanctions against warring states in the Balkans and provided command and control support for humanitarian flights and airborne radar aircraft.

Surface warships with embarked Coast Guard law enforcement detachments performed maritime interception operations from the Adriatic and Red Seas to the Persian Gulf. In 1993 alone, some 8,500 boardings were conducted in the Middle East, and 1,000 cargo ships carrying materials bound for Iraq were diverted for inspection. The pace did not abate as the United Nations–sanctioned blockade continued. In the next three years, Navy and Coast Guard law enforcement teams conducted more than 21,000 interceptions of commercial ships suspected of carrying contraband intended for Iraq.

Counterdrug operations in 1993 involved over 4,500 ship days of support in the Caribbean, Gulf of Mexico, and Eastern Pacific and contributed to the seizure of forty tons of cocaine. Navy and Coast Guard cooperation has been close whether the target is drugs or international contraband. Naval participation in maritime interception operations has added another dimension to modern shipboard training.

By the mid-1990s, surface combatants in the Adriatic enforced arms embargoes and guarded the seaward approaches to the crisis zone. Operations Sharp Guard, Joint Endeavor, and Silver Wake supported missions in Bosnia-Herzegovina, Croatia, Serbia, and Albania. Surface warships used state-of-the-art weapons—including the new Block III Tomahawk missile that featured improved accuracy through the use of Global Positioning System (GPS) guidance—in support of United Nations and NATO efforts in the region.

In the waters near Iraq, surface combatants frequently blunted Iraqi bluster in many interdiction operations. In November 1994 the Navy established its first permanent forward-deployed destroyer squadron staff in the Persian Gulf. Typical of the increasing dimension and scope of operations through the decade and into the twenty-first century, that same year, Navy ships showed the flag in nearly 100 countries, supported thirteen distinct operations from Haiti and Cuba to the waters off North Korea, and participated in multinational exercises in the Persian Gulf, Baltic, Black, North, and Norwegian seas. The first Partnership for Peace naval exercises expanded NATO's naval influence. Remarkable to the point of amazing for old Cold War warriors, the United States and the Russian navies were in the same exercise.

Toward the end of the 1990s presence operations often shifted to actual combat, with Operations Desert Fox in Iraq and Allied Force in Kosovo. But there was also a decided emphasis on exploring new concepts and emerging technologies and systems to determine future needs. A series of Fleet Battle Experiments tested new technological, cultural, and operational implications of warship design and changed the warfighting focus toward information warfare and information superiority.

In response to the truck bombing of American embassies in Africa, six Navy warships were ordered to Tomahawk launch baskets off Sudan and Pakistan to respond to a new threat—terrorism. Their targets were terrorist camps in the rugged mountains of Afghanistan near the storied Khyber Pass and a Sudanese drug plant suspected of nerve gas chemical production and ties to Saudi extremist Osama bin Laden. The ships were spread throughout the Persian Gulf, Arabian Sea, and Red Sea when they received their orders. The ships darkened their running lights and turned off their radars to dash in secrecy to their assigned launch positions. The latest satellite-directed Block III Tomahawk missiles were launched with coordinated precision, detonating against their targets two hours later.

The actions of surface combatants in the nation's terrorist response strikes of August 1998 were typical of the evolving stance of American naval power in what has been called an era of "sort-of peace," where a key attribute is the ability to bring credible, visible forces to bear as both a symbol and as proof of American interests and resolve. By being directly involved in nearly every international crisis or conflict, the Navy's front-line warships have contributed substantially to the stability and prosperity of our economy and well-being.

Airman Brian Nesby from Dubuque, Iowa, stows a fire hose after a drill on the flight deck of USS George Washington *(CVN 73) as USS* Normandy *(CG 60) steams alongside. The large phased array radar of this Aegis-class cruiser is behind the flat face of the superstructure below the bridge.*

Left: *Aegis cruisers like USS* Philippine Sea *(CG 58) are integral parts of any battle group and are present whenever the carrier air wing is called upon for a power projection strike. Although times have changed and rings of screening destroyers no longer surround carriers, a carrier today seldom goes anywhere without ample Aegis-controlled firepower somewhere nearby.*

Two fire controlmen load belted ammunition into the forward Close-In Weapon System (CIWS) mount on board USS John S. McCain *(DDG 56). CIWS provides the final line of shipboard defense against cruise missile attack by firing streams of heavyweight projectiles directly into the path of onrushing missiles.*

Opposite: USS Decatur *(DDG 73) launches a Standard Missile-2 Block IIIB during trials at the Pacific Missile Range Facility at Kauai, Hawaii. One of the keys to the effectiveness of the Aegis weapon system is its ability to launch multiple surface-to-air missiles rapidly from both forward and aft vertical launching systems.*

220

The Challenges

"The DDG 51 class destroyer quickly is becoming the workhorse of the fleet," emphasized the director of surface warfare in 1999. Not only was he pointing to the recent successes of a new class of warship, but also to its promise to be even more formidable in the future. The *Arleigh Burke* and *Oscar Austin* classes of Aegis destroyer—as well as Aegis cruisers—already are absorbing the next generation of modernization initiatives. Once these plans are completed, these multi-mission ships will be fully adapted to the emerging primary missions of the littoral, including Land Attack and Theater Ballistic Missile Defense (TBMD).

The capability to precisely attack land targets with a variety of weaponry is vital to the emerging imperative that surface warships be able to work within a joint service framework to operate effectively across a battlefield stretching from water's edge to hundreds of miles inland. Several new capabilities will allow land attack warfare to meet this heady goal. Chief among those will be vastly improved naval gunnery with the introduction of the Extended Range Guided Munition fired from upgraded 5-inch/62 guns on board Aegis destroyers and cruisers and the anticipated 155mm Advanced Gun System for the land attack destroyer. These new munitions feature a rocket-assisted projectile with precision guidance from a Global Positioning System/Inertial Navigation System buried within each shell. This improved guidance will allow these warheads to reach a range of over sixty miles with pinpoint accuracy.

Other programs will introduce the Land Attack Standard Missile, a land attack variant of the venerable Standard (SM-2) surface-to-air missile, or use of modified Army artillery missiles. Either can be fired from Aegis vertical launchers and complement two new variants of the Tomahawk missile, the Block III Tomahawk and the new Tactical Tomahawk that includes the capabilities for in-flight retargeting, real-time battle damage assessment, GPS guidance, and battlefield loiter.

Above: *USS* Cowpens *(CG 63) launches a Standard Missile during an exercise off the coast of Southern California. Although today's Standard Missile varies little in outward appearance from the Navy's first Tartar missile of the late 1950s, years of improvements have increased its range, lethality, maneuverability, and flexibility.*

Above, right: *Any modern Aegis sailor can identify with this scene. An operator's battle-space awareness increases dramatically with the fusion of a wide array of sensors into a single display in the ship's Combat Information Center.*

A slimmed-down nationwide shipbuilding industry has driven the introduction of a host of innovative shipbuilding practices from modular design to just-in-time supplies. These modern innovations have allowed the industry to stay competitive and to produce many of the world's best warship designs, such as USS Decatur *(DDG 73) shown here leaving Bath Iron Works, Bath, Maine, in a production environment limited to only a half-dozen new ships per year.*

The rapid proliferation of theater ballistic missiles among potential regional and littoral adversaries requires a dramatically increased naval capability for TBM defense. Aegis destroyers and cruisers with their advanced SPY phased array radar systems, versatile vertical launching systems, and inherent mobility can provide two complementary levels of defense. "Aegis Area TBMD" protects ports, airfields, and expeditionary forces ashore by intercepting ballistic missiles in the terminal phase of flight. A more advanced concept, termed "Navy Theater-Wide TBMD," evolves from the Aegis Area TBMD Program with modifications to the Aegis weapons system and integration of a new Lightweight Exoatmospheric Projectile warhead atop a three-stage SM-2 missile. Navy Theater-Wide TBMD provides an umbrella of defense across a much larger geographic region. Just a few Aegis cruisers or destroyers placed strategically in the Sea of Japan, for instance, could help defend all of Japan against North Korean theater ballistic missiles.

The anticipated Cruiser Conversion Program will bring these warfighting enhancements to the Navy's *Ticonderoga* cruisers. This mid-life upgrade program will allow the *Ticonderoga* class to keep pace with rapid technological advances inherent in theater missile defense, land attack, and long-range strike missiles and will ensure that these capable multi-mission ships will continue to serve in the front line.

A new afloat Area Air Defense Commander system has also been planned for *Ticonderogas* to improve their abilities to command air space close to land and to integrate their operations fully with shore-based air defense systems such as Patriot, Hawk, and the Army's Theater High Altitude Air Defense. This improvement will also allow full deployment of the sensor-netting technology known as Cooperative Engagement Capability (CEC) that extends the range of antiair intercepts and reduces the effectiveness of enemy stealth techniques. Netting several detection and missile control sensors through the use of CEC enables combatants to share real-time, fire-control quality data between platforms. This allows a central commander to combine fleeting or fragmentary radar returns to achieve a target track, allows for extended range intercepts of aircraft, and allows greater precision in engaging enemy aircraft or missiles over land.

Navy planning has also identified the need for a revolutionary class of warship to meet the challenges of littoral warfare. These efforts have aligned Navy planners with industry to design new classes of warships specifically optimized for the land attack mission and built upon a concept of operations that calls for the ship to get close to shore to fully exploit its revolutionary capabilities. Armed with an array of land attack weapons, these next-generation ships will

MILITARY SEALIFT COMMAND: *The Military Sealift Command provides ocean transportation of equipment, fuel, supplies, and ammunition to sustain U.S. military forces worldwide during peacetime and in war. On a daily basis, the command operates approximately 110 ships worldwide for the U.S. Navy in missions as diverse as fleet support, special mission support to U.S. government agencies, strategic prepositioning of U.S. military supplies, and ocean transportation of defense cargo. MSC is fully integrated with the combatant fleets and other U.S. military forces through four programs: the Naval Fleet Auxiliary Force, the Prepositioning Program, the Sealift Program, and the Special Mission Program.*

The Naval Fleet Auxiliary Force provides direct support to Navy active forces worldwide by delivering fuel, food, ammunition, and other supplies at sea, as well as providing towing and some salvage services. The command's expertise in underway replenishment is a critical part of keeping the Navy's surface combatants on station and ready. The force also features two hospital ships, USNS Mercy *(T-AH 19) and* USNS Comfort *(T-AH 20), normally in reduced operating status until needed. U.S. civil service mariners crew Naval Fleet Auxiliary Force ships, augmented by small U.S. Navy military detachments that support communications and helicopter operations.*

The Prepositioning Program provides operationally ready ships to the Army, Navy, Marine Corps, Air Force, and the Defense Logistics Agency. MSC's Afloat Prepositioning Force consists of thirty-seven ships, stationed at rapid response sites in the Mediterranean Sea, Diego Garcia in the Indian Ocean, and the Guam/Saipan area in the western Pacific.

The Sealift Program provides ocean transportation to the Department of Defense in peace, contingency, and war as well as ocean transport for humanitarian and peacekeeping missions. Sealift ships transport strategic combat equipment and supplies to sustain forward-deployed forces anywhere in the world.

MSC's Special Mission Program manages, operates, and maintains ships that carry out a wide range of diverse assignments for the Department of Defense and other federal agency sponsors including oceanographic survey, cable repair, acoustic research, missile range instrumentation, submarine support, ocean surveillance, and counter-drug operations.

Top: The Navy hospital ship USNS *Comfort* (T-AH 20) is refueled at sea by the fleet oiler USNS *Laramie* (T-AO 203). *Comfort* was returning from nearly two months' deployment for an exercise off the coast of Lithuania. *Laramie* provides underway replenishment services for the Atlantic Fleet. Both ships are part of the U.S. Navy's Military Sealift Command.

Middle: USNS *Shughart* (T-AKR 295), operated by the Military Sealift Command, was the first Large Medium Speed Roll On/Roll Off (LMSR) ship converted from commercial container vessel to sealift cargo ship. Its roll on/roll off design makes it ideal for transporting tanks, trucks, and other wheeled and tracked military vehicles. It provides approximately 300,000 square feet of cargo-carrying space. The ship is named in honor of Sergeant First Class Randall D. Shughart, United States Army.

Bottom: USNS *Algol* (T-AKR 287) delivers more than 8,000 tons of heavy equipment in support of hurricane relief efforts in Puerto Rico, unloading at Naval Station Roosevelt Roads. USNS ships are operated primarily by civilian crews and sail under the control of the Navy's Military Sealift Command.

The Sea Shadow experimental stealth test craft was built secretly in the mid-1980s to test various signature reduction initiatives for surface ships. Many of these improvements have been incorporated in the design of new surface combatants. (Photo: Greg E. Mathieson/MAI)

Opposite: Antenna maintenance high atop an Arleigh Burke *destroyer is a breathtaking evolution. Every piece of modern high technology equipment needs the attention of skilled technicians—even that at the top of a 120-foot mast.*

Quartermasters in battle dress lay out their ship's position and planned intended movement in a piloting situation during General Quarters. The heavy gloves and draped headdress are to protect exposed skin from flash burns, and the masks to protect against chemical inhalants.

provide sustained, offensive, distributed, and precise firepower at long ranges in support of forces ashore. With modern advances in information technologies, future warships will also be able to fully operate with other naval, ground, and land-based forces within the evolving interoperability tenets collectively known as network-centric warfare.

Future warfighting effectiveness will be gauged by a ship's ability to perform successful land attack missions by the use of a wide array of land attack weapons, including a next generation naval gun system. In the true tradition of a multi-mission destroyer, future warships will also employ capabilities to perform a variety of air, surface, subsurface, mine, and special warfare missions. For example, the next-generation destroyer is planned to employ an advanced integrated undersea warfare suite that may encompass ship quieting, torpedo countermeasures, a hull-mounted sonar with mine-detection capability, an advanced towed array sonar, and an integrated command-control and display system. The ship should be able to support armed helicopters and operate tactical unmanned aerial and underwater vehicles. It should be able to employ surface-to-air missiles and a cooperative engagement capability to establish and maintain local area air superiority.

Innovative ship designs will also take advantage of advanced stealth features, first pioneered in the mid-1980s aboard the Sea Shadow prototype, for improved survivability. Advances in electric drive technology, automated systems, multi-function radars, and active and passive survivability will also be pursued during the ship's design phase. A key goal for the next generation ship designs will also be to drastically reduce crew size from the 300 persons on the *Arleigh Burke*-class destroyer to a crew that numbers less than 100.

The People

Beyond the importance of its global missions and beyond the excitement of a force in transition, most point to the strength of the individual sailor and the uniqueness

Above: *Firefighting in specially designed shore-based trainers is an important element in the training of all surface warriors from seaman to captain. Firefighting and damage-control training never ends, and can be a key determinant in the equation of ultimate victory during combat at sea.*

Below: *A team from a destroyer based locally works an antisubmarine problem in the Single Ship ASW Trainer at the Fleet Anti-submarine Training Center, San Diego. In addition to teaching individual skills, in this case to sonarmen, the Fleet and Submarine Training Centers house devices and faculty that hone ships' companies performance in complex maneuvers and situations.*

Right: *Secretary of the Navy John H. Dalton answers questions from sailors during an all hands call with the crew of USS Boxer (LHD 4); a cross section of the ship, a cross section of the Navy, and a cross section of America.*

226

of the seagoing environment as the defining sine qua non for those who go to sea on board ships.

"America's naval forces are combat ready largely due to the dedication and motivation of the individual sailor," the Secretary of the Navy has said. Many view surface combatants as the traditional backbone of the Navy, and to them warship duty brings recognition and respect. "When the average American thinks of 'The Navy,'" summarized Commander Michael West, a former commanding officer of a frigate, "the instant image that comes to mind is of a ship. Not an airplane, not a frogman, not a supply center, not even an aircraft carrier. He thinks of a tough-as-nails gray ship making black smoke with a bone in its teeth."

Captain Ed Hebert, former chief of staff for the Naval Surface Force, Pacific Fleet, summed it up: "Today's ships run better than any before. Because of rigorous qualification programs, officers and enlisted alike master a broad spectrum of seagoing skills while gaining a comprehensive appreciation of the Navy's contribution to the nation's warfare capability. We have expanded the breadth of our average sailor's knowledge while simultaneously increasing the depth."

Through time immemorial, many a nation's pride and world position have been embodied in the hard wood and cold steel of its warships—a pride that is mirrored in the courageous sailors that have served in them. Our nation's physical and economic security depends on our freedom to use the seas and to deny their use by our adversaries. When America fights, it must fight with a global perspective and must be ready to reach across the oceans to meet its foes. Naval surface combatants provide credible forward presence, battlespace dominance, power projection, and force sustainment in well-designed and balanced packages of capability that can control three distinct and complex warfare environments—on, above, and below the ocean's surface.

> *Sign on, young man, and sail with me. The stature of our homeland is no more than the measure of ourselves. Our will is to keep the torch of freedom burning for all. To this solemn purpose we call on the young, the brave, the strong and the free. Heed my call. Come to the sea. Come sail with me.*

—ATTRIBUTED TO CAPTAIN JOHN PAUL JONES, C. 1779

Surface Warfare Viewpoints

The uniqueness inherent in duty on board surface warships of today's Navy can be measured in as many ways as there are sailors at sea. Challenged to identify a single element of life at sea in a warship "that makes it all work," many surface warriors came again and again to "the human element":

- "Watching a Caribbean moon come up over the placid horizon while on watch, you feel like you are part of a Jimmy Buffet song."
- "The surface ship duty means facing extreme challenges, with no script or prescription for success, and through the teamwork of the crew, sailing away with a feeling of satisfaction with the result."
- "Naval gunnery. It was so cool. John Wayne stuff at its very best."
- "The really memorable days aboard ship were the ones where the forces of the sea, or the complexity of the operation, or the leadership challenges faced were nearly, but not quite, too difficult to overcome."
- "The captain was an intense guy (we called him 'Rocket Man'), but very much a sailor's sailor—the ultimate tribute."
- "Leadership makes things happen aboard ship."
- "We once came to the rescue of a helpless merchant ship being attacked by Iranian Revolutionary Guard pirates."
- "You will lead men and you will lead them soon."
- "Today's warship officer operates at near personal saturation from the minute he or she reports aboard."
- "All the crew broke out the toys they'd bought for their own children to give to the Vietnamese children we had rescued."
- "All the 'yous' on a surface combatant today are essential parts of a greater whole, whose individual contributions to the success of their unit is indispensable."
- "Challenge and adventure are abundant aboard ship today, and will continue to abound in the future."
- "Over time, you develop a great deal of trust in your shipmates, trust that goes beyond the confines of the lifelines."
- "Taking care of sailors is what I do."
- "In today's world, there continue to be ample opportunities to exercise our capability to be on scene, or to get there quickly, with the ability to put ordnance on target or to provide command and control for a mission."
- "It is an important and exciting business."
- "Aboard ship we are riding the crest of the wave ushering in the Information Age."
- "Surface ship duty today provides a unique combination of fun and excitement, challenges and rewards, a combination founded on national security, rooted in tradition, forged in camaraderie, and sustained through sacrifice and dedication to duty."

(Photo: Surface Navy Association)

Two Block Foxtrot!
U.S. Carrier Aviation

Captain Rosario Rausa, USNR (Ret)

If there was a predominant color in the collective eyes of naval aviators of the early 1990s, it was that of desert sand. Iraq, with the fourth largest army on the globe, invaded its geographic neighbor, Kuwait, on 2 August 1990, and declared the sheikdom its nineteenth province. Almost immediately, in the White House and in the Pentagon, a recurring question was asked.

"Where are the nearest carriers?"

The answer: USS *Independence* (CV 62) and her battle group were operating in the Indian Ocean, 250 miles north of the island of Diego Garcia. USS *Dwight D. Eisenhower* (CVN 69) and her battle group were in the eastern Mediterranean. The ships were sortied to the area and by 5 August, *Independence* was in the North Arabian Sea, within range to launch strikes against Saddam Hussein's Iraqi forces. Two days later, *Eisenhower* was in the Red Sea. Subsequently, *Independence* moved north to the Gulf of Oman, just outside the Strait of Hormuz that led to the Persian Gulf.

"With the arrival of the aircraft carriers *Independence* and *Eisenhower* five days after the Iraqi invasion, ready to conduct sustained and effective military operations," noted retired Vice Admiral William Lawrence, "the line in the sand was clearly drawn, deterring further enemy advance beyond Kuwait." Coalition forces augmented American ships and aircraft as more and more ground troops, weapons, and support equipment were transported to the region in a massive buildup that portended outright hostilities.

General H. Norman Schwarzkopf, Commander in Chief, U.S. Central Command, later amplified Vice Admiral Lawrence's "lines in the sand" remarks when he said, "The Navy was the first military force to respond to the invasion of Kuwait, establishing immediate sea superiority. And the Navy was also the first air power on the scene. Both of these firsts . . . I believe, stopped Iraq from marching into Saudi Arabia." The aircraft carriers and their air wings lived up to their promise of mobility, versatility, and might.

Iraq refused to retreat from Kuwait. Consequently, a counter-invasion was planned, to be preceded by a mammoth air offensive. There was concern about

Above: *On deck of USS John F. Kennedy (CV 67) are 2,000-pound bombs and red-shirted ordnancemen standing by to load them onto the pylons of Attack Squadron 75 A-6E Intruders during the Gulf War. The bombs have laser-guided devices installed, which significantly enhance their accuracy.*

Opposite: *The controlled power and immense might of an aircraft carrier is manifest in this bow view of USS* Abraham Lincoln *(CVN 72) with F/A-18 Hornets in launch position on the bow catapults. The "Foxtrot" signal flags, two-blocked at the yardarms, announce air operations in progress.*

Below: *A "green shirt" hustles away from an F/A-18 Hornet after checking key points on the aircraft. Every launch from the catapult is a precision event calling for utmost care. Safety on the flight deck requires constant attention by every person working there.*

Top: *An A-7 Corsair II attack plane launches from USS* John F. Kennedy *(CV 67) in the Persian Gulf. The A-7 complemented the Intruders in striking enemy targets in Iraq and Kuwait, utilizing its great range and ordnance carrying capacity in the Gulf War.*

Above: *A fighter pilot from Strike Fighter Squadron 37, the "Raging Bulls," discusses her mission with another member of the squadron. The aircraft were launched from USS* Enterprise *(CVN 65) in the opening stages of an operation against Iraqi anti-aircraft sites.*

Above, right: *Carriers and their battle groups constituted an enduring and steady presence in the waters of Southwest Asia throughout the 1990s and were keystones to victory in the Gulf War. Portions of three battle groups are represented here. From left to right are USS* Thomas S. Gates *(CG 51), USS* Saratoga *(CV 60), USS* San Jacinto *(CG 56), USS* John F. Kennedy *(CV 67), USS* Mississippi *(CGN 40), USS* America *(CV 66), USS* William V. Pratt *(DDG 44), USS* Normandy *(CG 60), USS* Philippine Sea *(CG 58), and USS* Preble *(DDG 46).*

the ability of the Navy carriers to operate in the relatively confined and shallow waters of the Persian Gulf. But three days of successful operations within the Gulf by *Independence* proved that maneuvering for launch and recovery of aircraft could be achieved in this body of water just south of and adjacent to Kuwait and southern Iraq. When the counter-stroke's air attack on Iraq commenced on 16 January 1991, the *John F. Kennedy*, *Saratoga*, and *America* battle groups were on station in the Red Sea, the *Ranger* and the *Midway* battle groups in the Persian Gulf. The *Theodore Roosevelt* battle group was en route.

With some variation, each of the carrier air wings in the Gulf War generally consisted of the following: one or two medium-attack squadrons of A-6 Intruders; two strike-fighter squadrons of F/A-18 Hornets; two fighter squadrons of F-14 Tomcats; one electronic warfare squadron of EA-6B Prowlers; one airborne early warning squadron of E-2C Hawkeyes; one sea-control squadron of S-3 Vikings; and one antisubmarine warfare squadron of SH-3A Sea Kings. Two A-7 Corsair II squadrons, the last of their breed, were on board USS *John F. Kennedy* (CV 67) instead of Hornets.

4TH OF JULY: A glimpse of action during the Gulf War, Operation Desert Storm, is this account by Lieutenant Dan Wise, an A-7 pilot on board USS *John F. Kennedy*:

It was a night mission. The target was H-2 airfield in western Iraq and Commander John "Lites" Leenhouts, executive officer of our squadron, the VA-72 Blackhawks, was the strike leader. There were six A-7s from VA-72, six from VA-46 (seven MK-20 Rockeye bombs per Corsair) and two VA-75 Intruders with twelve MK-82s. We launched from Kennedy and over the middle of the Saudi desert took on fuel from a Kansas Air National Guard KC-135. The skies were clear, the moon full.

The A-7s pressed out from the tanker track followed closely by the A-6s. We were briefed to flare the airfield first, then bomb MiGs in open revetments. We flew close to each other, formation and position lights dim; tail-end charlie with lights off.

"Picture clear," called the Airborne Warning and Control System (AWACS). All our cockpit warning devices were silent.

"Tally Ho!" declared XO, "Target is 11 o'clock, five miles."

We could see the field in the bright moonlight but eight LUU-2 parachute flares (two million candlepower each with

four-minute descent time) turned night into day above the runways. Lieutenant Commander Bud Warfield and his wingman rolled in, each of their Rockeyes filled with 247 armor piercing bomblets. When they hit, it looked like popcorn bursting all around several MiGs in the open. As my wingman and I approached roll-in, my worst nightmare turned to reality. Some of that popcorn were muzzle flashes! Within seconds the entire airfield erupted with anti-aircraft artillery (AAA). My heart raced. I felt surrounded by flak. Mixed in with the AAA were numerous surface-to-air missiles (SAMs) which flew past us and fizzled out several thousand feet above. We dumped chaff continuously until the containers were empty. It was as if we were suspended in the middle of the grand finale of a 4th of July fireworks display.

Everyone held their breath as one by one the pilots checked in with an E-2 Hawkeye as we crossed back into Saudi Arabia. Everybody made it through and most importantly, inflicted heavy damage on H-2!

Above: Fighter Squadron 31 F-14s power straight up during a training flight. The Navy first began procuring Tomcats in 1969. The plane has been upgraded periodically ever since and remains one of the Navy's most potent weapons.

Intruders, Hornets, and Corsair IIs delivered bombs. Tomcats provided fighter cover, and mission planners utilized the invaluable data acquired through the F-14 Tactical Air Reconnaissance Pod System for assessing battle damage and mapping-out targets. The Prowlers suppressed enemy air defenses; the Hawkeyes were battlespace managers; the Vikings conducted armed surface surveillance; and some KA-6 Intruders also functioned as in-flight refuelers, or tankers.

Sea King helicopters were responsible for detecting submarine threats in the "inner zone" surrounding the battle group, but this threat was absent during the Gulf War. They provided search and rescue support and served as plane guards during launch and recovery sequences. A half-dozen SH-3 Sea King HS squadrons served on six carriers during the war. Three of these had Night Vision Goggle capability that enhanced their ability to see after dark. Even though the submarine threat was minimal, these units provided yeoman service as plane guard helos—hovering in position near the flattops during launch and recovery operations to rescue flyers in the event an aircraft crashed or ditched in the sea. They also functioned as logistics aircraft transferring people and goods from ship to ship, ship to shore, and vice versa. They flew maritime interdiction missions. Units in the Red Sea worked closely with special operations forces on Visiting, Boarding, Searching, and Seizing missions, laboriously monitoring all maritime shipping in the area. Two of the Sea Kings were

SH-3 Sea King helicopters from helicopter antisubmarine warfare squadrons provided "inner zone" ASW protection to battle groups during the Gulf War and worked closely with special operations forces in visiting, boarding, searching, and seizing of maritime shipping, among other missions. This SH-3 of Helicopter Antisubmarine Squadron 11 bears Old Glory as it passes USS America (CV 66) in the Persian Gulf.

Top: *Naval Aviation "Hero of the 1990s" is the EA-6B Prowler electronic jamming aircraft. A Tactical Electronic Warfare Squadron 135 Prowler flies over USS* Abraham Lincoln *(CVN 72) in this image. EA-6Bs had to be on station for major strikes to take place throughout the conflicts in Iraq and the western Balkans. The Prowler's main mission: suppress enemy air defenses.*

Above: *Members of Explosive Ordnance Disposal Mobile Unit 2 and Fleet Composite Squadron 8 practice insertion and recovery operations by means of the UH-3H version of the Sea King in 1997 in Puerto Rican waters. Working with special units like this one and Navy SEALs became more and more common in the 1990s, expanding the mission of helicopters. The aging Sea King's replacement is the SH-60 Seahawk.*

deployed on a destroyer to support Navy SEALs and participated in the destruction of several dozen mines and in the capture of thirty enemy prisoners.

In the Gulf War, EA-6B Prowlers were like the central character in a play. Events evolved around them. Their four-person aircrews—pilot and three naval flight officers designated electronic countermeasures officers—suppressed Iraqi air defenses with electronic jamming gear and with the extremely effective, High-speed Anti-Radiation Missiles (HARMs). The Prowlers were so vital that when EA-6Bs were not available to support a strike mission, that mission simply did not launch.

The unsung E-2C Hawkeyes were equally indispensable. Throughout the 1990s, they were the only fixed-wing, propeller-driven, turboprop airplane on the carriers, save for C-2 Greyhounds, which delivered cargo, people, and precious mail from home. The E-2C is manned by two pilots and three naval flight officers who specialize in airborne sensing and in command and control of the air battle space. Their three workstations sit alongside each other lengthwise in the darkened fuselage section where these officers monitor large radar screens and communicate with the tactical world outside. During the war and the blockade that preceded it, Hawkeye crews tracked an incredible number of contacts and managed the air spaces over the northwestern Persian Gulf, and adjacent littorals.

The S-3B Vikings had four-man crews: the pilot and one naval flight officer occupied the front two seats, while another naval flight officer and an enlisted sensor operator worked in the aft stations using their Inverse Synthetic Aperture Radar, infrared sensor, and armament suite to full advantage. The naval flight officer in the right front seat functioned as copilot, had a control stick, instruments similar to the pilot's, and a throttle so that he could relieve the pilot from flying the aircraft for brief periods. But his prime task involved a radar screen that enabled him or her to assist the tactical coordinator, who occupied one of the aft stations.

Normally, the tactical coordinator was the mission commander and used a big radar screen that provided a large view of the area under surveillance. He was the prime decision-maker, running the mission which, during the Gulf War, included sorting out and tracking thousands of contacts, all possible blockade runners.

The Viking's Electronic Surveillance Measures System enabled the air crews to collect intelligence data on enemy air defenses. The S-3Bs deployed Tactical Air Launched Decoys to lure the Iraqis into activating their radar. This helped companion aircraft, particularly the HARM-equipped EA-6Bs or F/A-18s, to electronically home in on surface-to-air missile sites and destroy them with HARM or other weapons. Around the clock, the S-3Bs monitored activities in harbor areas, along coastal installations and oil platforms. They were also able to detect convoys of Iraqi vehicles in the land areas near the coast, and aided strike planes in attacking these targets.

By the end of the decade antisubmarine warfare was eliminated as a mission of the Viking community, and the aircrew was reduced to three—a pilot and two naval flight officers—for non-tanking missions and to two—a pilot and naval flight officer—for in-flight refueling flights. In the three-person crew arrangement, the naval flight officer in the rear primarily handled surface surveillance responsibilities using the big screen.

When the ground war commenced on 23 February, USS *America* (CV 66), USS *Midway* (CV 41), USS *Theodore Roosevelt* (CVN 71), and USS *Ranger* (CV 61) were in the Persian Gulf, while USS *John F. Kennedy* (CV 67) and USS *Saratoga* (CV 60) operated from the Red Sea. Naval aviation historian Captain Steve Ramsdell wrote, "Carrier aviation played a major role in support of Coalition ground forces by lending credibility to the threat of an amphibious assault along Kuwait's coastline. The seriousness with which Iraq viewed that threat was significantly enhanced by the pattern of Navy and Marine Corps air strikes during the weeks prior to the counter-invasion. This threat occupied Iraqi Army divisions which could not be used to counter the land war. The credibility of an amphibious attack was most assuredly

Top: *E-2C Hawkeyes are airborne control towers, handling huge volumes of communications and managing the battlespace. These E-2Cs, with their distinctive "screwtop" radome markings, are shown shortly after the Gulf War and are from Airborne Early Warning Squadron 123.*

Above: *S-3B Viking as seen from below, with the aircraft's bomb bay doors open, exposing general-purpose bombs mounted on internal racks. The holes in aft bottom fuselage body in the shape of an inverted cross are for stowage of antisubmarine sonobuoy sensors.*

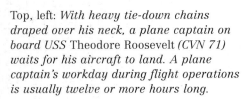

Top, left: *With heavy tie-down chains draped over his neck, a plane captain on board USS* Theodore Roosevelt *(CVN 71) waits for his aircraft to land. A plane captain's workday during flight operations is usually twelve or more hours long.*

Top, right: *In-flight refueling was necessary on many missions during the Gulf War. The Navy A-7 Corsair IIs refuel from a carrier-based KA-6 Intruder tanker shown in the lower part of picture, while others wait to link up with an Air Force KC-10 tanker aircraft.*

Above, left: *Armorer Joleen Trahan installs fins on a laser guided bomb on an F-14 Tomcat on USS* Theodore Roosevelt *(CVN 71). Female sailors serve in most ratings. The first contingent of women deployed was in USS* Dwight D. Eisenhower *(CVN 69) in the mid-1990s.*

Above, right: *Fighter Squadron 114 "Fighting Aardvark" Tomcat makes its way over burning oil fields in Kuwait during a combat air patrol after the Gulf War. Fourteen Tomcat squadrons saw combat in the Gulf War.*

enhanced by the destruction of Iraq's navy, largely accomplished by carrier aviation. By the end of the war, more than 100 Iraqi vessels had been sent to the bottom, and the Iraqi navy ceased to exist as a viable fighting force."

Captain (later Vice Admiral) Lyle Bien, the Navy's senior strike planner at the Central Command staff in Saudi Arabia during the war, noted, "The days and nights of air strikes (that preceded the ground assault) were devastating and paved the way to victory on the ground. But there is another key factor. Compare the nineteen-year-old American service person working eighteen hours a day on airplanes and tanks to his counterpart in the trenches in Iraq. Who was better led and motivated and believed in his mission—an American farm boy who knew little of the country of Kuwait, but a lot about the principles of freedom and democracy? Or his Iraqi counterpart who simply did not embrace the policies of Saddam Hussein? The answer was manifested in the unprecedented mass capitulation by the Iraqi troops."

The average age of the men and women who work on the flight deck of an aircraft carrier is nineteen. And the mean average age of the air wing's flight crews is only a few years greater. The ships' companies—without whom the aircraft would be land-locked—are equally young.

Although coalition forces were victorious in Desert Storm and the goal to liberate Kuwait had been achieved, Saddam Hussein remained in power, stubbornly refused to bend to United Nations sanctions, and resisted inspections intended to verify that Iraq was not building weapons of mass destruction. Consequently, in the

Previous page: *In-flight refueling, common during the Gulf War and in virtually all subsequent Persian Gulf and Adriatic operations, is a demanding evolution requiring intense concentration by the pilots involved. Here, an F-14B from Fighter Squadron 143 takes on fuel from a U.S. Air Force KC-135 over Iraq during an Operation Southern Watch mission. The Tomcat was based on board USS* George Washington *(CVN 73).*

Above: *Boiler Technician Fireman Clark Roderick helps light off one of the boilers in the main engine room on board USS* John F. Kennedy *(CV 67) operating in the Red Sea during the Gulf War.* Kennedy *was the last carrier built with a conventionally fired steam plant; all built after her have nuclear power plants.*

Top, right: *At Fallon, Nevada, vital combat training takes place on the Naval Strike and Air Warfare Center complex, which emulates virtually any hostile scenario carrier flyers might encounter. In this photo a Fighter Squadron 143 Tomcat releases a MK-83 1,000-pound bomb on a training target on the desert floor below. In the mid-1990s introduction of the LANTIRN—Low Altitude Navigation and Targeting Infrared for Night—system gave the F-14 new life, transforming it into a fully capable strike aircraft in addition to its role as an air superiority fighter.*

Right: *During a training flight south of the Salton Sea in California, a Fighter Squadron 24 F-14, with pilot Lieutenant Mark Burgess and Radar Intercept Officer Lieutenant Commander John Sheehan on board, fires salvo flares. The flares are used to decoy enemy surface-to-air missile sites as they attempt to track and fire at aircraft.*

years that followed, the Navy's presence in Southwest Asia, with aircraft carriers as the principle force present, continued, interspersed with periodic eruptions of hostilities prompting strikes against Iraqi targets, mostly missile sites. This constant, distant, low-intensity warfare rolled on for years. While rarely making headlines, the enforcement of the sanctions placed enormous demands on the crews, ships, and aircraft of the fleet.

A major reason for the success in the Gulf War was the pre-deployment training conducted at the Navy's elaborate weapons training complex in Fallon, Nevada, a region characterized by rough-hewn mountains and stretches of desert-like terrain. This facility featured simulated combat scenarios on bombing and electronic warfare ranges. The complex was upgraded in the middle of the decade with the consolidation of Top Gun (air-to-air combat training), Top Dome (airborne early-warning instruction), and Strike University. First designated the Naval Strike Warfare Center, this installation later became the Naval Strike and Air Warfare Center. Combat conditions were realistically emulated utilizing the latest technology and simulations of known threats around the globe. Pilots honed their skills while being carefully evaluated by veteran instructors who had at their disposal sophisticated

LANDING SIGNAL OFFICERS: *Landing Signal Officers (LSO) are a pilot's lifeline to a safe "trap," or arrested landing. LSOs are still referred to as "Paddles," because of the tennis racket-like signaling devices used on carriers to "wave" or guide the pilots to safe landings. These paddles were used until the late 1950s when they were replaced by the mirror and, ultimately, the Fresnel lens landing systems. LSOs observe countless approaches—on shore bases as well as in carriers—learning the nuances of the landing before they become qualified to control aircraft. Naval aviators themselves, they quickly learn to evaluate the oncoming pilot's approach—nose too high or too low, line-up too far left or right, rate of descent off the mark, power control erratic—and convey the necessary corrections to the pilot. LSOs also listen to the changing pitch of approaching engine sounds, and if those sounds indicate rough use of the throttle, or if insufficient power is being applied to the engine—or too much—the LSO advises the pilot accordingly.*

The pilot must fly the plane and is responsible for bringing it down safely, but the LSOs' imaginary hands are on throttle and stick right along with the pilot as he or she executes the most difficult phase of a flight from the carrier. There are several LSOs on the platform for every recover—one from the air wing staff, usually the senior LSO, and usually one each from the squadrons. The Air Boss in Primary Flight Control—referred to as the "Tower"—is also acutely tuned in to the activities at

the aft end of the ship, constantly concerned for safety. At night, the interplay between pilot and LSO is intensified. Visual reference points are diminished compared to daytime. In addition to the amber image of the "ball" on the mirror, the pilot has a string of line-up lights and runway lights for reference. The LSO watches the incoming aircraft's wing lights and a light on the nose wheel strut to gauge the plane's approach attitude. Landing aboard an aircraft carrier is never easy. But when the night is black, the weather is bad, and the deck is heaving, the challenges facing the pilot and the LSO are even greater. In those circumstances, the relationship between pilot and LSO is unique, enduring, and instrumental to safety of the fliers and the ship.

Aboard USS *Carl Vinson* (CVN 70), a landing signal officer guides an F/A-18 Hornet to a safe landing. He holds a telephone-like transceiver in his left hand to communicate with the pilot. In his right hand is a trigger with which he can activate blinking red lights on the Fresnel lens to wave off an incoming aircraft if necessary.

monitoring equipment that could track the flyers' every move in the various exercise areas. When it became apparent that newer and more capable surface-to-air missiles in the hands of potential foes forced attacking from higher altitudes than previous doctrine dictated, the center developed new parameters for all the strike fighters to use in their weapons delivery. Today, the Naval Strike and Air Warfare Center continues as a warrior brain center for naval aviation

At the outset of the decade, the collapse of the Soviet Union triggered its breakdown into component republics. The United States emerged as the sole superpower on the globe. The Gulf War added an exclamation point to that fact. Navy planners recognized in this new era a need for the re-shaping of the Navy's overall strategic policy, focusing on regional rather than global challenges. Aircraft carriers became lead agents in this endeavor, which was encapsulated in a white paper called "From the Sea." "From the Sea" and its later variation, "Forward . . . from the Sea," became the prevailing strategic theme for the naval service as the millennium approached.

Naval aviation historian Captain Richard Knott wrote, "'From the Sea' projected the role of the U.S. Navy and Marine Corps into the twenty-first century. It outlined a strategy wherein forward-deployed Naval forces would give priority to the littoral areas of the world to project power ashore when and where needed. Carrier battle groups, uniquely suited to this role, would provide a wide range of operations, from limited applications of force to, as demonstrated during the war

Look carefully—this Tomcat is upside-down over a Naval Strike and Air Warfare Center training range. On the center fuselage pylons are four BDU-45 bombs. The Tomcat's ability to conduct fighter as well as strike missions enhances its effectiveness and flexibility in the carrier air wing.

Sidewinder missiles, on the outer wing station of these Strike Fighter Squadron 136 Hornets, have the look of lethality about them. The Sidewinder was initially developed in the mid-1950s, has been upgraded through the years, and continues as a mainstay in the Navy arsenal.

with Iraq, 'enabling' actions that hold the line until deployment of follow-on forces, and, of course, all-out projections of force in large-scale operations."

An anticipated consequence of the Soviet collapse was the most severe reduction in U.S. military forces since the end of World War II. Knott summarized the effect of this draw-down on naval forces, "The careful and systematic draw-down of the U.S. defense establishment continued throughout 1992. As the U.S. base structure shrank worldwide, carrier battle groups increasingly became the only credible U.S. military presence in many parts of the world."

Yet America's worldwide commitments did not shrink. The threat from a major potential opponent like the Soviet Union may have diminished, but tensions rose and subsided in locales ranging from Taiwan in the Far East to the western Balkans, to Southwest Asia. The carrier battle group is a potent and flexible instrument capable of demonstrating the United States' determination to achieve stability and to ease tensions virtually anywhere on the globe. Consequently, the carrier

Rainbow sideboys: These sailors, wearing the jerseys of their specialty jobs, form part of the ceremonial personnel who welcome visiting flag officers and civilian dignitaries in USS Enterprise *(CVN 65). The purple jersey denotes fuel handlers; the blue is for aircraft handling crew, chockmen, and elevator operators; the yellow is for the flight deck officer, flight deck chief, aircraft handling officer, catapult officer, arresting gear officer, and plane directors; green jerseys denote the center deck operator, the deck edge operator, bow safety man, top-side safety petty officer, weight board operator, jet blast deflector operator, hook runners, deck checkers, and maintenance crew personnel. Plane captains who ensure proper aircraft inspection and servicing, cleanliness, and general condition wear brown jerseys. A red jersey denotes weapons handlers from the squadrons and the ship's company.*

238

battle groups were called upon with unprecedented frequency to "show the flag" and, as necessary, to employ military power.

In the mid-1990s, a new color and a landscape radically different from the tawny tones of the desert captured the attention of Mediterranean-bound flyers: the verdant mountains of the Yugoslav region. In this eastern European region age-old hatreds, which had percolated for generations, heightened to the boiling point. Intermittent hostilities were previews to inevitable greater conflicts, and the North Atlantic Treaty Organization countries joined forces to take action as necessary.

For carrier battle groups, the Adriatic Sea joined the Persian Gulf as a prime launch and recovery site for carriers supporting the NATO efforts in the Adriatic and United Nations' actions in the Persian Gulf. Weather could be nasty in either area. The meteorological conditions in southeastern Europe, particularly in winter, were troublesome primarily because heavy clouds could cloak mountain peaks or blanket the ground. In winter the countryside lost its luster, and strong, sometimes turbulent, weather cascaded across the land bringing cold, wet conditions. In spring and fall low ceilings and precipitation in the form of steady drizzle were common.

Carrier aviators could make their way to and from targets "in the clag," that is, in heavy clouds and/or precipitation. But the cloud cover prevented the aviators from seeing the surface-to-air missile sites so they could avoid any missiles launched and tracking toward them. Also, the Forward Looking Infrared (FLIR) systems, used by strike planes to identify and home in on targets, cannot penetrate visible moisture, i.e., clouds. Since the Rules of Engagement (ROE) required that missile sites had to be visible from the air in order to attack them, many missions were aborted.

In winter, 80-degree temperatures were common in the Persian Gulf, but in summer, a furnace-like 120-degree heat cloaked the flight decks. Those who labored on carrier flight decks, "on the roof," wore specially designed water containers, "camel backs," with a tube mounted near the individual's mouth so he or she could draw water without using their hands. For the remainder of the decade, carrier battle groups could expect to operate—and engage in combat—in both of these weather extremes.

In 1993, *Saratoga* and *John F. Kennedy* were ordered into the Adriatic Sea to establish a U.S. presence while supporting a United Nations effort to feed people in Bosnia-Herzegovina. In the autumn of the same year, *Eisenhower* and *America* deployed to Haitian waters to assist that impoverished country restore democracy. When Iraq attacked Shiite Muslims in southern Iraq from the air, *Independence*, first on the scene after the invasion of Kuwait, returned to the Persian Gulf to enforce President Bush's warning that if Iraqi aircraft entered the no-fly zone they would be shot down.

In the Western Pacific, the Navy's only permanently deployed battle group, based in Japan and spearheaded by *Independence*, was ordered to the Indian Ocean to support humanitarian relief in Somalia. Strikes against Serbian military targets in Bosnia in the summer of 1995 were led by *Theodore Roosevelt*. In March 1996, following China's live fire exercises off the coast of Taiwan, *Independence* again was dispatched to the vicinity of the Taiwan Strait to establish an American presence and to inhibit a conflagration between these discordant elements.

With unrelenting frequency, hostilities of varying size and impact reflected a prevailing unease among many nations and an unending commitment of the carrier battle groups. Missions included monitoring airspace over the Balkans, providing air cover and close air support for United Nations protection forces, and participating in efforts to enforce the military aspects of the Dayton (Ohio) Peace Accords

Neatly parked on the forward flight deck of USS Abraham Lincoln *(CVN 72) are the aircraft of Carrier Air Wing 11. The carrier can accommodate over eighty warplanes.*

USS Independence *(CV 62) departs Subic Bay, the Philippines. The naval complex at Subic Bay, including Naval Air Station Cubi Point, was a key way-point during the Vietnam War. The United States turned the base over to the Philippines in 1992.*

in the Balkans. Carrier planes made strikes in Iraq on several occasions as well as continuing the enforcement of United Nations sanctions.

These commitments on one side of the globe continued unabated as the world approached the millennium. America's defense strategy still required that U.S. military forces be able to conduct two major conflicts and one low-intensity conflict simultaneously. Plans called for eleven carrier battle groups and a twelfth carrier to serve as both a reserve and training carrier. Most significantly, the carrier battle groups have been endorsed at the highest levels as prime instruments in the nation's ability to project force—and presence—virtually anywhere on the planet.

A wealthy, successful businessman was invited aboard an aircraft carrier to observe flight operations. When the maneuvers were over he was in a state of awe and told the admiral who was his host that he could not believe the coordination and teamwork exhibited by the flight deck crew.

"If I had that type of cooperation, enthusiasm, and skill happening on my plant floor, there's no telling how much better our business could be, how much more we could accomplish!"

The young people on the Navy's carrier flight decks, which in recent years have come to include females as capable as the males, are thoroughly trained to do their jobs. But even though automation and high technology systems are in use in

Below: *Aviation ordnancemen from Attack Squadron 196 prepare to hoist a GBU-12 laser guided bomb onto the wing pylon of a squadron A-6E Intruder on board USS Carl Vinson (CVN 70) during training in the Indian Ocean in 1994. Even with the latest support equipment, the ordnancemen often have to hoist weapons onto pylons with human muscle.*

Opposite: *A safety checker on the flight deck signals the flight deck officer that the aircraft on the catapult, unseen at the right, is safe to go. Launching aircraft is a precise ritual involving dozens of people performing their tasks exactly in a defined sequence. Observers compare flight deck operations to a well performed ballet.*

Left, top to bottom: *Because the landing gear on this aircraft has been damaged, the S-3B Viking of Sea Control Squadron 29 depicted in this sequence had to "take the barricade" on USS* Abraham Lincoln *(CVN 72). This rare event is one for which flight deck crews must always be prepared. This aircraft has grabbed a landing wire, one of the four cross-deck pendants rigged across the landing area of the flight deck, but the barrier will arrest a plane even if no wire is engaged.*

Below: *USS* George Washington's *(CVN 73) flight deck crew positions a barricade during a practice drill. The barricade is used for emergency arrestments when an aircraft has difficulty with its landing or tail hook system. The crew practices regularly so that it can raise the barrier within minutes. The barricade may not be needed for months, but when the occasion arises, the training for its eventuality can pay off with the saving of the lives of a crew and a multi-million dollar aircraft.*

many phases of shipboard operations, the work is still physically draining. Plane captains carry heavy tie-down chains over their shoulders. "Purple-shirts" from the fueling division haul heavy hoses across the flight deck. Flight deck directors must exercise fierce and often exhausting concentration and become masters at signaling aircraft through narrow openings on the deck. When the ship adds power to achieve launch and recovery speeds, the forces of wind, jet-blast, the heat of jet-blast, and the ear-cracking noise of aircraft engines powering up and igniting afterburners for catapult launch, combine to make the flight deck a very high-hazard area.

In reference to plane captains, to whom much of the drudgery falls, one observer said: "With weighty tie-down chains draped over their shoulders, they walked from one end of the flight deck to the other, often in the face of twenty-five-knot winds. They toted cumbersome parking chocks, helped lug serpentine refueling

241

Above: *Aircraft are tremendously susceptible to corrosion damage from salt spray. A plane captain from the "Bluetails" of Airborne Early Warning Squadron 122 scrubs down the underside of the enormous radar dome on a squadron E-2C Hawkeye on board USS* George Washington *(CVN 73).*

Right: *Foreign Object Damage (FOD) walk-downs are regular events on board aircraft carriers. All hands participate in the search for "foreign objects which could cause damage" to aircraft, especially to jet engines as they spool up during start-up and launch evolutions. Here, personnel of USS* Nimitz *(CVN 68) in the Pacific in August 1992 do their duty.*

Above: *Firefighting is an important element in the training of all surface warriors from seaman to captain. Firefighting and damage control training never ends, and can be a key determinant in the equation of ultimate victory during combat at sea.*

Opposite, top: *This HH-46D Sea Knight was badly damaged during shipboard operations. The craftsmen and women of Naval Aviation Depot, Cherry Point, North Carolina, rebuilt the airplane, returning it to service.*

Opposite, bottom: *A T-45 Goshawk trainer is being prepared for a catapult launch from the bow catapult of the carrier assigned for training. This airplane replaces the aging T-2Cs and TA-4J.*

hoses, and occasionally had to push airplanes into position. They labored in an arena of spinning propellers that could slice a person to pieces in an instant, jet intakes with lethal suction power, and wind blasts from both jets and propeller-driven machines that would sweep a man overboard into the sea, a long one hundred feet below.

"Compounding the physical hazards was the pressure of meeting launch times, ensuring that aircraft were ready to go precisely as scheduled. In concert with their counterparts in the other air wing squadrons and personnel from the ship's own air department work force, the plane captains were at the very heart of carrier operations and always under the scrutiny of the captain and other senior officers."

Three levels of aircraft maintenance exist in naval aviation, two of them on board the aircraft carriers and at naval air stations ashore. The first is at the squadron level. Each squadron has a maintenance department manned by 150 to 200 enlisted personnel. These highly trained sailors service the aircraft; ensure they are safe for flight; conduct scheduled checks of the engine, hydraulic, electronic, oxygen, and fuel systems; repair and replace certain malfunctioning equipment; and perform all-important corrosion control. Exposure to sea spray, rain, sand-laden wind, and other elements causes corrosion in the aircraft that can detrimentally affect their structural integrity. Fighting corrosion is a never-ending job.

The second level of maintenance is the ship's or naval air station's aircraft intermediate maintenance department. With more capability, they work closely with the squadrons to keep the air wing's aircraft up and ready. Technicians in this department can make internal repairs to complex electronic equipment and, in many cases, manufacture precision parts needed for an aircraft.

The third and highest level of maintenance is conducted at naval aviation depots. Three large and effective depots exist: one at Marine Corps Air Station, Cherry Point, North Carolina; a second at Naval Air Station, Jacksonville, Florida;

and the third at Naval Air Station North Island, San Diego, California. Whole aircraft, aircraft engines, and a broad spectrum of aircraft components and support equipment are overhauled here. The depots are commanded by naval or Marine officers and feature some of the most skilled technicians and craftsmen in the aviation defense industry field. They can dismantle aircraft, replace worn-out or damaged sections and components, and totally rebuild them. Technological upgrades to airframes and to the inner workings of aircraft are installed at the depots. Months may be required to refurbish aircraft but when returned to the fleet their condition enables them to operate for many more years.

Like people, aircraft carriers need rest. On a scheduled basis some years apart, carriers must retire to shipyards like those in Portsmouth, Virginia, and Bremerton, Washington, for major repairs and improvements. The nuclear-powered carriers must go into the shipyard to refuel approximately every twenty years.

Training aviators is the job of the Naval Air Training Command, a widespread network of air stations, instructors, and aircraft. The "Cradle of Naval Aviation," where most historians agree naval aviation began in 1911, is Pensacola, Florida. All prospective pilots, naval flight officers, and enlisted aircrewmen are indoctrinated here, moving on to other bases for specialized instruction depending

243

Top: *The F-14 is the Navy's premier fighter aircraft and with the Phoenix missile system, the Tomcat has deadly teeth for any foes. This "Vampire" F-14B radar intercept officer is flanked by "Vandy 1," the world's only all-black F-14 of the operational evaluation testing squadron, VX-9. (Photo: Ted Carlson/Fotodynamics)*

Above: *The workhorse CH-46 Sea Knight helicopter is a master of vertical replenishment, "VERTREP"—moving food, bombs, parts, and other necessities from logistics support ships to warships.*

Above, right: *The Super Hornet's weapon load potential includes, besides a variety of bombs, the Sidewinder on the wingtip, the Sparrow missile with the white nose section, and Advanced Medium-Range Air-to-Air Missiles, mounted inboard toward the fuselage. The large tank directly under the fuselage is for fuel. Newer weapons the Super Hornet carries (but not shown in this view) are the Joint Direct Attack Munition, the Joint Stand-Off Weapon, and the Standoff Land Attack Missile–Extended Range.*

on the community to which they are assigned: strike-fighter, maritime patrol, rotary wing, airborne early warning, electronic countermeasures, or logistics transport.

All aviation officer candidates fly the T-34C Turbo Mentor in the primary phase of instruction. Rotary wing pilots then fly TH-57 helicopters for intermediate and advanced training. Strike fighter (F/A-18, F-14) pilots fly T-2C Buckeyes or the new T-45 Goshawk that is replacing the Buckeyes.

Naval flight officers get their instruction in T-44s and T-2Cs before completing their training. Those destined for E-2C Hawkeye or C-2 Greyhound duty go through their final training at the cognizant fleet replacement squadron and earn their wings there. In the case of the electronic countermeasures officers who fly in the EA-6B Prowler, they fly the twin-engine, jet powered T-1A, T-2C, and T-39 aircraft.

The length of training depends on the community to which an aviator is destined, but it usually takes a year and a half from indoctrination to the awarding of wings. Candidates must be college graduates, highly motivated, and physically fit to qualify for naval flight training. Aircrewmen are enlisted personnel who go on to various assignments, prime among them duty in helicopters as rescue swimmers, rescue hoist operators, or gunners in armed helicopters like the HH-60H Seahawk. The Training Command also schools the enlisted technicians who man the maintenance services of the fleet and operate the shipboard equipment.

Advances in technology led to upgrades in older aircraft, sustaining them as viable warfighting implements. The advanced F/A-18E/F Super Hornet is basically a new airplane. The F/A-18E is the single-pilot version of this new airplane, while the F/A-18F's crew is a pilot and naval flight officer. These Super Hornets are to be the centerpiece of future carrier air wings and the heart of naval aviation's revolution in strike warfare.

The new Seahawk helicopter vastly increases the capabilities that now deploy

on board carriers in two versions, the SH-60F for antisubmarine warfare duty and the HH-60H for combat search and rescue missions. The Seahawk has been a boon to the often unheralded rotary wing community whose pilots number nearly half the pilots in naval aviation. The HH-60H version of the Seahawk engages in special operations with SEALs, and other units, and is integrated into carrier air wing operations.

In 1995, reflecting the aging nature of aircraft carriers, USS *Independence* was the oldest active ship in the Navy, a first for an aircraft carrier. On the other hand, replacements for older flattops came on the line during the 1990s, the *Nimitz*-class USS *George Washington* (CVN 73), USS *John C. Stennis* (CVN 74), and USS *Harry S. Truman* (CVN 75). In the twenty-first century, the Navy is taking advantage of technology to develop new and better aircraft carriers. Under construction in Newport News Shipbuilding in Virginia is USS *Ronald Reagan* (CVN 76), another of the *Nimitz* class. CVN 77, yet unnamed, has been authorized and will begin construction in 2001. The last of the *Nimitz*-class carriers, she will incorporate a new, integrated combat system and an improved island structure with multi-function, phased array radars, and other flat plane antennae.

CVNX 1 will follow CVN 77 and will include a new nuclear propulsion plant as well as new electrical generation and distribution systems. The three-fold increase in electrical capacity will enable replacing the high maintenance, steam-powered systems with more efficient electrical ones. The replacement of steam catapults with electromagnetic catapults will reduce topside weight and require fewer personnel to operate and maintain. CVNX 2 will incorporate major changes in hull and internal arrangements, using re-configurable, modular construction. The planned changes will include a new flight deck design, an electromagnetic aircraft recovery system, and continuing advancements in electronics to reduce manning requirements and life-cycle costs.

If today's navy aircraft carrier is not a floating metropolis, it is at least a floating town. Populated by 6,000 uniformed citizens, roughly half from ship's company, half from the air wing—men and women—it can operate around the clock virtually anywhere on the planet covered by water. Although dimensions vary, the following numbers, based on *Harry S. Truman*, give an idea of the enormity of a carrier. The flight deck is 1,096 feet long—as long as the Empire State Building is tall. The flight deck is 251 feet at its widest point. The area of the flight deck is four and a half acres. From the waterline to the top of the mast is a distance equal to a twenty-story building. The carrier displaces 97,000 tons. Carriers are steam-powered; older ones use oil-fired boilers but all others, and those being built, are driven by nuclear power. *Truman* has two reactors. Four, five-bladed screws, each weighing 66,200 pounds, can drive the carrier at a top speed in excess of 30 knots.

Above, left: A SH-60H Seahawk helicopter from Helicopter Antisubmarine Squadron 7 flies plane guard on the port quarter of USS Theodore Roosevelt *(CVN 71). In the event of an aircraft mishap, the helicopter can rapidly swoop to the scene to rescue survivors. The flight crew includes a rescue swimmer.*

Above, right: Aircraft carriers are built at Newport News Shipbuilding in Newport News, Virginia. Here, in an example of modular construction, the island structure of USS George Washington *(CVN 73) is being lifted intact to be installed on the carrier's hull.*

The flight deck of USS Theodore Roosevelt *(CVN 71) covers about four and a half acres, but that does not leave much room when the air wing is embarked. Maneuvering this F/A-18 Hornet into a parking place requires many hands besides the tractor driver's.*

Top, left: *Head of the Air Department in an aircraft carrier is the "Air Boss," who is responsible for the safe conduct of flight operations. Commander Robert Snyder, shown here in a blue jersey—normally the air boss wears a yellow one—was Air Boss on USS* George Washington *(CVN 73). His station, aft on the island structure and referred to as "Primary"—for Primary Flight Control— allows him to view virtually the entire flight deck. He is in constant communication with the deck force below, the combat information center within the ship, and with the captain of the carrier on his bridge located forward on the island. The coordination between the Air Boss, the Landing Signal Officers, the flight deck crew, and the captain requires continuous communication.*

Top, right: *Flight deck crew members on board USS* Independence *(CV 62) hustle oxygen tanks toward parked aircraft for servicing. Aviators that routinely fly above 10,000 feet wear oxygen masks throughout their missions.*

Above: *Air Traffic Controller Second Class Jamie Bradley communicates to carrier-based aircraft from her console in the Carrier Air Traffic Control Center (CATC) in USS* Kitty Hawk *(CV 63). CATC controllers handle aerial traffic in the vicinity of the ship establishing departure routes and guiding returning aircraft to marshal points where they receive detailed approach information, and when the weather is bad, detailed guidance all the way to touch down in a controlled approach.*

A carrier's facilities and operational elements range from a cobbler shop to closed-circuit TV studio; weapons magazines deep down in the ship to an air traffic control center; a chapel to a vast and ever-critical engineering complex; galleys to ready rooms; berthing spaces to the captain's bridge—and hundreds of spaces in between. The ship contains roughly 2,700 compartments, 2,000 telephones, and an air conditioning plant weighing 2,900 tons and powerful enough to service 950 homes. The distillation plants can make 400,000 gallons of fresh water per day capacity, enough to serve 2,000 homes. There are more than 900 miles of cable and wiring in the carrier and 30,000 light fixtures.

The hardware means little without skilled and motivated people to operate it. In air traffic control, for instance, the controllers direct the flow of air wing aircraft through the sometimes crowded skies. A mistake made in air traffic control can have devastating results. The navigator, who works the plotting board on the captain's bridge, has no room for error. The supply department must feed this population and supply all its needs—from toothpaste to microchips. A Marine detachment on board is responsible for the security of the weapons stowed on the ship, among other duties. The engineering department has the never-ending duty to keep the vessel moving through the water and providing the many utility services. The medical department takes care of routine medical and dental problems, but must also be able to respond to a catastrophe.

Ship's company personnel labor as hard as those in the air wing, and a pervasive sense of teamwork normally exists as the two elements focus on the primary mission of the aircraft carrier—projecting air power wherever and whenever required. The carrier may be a floating town but it is a metropolis of power and might manned by a predominantly youthful assembly of hard-working, skilled, and dedicated men and women.

The result of the attention to detail in maintenance, training, and process is a remarkable record of safety. For the most part, accident rates have been declining for years. By the turn of the century, the mishap rate for Navy aircraft was the lowest in history, less than two major mishaps for every 100,000 hours flown. This remarkable achievement, in spite of the many deployments into danger zones and the enormous pressures imposed by combat operations, reflected great credit upon industry, naval aviation training, and the caliber of personnel who maintain and operate the precious aircraft of the fleet.

It is fitting that the last year of the decade witnessed carrier battle groups at their potent best. Five of these battle groups engaged in combat. Typically, at the

beginning of the new century, on any given day, one third of the ships of the fleet were at sea and half of those were deployed abroad.

In December 1998, *Enterprise* and her air wing mounted a four-night assault on Iraqi military targets in response to that government's refusal to comply with United Nations arms inspection requirement. Shortly after, during a planned attack as part of enforcement of the Iraqi no-fly zone, the Joint Stand-Off Weapon was introduced in combat. Three F/A-18 Hornet pilots from USS *Carl Vinson* (CVN 70) simultaneously fired a Joint Stand-Off Weapon and each scored a direct hit on the intended target, a major surface-to-air missile site. In subsequent operations, fourteen more Joint Stand-Off Weapons were fired, all precisely striking the target areas. The weapon led the Navy into the new century of strike warfare. Using inertial guidance and global positioning satellite accuracy, the Joint Stand-Off Weapon can be released from aircraft at great distances from the target with deadly accuracy and with minimum risk to the launching aircraft. The Joint Direct Attack Munition and the Standoff Land Attack Missile–Extended Range were weapons also introduced.

Suppression of enemy defenses has always been a key mission, but recognizing what these new weapons portend for the future, destruction of enemy defenses is now the goal. Rather than deterring an enemy surface-to-air missile from launching through electronic jamming or other means so that a strike flight could safely reach its target, the objective is to demolish it, permanently deleting it from the enemy's weapons' inventory.

The air campaign against Serbian aggression in Kosovo in 1999 appeared to be primarily a U.S. Air Force show. The theater seemed tailor-made for land-based air power. The geopolitical boundaries favored NATO. Allied countries surrounded the area in question. The access to numerous, well-equipped bases was politically easy and relatively convenient. Moreover, thirteen NATO allies contributed military forces to the effort, including 300 aircraft that flew approximately 15,000 sorties during the seventy-eight-day campaign. However, even in this environment favorable to land-based air power, naval aviation contributed 226 aircraft, or roughly two-thirds of the assets provided by all the allies combined. The Hornets, Prowlers, and Tomcats of Carrier Air Wing 8 flying from *Theodore Roosevelt* destroyed or damaged a total of 447 tactical targets and eighty-eight fixed targets. Prowlers from the carrier air wing and Navy and Marine EA-6Bs operating from Aviano, Italy, not only provided all the electronic warfare support, they fired nearly half of all the HARMs employed. Prowler support was vital for the missions

Top: *This F/A-18E Super Hornet is carrying 14,000 pounds of ordnance. Included in the weapons load are two 2,000-pound bombs, two air-to-ground Mark 88 anti-radiation missiles, and two Sidewinder missiles. Compared to its predecessor, the Super Hornet features increased fuel capacity, engine power, mission radius, and weapon stations. These characteristics increase the plane's ability to remain on station during combat air patrol scenarios.*

Above: *Attack Squadron 34 Intruder flight crews in their ready room on board USS* George Washington *(CVN 73) review navigation charts and kneeboard cards in preparation for a low-level training mission over Spain. In 1996, the squadron transitioned to the F/A-18 Hornet strike-fighter, becoming Strike Fighter Squadron 34.*

A plume of 800-degree fire from a Tomcat of Fighter Squadron 14 strikes the jet blast deflector on board USS Theodore Roosevelt *(CVN 71). The pilot has actuated his after burner and is about to be catapulted on a night mission over Kosovo during United Nations–sponsored operations in the Balkans.*

flown by U.S. Air Force and other NATO tactical aircraft. F-14s flew as Forward Air Controllers Airborne with notable success. Their mission was to detect targets on the ground, guide strike forces to the scene, establish the direction and timing of attack runs, altitudes to be used, and type ordnance to be dropped. And the Joint Stand-Off Weapon appeared again with a staggering 100 percent success rate.

Those who complete the screening process to become naval aviators are young men and women in outstanding physical and mental condition. But the most important commodity they must possess is the determination to become a naval aviator. The ground school curriculum through the training command is clear-cut and demanding. The pathway to gold wings does not consist of eight-hour days. As candidates gain confidence, moving along through the program, the road gets a bit smoother, but not much. At the end comes the carrier qualification phase for those selected for carrier-based duty.

It is the ability to take off from and land on a moving ship that sets naval aviators apart from all others. This evolution never becomes routine, particularly at night. During the Vietnam War electrodes were taped to the chests of pilots on

combat missions to measure their anxiety levels. Their anxiety during landing on the carrier at night exceeded that while under fire. In one sense these carrier pilots at the "pointed end of the spear," as a forward-deployed carrier strike force is sometimes called, are an elitist group, warriors of the highest order. Only a special kind of man or woman has both the skill and determination to be able to maneuver extremely expensive, powerful high technology flying machines from catapult launch to target area, back to the carrier, and then, from the high skies downward, land that machine in a space only 600 feet long, day or night, in all kinds of weather.

While it is a sad commentary on our civilization that wars happen with frustrating frequency, it is reassuring that the Navy's aircraft carrier battle groups are available to protect American interests or to conduct humanitarian operations on short notice, around the world, day or night. This presence is a credit to the defense industries that provide the fleet the tools with which to do the job. But above all else, it reflects with utmost honor on the dedicated performance of the hard-working young men and women who operate the ships and who maintain and fly the aircraft of the United States Navy.

A rainbow arches over a pair of Fighter Squadron 2 F-14D Tomcats on board USS Constellation *(CV 64) in the central Pacific in April 1997.* Constellation *was en route to the Persian Gulf on a regular six-month deployment.*

249

Dive! Dive!
Submarines in the New World Order

Captain James H. Patton, USN (Ret)

USS Seawolf (SSN 21), the quietest submarine in the world with twice the number of weapons of its predecessors. Originally planned to be a class of twenty-seven ships, the collapse of the Soviet Union resulted in that number being reduced to three—Seawolf, USS Connecticut (SSN 22), and USS Jimmy Carter (SSN 23).

When the Berlin Wall came down in 1989, the Submarine Force seemed to
have lost its mission and purpose for the second time in a half-century.
The first time occurred in the late 1940s, when conventional wisdom
held that the only mission submarines did well was interdict commerce
deep in an enemy's home waters. And since the next apparent peer competitor,
the Soviet Union, had interior lines of communication and little dependence upon
maritime trade, submarines were unnecessary. In a story of great tactical innovation
and technical invention, forward-thinking submariners, convinced that submarines
could do antisubmarine warfare—a critical mission considering the Soviet's large
and growing submarine fleet—developed the specific weapons and tactics to
accomplish that mission.

So well was their ASW mission accomplished that, after the implosion of the
Soviet Union, "new-think" held that the only mission submarines did well was to
threaten an opponent's navy. Considering that America's next military challenges
would involve projecting power ashore in major and minor regional conflicts against
entities with small if any forces, submarines were again seen as largely unnecessary.
The planned procurement of *Seawolf*-class submarines, which were much faster
and quieter than their predecessors of the *Los Angeles* class, and carried twice
the weapons, plummeted from twenty-seven to three: USS *Seawolf* (SSN 21),
USS *Connecticut* (SSN 22), and USS *Jimmy Carter* (SSN 23). Decommissioning of
existing SSNs, many well short of their useful life, resulted in force levels being
nearly halved—from about one-hundred to roughly fifty. Much of the supporting
infrastructure—submarine squadrons, bases, and submarine-associated Navy
laboratories—were also closed and consolidated as part of the peace dividend.

In many respects, the traditional silence with which the Submarine Force
did its work was its own worst enemy. For forty years, submarine peacetime
and planned wartime operations were so cloaked in secrecy, and their value so
taken for granted, that added to an intrinsic reluctance to talk was an inability

USS Alaska *(SSBN 732) returns from
patrol through the Straits of Juan de Fuca
and Puget Sound. Although the Bangor,
Washington, base is one hundred miles from
open ocean, the waters are deep enough
for submarines to transit submerged most
of the way if advisable.*

Crew members from USS Billfish *(SSN 676),
a* Sturgeon-*class SSN, walk on the icecap
at the North Pole. The* Sturgeon *class was
designed for through-ice operations including
the ability to rotate the fairwater planes to
the vertical to facilitate breaking through
the ice. The top of the sail was specially
hardened, and masts and antennas could
be lowered below this cap to shelter.*

251

Exercise Mark 48 torpedoes being readied for loading. Exercise torpedoes are designed to surface at the end of their programmed run, and are refurbished, refueled, and reused. Most U.S. submarines can carry up to about two dozen weapons.

to articulate the value added by submarines in a post-Soviet world. For example, at a war game at the Naval War College, players considered submerged, covert transits of passages such as the Strait of Hormuz by nuclear attack submarines impractical because such waters were deemed too shallow and too narrow. Following a clarification of submarine capabilities by operational commanders, such operations became routine within a year.

Since submarines had greatly aided the deterrence of global war for four decades, a common misperception was that deterring regional war on a global basis would be a less demanding task. That perception was wrong. Much of the new tasking is harder but just as valuable, so much so that high-level reviewing agencies with access to the nature and results of submarine operations have resoundingly endorsed the submarine's utility in the current environment. The Defense Science Board, for example, described the nuclear attack submarine as the "crown jewel" of the defense establishment. In addition, many small and mid-size countries have recognized that the most cost-effective way to contest entry into their littoral waters is with very quiet non-nuclear submarines with modern torpedoes and antiship cruise missiles. These platforms often have some degree of air independent

Above: *What the approach officer sees as he orders a practice torpedo fired at the aircraft carrier with whom he is exercising. If his intent is to use the full range capability of the Mark 48 torpedo, the size of the silhouette of the carrier will be less than twenty percent of that in this photograph.*

The physics of sound in the sea are very complicated yet they govern much of a submarine's operations, sensors, and weapons performance. Modern torpedoes are precision-guided munitions that use sonar to detect and then steer to hit the target. People must build the instructions for the torpedo's computer, for though computers can assist, the environment is too complex for automatic instruction.

Left, top to bottom: *Torpedoes are fired against real targets regularly to ensure the weapons perform as expected when needed. Every operation, real and exercise, demonstrates that making holes in the bottom of a ship to let water in is vastly more effective than making holes in the top to let air out.*

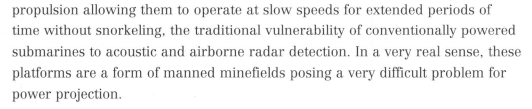

propulsion allowing them to operate at slow speeds for extended periods of time without snorkeling, the traditional vulnerability of conventionally powered submarines to acoustic and airborne radar detection. In a very real sense, these platforms are a form of manned minefields posing a very difficult problem for power projection.

253

The upper level of the missile compartment on USS Michigan *(SSBN 727) is a common place for joggers on the ship to run laps. Submariners have nicknamed this compartment "Sherwood Forest."*

A submarine broaches following a test of her emergency blow system. Following the loss of Thresher *in 1963, all U.S. submarines were built or backfitted to have the ability to rapidly deballast in the event of a flooding casualty. The system is tested each quarter on every submarine.*

Today, as in the past forty years, the capabilities that the nuclear submarine offers military planners are stealth (presence is typically unknown), mobility (arriving quickly), and endurance (operating on location covertly for months). The submarine is also unique in that it requires no escorts or supports, has virtually no logistic requirements once deployed, and one unit is a militarily significant quantity—unlike one tank, one airplane, or one surface warship. Since submarines are now being built with nuclear cores that will last the entire lifetime of the ship, fuel is not a recurring expense. It costs no more to have the ship at sea than it does to have it in port.

Because routine submarine operations are covert, submarines are "The Great Black Fleet." With an average of half of the force at sea every day and half of those on some kind of local operation, a quarter of the force is therefore deployed out of home waters. Even with a force level of fifty, these deployed units, if spread somewhat homogeneously over the world oceans, would always place some unit no more than about a thousand miles from any littoral, within Tomahawk cruise missile range, and no more than two days' steaming distance. Since in this post-Soviet era the intelligence community has revised its promise of unambiguous strategic warning from two weeks to two days, such an employment concept fits well with modern naval missions. As for units attached to carrier battle groups, existing and evolving connectivity capabilities allow a unit to be well out of the immediate vicinity and yet remain under operational control. In many scenarios nuclear submarines attached to a carrier battle group can best support that command by preparing the battlefield thousands of miles distant.

The mystique of submarining got a significant public boost when the U.S. Naval Institute published its first work of fiction, Tom Clancy's *The Hunt for Red October*. The Paramount Pictures movie is now a classic. The result was the immediate increase in the number of volunteers entering submarine service. Submariners were amused to observe that almost the only thing reviewers saw as incredulous was a submarine leaping half out of the water following an emergency blowing of main ballast tanks. Yet this evolution is performed by all submarines once a calendar quarter to validate the proper functioning of a system, a legacy stemming from the tragic loss of USS *Thresher* (SSN 593) in 1963.

A major display in the Smithsonian's National Museum of American History is another tribute to the Submarine Force's often-unheralded participation in the Cold War. Opened in the spring of 2000 to coincide with the Submarine Force's one-hundredth anniversary, this display visually and audibly captures previously secret operations carried on during the four decades of the Cold War. Those close to submariners during this era, including spouses, knew little of the nature of these operations. After 300 days a year at sea, the answers to the questions, "Where did you go?" invariably was, "Out," and to "What did you do?" was, "Nothing."

Reductions in strategic armaments began long before the Cold War ended. However, even with the end of Soviet Union, existence of nuclear weapons mandated that the country's nuclear deterrent had to be maintained. But what was once a massive nuclear-armed triad of silo-based intercontinental ballistic missiles, many long-range bombers, and forty-one ballistic missile submarines, has evolved primarily to fourteen *Ohio*-class submarines each armed with twenty-four long-range and extremely accurate Trident missiles. Although some land-based missiles and nuclear weapons-capable bombers still exist, the majority of this country's nuclear weapons are based in submarines. Backfitting the first four of the eighteen *Ohio*-class submarines from the original Trident missile to the newer Trident II has long been abandoned. The removal of these ships from service rests on arms limitation treaties and proposals still under consideration. But even after they leave the ranks of the strategic forces, these submarines will have significant life remaining. Now under consideration is a proposal for their conversion to tactical vice strategic platforms, armed with up to 154 land-attack Tomahawk missiles and able to deliver as many as sixty Special Forces personnel in two Advanced Swimmer Delivery Vehicles.

Nothing better characterizes the U.S. Submarine Force than the degree and quality of the associated training, particularly since the advent of nuclear power. The Naval Submarine School at Groton, Connecticut, has both officer and enlisted students and teaches the widest range of subjects and students in the Naval Training Command. Nuclear Power School at Orlando, Florida, teaches college-level math, chemistry, and nuclear physics to enlisted high school graduates and postgraduate

An exercise missile is fired from USS Ulysses S. Grant *(SSBN 631) near Cape Canaveral, Florida. Regular exercises demonstrate the missile system's accuracy and reliability, and the crew's expertise in employing it. Such exercises made deterrence credible during the Cold War, and continue to do so.*

Many modern submarines have transited the Panama Canal. All of the Ohio *class were built in Connecticut, but half of them are based in the Pacific. One, USS* Nevada *(SSBN 733), negotiates Gaillard Cut en route to the base at Bangor, Washington.*

Top: *Specialized "wet trainers" at submarine training facilities expose crew members to repairing sea water leaks at pressures up to 200 pounds per square inch.*

Above: *Preparing six meals a day in a space about the size of a large pickup truck or van is a challenge. Add that most meals serve between forty and a hundred people, and the size of the challenge becomes clearer. There are no secondary suppliers on submarines and little space to stow supplies. The galley is the bakery and scullery as well as kitchen and butcher shop.*

Above, right: *Submarine food is considered the best in the services, and good food is generally available all day. Here, the captain and officers enjoy a meal with holiday decorations on board the USS* Blueback *(SS 581).*

level courses in the same subjects to recently commissioned officers, most from technical and engineering colleges of the first caliber. Both enlisted and officer personnel who will operate the reactor plants then undergo six months of hands-on technical training and qualification examinations at land-based naval nuclear power plants or special training ships before reporting to their first assignment. Extensive formal training facilities exist ashore in every submarine homeport, and training devices on board the ships permit replication of many scenarios and evolutions for teaching purposes.

On board ship, an intensive qualification program exists, not only to certify individuals to stand specific watches or operate designated equipment, but also to demonstrate a thorough knowledge of the ship's systems and emergency procedures.

TACAMO—THE AIRBORNE COMMUNICATIONS STATION: TACAMO, allegedly an acronym for "TAke Charge And March Off," is a mobile communication system that adds survivability to the already robust communications architecture that ensures, should the necessity arise, that ballistic missile submarines on patrol receive orders to launch under any condition. Continually airborne from the late sixties to the early nineties, these aircraft provided connectivity between the National Command Authority and the submarine missile forces even in the most extreme conditions where all other communications systems had been destroyed by a "bolt out of the blue" surprise attack. To ensure an airplane was airborne 100 percent of the time over both the Atlantic and Pacific, alert planes and crews were always standing by at Travis Air Force Base, California, or Patuxent River Naval Air Station, Maryland, and other fields on both coasts.

The specially configured C-130s that served during the bulk of the Cold War and their reliefs, the E-6A Mercury, push the aircrafts' aerodynamic envelope when required to transmit. Transmissions are required frequently for training and system validation. When transmitting, the airplane must maintain a tight circle (a 25- to 40-degree bank at ten knots above stall speed—a 1.5G pull on the crew) while streaming a mile-long antenna hanging as vertically as possible. The message is then transmitted by very low frequency (VLF) radio on circuits constantly monitored by the deployed strategic missile submarines on alert. These aircraft are considered so critical to the total nuclear defense structure, that when standing by at a Strategic Air Command (SAC) base, the TACAMO is the first in line to take off in an alert—ahead of the SAC bombers.

In 1989 the Boeing E-6A replaced the C-130s in this assignment, and homeport for squadrons on both coasts was shifted to Tinker Air Force Base, Oklahoma. Although no longer operating to maintain 100 percent airborne coverage, aircraft are deployed continuously on field alert at Tinker, Patuxent River, and other locations. Now configured for duty not only as airborne radio stations, the new aircraft relieved the Air Force's Airborne Command Posts. In their new role, TACAMO carries the Strategic Command Battle Staff, code named "Looking Glass," and is able to launch land-based missiles from silos in the center of the country and control bombers assigned to the Strategic Command.

The E-6A TACAMO is the Navy's largest airplane. Flying with a crew of sixteen plus an airborne battle staff, and capable of refueling in the air, the aircraft can stay airborne for seventy-two hours. Communications equipment on board ranges from extremely high frequency satellite systems to the only very low frequency transmitter operating on a mobile platform.

On average, a year of practical training is required to earn the proud emblem of the submarine service—dolphins, silver for enlisted and gold for officers.

Advanced training and qualification continues on board and ashore. Enlisted personnel study for advancement in rank and to qualify to stand more responsible watch stations. Officers generally attend an advanced course at the Submarine School in preparation to serve as a department head. A difficult comprehensive examination at the Office of Naval Reactors must be passed before assignment as an engineer officer, and even prospective commanding officers must undergo further training at both Naval Reactors Branch and the Type Commanders' Course before being allowed to serve as a captain.

Six submarine bases exist in the United States—four for attack submarines (SSNs) and two for ballistic missile submarines (SSBNs). The attack submarines' homeports are New London, Connecticut; Norfolk, Virginia; San Diego, California; and Pearl Harbor, Hawaii. The homeports for strategic submarines are Kings Bay,

The insignia of the Submarine Force, Dolphins—designed by then Captain Ernest J. King in the 1920s—represents a great deal of effort on the part of its recipients. Less than five percent of the Navy's personnel are qualified in submarines.

Below: *The USS* Columbus *(SSN 762) underway on the surface. Many of the ship's masts, periscopes, and antennas can be seen in their stowed position. The fairing running down the starboard (right-hand) side of the ship houses an acoustic array, which is streamed after the ship submerges. Also visible are some of the twelve vertical launch tubes at the very front of the bow. These tubes were added to later ships of the class for Tomahawk cruise missiles. Those missiles can also be stored inboard and fired from the ship's four torpedo tubes.*

Below, right: *Even people who have served on these ships do not gain a true appreciation of their size until they see them on the blocks in drydock. USS* Minneapolis-St. Paul *(SSN 708) is docked in the floating drydock, USS* Resolute *(AFDM 10), at Naval Station, Norfolk.*

Georgia, and Bangor, Washington. Deployed submarines are supported at La Madelena, Sardinia; Guam in the Marianas; and Yokuska, Japan.

All these sites have maintenance facilities, either on shore or in a submarine tender. Before 1990, these tenders provided most support serving as logistic caches, arsenals, and workshops. Today, only two tenders remain active and most maintenance activity has been moved ashore.

During the mid-1970s, at the height of the Cold War, the submarine-launched cruise missile entered into nuclear arms equations almost as a bargaining chip. Although the nuclear capability was eliminated in an arms limitation agreement, other variants of the concept of a tactical missile were explored. By 2000, the conventionally armed and extremely accurate Tomahawk became well known to readers and watchers of the media. By then such weapons were carried not only by submarines but also in cruisers and destroyers, and became the weapons of choice for quick and accurate strikes at fixed targets. The increasing role of submarines in such strikes is evident. During the Gulf War in 1991, four percent of the Tomahawks fired into Iraq

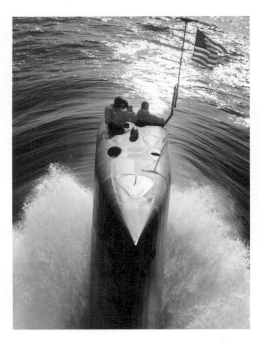

258

were launched from submarines. During the 1999 Kosovo/Serbian operations, that percentage had risen to twenty-five percent. Research continues into other long-range strike weapons systems, either new or modifications of existing ones such as the Army's Advanced Tactical Missile System. These efforts seek to enable call-fire support for special forces, Marine, or Army units ashore, with ordnance arriving on targets hundreds of kilometers away in only a few minutes after the target is identified.

Having supported swimmer operations during World War II and since, missions with the special forces, Navy SEALs, or Army/Air Force counterparts are not new. Because their numbers are small, these forces must come into action covertly; that aspect of their character is obviously enhanced by using the submarine as the transport vehicle. Substituting surprise for mass is a fundamental of submarine warfare in all its aspects.

Submarines have always been expensive and difficult to build, and their weapons and sensor systems take a long time to develop and implement. Post–Cold War military economies imposed limits on both design and construction costs so that

Above, left: *A Tomahawk cruise missile being loaded into a* Los Angeles-*class SSN. Submarine-based Tomahawks make up a significant portion of the Navy's inventory of these weapons.*

Top and above: *Over 85 percent of the space inside the submarine is occupied by machinery and equipment. Pipes and electrical wiring are everywhere, and sailors must know what is inside each, where to isolate it if there is a casualty, and what backups must be employed in an emergency. Studying to learn the equipment and procedures occupies most of the time not involved in operations or maintenance for the first two years of assignment to a submarine. Quiet, private places are rare: next to a torpedo or torpedo tube is not unusual.*

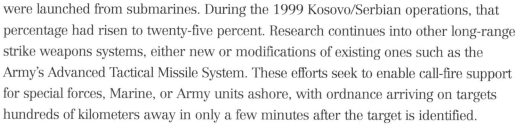

Opposite, top: *Two* Permit-*class attack boats, USS* Pollack *(SSN 603) and USS* Guardfish *(SSN 612), alongside their tender USS* Dixon *(AS 37). Submarine tenders are significant industrial complexes capable of virtually any repairs or maintenance. In addition they are storehouses for food, weapons, and a wide variety of goods and services. Only two tenders remain in service—one in Guam in the Western Pacific and one in Sardinia in the Mediterranean.*

Left: *One of two, the deep submergence rescue vehicle* Avalon *can piggy-back on a "mother" submarine, reach a bottomed submarine throughout its operating depth, and transfer twenty-four crew members on each trip. These mini-submarines can be air lifted in Air Force C5 transports.*

Above: *A port bow view of the nuclear-powered attack submarine USS* Buffalo *(SSN 715) underway during sea trials.*

Right: *Fires at sea are fearsome: in a submarine's closed atmosphere they are disastrous. Training facilities ashore, like this one at the Submarine School, allow techniques and procedures to be practiced, and self-confidence gained.*

Below: *There is little room to spare when a submarine begins a long patrol. On board the USS* Will Rogers *(SSBN 659), the missile compartment also serves as a makeshift pantry and bunkroom. (Photo: Steve Kaufman)*

customary methods were no longer adequate. Computer-based processing is now incorporated in every aspect of submarine design and construction. Previously a submarine hull was built on an inclined shipway and launched with only the largest major components inside. Then the rest of the internal systems were brought down piece by piece to be passed through a hatch or similar small opening and painstakingly assembled inside. Almost like building a ship in a bottle on a grand scale, this inefficient approach was eliminated when computer-aided design and manufacture made end-loading feasible. Today, entire systems in a compartment are pre-assembled in facilities remote from the shipways, sometimes where the entire assembly can be rotated to permit access. When completed, the assembly is slipped into the partially constructed cylindrical pressure hull inside a building hall on a gigantic railway before the next portion of the hull is welded on. Where previously the pipefitter had to allow an inch or so of extra length on each piece of pipe—which had to be painstakingly ground off for a precision fit—everything now matches almost exactly to the ends of those pipes already in place.

In a similar fashion, past practices in developing the specifications for submarine electronics, fire control, and processing capability resulted in fine equipment built to rigid standards that was several generations behind the state of the art when delivered to the fleet. Ship's computers were less capable than the crew's personal computers. But commercial products did not meet the shock, vibration, and environmental requirements necessarily demanded in the military environment. To take advantage of advanced commercial off-the-shelf equipment, today's military environmental and shock requirements are incorporated in the cabinets that hold the equipment rather than in the equipment itself. This concept enabled a vast improvement in sonar systems installed on submarines at a fraction of the previous cost and time. With this design, as commercial equipment improves, much less effort will be needed to further upgrade these systems.

USS Billfish *(SSN 676) under renovation in the floating drydock* Shippingport *(ARDM 4) in New London, Connecticut. When the construction of a submarine is substantially complete, the ship is moved to a drydock such as this to be launched. (Photo: © Yogi Kaufman)*

The crew's mess is the only place larger than a desktop not involved in operations around the clock when at sea. It is the only gathering and recreational space for the crew and serves as the study hall and schoolroom for the ship. Board games like Monopoly have been known to last an entire deployment, and card games are universally popular. Cribbage tournaments are particularly cutthroat affairs, and serious bridge can be found in many ships.

Opposite: *The submarine in this drydock at the Newport News Shipbuilding Company is completing her construction period. After the ship's sea trials, submarines are docked and inspected to ensure the exterior fittings have not been deformed. Very fast submarines have been known to lose pieces during their high-speed trial runs.*

Left: *The submarine's atmosphere is a closed system; fire or release of toxic gas poses the immediate threat of asphyxiation. In a general drill, the Ship's Control Party of USS* Nebraska *(SSBN 739) has donned masks and connected hoses to the Emergency Breathing System, which provides an independent reservoir of air.*

War games are conducted by all services to identify issues and insights involved with warfighting a decade or two in the future. A consistent theme emerging from these efforts is the great value of stealth. Modern weaponry, such as theater ballistic missiles, weapons of mass destruction, and integrated air defense systems, is proliferating in second- and third-tier countries; basing is less likely to be available in theaters of interest; and there is a clear preference to avoid personnel casualties. Weapon systems that adapt to these considerations increase in value. The nuclear submarine is the most obvious example of such a system.

The Missile Control Center of USS John C. Calhoun *(SSBN 630). A submarine on alert is ready to launch missiles within minutes of the president so ordering.*

Two intrinsic traits that the nuclear submarine brings to any operation are great mobility and long endurance. At the earliest signs of a potential problem, a submarine can be positioned quickly close to the area and remain there for an extended period of time. Not only does the submarine provide the national command authority a force on-station in near-real time, but the submarine's passive sensors allow unobserved monitoring. This type of covert intelligence, surveillance, and reconnaissance has proven invaluable in the past, and promises to be even more so in the future.

Research and development for future submarines include shifting to electric drive, increasing payload by a factor of ten to include significant employment of "adjuvant" or off-hull vehicles, furthering the ability to covertly detect, localize, and neutralize sea mines, and finally providing rapid fires ashore in support of early entry teams. The submarine that follows the *Virginia* class promises to be a remarkable vehicle. Whatever this ship becomes, it is certain that those characteristics that make today's submarine powerful—stealth, endurance, and mobility—will remain hallmarks.

United States submarines in the post–Soviet era, though fewer in number, have been assigned a wider variety of tasks. Because the older hulls have been decommissioned, both the attack submarines and ballistic missile submarines now consist of only relatively new units. The three submarines of the *Seawolf* class are

Left: *A forty-foot hull section is manipulated at a Quonset Point, Rhode Island, fabrication facility. Such automation not only greatly facilitates construction, but lowers costs substantially.*

Right: *The professional expertise needed to operate complex submarines is not taken for granted, or easily obtained. Students at Nuclear Power School at Orlando, Florida, study the details of the machinery they will operate: here, steam turbine blades and seals.*

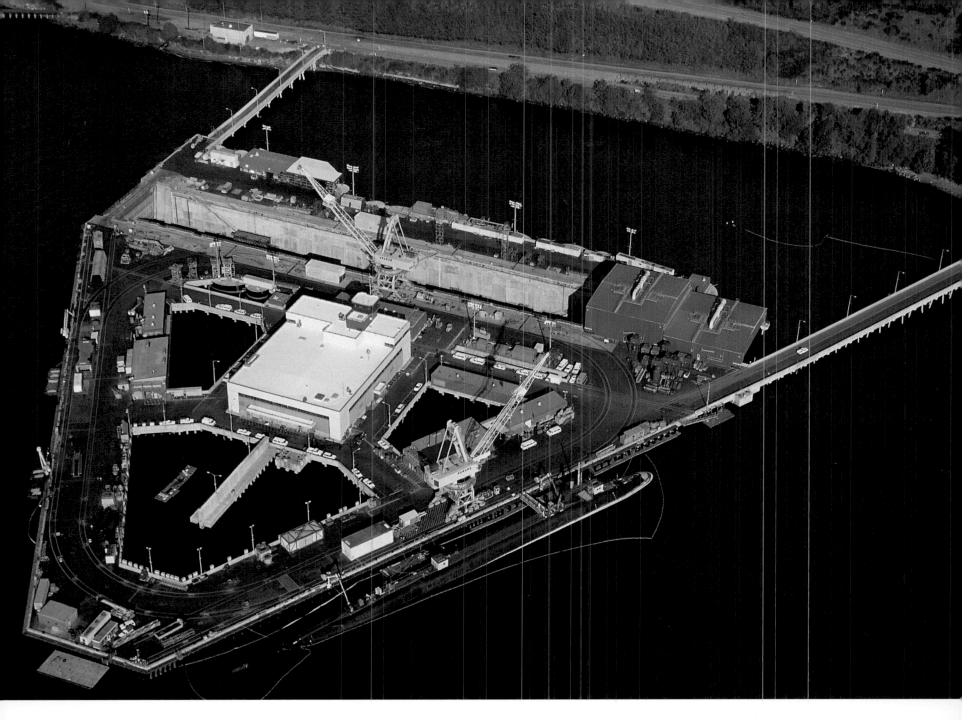

the largest, quietest, and fastest attack submarines in the world: *Seawolf* is said to be quieter at 20 knots than a *Los Angeles* class is when moored. The keel of the first of a new class of attack submarine, USS *Virginia* (SSN 774), was laid down in 1999. Although *Virginia* will be smaller and slower than its predecessor USS *Seawolf*, none of *Seawolf*'s extraordinary quietness will be relinquished.

All services are recognizing what a platform with stealth, mobility, firepower, and endurance can do when properly integrated into joint operations. Submarines can be tasked to locate and even covertly disable sea mines that deny access to surface ships to the littoral. Aviators, Navy and Air Force, can expect forward-deployed submarines to do much of the suppression of enemy air defenses that airplanes would otherwise have to accomplish before executing their primary missions. Marine and Army ground forces can anticipate a significant contribution to their fire support through submarine-launched cruise or tactical ballistic missiles. In addition, particularly during peacetime and the pre-hostility phase of any conflict, submarines will continue to provide the same non-provocative, high-quality intelligence, surveillance, and reconnaissance for which they are unsurpassed.

The Trident Refit Facility at the Submarine Base, Bangor, Washington, with a ballistic missile submarine moored alongside. The home of Submarine Group Nine, the Pacific strategic deterrent force, the base includes housing and the Trident Training Facility up the hill in the woods.

New Attack Submarine USS Virginia *(SSN 774) class will carry only about half the weapons capacity of its predecessor* Seawolf—*about the same as classes prior to* Seawolf —*but will relinquish none of* Seawolf's *extraordinary quietness.*

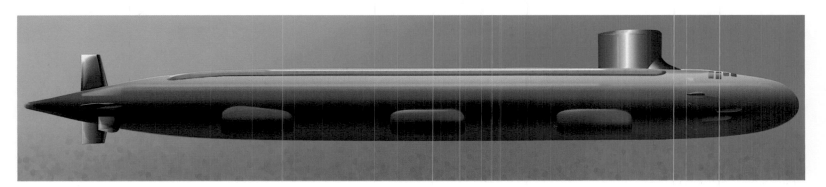

265

Land the Landing Force!

Amphibious Assault at the Turn of the Millennium

Captain George Galdorisi, USN (Ret)

The Past is Prologue

GATORS . . . Amphibs . . . tracks. The very names conjure up visions of scores, perhaps hundreds, of ships, boats, and craft moving toward a landing beach at an agonizingly slow speed reminiscent of the World War II–era assaults brought to the screen so vividly in movies such as *Saving Private Ryan*. It is an enduring image.

.   Until recently, this image was fairly accurate. The way the Navy and the Marine Corps organized, trained, and executed the amphibious warfare doctrine bore more of a resemblance to this mid-century paradigm than to the way warfare was evolving at the end of the twentieth century. Although some forward-thinking leaders worked hard to change the doctrine, strategy, and tactics, for much of the second half of the twentieth century, the American way of amphibious warfare envisioned the Navy and the Marines fighting the last war—the good war—again.

The Gulf War and the New Amphibious Assault Force

Journalists who chronicled the Gulf War focused primarily on the high-profile action—the bombing campaign, the cruise missiles hitting downtown Baghdad, and the lightning, armored assault through the desert. Most ignored the crucial role that the amphibious assault forces played in providing the leverage for that victory. This is unfortunate, and only partially because many of the actions of the sailors and Marines who made up those forces are overlooked. Desert Storm was a harbinger of the way the Navy–Marine Corps team that comprised the amphibious

Amphibious assault vehicles move from USS Gunston Hall *(LSD 44) toward a beach in Greece. New systems such as the new* San Antonio *(LPD 17), class amphibious transport dock, the V-22 Osprey, the Landing Craft, Air Cushion (LCAC), and the Advanced Amphibious Assault Vehicle (AAAV) promise to ensure that no beach will be out of reach.*

Opposite: A landing craft, air cushion (LCAC) approaches the gate of USS Peleliu *(LHA 5) preparing to come aboard. Amphibious assault ships like* Peleliu *carry a battalion of Marines and the helicopters and landing craft to take them into combat. (Photo: Dave Gatley/MAI)*

Cockpit view from an LCAC as it makes its approach to the well deck of USS Essex *(LHD 2) during RIMPAC exercises off Hawaii. (Photo: Rick Mullen)*

Top, right: *A landing craft, air cushion (LCAC) from Assault Craft Unit 4 heads toward the beach in Croatia during NATO–sponsored operations in the Balkans. These speedy vehicles can lift 60 tons at forty knots for over 200 miles. Their air cushion allows them to move up the beach to discharge their cargoes well clear of the water.*

Right: *Close cooperation within the Navy– Marine Corps team makes vertical assault successful. A CH-53E prepares to launch from the deck of USS* Denver *(LPD 9).*

Opposite, bottom: *A landing craft, air cushion (LCAC) heads toward shore after leaving the well deck of USS* Kearsarge *(LHD 3) as a second maneuvers to enter. These vehicles carry the 26th Marine Expeditionary Unit to Litoror, Greece, as part of NATO operations in Kosovo.*

assault force would be used throughout the 1990s and into the next century. Further, it is important to note accurately the way the amphibious assault force supported both the president's national security strategy and the Chairman of the Joint Chiefs of Staff's national military strategy.

Amphibious assault forces performed brilliantly in the Gulf War in what they accomplished directly and in what they enabled other coalition forces to do. The heroics of the Marines in blunting the Iraqi attack on Khafji in January 1991 are well chronicled, as are the lightning, coordinated attacks through Kuwait in February of that year—attacks that both stunned the Iraqi adversary and surprised the coalition planners. No one thought the Marines could advance as quickly and as successfully as they did—no one, that is, except the Marines themselves.

Less well heralded was the strategic advantage conferred by the amphibious task force whose presence tied up divisions of Iraqi troops along the western shoreline of the Persian Gulf, making the "left hook" through the desert as successful as it was. Documents captured from retreating Iraqi troops—as well as analysis conducted after the war—show the extent to which the very real and very visible threat of amphibious invasion from the sea complicated Iraqi defensive strategy and tactics tremendously.

The Gulf War also focused attention on many of the special capabilities of the Amphibious Ready Group/Marine Expeditionary Unit (Special Operations Capable), in short the ARG/MEU(SOC). These teams performed a wide range of actions from gas and oil platform takedowns, to amphibious raids and feints, to maritime interdiction operations, to specialized demolition operations. These and other operations highlighted during the Gulf War, became the paradigm for the amphibious assault force throughout the last decade of the century.

During the 1990s, the amphibious assault force became the force of choice in response to crises across the globe in areas as diverse as Somalia, Haiti, Bosnia, and Kenya, to name a few. The capabilities of the ARG/MEU team are truly unique and often represent the only force—from any nation—that can respond equally well providing forward presence, crisis response, power projection, special operations, humanitarian operations, and disaster relief, as well as the ability to task organize and function in many other capacities.

Not Your Grandfather's Amphibious Assault Force

Throughout the Cold War, and into the post–Cold War era, the first question that the national command authorities have asked in virtually every international crisis is, "Where are the carriers?" Increasingly, the question has evolved to, "Where is the carrier battle group—and where is the amphibious ready group." The missions that our military must perform today—and tomorrow—are in the littorals, where an amphibious ready group, supported by a carrier battle group, is the indispensable element to accomplish a host of missions.

The new national security paradigm focuses on using amphibious assault forces as the nation's enabling force—the 911 force—designed as the rapid response force to kick the door open and hold it open. This model has many other facets—

Landing craft, air cushion (LCAC) vehicles move Marines and their equipment to the beach rapidly, enabling the Marine Expeditionary Unit (Special Operations Capable) (MEU/SOC) to quickly build up combat power ashore. The light armored vehicle coming off this LCAC provides rapid exploitation of openings from the beachhead.

Above: USS Wasp *(LHD 1), the first multi-mission amphibious assault ship, is truly a vessel for all seasons, with its flight deck accommodations for landing force helicopters, Harriers, and Osprey tilt-rotor aircraft, and its ample well deck for launching air-cushion landing craft and assault amphibian vehicles.*

and a wide array of missions across a broad spectrum from peacetime operations to all-out war. The ability of the Navy–Marine Corps team to serve as the force of choice for the twenty-first century is critically dependent on three things: the sailors and Marines of the force, the missions that this force undertakes, and the world-class equipment that this force has at its disposal.

The men and women who make up the amphibious assault force are the indispensable element that makes this team unbeatable. The missions that this force has proven itself capable of performing make it certain that the Navy–Marine Corps team not only will be on call but will be active across the globe. The equipment, current and planned, that these forces use to accomplish their mission will give the amphibious ready group/Marine expeditionary unit team the edge over any foe in any situation.

People—Today's Amphibious Assault Sailors and Marines

It is no accident or coincidence that in their command briefings, every Navy amphibious group commander describes the Marine rifleman as "the ultimate smart weapon—the amphibious main battery." Put another way by General Charles C. Krulak, the Marine Corps' thirty-first Commandant, "Ultimately, it is the individual Marine—not machines or technology—that defines our success in war." It is also no accident or coincidence that in today's Marine Corps, as a matter of organizational doctrine, every Marine is a rifleman. In a service that is not large, this is not just a matter of convenience but a matter of necessity.

These Marines and the sailors who constitute the Navy arm of the amphibious assault force—the seamen who man the ships, the assault coxswains who drive the landing craft, the beachmasters who control the landing areas at the waterline, the Navy corpsmen who go into combat with their Marine brothers-in-arms— are a special breed within our military. They are essential elements of this force, the first to fight, the ones who can step ashore or fly inland from the sea to do the work of the republic.

Amphibious Assault Force Missions

The amphibious assault force—the amphibious ready group/Marine expeditionary unit team—often supported by a carrier battle group and by Air Force and Army forces, has evolved a host of missions that have become the regular military responses of the United States and our allies in this new millennium. The ARG/MEU team brings a robust, immediate response capability that also serves as an enabler for follow-on forces. Well prepared in both conventional and special operations, this force trains with all of the Navy's numbered fleets as integral parts of these Navy commands during normal and surge deployments. Additionally, as a key forward deployed asset, these amphibious assault teams are available to unified commanders worldwide.

The amphibious ready group/Marine expeditionary unit team is prepared to conduct operations in a benign or hostile environment—or anywhere in between—in response to tasking by the national command authorities. Their primary role is projecting naval power ashore through a full range of amphibious operations. In addition, the ARG/MEU team maintains its readiness to perform a wide range of missions other than war. These are the real-world missions that our amphibious assault forces find themselves conducting with increasing regularity.

This training is robust, dynamic, and challenging. The two-dozen Marine expeditionary unit missions are the focus of training for the Navy–Marine Corps team during the six months prior to deployment. If a mission is not successfully demonstrated during final pre-deployment work-up, the team undergoes

The Marine rifleman is the main battery of the ARG/MEU team and is trained to operate across a broad spectrum, from peacekeeping, to humanitarian operations, to noncombatant evacuation operations, to all-out warfare. (Photo: Greg Mathieson/MAI)

Opposite, top: *The V-22 Osprey provides the amphibious assault force with heavy lift to battlefields well beyond the beach line. The Osprey can lift a 155mm Howitzer or twenty-four combat-loaded Marines and move at 300 knots. (Photo: U.S. Naval Institute)*

Opposite, bottom: *Main control in USS* Essex *(LHD 2) is the center of the activity of the propulsion plant. Powered by two steam turbines,* Essex *can make more than twenty-four knots. Without engineers, the ship does not move. It becomes simply a steel camp that could be turned over to the Army.*

Left: *Landing craft utility LCU 1630 from USS* Fort McHenry *(LSD 43) carries armored vehicles during an amphibious assault exercise with sailors and marines from the Republic of Philippines. Exercising with forces of other nations is a major diplomatic mission of the Navy and Marine Corps.*

271

AMBHIBIOUS READY GROUP—MARINE EXPEDITIONARY UNIT
TASK ORGANIZATION AND FORCES ASSIGNED:

AMPHIBIOUS READY GROUP

- *Amphibious Squadron Command Element and embarked detachments, including air control, special warfare, beachmaster unit, assault craft unit, explosive ordnance disposal, and fleet surgical unit.*

- *LHA/LHD—Multi-Mission Amphibious Assault Ship—Over 40,000 tons displacement, 1,000 ship's crew/1,870 troops, three LCAC capacity, nine flight deck spots.*

- *LPD—Amphibious Assault Transport Dock—Over 16,000 tons displacement, 420 ship's crew/920 troops, one or two LCAC capacity, six flight deck spots.*

- *LSD—Dock Landing Ship—Over 15,000 tons displacement, 380 ship's crew/470 troops, four LCAC capability, two flight deck spots.*

*MARINE EXPEDITIONARY UNIT
(SPECIAL OPERATIONS CAPABLE)*

- *Command Element—Capable of providing local command and control, communications with adjacent units in the region, and linkage upward through the chain of command to the regional commander in chief and the national command authorities.*

- *Ground Combat Element—The infantry battalion and its combat support units, including artillery, armor, engineers, amphibious assault vehicles, and reconnaissance.*

- *Aviation Combat Element—A composite squadron with attack and transport helicopters, and vertical/short takeoff and landing aircraft.*

- *Command Service Support Element—Capable of providing a full range of logistical support from the sea or ashore. Typically embarks with fifteen days of supplies and equipment.*

Chief Aviation Boatswain's Mate Rick Poedtke briefs his flight deck crew in USS Tarawa *(LHA 1) on their duties in coming activities. This picture illustrates why some believe the Navy is run by Chiefs.*

Opposite: *Haggard but in good spirits after a week-long ordeal evading capture in the Bosnian hills, Air Force Captain Scott O'Grady debarks from his rescuing CH-53 and walks across the deck of USS* Kearsarge *(LHD 3). O'Grady's rescue by amphibious assault force units is testimony to the inherent flexibility of these forces. (Photo: U.S. Naval Institute)*

immediate retraining until the ability to perform the mission is successfully demonstrated.

In the decade following Desert Storm, the striking arm of the amphibious assault force—the Marines—has been in action more than eighty times, an average of almost one engagement a month.

These engagements have occurred across the globe, spanning primarily—but not exclusively—littoral areas within reach of the surface and aviation arms of the amphibious ready group/Marine expeditionary unit. They have operated in diverse areas: Liberia, Monrovia, Dakar, Senegal, Bangui in the Central African Republic, Yaounde, Cameron, Bohinjska Bela, Slovenia, Haiti, East Timor, and more. Though only points on a map to many people, each area represents a part of the world where instability and often conflict necessitated the steadying hand that American forces provided, and no force could match the presence, speed of deployment, and wide range of capabilities of the ARG/MEU.

Marine expeditionary unit operations, typically facilitated by a supporting amphibious ready group, have covered the spectrum of humanitarian operations, including aid and relief to Somalia, Bosnia, and Kenya and to Kurds in northern Iraq. These same teams have provided disaster relief to Chuuk Island in Micronesia, to Bangladesh after severe monsoons, and to Guam after Typhoon Omar devastated that island.

The same Marines and sailors who focused on humanitarian assistance and disaster relief changed gears and rescued Air Force pilot Captain Scott O'Grady after he was shot down over Bosnian Serb territory, an operation that demanded precise timing, close coordination between land and air forces engaged in the rescue, and a readiness for action. On a larger scale, these Navy–Marine Corps teams conducted noncombatant evacuation operations in littoral areas worldwide.

Top: *A combat-loaded landing craft, air cushion (LCAC) in the well deck of an amphibious assault ship represents America's ability to project power into the littorals around the world at the beginning of this millennium.*

Above: *Sailors operate the landing craft that bring the Marines ashore. Directing their manuevering onto the beach is the task of Navy beachmasters. One of these intrepid souls who stand in the face of on-coming landing craft and their loads of Marine equipment, Seaman Jennifer Bray of Cincinnati takes a breather before the next wave of landing craft, air cushion (LCAC) vehicles comes ashore.*

MARINE EXPEDITIONARY UNIT (SPECIAL OPERATIONS CAPABLE)
CONVENTIONAL AND SPECIAL MISSIONS

- *Amphibious Raids*
- *Limited Objective Attacks*
- *Show-of-Force*
- *Non-Combatant Evacuation Operations*
- *Reinforcement*
- *Security*
- *Mobile Training Teams*
- *Fire Support Control*

- *Tactical Recovery of Aircraft & Personnel*
- *Visit, Board, Search, and Seizure*
- *Recovery Operations*
- *Signals Intelligence*
- *Civic Actions*
- *Tactical Deception*
- *Counter-Intelligence*
- *Human Intelligence*

- *Initial Terminal Guidance*
- *Military Operations in Urban Terrain*
- *Humanitarian Assistance*
- *Airfield/Port/Key Facility Seizure*
- *In-extremis Hostage Recovery*
- *Gas and Oil Platform Operations*
- *Specialized Demolition Operations*
- *Electronic Warfare*

Above: *Marines train continuously for a wide range of missions, but at the basis of their power is their individual personal abilities. Marine riflemen are famous for their skill as individual marksmen, the cornerstone of their fame as light infantry.*

Below: *The landing craft, air cushion (LCAC) provides the heavy lift as Marines storm a landing beach during an amphibious assault exercise. Landing Marines is one of the strongest signals that the United States can send in the age of littoral warfare. (Photo: U.S. Naval Institute)*

Below, right: *A Pioneer unmanned aerial vehicle comes in for a landing in the net on USS* Ponce *(LPD 15). These vehicles conduct reconnaissance and offer a means to scout over the horizon without manned aircraft. Space based sensors combined with unmanned aerial vehicles provide the broad area surveillance and precise locating data necessary to employ precision guided weapons.*

Naval Expeditionary Forces— Equipped for the New Millennium

While the members of the Navy–Marine Corps team might be unknown to the general public, and the missions of the amphibious ready group/Marine expeditionary unit may suffer from some lack of visibility, what has not escaped notice is the tremendous upgrade in the capabilities of the Navy and Marine Corps platforms, systems, sensors, and weapons used by the amphibious assault force to take the fight to the enemy. Here the strides made have been significant and noteworthy.

For the Navy, amphibious shipping has been one of the biggest success stories as the Navy has rightsized its forces. Gone are the single-screw amphibious assault ships (LPHs), the unstable tank landing ships (LSTs), the single mission amphibious cargo ships (LKAs), and a plethora of older craft that provided capabilities that were often only marginally better than their World War II predecessors.

The ships that make up today's amphibious ready group are some of the most capable in the Navy inventory. The newest flagships, the highly capable amphibious assault ships (LHDs), carry over 1,700 troops and can deliver these troops and their equipment in speedy air-cushion landing craft (LCAC) and in the H-53s and H-46s of the Marine expeditionary unit's air combat element. Importantly, the medical facilities on this amphibious ready group centerpiece rival a moderately sized hospital ashore—with six operating rooms and a 600-bed ward. The venerable, but still capable, *Austin* (LPD 4) class is soon to be replaced by the *San Antonio* (LPD 17) class, which will displace twice as much as its predecessor and have the capacity to embark two LCACs. It will also have far more robust

medical capabilities than its predecessor, with two operating rooms and a 100-plus bed ward. Rounding out the amphibious ready group is either the *Whidbey Island* (LSD 41) class or the *Harpers Ferry* (LSD 49) (CV) (cargo variant) class.

These ships work well together as a cohesive entity, but are also highly capable of independent operations. Operations conducted by separate entities of the *Boxer* Amphibious Ready Group were amply demonstrated during Horn of Africa Operations in 1999. In that operation, the amphibious ready group team was able to organize in a manner that allowed *Boxer* (LHD 4) to operate in the Red Sea off Eritrea and Ethiopia, USS *Cleveland* (LPD 7) to operate in the Gulf of Aden off Djibouti, and *Harpers Ferry* (LSD 49) to operate off Mombassa, Kenya. Each ship was able to operate independently in diverse areas where mutual support was impossible.

The amphibious ready group brings other tools to the fight that are often not as "visible" as these large, highly capable ships, but are equally impressive. Unmanned aerial vehicles (UAVs) provide over-the-horizon targeting and battle-damage assessment. Recently developed counter-mine equipment embarked in LCACs provides these amphibious ready groups with a good capability to prevent enemy mines from derailing an amphibious operation. Self-defense capabilities, especially point defense, of these ARG ships are among the best in the fleet.

Perhaps the biggest change in the composition of the Navy's amphibious ready groups has been the evolution and installation of truly robust communications, improving command and control and intelligence capabilities. The capabilities in today's amphibious ready groups now rival, in some areas exceed, those of our carrier battle groups. These capabilities not only provide seamless communications within the amphibious ready group and with the Marine expeditionary unit forces on the ground, but also access a wide array of off-ship intelligence that enables the team to tap all available information in developing their situational awareness. This ability enables our amphibious assault forces to be an intelligent tip of the spear when a crisis erupts.

The tools that the Marine expeditionary unit brings to the fight are equally impressive and enable the Marines to operate successfully across an incredibly

Top: *The AH-1E Super Cobra, shown here dispensing decoy flares during a training mission, provides a powerful punch to support the Marine rifleman on the ground. As an inherently "light" force the amphibious assault force delivers most ordnance from aircraft or support ships rather than from tanks or artillery on the ground. (Photo: John W. Alli)*

Above: *The powerful CH-53 helicopter and the* Austin-*class amphibious transport dock (LPD) are aging but capable weapons that have served as a bridge to bring the amphibious assault force into this century. These soon will be replaced by the V-22 Osprey and the* San Antonio *(LPD 17) class respectively, providing additional combat power. (Photo: U.S. Naval Institute)*

wide spectrum of conflict from peace to war. From AV-8B Harriers to the venerable CH-46 helicopter, the air assets that the Marine commander has at his disposal are well suited to accomplish a plethora of missions—from assaulting a beach, to taking the fight beyond the beachline, to reaching inland to conduct any conventional or special missions.

On the ground, the Marines boast some of the most modern warfighting tools in existence, tools that enable the Marine rifleman, the main battery, to operate effectively and to be supported by the full weight of the ARG/MEU team. As with Navy platforms, beyond firepower, the Marine on the ground uses a command and control capability that takes full advantage of emerging technology to more effectively accomplish his mission.

The robust capabilities of the ARG/MEU team will be further enhanced by new systems, sensors, and weapons coming on line during the first decade of this century. The new *San Antonio* class designed to replace the *Austin* class has been designed from the keel up as a multi-mission platform with state-of-the-art communications and information technologies. Displacing 25,000 tons, but drawing only twenty-three feet fully loaded, this new class of amphibious assault ship will add flexibility and capability.

On the Marine side of the equation, two new platforms will enhance current capabilities. The MV-22 Osprey will replace the CH-46 Sea Knight helicopter to add a completely new dimension. This high-speed, tilt-rotor, vertical takeoff and landing aircraft can transport twenty-four combat troops or more than five tons of cargo at speeds and distances that expose entirely new areas inland to the offensive punch of the Navy–Marine Corps team.

Perhaps less heralded, but of no less importance than the MV-22, is the Advanced Amphibious Assault Vehicle (AAAV). Based on a completely new craft

design, this vehicle will allow the Marines in surface assault waves to move rapidly, in the same fashion as their heavy equipment moves in the highly capable LCAC. The combination of these two craft make over-the-horizon assault from the surface viable enabling the Marines to more fully exploit operational maneuver from the sea.

Amphibious Assault Force— A Focused Future

Today's amphibious assault force, the amphibious ready group/Marine expeditionary unit team, boasts capabilities that were only a dream as little as a decade ago. Emerging capabilities will make this team even more powerful and capable of not only conducting present missions more effectively, but will open up a host of possibilities for additional missions for America's rapid reaction team.

The key word in this equation is "team." Perhaps nowhere else in the United States military—or the military of any other nation for that matter—are two separate services so inextricably linked as the Navy and Marine Corps sides of the amphibious assault force. Neither can do its job without the other, but teamed together, these forces are ideally suited to do the work of the republic in peace, during disasters, in crises, and in war.

That these new and robust capabilities for the Navy and Marine segments of the amphibious ready group/Marine expeditionary unit have come on line so quickly is singular testimony to the enormous importance that our nation places in our amphibious assault force. These forces are important ingredients in our ability to operate as the indispensable power in an increasingly insecure world.

Top: *The AV-8B Harrier provides organic close air support to the Marine riflemen on the ground. This airplane, coming in for a landing on USS* Pelelieu *(LHA 5) can take off and land vertically.*

Above: *Marines of K Company, 26th Marine Expeditionary Unit (MEU), come ashore in zodiacs. These rubber raiding craft carried by amphibious ready group ships allow Marines to land covertly on enemy shores. (Photo: © Greg E. Mathieson/MAI)*

Mare Nostrum
Ocean Surveillance, Maritime Patrol, and Intelligence

Captain Andrew C. A. Jampoler, USN (Ret)

During earlier centuries, ocean surveillance meant peering intently at the surface of the water, first with the naked eye, then through a telescope, and then binoculars. Leif Ericsson, off Markland (Labrador) in 1001, and Admiral Sir John Jellicoe, off the Dogger Bank more than 900 years later, both learned through what they or others saw. Infrequent special cases aside, intelligence during this same period was not much more than occasional observation coupled to current rumor, and leavened by wishful or fearful thinking. Comprehension of the other side's strategic capabilities, plans, and tactical dispositions was confused, incomplete, and stale, when it was not simply wrong.

In the Cold War, the Soviet Union challenged the United States everywhere. At sea, from practically nothing—and with a heritage early in the twentieth century of humiliating defeat in the Sea of Japan—the Soviet Navy grew ultimately to challenge Western dominance. Cautious and deliberate, the Soviet's priority was submarines first, surface combatants next, and sea-based aviation last. If loosed on the high seas, the USSR's surface combatant fleet might have caused serious mischief until defeated, but the centerpiece of Soviet naval power then was, and as Russian sea power remains today, its submarine fleet.

In the face of this threat, the primary mission for the U.S. Navy was clear: know where the Soviets are at sea, know what they are doing there, and be able to send the appropriate force in time to stop them, if necessary. To fulfill this mission, the United States needed to know the capabilities of the Soviet fleet, where it operated, and when and how the Kremlin intended to use it and its other naval forces. Much of this essential knowledge could come only from a peacetime ocean surveillance program of unprecedented scope and depth.

No other nation ever set itself the task of real-time, full-time surveillance of key hostile naval bases, transit lanes, and operating areas worldwide in peacetime. But only through around-the-clock surveillance, year in and year out, could the United States avoid painful or even fatal surprise. Only through permanent surveillance could the data be collected that would provide clues to how the Soviets planned to use their fleet in wartime, and how capably they could execute their contingency plans.

Opposite: A P-3C of Patrol Squadron Five passes over a U.S. submarine running on the surface en route to her diving point. Teaming the cueing from wide-area sensors of the Undersea Surveillance Command, the large-area search and rapid arrival capabilities of the maritime patrol aircraft, and the localization and weapons delivery potential of submarines, the Navy created an effective broad-ocean anti-submarine warfare force.

Above: Scout cruisers like USS Marblehead (CL 12) culminated the design of fast long-legged ships to serve as scouts for the battle line. Before aircraft, contact with the enemy depended on physical encounters. As a result, few naval engagements occurred on the high seas; most were near choke points or ports. (Photo: National Archives)

Below: Seaman Cody Brannan from Victoria, Texas, stands lookout watch aboard the aircraft carrier USS John C. Stennis (CVN 74) as the ship transits the Atlantic Ocean en route to operations in the Persian Gulf. Even with satellites and sophisticated electronics devices, the human eye remains the most intelligent and discerning sensor.

Above: *A P-3 Orion from Patrol Squadron Forty-five parked below the fabled Rock of Gibraltar en route to operations in the Mediterranean Sea. Maritime patrol forces played a major role in operations over the Adriatic Sea, adjacent to the former Yugoslavia, during the late 1990s, as they would in any future contingency. Watching for violators of international embargoes has replaced anti-submarine warfare as the major mission assignment in these deployed assignments.*

Right: *Technologies pioneered in ocean surveillance are now common throughout the Navy. Reducing the time delay between sensors, the sources of information, and decision-makers is a key component of command in the information age.*

280

By the mid-1980s, U.S. Navy commanders generally knew whose ships and submarines were at sea and roughly where. Better still, fleet and force commanders also knew the capabilities of the submarines they faced in detail, and had a clear understanding of how the Soviets planned to use their navy in wartime. This success required much that was new, and included the development of:

• New platforms and sensors, to exploit any discernable environmental disturbance, no matter how minute.

• New intelligence collection systems, generally satellite-based, and including remarkable, real-time surveillance and signals intelligence capabilities.

• Data fusion centers, where these sensors' data could be combed, evaluated, and combined into a single, coherent plot of what was underneath the seas. Fast, computerized data processing, automating and accelerating the evaluation and analysis of huge files of data, was essential to winnow tenuous signals from out of the babble of background noise.

• The creation of dedicated institutions and organizations to conceive, develop, manage, and operate the resulting systems, and the necessary communications links between them.

Although the Navy has done much in the troubled decades since the end of World War II, arguably its greatest contribution to national security was in pulling the fangs of the Soviet submarine force. The effort drew on the technical genius of two generations ashore and on the seamanship and dedication of two generations at sea. The enormously complex problems inherent in finding modern submarines—history's first truly stealthy weapon system—were understood, and if not solved, at least became manageable.

With Mount Etna, on Sicily's eastern shore, erupting in the background, an Orion of Patrol Squadron Ten home-ported in Brunswick, Maine, assigned to the U.S. Sixth Fleet returns to Naval Air Station Sigonella after another surveillance mission. Sicily's location in the Central Mediterranean has made it a strategic focus for centuries. P3's also operate from Spain and Crete as well as bases in the Pacific and Arabian Peninsula.

In the sonar room of USS Atlanta *(SSN 712) sonarmen classify contacts by listening to them, observing their signatures on a video screen, and, if necessary, analyzing them with the aid of computer programs. Blue lighting enhances the video displays. Their work is a combination of science and art. A submarine sonarman trains for over a year before reporting to his ship to practice this highly technical trade.*

Below: *Underwater acoustic arrays and the associated computer processing were a major scientific and technical development during the Cold War. Today, the Undersea Surveillance Command monitors the oceans with fixed and mobile arrays. The data from these sensors is processed at operation centers on both coasts and overseas; the resulting information is used to vector maritime patrol aircraft and submarines to search areas and to alert ships to the locations of potentially unfriendly submarines.*

Through nearly continuous innovation, the United States Navy developed an effective antisubmarine warfare capability across the full range of scenarios for war at sea. This required oceanographic research, systems development and procurement, and training on an enormous scale. A high degree of effective tactical cooperation among complementary platforms—submarines, surface combatants, and aircraft—developed over time. Ocean surveillance provides the data to support intelligence cueing, shrinking the ocean to manageable size for effective search. But probability areas are not enough. Certainty can only come from on-scene verification by a trained crew, which could deliver a weapon if directed to do so.

Which trained crew to select depends on which ship, submarine, or aircraft is on station or available most quickly and which can search most efficiently. Attack submarines are superb ASW platforms, but cannot be fielded in sufficient numbers entirely to cover the territory to be searched. Surface combatant escorts, ASW helicopters, and carrier-based antisubmarine aircraft are essential to protect forces in mid-ocean, but are limited to the immediate vicinity of their location. Maritime patrol aircraft have the combination of long-range, quick responsiveness, and large payload to support the battle group's outer defenses, and the sensors and weapons to solve the transiting or on-station missile-equipped submarine problem. Combining data from many sources and deploying forces of different capabilities over long distances requires skills that only come from practice.

Today, forty-two nations operate more than 500 submarines. Some are friends and allies; others are not. The Soviet Union's collapse changed the hostile submarine threat less than is commonly assumed. The Russian Navy operates the best of the submarine fleet left behind in the rubble of the expired Soviet order—more than 120 modern submarines. The Russians have continued this capability at the expense of modernization of other strategic forces, their army, and other navy capabilities. Others investing in submarines may not always have friendly intentions. Surveillance for other purposes, to enforce embargoes against rogue states or groups, and to intercept drug traffic have grown a hundred fold in the last ten years of the century. Full-time ocean surveillance and other intelligence collection by uniquely capable naval forces remain requirements as the world enters the next millennium.

In the face of this challenge, today the United States commands the oceans of the world as no power ever has before, not imperial Rome in the Mediterranean, not Great Britain in the era of Pax Britannia after Trafalgar. More than good fortune, this essential strength flows from several sources:

• A naval tradition that predates the country itself. From this tradition emerge annually the men and women that make the Navy work, who stand its watches and accept its burdens. The U.S. Navy's officers and petty officers constitute an unequalled reservoir of expertise.

• Knowledge about the ocean. Over decades of research, huge sums were spent to understand what questions to ask, to divine the answers, to buy the necessary force structure, and to operate it to proficiency.

• The emergence of technological innovation. This vigorous process provides the tools with which to ask questions and obtain answers, and to convert these answers to hardware and tactics.

As long as these conditions remain and wise decisions are made, the United States can continue to work its will at sea, and from there, upon the neighboring shore during the new century that will certainly confront the nation with problems not even imagined and, perhaps, not yet imaginable.

Opposite, top: *The Oceanographer of the Navy has been a prime mover in ocean sciences since Lieutenant Matthew Maury published the first* Winds and Currents Charts *in 1848. USNS* Pathfinder *(T-AGS 60) is one of eight deployed survey ships. These ships map the ocean floor, sample the water column, and measure acoustic properties. The knowledge gained in this research is fundamental to surveillance in the deep.*

Effective reconnaissance and surveillance requires operations around the clock in every kind of weather. This P3C Orion prepares to take off from Naval Air Station Jacksonville to fly a mission that will cover a huge swath of the Atlantic Ocean and require landings at Naval Air Stations Roosevelt Roads, Puerto Rico, and Keflavik, Iceland.

Weapons That Wait
Mine Warfare in the 21st Century

Rear Admiral Charles F. Horne III, USN (Ret)

Officers inspecting the hull of the amphibious assault ship USS Tripoli *(LPH 10) as the vessel sits in drydock awaiting repairs after striking an Iraqi mine during the Gulf War.* Tripoli *was able to continue operations after damage control crews stopped the flooding caused by the explosion. The damage on her forward starboard side demonstrates the adage, "Every ship can be a mine sweeper once."*

USS Guardian (MCM 5) is one of the fourteen ships in the Avenger class of minesweepers. Begun in the early 1980s and completed in 1999, these wooden-hulled ships have the ability to hunt, sweep, and neutralize mines.

Mine warfare played a more important role during the Cold War than most Americans realize. From the Korean War through the Vietnam conflict and the Gulf War, fourteen U.S. Navy ships were either damaged or sunk by enemy mines. During this same forty-four-year period, only one U.S. Navy ship was damaged by a missile, one by a torpedo, and two by aerial attack. Of equal importance, mines significantly impeded or delayed major U.S. Navy fleet operations and amphibious assaults. In Korea, the seventy-two ships of the Joint Task Force of the Seventh Fleet were delayed six days in making a key amphibious landing at Wonsan, prompting the Seventh Fleet commander to exclaim, "We have lost control of the seas to a nation without a Navy." During the Gulf War, the mine threat posed by Iraq, resulting in serious damage to USS *Princeton* (CG 59) and the USS *Tripoli* (LPH 10), so imperiled operations that an amphibious assault from the sea into Kuwait was not attempted.

Since the Gulf War, significant efforts have been made addressing how to overcome this asymmetric and critical threat to sea control, maritime dominance, and projection of power from the sea. The Chief of Naval Operations' comprehensive report on the shortfalls in the U.S. Navy's ability to conduct effective mine countermeasures in littoral warfare began the efforts to improve the U.S. Navy's mine countermeasures capabilities at sea and in real time—in order to enable the Navy to go "anytime, anywhere."

The first objective for improvement in mine countermeasures (MCM) capabilities was to improve the existing dedicated forces. Fourteen new mine counter-measures ships—the MCM 1 *Avenger* class—have been constructed. All these state-of-the-art ships are now in service, and are the best minehunters and minesweepers in the world. In addition, twelve new coastal minehunters, the MHC 51 *Osprey* class, have been built and are now at sea. Coupled with these top-of-the-line mine countermeasures ships are two squadrons of the world's most capable Airborne Mine Countermeasures (AMCM) helicopters, the MH-53Es.

Mines are an inexpensive but potent threat to our Navy. Fifty countries have mines in their arsenal. Produced in over thirty countries, mine sales have increased 40 percent since the Korean War, and the momentum continues.

285

Above: *Dolphins are part of the Very Shallow Water Explosive Ordnance Disposal Teams. The animals must be kept cool when out of the water, which often happens when they are being transported to their workplace.*

Below: *USS* Inchon *(MCS 12), the Navy's only mine countermeasures command and support ship, underway in the Gulf of Mexico.* Inchon *originally was an amphibious assault ship. The small size of the mine countermeasures ships means that they need a large support ship to accompany them when deployed.*

In 1993, all these dedicated mine countermeasure forces were ordered to Ingleside, Texas, where for the first time they occupied the same homeport. Since then, these ships and helicopters have been training and operating together as a closely integrated team. Then two years later, in 1995, thanks to the personal efforts of Chief of Naval Operations Admiral Frank Kelso, the USS *Inchon* (LPD 12) was converted to a Mine Countermeasures Command and Support Ship (MCS 12) to serve as the flagship of these dedicated air and surface mine countermeasures forces. Finally, to complete the closely linked cooperation necessary between development and deployment, located nearby at Panama City, Florida, is the Navy's Mine Countermeasures Laboratory.

Closely teamed with the mine countermeasures forces in Ingleside are the Explosive Ordnance Disposal (EOD) teams—divers who are trained experts in mine warfare. These teams are a critical part of the dedicated mine countermeasures forces and deploy with them as an integral part of their organization. In addition to these divers, the Very Shallow Water detachment in San Diego consists of divers and marine mammals, along with special unmanned underwater vehicles to do the vital reconnaissance and neutralizing of mines in very shallow water.

The long transit times across the Atlantic and Pacific made it prudent to forward deploy some of these dedicated mine countermeasures units to reduce the response time to crisis. Two *Avenger*-class ships were deployed to the Fifth Fleet in the Persian Gulf and two more were assigned homeports in Sasebo, Japan, for contingencies on the Korean peninsula. Even with these forward-deployed ships, it remained clear that the U.S. Navy battle groups and amphibious readiness groups needed indigenous mine-hunting and mine-avoidance capabilities.

In littoral warfare, response time lines can be critical. Waiting as much as thirty or forty days for the dedicated mine countermeasure forces from Ingleside, or even the two to five days for those from the two forward deployed sites, may not be appropriate. To address this problem, organic surface, subsurface, and air

mine-countermeasures capabilities indigenous to the battle group and amphibious ready group surface ships, submarines, and helicopters are being created.

A Remote Mine Hunting System—an independent semi-submersible unmanned vehicle—will operate from destroyers. Capitalizing on the submarine's inherent stealth, unmanned underwater vehicles launched and recovered from its torpedo tubes will provide clandestine mine reconnaissance for the battle group days ahead of its arrival in the area. Airborne organic mine counter-measures programs include towed sonars that will identify as well as locate mines. The CH-60 helicopters assigned to the battle groups and amphibious ready groups will be able to tow these devices. Eventually a complementary Airborne Mine Neutralization System will enable a helicopter to send down small underwater vehicles to hunt the discovered mines and destroy them. Airborne lasers will be able to track floating and moored mines within forty feet of the water's surface and then destroy them with direct gunfire, and the Organic Air Surface Influence System, towed by CH-60 helicopters, will sweep magnetic and acoustic influence mines. Finally, to attack the very difficult problem of mines close to shore, explosive clearing devices launched from landing craft, air cushion (LCAC) vehicles are being developed.

To properly employ these new organic mine countermeasures, awareness and knowledge of mines and mine countermeasures tactics is needed. The Chief of Naval Operations' 1995 white paper on mine warfare stated, "Our most immediate goal in this vital naval warfare area is to mainstream mine warfare, and especially mine countermeasures, into Navy and Marine Corps planning for, and execution of, Joint and Combined force operations in the littorals." In 1998, the Chief of Naval Operations directed that henceforth mine warfare would be a "core competency." Mine warfare is being incorporated in schools and exercises at all levels. A major cultural and operational shift is in progress to make mine warfare equal to antiair warfare and antisubmarine warfare.

While mine warfare continues to be a major threat in the twenty-first century, it is being addressed with the new and exciting "mix" of dedicated and organic mine countermeasures capabilities along with the needed concomitant cultural changes to make mine warfare a core competency of all sailors and Marines. In implementing these vital mine countermeasures programs and the needed cultural changes, the Navy and Marine Corps are acting to meet the goals set forth by the Chief of Naval Operations that "The U.S. Navy will influence directly and decisively, events ashore from the sea—anytime, anywhere."

Stealth from the Sea

Rear Admiral George R. Worthington, USN (Ret)

SEAL is an acronym for "Sea-Air-Land," the regions in which SEALs perform their missions. The members of this naval warfare specialty are usually assigned to carry out maritime special operations as directed by the national command authorities, the Joint Chiefs of Staff, and the geographic commanders in chief. Organized as U.S. Navy SEAL Teams, SEAL Delivery Vehicle Teams, and Special Boat Squadrons, they work directly for numbered fleets and regional joint Special Operations Commands. The SEAL Delivery Vehicle Teams operate free-flooding, underwater vehicles that transport SEALs and other special operations personnel into sensitive areas. The Special Boat Squadrons support SEAL insertion and extraction, and conduct coastal patrol and interdiction in littoral regions. Usually each unit is oriented to a specific geographic region, although actual deployments depend on emergent requirements.

SEAL Teams One and Two were established in 1962 as part of the Department of Defense–wide initiative to enhance United States' capabilities to counter Communist-inspired insurgencies occurring at the time in the developing world. SEAL team members were drawn from the then existing fleet Underwater Demolition Teams (UDTs), the elite Navy "frogmen" units that had their beginning in 1943 as a result of intelligence deficiencies during the amphibious assault at Tarawa. The first frogmen served in outfits dubbed "Combat Demolition Units" and saw combat throughout the remainder of the war in both Pacific and Atlantic campaigns locating and clearing beach obstacles prior to amphibious landings. Underwater demolition teams performed these basic tasks in World War II after 1943. During the Korean War, in addition to supporting the Inchon landings, UDT members performed inland reconnaissance and demolition missions—all missions performed today by SEALs. During the Vietnam War, SEALs performed beach reconnaissance, small unit raids, and administrative demolition support. SEAL teams were among the most decorated units in the conflict: three Medals of Honor were awarded within this small group of men.

Special boat squadrons came of age during the Vietnam conflict when they supported SEAL missions throughout the Mekong Delta. Subsequently, they have accompanied SEAL teams in a variety of missions and routinely support SEAL platoons as part of fleet deployments and exercises. They use a mix of combatant

Above: A thirty-foot Rigid Inflatable Boat takes to the air on a mission to insert a SEAL squad in a typical "over-the-beach" operation. These units are normally staged from Navy amphibious ships.

Opposite: A U.S. Navy frogman loads a demolition pack on a type of beach obstacle common in World War II, clearing the way for landing craft to reach the shore in an amphibious assault. Today this function as well as beach reconnaissance and raids are performed by SEALs. (Photo: U.S. Naval Institute)

The physical training during Basic Underwater Diver/SEALs training focuses on teamwork and skill as much as endurance. Individual motivation is a key ingredient. (Photo: Dave Gatley/MAI)

Above: *Drown-proof training has been a part of SEALs instruction since Vietnam, because of drowning incidents in hostile situations. Here, trainees learn that they can survive for long periods of time in the water—even with hands and feet bound. (Photo: Greg E. Mathieson/MAI)*

Above, right: *This Mark V special operations craft, the latest addition to SEAL insertion platforms, is a medium-range vehicle for SEALs and other special operations personnel. It provides rapid mobility in shallow water areas and can be deployed by C-5 aircraft anywhere in seventy-two hours.*

Opposite, top: *SEALs return to a submarine on an open swimmer delivery vehicle. All users of this delivery system must be qualified divers. Recovery is made by grabbing a buoyed line trailing from the submarine and following it down to the hull and maneuvering into the recovery chamber.*

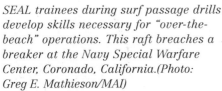

SEAL trainees during surf passage drills develop skills necessary for "over-the-beach" operations. This raft breaches a breaker at the Navy Special Warfare Center, Coronado, California.(Photo: Greg E. Mathieson/MAI)

craft ranging from combat rubber raiding craft through mid- to long-range craft and commissioned ships. The patrol craft were designed to give the Navy a more prominent presence in littoral regions worldwide. They are assigned varied missions in keeping with their basic roles supporting SEAL teams and coastal patrol and interdiction.

Navy SEAL candidates undergo the most grueling physical training within the armed forces. Teamwork and the belief that quitting is not an option are the hallmarks of those who complete this training successfully. In addition to the basic twenty-five-week course, SEAL candidates attend the U.S. Army Basic Parachute Course at Fort Benning, Georgia, following which they undergo specific advanced training in their parent teams. At the end of a probation period, during which they are closely observed for adaptability and suitability for special operations, successful candidates are awarded the coveted SEAL breast insignia.

Between Vietnam and the Gulf War, SEALs continued to operate over the beach with an increasingly wide variety of vehicles and from a broad array of launch platforms. These insertions are carried out from submarines and surface craft. SEALs also parachute from fixed-wing aircraft or drop from helicopters. Submarine insertion is the most clandestine method but is the most demanding on the team in terms of preparation, complexity, and duration.

SEALs are often involved in foreign internal defense missions. In these assignments, they interact with foreign forces, engaging in combined and joint cross-training exercises with European allies and Pacific nations. Many SEALs have qualified in a variety of foreign languages; for example, one commander of the Naval Special Warfare Command studied Arabic. The SEAL team oriented on Latin America requires all incoming personnel to be fluent in Spanish. In addition to teaching specific warfare capabilities, SEALs also set examples of democratic principles and equal opportunity.

The predominant effort made throughout the 1980s and continuing today is improving the SEAL teams' underwater capability. Great gains have been made, most because of the initiative of individuals within the SEAL delivery vehicle commands. SEALs and their forebears, the frogmen, operated from submarines for years. SEAL teams had used a variety of underwater vehicles for swimmers since the Korean War, generally with lackluster results. With the development of sophisticated, free-flooding delivery vehicles, however, SEALs gained real underwater operational capability. Using the SEAL delivery vehicle, SEALs can penetrate harbors and coastal regions undetected. Using submarine dry deck shelters, SEALs and, specifically, SEAL delivery vehicle teams achieve a level of operational capability in underwater insertion unmatched in the world.

The arrival of state-of-the-art underwater systems represents a quantum advance in underwater operational capabilities. The advanced SEAL delivery system is a mini-submarine capable of transporting SEALs further and in more habitable conditions than those afforded by the free-flooding SEAL delivery vehicle. Because it is a dry boat, operators do not have to be qualified divers allowing Army and Air Force special operations personnel to be transported.

From glass faceplates of World War II, dry suits of Korea, jungle fatigues of Vietnam, to the wet and dry submersibles, laser range finders, and information-age laptop computers of the post-Cold War era, the naval special warfare warrior adapts to keep pace with technologically maturing threats. The uncertainty of the next warfare environment promises to create many new tasks for the energetic SEAL, with trends toward working in urban areas and in countering the proliferation of weapons of mass destruction.

The journey from the dark days of 1943 to the beaches of Kuwait has been arduous, but naval special forces, more relevant than ever before, entered the second half-century of service on the leading edge of operational capability, individual dedication, and underwater technology. While developing improved capabilities through technological innovation and dedication, SEALs preserve the grit that made them famous from Okinawa to Normandy, from Korea to Vietnam, from Kuwait to Bosnia.

Below: *An advanced SEAL delivery vehicle enters a dry deck shelter mounted on the submarine's hull. This vehicle is a miniature submarine that delivers the swimmers closer inshore than the submarine can go. Even with this equipment, these dangerous missions can last longer than ten hours.*

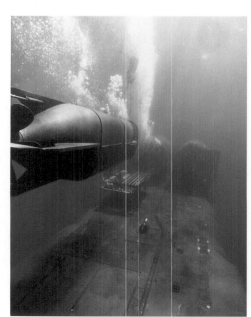

THE
Supporting Cast
Doctors…Lawyers…and Storekeeper Chiefs

Captain John Edward Jackson,
Supply Corps, USN (Ret)

In many ways, the Navy can be visualized as a virtual city of 370,000 uniformed
citizens, with another 200,000 reservists who join the population when called
to active duty. This city exists for one main purpose: to wield military power as
directed by the nation's civilian leaders. To do so requires not only bombs and
bullets, but also the full range of support services found anywhere in America:
doctors, lawyers, shopkeepers, bankers, restauranteurs, and more. The feeding,
care, and support of Navy personnel is an important task taken very seriously by the
uniformed men and women entrusted with these responsibilities. These specialists
are organized into functional groups within the Navy and Naval Reserve, defined by
an officer's staff corps and the associated enlisted ratings, or in various categories of
line officers dedicated to missions not leading to command at sea.

The Healthcare Providers

Although today's Navy consists of far more than ships at sea, the service's
organization and ethos are derived from shipboard traditions. Throughout history
ships usually carried with them crew members who did not take up the sword
in battle, but instead served to bind the wounds and cure the ills of their fellow
shipmates. So it was in the United States Navy from the beginning. In 1775, the
Continental Congress, in creating the Continental Navy, directed that surgeons and
surgeon's mates be carried on board all ships. The Rules for the Regulation of the
Navy of the United Colonies of the United States required that "a convenient place
shall be set apart for sick or hurt men . . . and some crew shall be appointed to
attend and serve them to keep the place clean." This designated place soon came
to be called the "sick bay," and qualified physicians were recruited to serve there,
often on a cruise-by-cruise basis. Among the pioneers of Navy medicine was
surgeon Joseph Harrison of the Continental sloop *Alfred*, considered to be the first
medical officer of the U.S. Navy. He and his fellow surgeons were aided by a
group of enlisted crewmen, referred to as loblolly boys, waisters, baymen, and
faithful attendants. These medical assistants were the forerunners of today's
Hospital Corpsman (HN). In 1842, the Navy established the Bureau of Medicine

*The Union Army, with assistance of the U.S.
Sanitary Commission, outfitted a captured
Confederate transport as a hospital ship.
She featured a 300-ton icebox, laundry
facilities, a specialized amputation room,
and even an elevator to move patients
between decks. Transferred to the Navy in
1862, USS Red Rover became the Navy's
first hospital ship. Over 2,500 casualties
ultimately received care on this floating
sanctuary. (Photo: Naval Historical Center)*

Opposite: *This painting of USS Cahaba
(AO 82) refueling USS Iowa (BB 61) and
USS Shangri-La (CV 38) hangs at the
Naval War College, where the lesson that
"amateurs talk tactics, professionals worry
about logistics" is taught. No campaign
demonstrated that truism more than that
in the Western Pacific in 1945, where
supplies had to be brought thousands of
miles to the scene of action. (Painting:
Andrew Small, Naval War College)*

*Long-term medical care began to be
provided to Navy personnel in 1830, when
the first naval hospital was constructed at
Portsmouth, Virginia. Others followed at
Philadelphia; Portsmouth, New Hampshire;
Chelsea, Massachusetts; and Brooklyn, New
York. The Bureau of Medicine and Surgery
was established in 1842. (Photo: Bureau of
Medicine and Surgery Archives)*

293

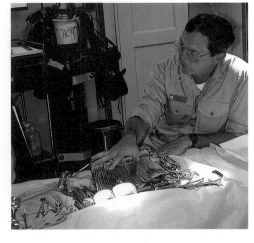

Commander Bruce Potenza (MC), USN, examines surgical instruments on board USS Kearsarge *(LHD 3). Doctor Potenza, whose specialty is trauma and critical care, was activated from Fleet Hospital Unit 23 at the Madison, Wisconsin, Naval Reserve Training Center.* Kearsarge's *Amphibious Ready Group provided humanitarian assistance after an earthquake in Turkey.*

and Surgery to ensure "the maintenance of the health of the Navy and Marine Corps, and the care of the sick and injured in peace and war."

The Civil War brought immense challenges to military medicine. Living and working conditions afloat changed little from the days of the Continental Navy, and diseases such as yellow fever decimated the crews of ships stationed in the Gulf of Mexico. Ashore, conditions were somewhat better, but still far from ideal. The Civil War demonstrated the hazards for the medical staffs. Thirty-three of the nearly 150 medical officers who served in the Federal Navy during the Civil War were killed in action. After the war, medical care, living, and working conditions on board ships improved as the Navy transitioned from sail to steam, and in 1871, to improve and standardize the management of its medical care system, the Navy founded the Medical Corps.

Reserve commissions swelled the ranks to meet the demands of World War I. Navy combat medical teams that supported the 4th Marine Brigade in France treated over 13,000 casualties over a nine-month period under severe combat conditions. When Lieutenant Orlando Henderson Petty's dressing station was bombarded with artillery and gas, he continued to aid and evacuate wounded Marines despite a damaged gas mask. Doctor Petty became one of the first reserve officers awarded a Medal of Honor in the war.

After demobilization reduced the medical corps to less than 900 officers, the corps grew at a staggering pace in 1942 and 1943, reaching a peak of 13,700 officers by 1945. At the end of World War II, the Navy Medical Department (officer and enlisted) totaled nearly 170,000—a personnel strength larger than the entire U.S. Navy before Pearl Harbor—who were treating a peak patient load of over 110,000 patients daily. But while the throughput was huge, the care was

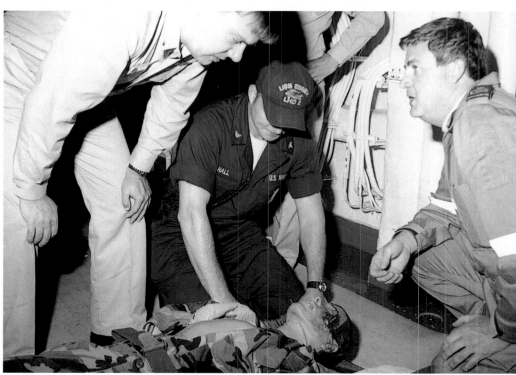

excellent. Of every hundred sailors and Marines wounded in World War II, ninety-seven ultimately recovered.

Navy corpsmen stationed at sea and ashore with Marine combat units deserve much of the credit for the high recovery rate. Highly trained, these men provided immediate first aid to wounded sailors and Marines and stabilized injuries to allow evacuation to hospital facilities. In saving lives, these men did not hesitate to risk their own. The heroism of those serving with the Marines was renowned throughout the Pacific. Medals awarded for their bravery were legion. On Iwo Jima, for example, Pharmacist Mate Second Class George Wahlen collapsed in his own pool of blood after tending to a wounded Marine, while Pharmacist Mate Third Class Jack Williams treated another Marine despite being hit three times. The two reservists received the Medal of Honor; Williams posthumously. World War II claimed the lives of 1,046 corpsmen. Such performance continued during the Korean, Vietnam, and Gulf Wars. Navy corpsmen continued to perform unselfishly, contributing to even higher survival rates. Front-line work with the Marines continued to exact a harsh toll; 110 were lost in Korea, and another 690 corpsmen were killed in Vietnam.

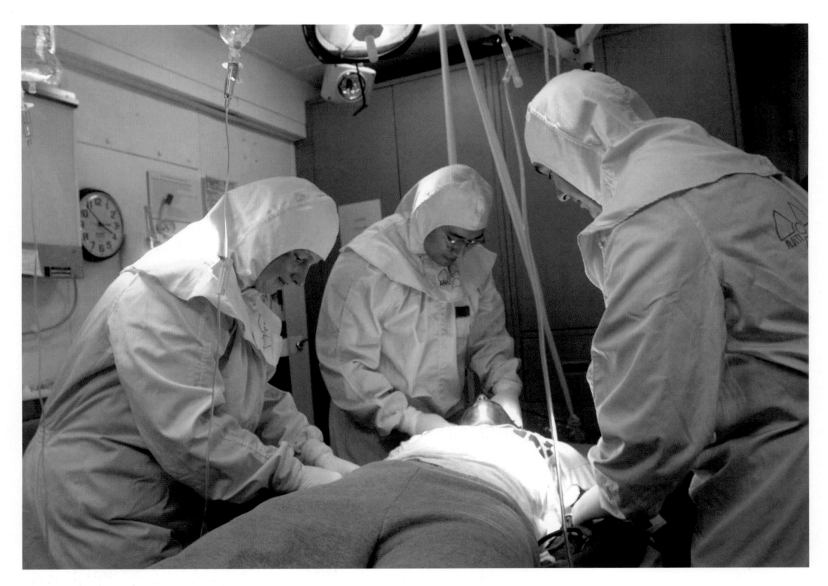

Navy doctors remain on the leading edge of medical technology. In research labs and in field operations, new and innovative concepts to improve patient care are nurtured and implemented. Fully equipped hospital ships in the reserve fleet are ready to sail in times of conflict and to provide humanitarian assistance during operations other than war. When large-scale medical care is required ashore, modern modular hospitals can be transported to the scene, assembled and ready to receive patients within hours of mobilization. The Navy is leading the way in developing the concept of telemedicine, where the patient and the caregiver are separated by geography, but joined by technology. Examples of these developments are patient medical history on a chip; portable, lightweight, and miniaturized technologies for emergency care in deployed settings; and the Field Medical Surveillance System to collect data on diseases and illnesses that occur during foreign deployments or conflicts.

Drills are a daily part of life on a warship and the medical department is no exception. Handling casualties who may have been contaminated by radioactive material is a complex and difficult task that requires practice. This radiation decontamination team on board USS Harry S. Truman *(CVN 75) prepares the patient so that other medical personnel can treat wounds without endangering the patient or themselves.*

Suggestions to employ women as nurses on Navy ships and stations can be traced back as far as 1814, when Doctor William Barton recommended that, "The nurses should be women of humane disposition and tender manners; active and healthy. They should be neat and cleanly in their persons; and without vice of any description." However, care continued to be rendered by doctors assisted by loblolly boys, male nurses, and other attendants until the horrific medical conditions experienced during the Civil War led to a call for nurses with formal training and certification. By 1875, the Naval Hospital at Pensacola, Florida, employed male nurses in a ratio of one nurse for every eight patients. Through the remainder of the nineteenth century, the Navy used contract-hired nurses and civilian volunteers to provide traditional nursing services.

This arrangement, however, failed to provide an adequate level of professionalism. Responding to this inadequacy, Congress acted to establish the Navy

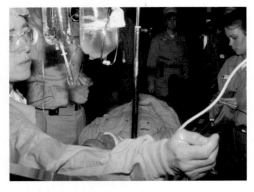

In the casualty receiving area of USNS Mercy *(T-AH 19), nurse anesthetist Lieutenant Commander Cynthia Feller (NC), USN, and her assistant Hospital Corpsman Third Class Brooke Warren, prepare to treat a mock casualty during a general drill.*

296

Nurse Corps in 1908. Shortly after passage of the legislation the first twenty nurses were appointed. Fondly referred to as the "Sacred Twenty," they held no rank, although they were treated as commissioned officers. These trailblazers faced considerable opposition from men who resented the invasion of these women into the all-male world of the American seaman, but they soon earned the respect of their patients, co-workers, and supervisors. In January 1935, the last of the Sacred Twenty, Chief Nurse Myn Hoffman, retired from active duty. By then the traditions of professional Navy nursing were firmly established.

The 427 Navy nurses on active duty in 1939 formed the nucleus of the wartime nurses who played a vital role in the lives of America's warriors during World War II. Late in 1942, nurses were assigned permanent relative rank as an indicator of their growing importance. At the end of the war, the corps numbered over 11,000 nurses serving in naval hospitals, dispensaries, and hospital corps schools within the continental United States, as well as on twelve hospital ships and in over two dozen overseas bases and activities.

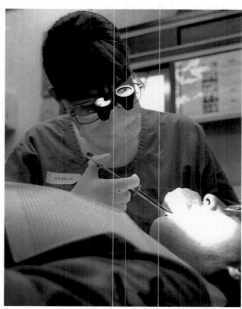

Demobilization led to the recall of naval reserve nurses to active duty to support medical facilities in the Korean War. At the time, the corps was restricted to women. With men entering the profession in significant numbers, this restriction was dropped in 1964. Both male and female nurses served with distinction in Vietnam and later in the Gulf War.

While doctors and nurses were concerned with the health of the entire person, other specialists focused on specific portions of the human body. In 1873, a Navy medical inspector summarized the overall state of oral hygiene when he remarked: "The hair, beard, and teeth are all neglected on board ship. It would be a difficult matter to compel old sailors to cleanse their teeth, but all the boys should be obliged to purchase tooth brushes, and to use them regularly." Until 1912, civilian dentists under Navy contract provided treatment ashore, while afloat some surgeon's stewards gained a degree of training in oral procedures and provided rudimentary dental services as needed. After years of argument and delay, Congress authorized a Navy Dental Corps on 22 August 1912. Emory A. Bryant, a doctor of dental surgery in Washington, D.C., was appointed as "acting assistant dental surgeon."

Dental corps officers were assigned to the various combat medicine teams sent to support the 4th Marine Brigade in France. The first U.S. naval officer to die in combat in World War I was a dental corps officer, Lieutenant (junior grade)

Top, left: Preventive care is a major facet of Navy medicine. Growing threats of biological warfare have added to the already important immunizations against diseases in areas rarely frequented by Americans. This ensign on board USS Nicholson *(DD 982) demonstrates the usual enthusiastic response to receiving such shots, commonly referred to as "Suck it in!"*

Top, right: In the Naval Hospital, Roosevelt Roads, Puerto Rico, Dental Technician First Class Guy G. Gilman prepares a wax model on a five unit porcelain fuse to metal bridge; the first step in making artificial teeth. The craftsmanship and technical skill required in such efforts are as complex and demanding as any trade or rate in the Navy.

Above: Lieutenant Theresa Bean (DC), USN, performs a root canal on a patient on board USS Theodore Roosevelt *(CVN 71) in the Persian Gulf. With five thousand people on board the carrier and another thousand in the ships in company for which the carrier serves as the major medical facility, this kind of significant surgery is not an unusual event.*

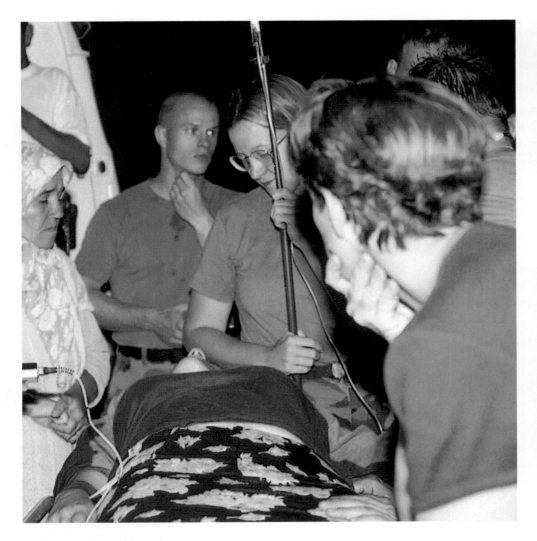

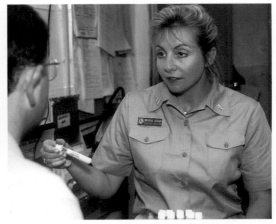

Above: *Corpsmen and Marines from USS* Kearsarge *(LHD 3) ashore near Izmir, Turkey, provide aid to victims of a major earthquake. Navy medicine—by nature of association with seagoing forces—is highly mobile. Providing medical treatment very quickly is a major mission capability so immediate aid in cases of civil catastrophe is a natural attribute.*

Top, right: *Lieutenant Brenda Adams, a Medical Service Corps dietitian conducting research on weight-loss programs that focus on behavior rather than physical training, shows the amount of fat in three ounces of fried chicken to a chief petty officer on board USS* Enterprise *(CVN 65) in the Mediterranean Sea. Lieutenant Adams has her work cut out for her. Navy galleys produce delicious pastries in the early morning hours, properly "bear claws" or "glazed doughnuts"; their consumers lovingly refer to these as "Fat Pills."*

Lower, right: *Hospital Corpsman Isabel Ramirez prepares prescriptions in the pharmacy of the Sick Bay on USS* Theodore Roosevelt *(CVN 71) during deployment. The medical department on a carrier provides care for 5,000 members of the ship's company and air wing as well as major medical facilities for the crews of the other ships in the battle group.*

Weed Osborne, who was awarded the Medal of Honor for attempting to rescue a wounded Marine officer in the field during the advance on Bouresches, France.

From just over 500 dental corps officers in June 1941, the corps reached a peak of over 7,000 officers on duty in 1945. Sixteen died in combat. The scale of the war is hard to imagine today, but a measure of the scope of effort in those five years was the nearly 30 million dental restorations of all kinds completed and the more than 4 million teeth that were extracted!

In January 1948 the Navy established the Dental Technician (DT) school in Great Lakes, Illinois, and in April of that year, dental technicians were separated from the hospital corpsman rate. These actions ensured the continued professionalism of this important enlisted rating. At the beginning of the twenty-first century, just under 1,400 dental corps officers provide state-of-the-art preventive and restoration services.

The full-service healthcare team within the Navy also includes a number of highly educated and specially trained practitioners who provide clinical services or perform medical administrative functions. The composition of the Navy Medical Department changes as new medical specialties develop and as the need for dedicated professionals with various levels of medical training and education become evident. The first group so recognized was the pharmacists, authorized as warrant officers in 1898.

As part of the build-up associated with World War II, nearly 1,500 officers in the grades of ensign through lieutenant were commissioned in the Hospital Corps. These officers worked in a broad range of assignments in healthcare, administration, and logistics. After the war, these became the Medical Service Corps, professionals who serve as healthcare providers, scientists, and administrators. Many provide direct patient care as physician assistants, pharmacists, optometrists, clinical psychologists, physical therapists, and other specialties. Others serve in the area of healthcare science, in fields such as industrial hygiene, environmental health, aerospace physiology, medical technology, and other specialties. Healthcare administration fields, such as general administration, plans and operations, fiscal services, and medical logistics, among others, are also part of the Medical Service Corps. Twenty-three percent of the officers within the Navy Medical Department are members of this corps.

The Business Managers

As long as ships have gone to sea, they have been procured, prepared, and provisioned by outfitters and merchants specializing in maritime materials. At various times these have been referred to as ship's clerks, pursers, super-cargoes, paymasters, or supply officers.

In the reforms of 1842, Congress directed establishment of a number of bureaus, with many logistical matters assigned as the responsibility of the Bureau of Provisions and Clothing. As ships became more complex, and naval operations began to range far from friendly shores, the demands on the Navy's support structure became progressively greater. Navy pursers eventually assumed the title "paymasters," and formed the Navy Pay Corps. These officers and their enlisted assistants occupied key shore assignments and afloat billets charged with providing the material needed to sustain both men and machines. They served in combat as

Illustrating the importance and complexity of logistics for operations at great distances, USS Arctic (AOE 8) *sails the Ionian Sea supporting USS* Theodore Roosevelt (CVN 71) *and her battle group. The fast combat support ship can carry more than 177,000 barrels of oil, 2,150 tons of ammunition, 500 tons of dry stores, and 250 tons of refrigerated stores.*

Left: *In this group of naval personnel in 1841, the purser, second from left, in an undress uniform, is in a discussion with the commodore and another officer—both in full dress. The third officer in full dress is a surgeon, precursor to today's medical corps officers. Pursers were the forerunners of today's supply corps officers. ("Military Uniforms in America," Charles McBarron, courtesy The Company of Military Historians)*

Tench Francis was the first purveyor of public supplies, appointed to his post in 1795 after Congress passed the Naval Armament Act authorizing the construction of six frigates. A Philadelphia merchant, he procured all the materials necessary to construct, outfit, and operate the frigates; everything from 2,400 tons of live oak from the state of Georgia for ship hulls and masts, to hardtack and salt pork for the crew's sustenance.

Top, left: *"It's in here somewhere!" Store-keepers on Guam in the 1950s research the nature and location of a part required to complete a repair. Modern technology helps the search process, but great attention to detail is still necessary to be sure storage locations are recorded accurately so that material can be found quickly.*

Top, right: *The scope and depth of the repair parts required to operate a modern navy can be imagined looking at the shelves of the supply warehouses at the Naval Supply Depot, Mechanicsburg, Pennsylvania, in 1950. When ships live beyond twenty-five years, manufacturers of much of the original equipment disappear before the equipment goes out of service. Balancing inventory investment versus repair parts availability is a constant challenge for the Supply Corps logistic managers.*

Above: *This CH-46D helicopter is lifting supplies in the cargo slings from USNS* Tippecanoe *(TAO 199) to USS* Belleau Wood *(LHA 3). USS* Germantown *(LSD 42) is in the background. This helicopter can lift 10,000 pounds in the sling or transport twenty-five people inside.*

part of the crew. Paymaster's Steward Michael Aheam was an early recipient of the Medal of Honor for exhibiting "marked coolness and good conduct" on board USS *Kearsarge* during her triumph over CSS *Alabama* off Cherbourg, France, on 19 June 1864.

These logistics specialists of the Navy Pay Corps were re-designated as the Navy Supply Corps, the term still used today.

During World War II, supply corps officers played a major role both in industrial production within the continental United States and in managing a logistics pipeline that conveyed the arms and equipment to the war zones. The size of the task was staggering. Just to feed Navy men ashore and afloat depended on delivering 25,000 tons of fresh and frozen food a month across the Pacific, along with twice that amount of dried consumables. By July 1945, a total of 2,930 ships were assigned to the support squadrons alone. The records of Pacific Fleet logistics ships document the transfer of 27 million packs of cigarettes and 1.2 million candy bars during one thirteen-day period. Fleet Admiral Ernest J. King would state: "The war has been variously described as a war of production and a war of machines. Whatever else it is, so far as the United States is concerned, it is a war of logistics." Over 17,800 supply corps officers were needed to manage the naval logistic war.

Modern supply corps officers and enlisted personnel of the supply ratings are involved in virtually every aspect of the operations on board a commissioned ship. For example, on an aircraft carrier deployed for six-months:

• Storekeepers will order, receive, store, and issue over 125,000 items worth over $250 million, ranging from nearly microscopic electronic components to deck and engineering equipment weighing several tons.

• Ship's servicemen will maintain and operate vending machines that will sell over 600,000 cans of soda. They will man a half-dozen retail outlets and stores, a six-chair barbershop, a full-service laundry and dry-cleaning plant, and a mini-arcade of video-entertainment games.

• Mess management specialists will prepare and serve over 3.2 million meals. On any given day the crew will consume 5,000 cups of coffee, 1,500 eggs, 5,000 ice cream cones, and 10,000 glasses of milk.

• Disbursing clerks will manage a payroll for over 6,000 people, dispensing in excess of $5 million a month through direct deposit, cash, checks, and a network of on-board Automatic Teller Machines.

• Data processing technicians and data systems technicians will operate and maintain mainframe computers and an elaborate shipboard network consisting of hundreds of personal computers and workstations.

• Postal clerks will receive and deliver hundreds of thousands of pieces of mail and tens of thousands of packages from home.

With fully loaded storerooms, a modern combatant is self sufficient for weeks or even months at a time. But in routine peacetime operations, ships are refueled and replenished on a regular basis, and in war ammunition and fuel may have to be replenished as often as every other day. Depending on location and

This painting captures the intensity of the logistics operations associated with amphibious landings of World War II. The bow doors and ramps of the landing craft medium LCM 201 in the foreground and the tank landing ships (LSTs) in the background allowed these ships to discharge the tanks and trucks in their holds directly onto the shore so that manhandling of cargo was reduced. (Painting: Andrew Small, Naval War College)

Opposite, center right: *Today, most administrative actions that once required paper are accomplished electronically. This storekeeper on USS* Spruance *(DD 963) accesses inventory records afloat and ashore using his computer.*

301

Above: *One facet of the Navy slogan "Anytime Anywhere" is demonstrated by Mess Management Specialist Lau bringing food to the Officer of the Deck and Lookout on the bridge of USS* Jefferson City *(SSN 759). No member of the crew is more important or more prized than a good cook. Though he may be derided by his own crew, the same crew will brag about his merits throughout the fleet. Arguments over their chefs' abilities have led to hostilities between crews more often than arguments over merits of captains.*

Above, right: *Sorting mail on board USS* George Washington *(CVN 73) in the Persian Gulf, Yeoman Second Class Marion Hicks, Postal Clerk Second Class Tony Spencer, and Personnelman Third Class Parome McGill prepare the most looked forward to event on board ship other than mooring in homeport. With the advent of e-mail capability on most major ships, mail call is less important an event than in years past—but not much. E-mail brings word, but not the children's hand-lettered posters and letters, and homemade cookies still come only in boxes.*

Opposite, top: *Navy chaplains serve in the field with the Marines as well as on board ship, conducting divine services in many climes and circumstances. The altar for this Mass at a fire base in Vietnam is made of ammunition cases and boxes of canned goods.*

mission, a surface ship normally can expect to be re-supplied at least every few weeks. One of the most demanding of at-sea evolutions, the underway replenishment, or UNREP, brings huge ships within yards of one another linked together by cables and hoses to transfer fuel, water, and supplies. Many replenishment ships carry helicopters that serve as flying cranes to move material from one ship to another. These vertical replenishments require extraordinary flying skills on the part of the aircrews, and strong backs and stamina on the part of the receiving crew that must unload and stow the materials into shipboard storerooms.

Ashore, teams of talented officers, enlisted personnel, and civil servants operate a vast network of inventory-control and stock points, data processing centers, regional contracting offices, petroleum storage and delivery facilities, Navy Exchanges, personal property offices, food service outlets and dining halls, and hazardous-material handling facilities. Much of what contributes to the overall quality of life of Navy personnel is managed and directed by the Navy Supply Corps. Whether it is the cook who works all night so the crew can have hot pastries in the morning, the postal clerk who forgoes his leave during the holidays to process mail from home, or the disbursing clerk who opens his safe on a weekend to provide advance pay so a sailor can go on emergency leave, these uniformed logisticians provide the material and services essential to maintain and operate the world's best Navy.

The Combat Clergy

As with any large and diverse society, Navy sailors require spiritual support. This support is provided by ordained men and women known collectively as chaplains. Former Navy Chaplain Sydney Key Evan stated, "The Navy chaplain has particular help in his work. The very ocean itself comes to his aid. In its calmer aspects it suggests the serenity, mystery, immensity, and irresistible energy of God, and in

Left: *Commander Patrick Hahan (CHC), USN, celebrates Mass at Camp Montief near Cernica, Kosovo. Marines went ashore as part of the NATO forces trying to bring peace and stability to the Balkans. In addition to conducting divine services, chaplains are called on for a wide variety of difficult personal circumstances, from counseling the bereaved parent distant from a dying child to explaining the provisions of just war to a combat unit.*

Above: *Father Steven Rock of Andover, Massachusetts, Chaplain of USS* Theodore Roosevelt *(CVN 71) administers the Sacrament of Confirmation to Interior Communications Technician Third Class Brian Erb. The Chaplain Corps encompasses over 1,200 chaplains, active and reserve, representing approximately 100 faith groups.*

its wilder moods His power, majesty, and awfulness. In all moods it is a constant reminder of man's littleness and dependence, and has ever been one of his chief stimuli to resourcefulness, courage, heroism, and self sacrifice."

Clergy have ventured offshore for centuries to minister to their seagoing flocks. In Great Britain in the late 1600s, the Secretary of the Admiralty Office was directed, "to notify the Church authorities of every ship ordered to sea that there might be a chaplain appointed to each, properly equipped with the King's warrant."

Military funerals are moments of great ceremony—nowhere more solemn than at the Arlington National Cemetery. Chaplains assigned there often perform their rituals several times a day. Devoted partners who share the joys and sorrows of life with their far-flung flock, Navy chaplains share the joys of marriage, birth, and fellowship and ease the pain of family separations, illness, and death.

A chaplain baptizes a Marine at the An Tan Bridge, Chu Lai, Viet Nam. Most chaplains bear witness to the adage that "There are no atheists in foxholes."

In the United States the regulations of the Continental Navy stated, "The Commanders of the ships of the thirteen United Colonies are to take care that divine service be performed twice a day on board and a sermon preached on Sundays, unless bad weather or other extraordinary accidents prevent." The first chaplain known to have served in the Continental Navy was the Reverend Benjamin Balch, a Harvard graduate and a Congregational minister who reported aboard the frigate *Boston* in October 1778. Over the decades, the role of the chaplain evolved to encompass visiting ill patients in sick bay, holding Bible study during the crew's off-duty hours, and teaching secular and liturgical subjects, as well as conducting divine services.

While the chaplain's formal tasks deal primarily with the spiritual and the cerebral, they live and work alongside their fellow officers and men, and as such, they play a part in the day-to-day life of the ship or station at which they serve. In times of battle they provide encouragement, prayer, final solace for their shipmates, and at times perform acts of great heroism. Commander Joseph Timothy O'Callahan helped save the aircraft carrier USS *Franklin* (CV 13), operating off the coast of Japan in March 1945. When two armor-piercing bombs ripped into "Big Ben" below decks, Chaplain O'Callahan worked his way up onto the flight deck where, in the midst of exploding ammunition and suffocating smoke, he calmly organized and led fire parties at a critical juncture, directed the flooding of several magazines threatened by the fire, and ordered ammunition to be tossed over the side. O'Callahan received the Medal of Honor for his heroism in this action.

As with corpsmen, Navy chaplains are assigned to Marine units. Many have distinguished themselves with acts of heroism during combat. When North Vietnamese soldiers ambushed Lieutenant Vincent Robert Capodanno's Marine battalion in September 1967, the chaplain came to the aid of several wounded

Seaman Carmelita Ellis singing at the Easter sunrise service on the fantail of the submarine tender USS *Holland* (AS 32) while en route to Sasebo, Japan. All large ships like carriers and tenders have chaplains assigned. Small ships sometimes share a chaplain when in company, but ships operating alone rely on lay leaders to conduct services.

Eternal Father, Strong to save,
Whose arm hath bound the restless wave,
Who bid'st the mighty Ocean deep
Its own appointed limits keep;
O hear us when we cry to Thee,
For those in peril on the sea.

Other verses added during and since World War II are dedicated to particular specialties and tasks. Samples include:

Lord, guard and guide the men who fly
Through the great spaces in the sky,
Be with them always in the air,
In dark'ning storms or sunlight fair.
O hear us when we lift our prayer,
For those in peril in the air.

Lord God, our power evermore,
Who arm doth reach the ocean floor,
Dive with our men beneath the sea;
Traverse the depths protectively.
O hear us when we pray, and keep
Them safe from peril in the deep.

Marines, pulling some to safety and performing last rites for others. Shielding a wounded corpsman, Reverend Capodanno died with twenty-seven bullets in his body. He too was awarded the Medal of Honor. The Chaplain Corps, though small in number, is large in its impact on the lives of America's sailors.

The Civil Engineers

Ships and aircraft require bases to return to and prepare for the next cruise, flight, or battle. The facilities of the Navy's shore establishment go by dozens of names—naval base, naval air station, naval training center, naval shipyard, fleet and industrial supply center, naval hospital, and more. Each facility exists to support either the equipment or the operators and their families. A naval facility can range from a small, gray metal desk in a strip-mall office manned by a lone recruiter to a huge complex of buildings, airfields, and piers on thousands of acres supporting a population of tens of thousands. The task of designing, building, and managing this multi-billion-dollar infrastructure falls to the officers of the Civil Engineer Corps, working under guidance from the Naval Facilities Engineering Command.

This organization, established in 1966, is the direct descendent of the Bureau of Yards and Docks, which built and managed the Navy's shore establishment since its founding in 1842. By 1890, the Navy shore establishment consisted of thirteen Navy yards and stations, 439 workshops, numerous storehouses, seven miles of wharf line, ten drydocks, nineteen marine railways, 150 oxen and horses, and ninety-six houses for officers' residences. This impressive array of facilities expanded beyond all expectations as the nation moved into the twentieth century. In World War I, the bureau built twenty-four aviation facilities in France, England, and Ireland; oil storage facilities and communications towers in France; thirty-five

Equipment Operator Second Class Ronald Chaffee operates an excavator at a project site on Guam, Marianas. The Seabees, organized at the beginning of World War II, became famous for building airfields, port facilities, and bases in the campaign across the Central Pacific. Today, there are nearly two thousand active duty and reserve construction engineering corps officers and 17,000 active-duty and reserve-enlisted Seabees.

Seabees insert a portable floating pier on the beach in Rockhampton, Australia. These Seabees are participating in a combined military training exercise involving 28,000 personnel, 252 aircraft, and forty-three ships, designed to train U.S. and Australian staffs in crisis action planning and contingency response operations.

In the island-hopping campaign that was the Pacific War, it frequently fell to Navy construction battalions (abbreviated CBs and usually written as Seabees) to do the heavy work in the forward areas. At times they had to fight as well as build. Above, Seabee Vance Shoemate stands by during the unloading of coral for runways on the island of Tinian in the Marianas. Tinian was the launching point for the B-29s that dropped atomic bombs on Hiroshima and Nagasaki in August 1945.

The Seabee Memorial stands alongside the entryway to the National Cemetery at Arlington, Virginia. Raised by popular subscription after World War II, the memorial salutes the exploits of the Navy's combat construction battalions.

training facilities; and a host of emergency hospitals. Once the war came to a close the bureau took the lead in the salvage and disposition of surplus materials, the berthing of deactivated ships, the closing of overseas stations, and the establishment of veterans' hospitals to care for the long-term wounded.

World War II initiated a $9 billion military construction program. Awarding contracts to commercial firms to construct facilities in remote locations and war zones was quickly deemed impractical. The Chief of Civil Engineers, Admiral Ben Moreell, organized construction battalions, the Seabees, construction experts who could defend what they built. In the Pacific, the Seabees built 111 major airstrips, 441 piers, 2,558 ammunition magazines, 700 square blocks of warehouses, hospitals to serve 70,000 patients, tanks for the storage of 100-million gallons of gasoline, and housing for 1.5 million men. The Pacific Seabees suffered 200 combat deaths, and earned over 2,000 purple hearts. These combat builders will long be remembered, in part because of John Wayne's portrayal in the 1944 film *The Fighting Seabees*.

For the next five decades, wherever the Navy went ashore, the Seabees were there. Korea to Vietnam to Kuwait—the Civil Engineer Corps/Seabee team built and maintained the facilities needed to keep the Navy deployed and functioning in combat and in humanitarian operations. The names of the enlisted ratings describe their skills: builder, construction electrician, construction mechanic, engineering aide, equipment operator, steelworker, and utilitiesman.

As in World War II, the Seabees were subjected to enemy fire during the more recent conflicts. On 10 June 1965, Construction Mechanic Third Class Marvin G. Shields fought with "gallantry and intrepidity" when an Army Special Forces compound came under intense fire from a Viet Cong regiment. Shields served to supply his fellow Americans who needed ammunition and returned the enemy fire for a period of approximately three hours, at which time the Viet Cong launched a massive attack at close range. Wounded in this firefight, Shields unhesitatingly volunteered to knock out an enemy machine-gun emplacement, saving the lives of many fellow servicemen. Mortally wounded by hostile fire while returning to his defensive position, Shields received the Medal of Honor posthumously.

In the 1970s national concerns about pollution and the environmental damage caused by our industrial society caused policies to be established to ensure that Navy facilities would be good stewards of the environment. The Civil Engineer Corps monitors compliance with existing regulations and conducts

Above: *Courts-martial, once the province exclusively of line officers, are now military trials at which the presiding officer serves as the foreman of the jury and the legal matters are in the hands of trained attorneys. The trial judges are experienced officers who have completed formal qualifications and been appointed to the office by the Judge Advocate General.*

environmental restoration when necessary. This new mission is added to an annual volume of business of $8 billion. As has been true for over a half-century: Seabees Can Do!

The Judge Advocates

For nearly two centuries, administration of legal affairs and the resolution of legal problems were handled by Navy officers of the line who had the necessary experience and knowledge of naval matters to ensure proper actions in light of maritime considerations. This system worked well for the most part, but as the nature of legal issues became more complex the establishment of a cadre of uniformed attorneys was warranted. The Navy Judge Advocate General Corps today consists of over 700 attorneys and nearly 500 legalmen who provide legal support and advice on issues ranging from International Law of the Sea to individual wills, trusts, and family law. Increasingly these officers are being assigned to operational staffs and deploying units to advise commanders on the complex legal issues that arise in coalition and multinational operations.

Above: *At the Oceans Law and Policy Department of the Naval War College's Center for Naval Warfare Studies, officers of the Judge Advocate Corps research and provide education on issues relating to the Law of the Sea, Admiralty Law, and other maritime matters. This department also serves as a source of analytical support to the Departments of the Navy and Defense on broad ocean law and policy issues.*

Left: *Courts-martial of enlisted men were often held in the open, attended by the Marine guard, and watched by the crew. Administration of justice was swift and often harsh. When use of the physical punishment was outlawed in 1850, concerns were voiced about how discipline would be maintained. Courts-martial composed exclusively and entirely of line officers ended with replacement of the Articles of War, known as the "Rocks and Shoals," by the Uniform Code of Military Justice after World War II.*

307

The Educators, Administrators, and Others

The Navy's supporting cast also includes a number of other specialists and technicians who do not belong to a staff corps category, yet are not warfare specialists. Engineering duty officers supervise construction and overhaul of ships and aircraft, or function to oversee design and acquisition of equipment or combat systems. Other officers of the restricted line include the public affairs officers and fleet support administrative specialists who supervise shore activities and the necessary bureaucratic work endemic to a large organization. Sailors who work in career fields such as yeoman, personnelman, musician, journalist, and Navy counselor at times are led by officers of the line, but at other times by officers who are administrative specialists or technically skilled in the appropriate fields. Each contributes to the team that enables the Navy to accomplish its overall mission.

The Navy's support infrastructure includes scores of schools and training establishments, ranging from enlisted basic recruit training "bootcamp" at

RECRUITING—IT ALL STARTS HERE: *"Nothing happens until somebody sells something!" is the punch line of an inspirational speech for salesman. Making something happen in the Navy starts with enlisting, training, and assigning people. For the Navy, the starter in this process, the* salesman, is the recruiter—officer or enlisted. Aided by thousands of former sailors who are ready references and endorsers, these dedicated officers and petty officers pound the pavement across the nation telling the Navy's story, answering questions, enrolling the eager, and encouraging the hesitant. Hours are long *and competition fierce—from colleges and workplaces seeking talented people as well as from the other services. In the heat of this battle, the Navy recruiter has many tools and attractions, but he is the only one who can say, "Join the Navy, see the world!"*

Upper left: Fire Controlman First Class A. F. Luann talks to a prospective recruit at the SEAFAIR Exhibition in Seattle, Washington. After mental and physical tests, recruits meet with classifiers who try to fit individual aptitude and interest with the Navy's more than ninety different job specialties. Recruits all go on to basic skill development schools following recruit training. In some technical areas, schooling lasts up to two years before the sailor is ready to occupy a billet in a crew.

Left: Recruit Training, Great Lakes, Illinois, is much the same as the entrance schools of other services plus water. Recruits are evaluated on their ability to swim and must leap from an elevated platform in a simulated abandon ship drill.

Great Lakes, Illinois, through undergraduate education at the U.S. Naval Academy in Annapolis, Maryland, and graduate education at several highly respected institutions.

The technical training establishment teaches all the vast variety of trades necessary to operate the engineering marvels that fly above, navigate on, and dive beneath the seas in the most complex machines that man has made. Thousands of courses convene each year teaching general and specific skills to hundreds of thousands of sailors. Few spend a year in the Navy without attending some kind of technical school or participating in a formal educational activity. Schools also train teams from specific ships in activities as diverse as controlling aircraft over a combat theater, conducting a search for and an attack on a submarine, or practicing for launch of intercontinental ballistic missiles.

Graduate education is provided by the Naval Postgraduate School in Monterey, California, and by the Navy's highest-level educational institution, the U.S. Naval War College in Newport, Rhode Island. Each year, through resident study on the Newport campus and nonresident study through the College of Continuing Education, over 2,000 senior officers enhance their skills as decision-makers in the complex worlds of national security and strategic study.

Opposite, top: *Established by Rear Admiral Stephen B. Luce in 1884, the Naval War College in Newport, Rhode Island, is the oldest war college in the United States. The college serves as the highest level graduate institution in the Navy's extensive education and training system. The Navy Doctrine Development Command charged with keeping Navy operational practices current is collocated with the college.*

Opposite, bottom: *Personnelman First Class Corey A. Hamilton (AW), USN, with his son at a retirement ceremony at Tinker Air Force Base, Oklahoma City, Oklahoma. Personnelmen are custodians of the service records, promoters of opportunities, and caretakers of fringe benefits. The skill and manner with which these petty officers perform their duties has great influence on individual morale. A chief personnelman opened the door and applied the push that started Admiral Mike Boorda on the road from petty officer third class to Chief of Naval Operations.*

The Civil Servants

No discussion of the Navy's support structure would be complete without paying tribute to the contributions of the civilian employees of the Department of the Navy. Over 195,000 career civilian employees work on the bases, stations, shipyards, air rework facilities, training commands and other complexes, in the bureaus and systems commands, as well as on the ships of the Military Sealift Command. Without them, Navy operation would cease. Their service runs the gamut from the clerks, technicians, and administrators so critical to day-to-day operations, to the research scientists, educators, and administrators who focus on the Navy's future needs. In nearly every Navy command ashore civil servants provide corporate memory, operational experience, and long-term stability. The relative permanence of this civilian workforce provides a degree of organizational continuity that effectively complements the rotational assignments inherent in the careers of uniformed personnel. It is neither facetious nor derogatory to state that active-duty personnel may come and go, but the civilian workforce will always be there! These members of the supporting cast are as loyal, as patriotic, and as dedicated as their more visible and uniformed teammates.

The Role of the Supporting Cast

Analysts and policymakers have wrestled with the proper ratio between support and warrior, tooth-to-tail, since Alexander the Great. The tooth represents the actual fighting forces and the tail stands for the support infrastructure needed to keep the fighters ready to engage the enemy. The Roman legions had a huge preponderance of tooth, and very little tail. The spear-carrying infantryman pretty much fended for himself, foraging off the land, and seizing food from the locals. As warfare became more complex, however, and as machines began to shape the battlefield, more support (or "tail") was needed. Sailing ships needed only wind—a free if unreliable commodity. But steam ships needed fuel. That meant bases first, then colliers, and now oilers. Complex electronic equipment demands replacement parts, skilled technicians, and a logistics organization to get the right supplies to the right location at the right time. In the new century, the strike airplane that puts explosive on target carries only one or two warriors. While saluting the courageous pilot and acknowledging his or her critical role in striking the target, the contributions of the entire team that worked to prepare both man and machine for the challenges of armed conflict need be recognized. These backstage players . . . the supporting cast . . . provide the physical and spiritual support that enables the warrior to face the enemy and emerge victorious.

Above, left and right: *Common to all ships is the need to keep the water out. Damage Control Trainers allow new sailors to learn basic techniques and experienced teams to practice their skills. Trainees in the Damage Control Trainer at Great Lakes push hard against the water pressure while at Submarine School, Groton, Connecticut, students work feverishly to contain a sea water leak before their compartment is flooded. Such experience cannot be gained in any way other than in such complex training devices. The return in self-confidence and team motivation is priceless.*

Opposite, top and lower left: *War games are an integral part of the Naval War College's mission—both as educational techniques and as research tools. Games in the 1920s and 1930s thoroughly prepared naval officers for the war with Japan. Admiral Nimitz reflected, "... nothing that happened during the war was a surprise...except the kamikaze." Games in the "Information Age" rely on computer technology and large data banks.*

Opposite, lower right: *Training devices allow neophytes to learn in safety, allow mistakes to be made without damage other than embarrassment, provide for exercises when the ship is in port, and permit creation of situations that cannot be duplicated on board ship. This Fire Control Coordinator of a submarine Fire Control Party seems to be encountering some difficulty communicating his thoughts to the console operator in the Combat System Trainer at the Submarine Training Facility in San Diego—better here than in combat.*

311

The Heritage

Partakers
of the Glory
Customs and Traditions

Vice Admiral William P. Mack, USN (Ret)

> *"May we not who are of their brotherhood claim that in a small way at least we are partakers of their glory? Certainly it is our duty to keep these traditions alive and in our memory and to pass them on untarnished to those who come after us . . ."*

—Rear Admiral Albert Gleaves, USN

Traditions and the customs that embody them exert a profound influence on human behavior. The esprit de corps engendered is particularly marked and important in military organizations, especially in time of war. Peacetime emphasis on the Navy's many unique and colorful traditions and customs inspires behavior that carries over in the stress of battle. A distinctive feature of American naval history is its continuum of success during peace and at war. The people, ships, and aircraft responsible for those successes are memorialized in the traditions and customs of the service.

Traditions are steeped in history and are part of the fabric of an organization. While a new navy can borrow many of its customs, it has to establish its own traditions. These traditions usually evolve from events that happen during wars or other memorable events. In over two centuries of service the most important tradition that the United States Navy has established is its reputation to fight aggressively.

What is it that inspires generation after generation of American seamen to persevere in combat and triumph, sometimes against enormous odds? Partly, it is a value system based on courage, honor, and commitment memorialized in inspirational words or phrases, many of which entered the naval vernacular in the heat and stress of battle. These phrases are committed to memory early in initial training and become etched into the souls of countless men and women who have served.

John Paul Jones fathered the oldest of these memorable phrases during the famous battle between his ship, *Bonhomme Richard*, and the British frigate *Serapis*, off Flamborough Head, England. Responding to a call to surrender, Jones told his senior lieutenant, Richard Dale, to relay, "I do not dream of surrender, but I am determined to make you strike." Dale said later that he replied to the other captain, "I have not yet begun to fight." When Captain Jones was asked if Dale's relay was the true version of what he said, he answered, "That sounds good. Let it stand." And so it has been a part of Navy folklore ever since.

Above, left: *On 3 August 1804, Stephen Decatur led a boarding party against a Tripolitan gunboat. During the hand-to-hand fighting Decatur was nearly killed. Seaman Daniel Frazier fended off the mortal blow. USS* Frazier *(DD 607), built in 1941 at Bethlehem Steel Shipyard, San Francisco, was named after him. ("Decatur Boarding a Tripolitan Gunboat," D.M. Carter, Naval Art Collection)*

Above: *Stephen Decatur was a mere twenty-five years old when he sailed* Intrepid *into Tripoli harbor on 16 February 1804. Decatur's daring attack so captured the American imagination that his name graces hundreds of towns, streets, and schools across the country. His home in Washington, D.C., maintained by the National Historic Trust, is open to visitors.*

Opposite: *Buried in France after his death, the body of John Paul Jones was returned in 1905 and placed within this crypt located beneath the Naval Academy chapel. It is one of many "shrine-like" places where people can reflect upon the sacrifices made by past generations of sailors, and which perpetuate the traits of courage, honor, and commitment that have become the hallmarks of American naval heroes.*

Pages 312–313: USS Constitution, *the world's oldest commissioned warship afloat—never defeated in battle—underway in Massachusetts Bay, while the Navy's Blue Angels Flight Demonstration Squadron passes overhead. Commissioned on 21 October 1797,* Constitution *makes an annual turnaround cruise in Boston Harbor. In the summer of 1997 she set sail unassisted for the first time in 116 years. ("Queen of the Fleet," Erick M. Murray, Navy Art Collection)*

315

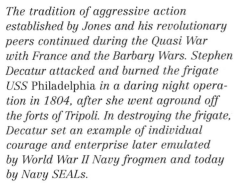

Oliver Hazard Perry was an American naval hero who achieved fame before age thirty. While the majority of today's naval officers will not achieve command until later in life, as depicted above, they still are given important and grave responsibilities at a young age and are expected to perform in the tradition of Jones, Decatur, and Perry.

Another well-known Jones quote combined his frequent declamations, "I want to sail in a fast ship!" and "I want to sail in harm's way." He repeated these two sayings in statements and correspondence until there was no doubt as to his intentions. This announcement became a motto underpinning a tradition of aggressive behavior expected of individual ship captains in the United States Navy.

With the outbreak of war with Great Britain in 1812, American seamen more than held their own against the Royal Navy as the frigates USS *Constitution* and USS *United States* and other warships enhanced the U.S. Navy's reputation with a string of victories over comparable British ships. Yet another famous phrase entered the Navy's lexicon in a defeat. Captain James Lawrence's frigate USS *Chesapeake* met HMS *Shannon* in single ship combat. In this duel, seasoned gunners of *Shannon* savaged the American ship with accurate fire, mortally wounding Lawrence and many of his shipmates. Lawrence succumbed, but not before urging his men to fight on with the five immortal words, "Don't give up the ship."

The tradition of aggressive action established by Jones and his revolutionary peers continued during the Quasi War with France and the Barbary Wars. Stephen Decatur attacked and burned the frigate USS Philadelphia *in a daring night operation in 1804, after she went aground off the forts of Tripoli. In destroying the frigate, Decatur set an example of individual courage and enterprise later emulated by World War II Navy frogmen and today by Navy SEALs.*

Three months later, twenty-seven-year-old Oliver Hazard Perry led a flotilla into battle against the British on Lake Erie. On his ship, named for Lawrence, he flew a flag made of rough muslin with the fallen captain's famous words emblazoned on it. After using Lawrence's dying words to inspire his men on to victory, Perry penned a dispatch to his superior that captured the young nation's imagination and entered into Navy lore: "We have met the enemy and they are ours: two ships, two brigs, one schooner, and one sloop."

Historians continue to debate the actual words exclaimed by David Glasgow Farragut during the Battle for Mobile Bay on 5 August 1864. Moored Confederate mines, called torpedoes at the time, struck fear within many northern sailors. "Damn the torpedoes! Full speed ahead!" became another inspirational phrase passed down to reinforce the reputation of Americans sailors as aggressive fighters.

Above and right: *Teamwork is at the heart of operating a ship, whether it be in battle at Manila Bay in 1898* (above) *or in a routine missile countdown simulation in USS* Pennsylvania's *(SSBN 735) Missile Control Center (MCC)* (right). *On a strategic ballistic missile submarine, the willing participation of over forty people is required in order to launch a missile.*

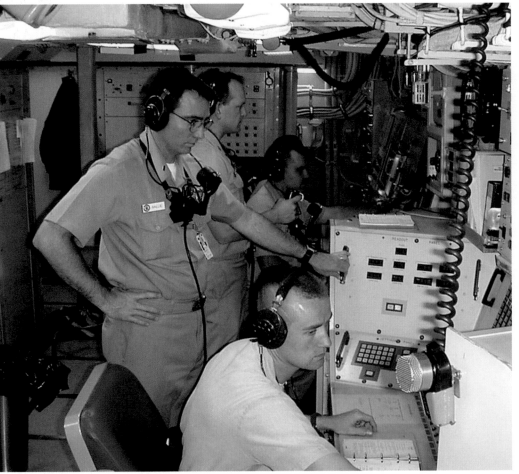

Admiral George Dewey became a national hero with the victory of his Asiatic Squadron at Manila Bay. Dewey was known for calm delegation of authority to his ships' captains and crews. With him are Samuel Ferguson, Apprentice Signal Boy, John A. McDougall, Marine orderly, and Chief Yeoman Merrick W. Creagh. Reliance on junior officers and enlisted sailors to execute important and complex tasks continues to this day.

One reason American naval commanders have been able to act aggressively is the trust and confidence they have in their well-trained subordinates. This tradition of professionalism was illustrated on 1 May 1898, when Commodore George Dewey, embarked in the cruiser *Olympia*, boldly steamed his Asiatic Squadron into Manila Bay. As his ships came within range of the enemy, he calmly called down to Captain Charles V. Gridley, "You may fire when ready, Gridley."

That Dewey was able to attack at Manila immediately upon being notified at the outbreak of war is a credit to his preparation and routine readiness. More often than not, over two hundred years, the Navy has been able to react capably and on short notice to challenges. When Destroyer Division 8 arrived at Queenstown, Ireland, on 4 May 1917, less than a month after the declaration of war, the British commander asked Commander Joseph K. Taussig when his vessels would be ready for escort duty. His response, "We are ready now, sir!" became a watchword for future operations.

A tradition of vigilance came with the outbreak of World War II. The words "Remember Pearl Harbor" or "December 7th" evoke special meanings for American sailors. Since then, American naval leaders have tried to avoid any complacency that could expose the fleet to such blows in the future. In the wake of the Pearl Harbor tragedy, the Navy quickly rebounded, the tradition of aggressiveness unabated. As the commander of a destroyer division operating nightly in the waters north of Guadalcanal known as the "Slot," Captain Arleigh Burke routinely led his division at high speed, leaving the refueling area off Guadalcanal and transiting up the slot to find Japanese ships. He announced on the tactical radio circuit as he maneuvered up the slot, "Stand clear, I am coming through at thirty-one knots."

As a result of their triumph in World War II and their support of the United Nations effort to defend South Korea, naval officers and enlisted personnel in the

Top, left and right: *The ability to fight on short notice, "We are ready now," typified by Commander Joseph K. Taussig in World War I (as told on pages 70 and 71) was demonstrated again by* USS Theodore Roosevelt *(CVN 71) in operations in the Balkans in 1999.*

Above, left and right: *Lacking sophisticated sensors, the United States Navy and Army failed to detect attacking Japanese naval aircraft launched from six aircraft carriers northwest of Oahu. Since World War II, a vast array of sea, air, and even space-based electronic sensors feed information to the Combat Information Centers of ships such as* USS Theodore Roosevelt *(CVN 71).*

319

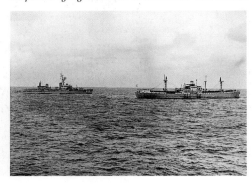

Above: *Then Captain Arleigh Burke reads on the starboard wing of the bridge of USS* Charles Ausburne *(DD 570), flagship of Destroyer Squadron 23, "The Little Beavers," in the Solomon Islands campaign in 1943. With a reputation as a bold destroyer squadron commander, enhanced by his abilities as a keen staff officer, Admiral Burke served as Chief of Naval Operations from 1955 until 1961. (Photo: Naval Historical Center)*

Below: *Interdiction of hostile merchant marine ships has been a mission of the U.S. Navy since the American Revolution. USS* Joseph P. Kennedy, Jr. *(DD 850), named for the president's brother lost in World War II, stopped the freighter* Marcula *as part of the American "quarantine" of Cuba to block Soviet cargo ships carrying missiles and nuclear warheads.*

early 1960s could take great pride and confidence in the ability of their ships and aircraft. When President John F. Kennedy questioned Chief of Naval Operations George W. Anderson about the fleet's ability to implement a Cuban quarantine, Anderson answered without hesitation, "The Navy will not let you down," and no further discussion or explanation was offered or expected.

With many colonials tracing their roots to England—a nation with the world's most powerful navy at the time of the American Revolution—the fact that many British naval customs were adopted by the new nation at the outset should not be surprising. Indeed, a committee of the Continental Congress, called the Marine Committee, used procedures modeled after the existing British regulations. With the adoption of the Articles of Organization on 28 November 1775, the Marine Committee proceeded to form the young Continental Navy. With the beginning of naval operations in wartime, the American Navy began developing its own character, and over time, created customs of its own.

Many customs are associated with ceremonial events, and few ceremonies match the splendor of a ship's commissioning. A ship is commissioned when afloat and after being completed by a shipyard or a builder. At the uttering of that final phrase, "Commission the ship," the mass of steel, wire, and equipment becomes an entity, a "United States Ship." From then on, until she is decommissioned, she is the responsibility of a succession of commanding officers. Whatever the size or shape of the ship, the elements of the ceremony are fixed in custom.

Prior to commissioning no jack or commission pennant is displayed. The

Colors

ENSIGN: *The word comes directly from the old Norman ensigne meaning "flag"; the ensign designates the nationality and is the principal flag. On American ships, the ensign is the national colors and is flown from the gaff at the mainmast when underway and from the staff*

at the fantail during daylight hours when moored or anchored. The colors are shifted at the moment the ship is underway, when the last line leaves the bollard or cleat on the pier or when the anchor is aweigh. Hauling down or "striking" the colors in battle indicates a warship has surrendered.

JACK: *A rectangular flag flown at the bow when moored. On American ships, the jack is the blue union component of the national colors. The exception is the jack flown by the ship with the longest total active service (other than*

USS Constitution*). This special jack is adapted from the colonial colors with horizontal red and white stripes and a rattlesnake above the words "Don't Tread On Me."*

COMMISSIONING PENNANT: *A long, narrow pennant, blue with seven white stars next to the hoist and a red and white trailer, flown continuously from the peak of the mainmast from commissioning until the ship is decommissioned. This is the official mark of a commissioned ship belonging to the United States Navy.*

BROAD COMMAND PENNANT OR BURGEE: *Flown on the flagship of a commander of a squadron or flotilla. A small flag of white with blue borders on which is emblazoned the number of the flotilla or squadron.*

DRESS SHIP: *For ceremonial occasions, in addition to the normal sets of colors, the ship is decorated using the signal flags rigged from the jack staff forward over the masts and to the stern. On national holidays, ships not underway dress ship.*

UNIT CITATION PENNANTS: *Ships awarded Presidential, Navy or Meritorious Unit Commendations recognizing extraordinary service fly pennants marking those awards.*

Upper left: The color guard on USS *Enterprise* (CVN 65), moored at Naval Station, Norfolk, prepares to lower the ensign at sunset. In port, colors are hoisted at 0800. When underway, colors fly continuously.

Left: With the historic jack displayed behind him in the hangar bay of USS Kitty Hawk (CV 63), the Secretary of the Navy addresses the crew.

Bottom, left and right: USS *Constitution* celebrating Washington's Birthday in Malta in 1837 (right) and USS *Alaska* (SSBN 732) tied up alongside the submarine tender USS *McKee* (AS 41) in Seward, Alaska, on Independence Day. *Constitution* and *McKee* have dressed ship. The submarine without masts or signal flags flies larger than normal colors at the regular places.

"In the name of the United States of America I christen thee Roosevelt," proclaims Mrs. Nancy Roosevelt Ireland as she shatters the ceremonial bottle of champagne against the guided missile destroyer named after her grandparents, Franklin and Eleanor Roosevelt. The ship's christening takes place when the hull is put in the water. In the nineteenth century, both men and women acted as ship sponsors, but in the twentieth century the honor has been reserved for women. When a ship is named for an individual, a relative is usually asked to perform the ritual. Bad luck is said to attend a ship if the bottle is not broken.

Right: A ship can be commissioned and decommissioned many times. The battleship USS Iowa *(BB 61) was originally commissioned in February 1943. After World War II the battleship was decommissioned and placed in "mothballs." It was then recommissioned to serve in Korea, decommissioned, and then brought back again in the 1980s to augment an expanding fleet.*

Below: President John F. Kennedy was the first of five consecutive presidents who had naval service on their resumés. As a lieutenant (jg), Kennedy skippered PT-109 when it was sunk in action in the South Pacific during World War II. Kennedy was awarded the Navy–Marine Corps Medal in recognition of saving lives at the risk of his own. Speaking to sailors on USS Kitty Hawk *(CVA 63), the president said, "I can imagine no more rewarding career. And any man who may be asked in this century what he did to make his life worthwhile, I think can respond with a good deal of pride and satisfaction: 'I served in the United States Navy.'"*

crew is paraded so they can see and participate in the ceremony. The official party, including the prospective commanding officer, the senior naval officer who accepts the ship for the Navy, the builder's representative, and other distinguished guests mount the official platform or board the ship without formality. After an invocation by a chaplain, the builder's representative "delivers" the ship, the senior officer accepting the ship reads the order to accept delivery and directs the prospective commanding officer to commission the ship. Attention is sounded, and the national anthem is played. The ensign, jack, and commission pennant are then broken.

The prospective commanding officer reads his orders from the Navy Department to take command, salutes the officer conducting the transfer, and reports, "Sir, I assume command of this ship." Immediately he orders the executive officer to "Set the watch," and the crew ceremoniously boards the ship.

Honors and speeches follow as the ship assumes an identity. Development of that identity is closely linked to the ship's unbroken chain of commanding officers until the ship is decommissioned years later. Each transfer from one commanding officer to the next takes place in a similar ceremony. After the new commanding officer has time on board to meet the officers and crew, to be briefed on the condition of the ship, and to make certain required inspections, the actual transfer of responsibility takes place in a long-standing, prescribed, formal public ceremony. The uniform is usually full dress, in keeping with the dignity of the occasion. All the officers, chief petty officers, and enlisted men and women are paraded in a location that has an unobstructed view of the ceremony. The departing commanding officer bids farewell and expresses his appreciation to the officers and the crew, while the crew in turn sees and hears the new commanding officer. The new commanding officer stands, reads his orders, salutes the outgoing commanding officer, and says, "I relieve you." At this public exchange, responsibility for the ship and crew moves from one person to the next. The new commanding officer turns to his senior, if present, and reports, "Sir, I have relieved as commanding officer."

The commission pennant of the relieved commanding officer is hauled down, and the commission pennant of the new commanding officer is hoisted. The master chief of the command or the chief quartermaster presents the old commission pennant to the now former commanding officer as a token of the crew's respect. The new commanding officer makes a very short speech—brevity is customary. The chaplain closes the ceremony with a short prayer.

In former days, few outside guests were present. At the conclusion of the ceremonies, the former commanding officer repaired to the captain's cabin, changed his uniform, and reappeared on the quarterdeck. Senior officers of the ship acted as sideboys, and junior officers manned the pulling boat. But these customs have faded with the years.

Sometimes circumstances dictate the removal of all fanfare, but the

"I will now read my orders!" intones Commander Joseph M. Reeves taking command of the USS Oregon *(BB 3) in 1914. Assuming command of a ship or air squadron represents a high point in a naval officer's career. While some may go on to become admirals and oversee vast bureaucracies and hundreds of personnel, when asked after retirement, most officers will fondly reflect on the days they had command at sea as the most personally satisfying of their career. (Photo: Naval Historical Center)*

Below: *Admiral Joseph M. Reeves is rowed ashore by officers of USS* Pennsylvania *(BB 38) after being relieved as Commander in Chief, U.S. Fleet, in 1936. This old custom died with the end of pulling long boats as part of ship's equipment`. (Photo: Naval Historical Center)*

King Neptune and his court arrive on board USS Wasp *(CV 7) as the ship crosses the equator. Even in war the rituals of turning pollywogs into shellbacks are carried out. By tradition, the person aboard who has been a shellback the longest acts as King Neptune and the next in seniority is his messenger, Davy Jones. (Photo: Naval Historical Center)*

The crew of USS Pogy *(SSN 647) sports blue noses as they return to San Diego from a trip to the North Pole. Traveling north above the Arctic Circle or south below the Antarctic Circle qualifies one to be a "blue nose."*

essentials of the ceremony are fixed even in time of battle. Just minutes before the change of command of the United States Seventh Fleet during the Vietnam conflict, the flagship, missile cruiser USS *Oklahoma City* (CG 5), located off the coast of North Vietnam, was engaging enemy batteries ashore. The ship pulled off shore a safe distance, the relieving fleet commander flew in from Danang by helicopter, and a short briefing was conducted. The ceremony took place immediately after the briefing, the departing commander flew off by helicopter, and the ship returned to conducting shore bombardment.

Changes of command are not the only ceremonies that can occur while underway. Of all the ceremonies conducted at sea, most notable is the crossing the line ceremony, which occurs when the ship crosses the equator. Those who have already crossed the line are known as "shellbacks," and those who have not are "pollywogs." The ceremony, when conducted by a well-drilled and capable crew, can be spectacular and fun for all hands.

These ceremonies are of such ancient vintage that their specific derivation is lost. The ceremonies used to be very rough and were designed to test inexperienced young sailors to see if they could endure the hard life at sea. Supposedly the ceremony began as a pagan ritual passed from the Vikings, to the Anglos, to the Saxons, and finally to the Normans. In the beginning the ceremony was designed to propitiate Neptunus Rex, the mythological god of the sea. In the ceremony, Neptune (that person who has been a shellback the longest) is decked in a beard of frayed rope, colorful robes, and crowned as a king. The next in line of seniority is his messenger, Davy Jones. Other shellbacks serve as members of his court, or are

dressed as mermaids. Ceremonies are preceded by elaborate printed summons for each pollywog. At the beginning of the ceremony, the navigator declares that the ship is "crossing the line," and Neptune and his court come aboard by some device appropriate to the type of ship.

The ship is symbolically turned over to Neptune and the ceremony proceeds under his direction. Each pollywog undergoes an examination and receives a punishment; while these were rigorous in the past, humor and mutual enjoyment are the aim of present-day rituals. At the completion of the ceremony King Neptune and his court "leave the ship and return to the sea." Each new shellback receives an elegant certificate of his initiation, which is treasured for years.

Funerals for naval personnel conducted ashore follow a military format established by the Army, but the ceremony associated with burial at sea follows the very old traditional customs of the Royal Navy. Every year the Navy honors many requests for burials at sea. Today's ceremonies are reserved for the remains of veterans, but up until World War II, burial at sea usually involved a member of the crew. Long voyages, poor sanitation and diet, and more physical hazards meant a death at sea was not uncommon. Without refrigeration, a dead body

Below, left: Partaking in the Navy's most solemn custom, grieving sailors gather on USS Kalinin Bay (CVE 68) after the Battle of Leyte Gulf in October 1944 to commit their fallen shipmates to the sea. (Photo: National Archives)

Below: Burial at sea continues to be practiced where veterans request such a disposition of their remains. USS Bataan (LHD 5) is the platform from which the body of Commander Robert S. Allison is committed to the deep.

The remains of Captain Charles "Pete" Conrad, USN (Ret), a naval aviator and astronaut, are brought to his gravesite with full military honors. The ceremony for burial of Navy personnel ashore follows the ritual designed by the Army; including a horse-drawn artillery caisson at Arlington National Cemetery.

Gun salutes are rendered to national flags and important officials. Edward Moran's painting (below) depicts the first French salute to the American flag when Ranger *arrived in France in 1778. USS* Virginia *(BB 13) at full dress ship (above) salutes President Theodore Roosevelt in 1906. Large warships are still equipped with saluting batteries to render honors. (Photo: Naval Historical Center)*

posed a health risk soon after death. A sailmaker promptly prepared the body for burial by sewing it in a canvas hammock, taking the last stitch through the nose. A projectile was placed at the feet and slits made in the canvas to ensure that the body would sink. The crew formed for the ceremony on the main deck, and the body was brought to the area by pallbearers and placed on a mess table next to the lifelines. Scriptures were read, prayers given, and the captain spoke a few words of inspiration. A chaplain gave a benediction to close the service and at his nod the pallbearers tipped the table so the body would slide over the side. Gun salutes would be fired along with a bugle rendition of Taps.

Gun salutes are rendered at sea and ashore. Gun salutes were originally friendly gestures by the first to salute, because the salute rendered a ship powerless during the honor. In the days of sail, guns were always kept loaded. After the gun salute an appreciable time was required before the guns could be loaded again and used offensively.

It is a very old superstition that the gun salute should be an odd number. The number of guns varied over the years and was finally settled by the United States on 18 April 1875 as twenty-one for a country or head of state salute and a "gun for gun" return. Personal salutes were set at lesser numbers according to the rank of the person saluted.

The salutes by one ship to another started when the waters from Norway to Cape Finisterre were claimed as "English Seas." Before Norman days, sails in these waters were lowered to the vessels flying the English flag as marks of respect to English sovereignty. The act rendered the vessel helpless until its sails were raised again. From this ancient custom grew the present action of tossing oars, lying on oars, stopping engines, letting fly sheets, and finally lowering the flag as a mark of respect to the nation of the ship saluted.

Today, ships passing close to each other dip their flags when abreast and quickly haul them up. Merchant vessels customarily dip their flags first when passing warships, and the warship answers the dip. War vessels do not dip to each other, but render passing honors through a mutual salute. Warships sound attention and remain at attention until the ships have passed. Officers on the bridge render a hand salute.

When official visitors board or leave a ship a ceremony known as "tending the side" is performed. The boatswain's pipe is used to announce the approach of a boat carrying a visitor. The coxswain of the boat raises a number of fingers to inform the officer of the deck of the rank of the visitor. The officer of the deck mans the side with the appropriate number of sideboys, and the boatswain's mate then pipes as the visitor climbs the accommodation ladder and passes through the sideboys. The pipe ends when the visitor salutes the colors.

"Good order and discipline" must be maintained in any military organization to assure success in combat. Good leadership and a strong chain of command keep everyone working together to achieve a positive result, with rules and regulations in place to serve as guidelines. For many years the Navy was governed by the Articles for Regulation of the Navy or more familiarly, "Rocks and Shoals."

"Atlantic Fleet, arriving!" Arrival and departure honors rendered on ceremonial occasions involve sideboys who "tend the side." The number of attendants reflects the rank of the official being honored—a remnant from the days when older officers were unable to scramble up the side and had to be hoisted aboard warships. "Older" generally meant "heavier," and so more hands were needed to hoist the older officers. In this case Admiral Royal E. Ingersoll merits eight sideboys as he steps aboard USS Iowa *(BB 61) in 1943. (Photo: National Archives)*

Manning the rails is an old and formal method of rendering honors. USS W. S. Sims *(FF 1059) mans the rails as the ship enters Antwerp, Belgium, on a port call.*

Opposite, top: *Formality varies from ship to ship but meals are the major social events of the day on a long voyage. In small ships like this submarine, the captain is a member of the Wardroom, occupying the chair at the head of the table, and the food is the same as in the crew's mess. In larger ships, the Wardroom has its own galley and menu. Customarily, business is not discussed at meals, and the subjects of sex, religion, and politics are avoided. (Photo: © Yogi Kaufman)*

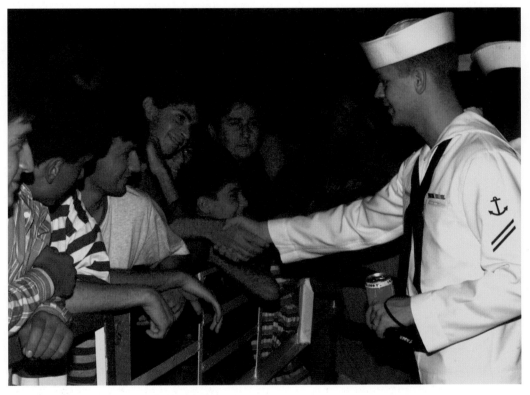

Top and right: *The author, as Commander Seventh Fleet, and his wife are guests of honor at a formal ceremony in Japan (top). Senior officers are often called upon to take part in formal rituals in foreign lands and strange cultures. At a port call in Batumi, Georgia (right), Seaman Tracy Tabor does his part to establish friendly relations with potential friends and allies.*

Sailors have not had to grit their teeth on hardtack and salt pork for many years. Meals are high points of social activity on board ship, and good food is important to crew morale.

After World War II, these articles were superseded by the Uniform Code of Military Justice. Today, the administration of justice is based on that law.

Courts-martial still exist, but now reflect the standards of American civil jurisprudence with professional judges presiding and the court acting as a jury. For less grievous infractions, commanding officers can conduct non-judicial punishment (NJP) or "Captain's Mast." Depending on his rank, the commanding officer has options for punishment ranging from restriction to the ship to pay forfeitures. One option, unique to the Navy, is a punishment of three days confinement with only bread and water served.

Bread and water is a remarkable punishment, given the variety of foods normally available to sailors on the mess or "chow" line. What sailors eat and drink has evolved, mainly due to the introduction of refrigeration and, more recently, to attention to diet. Sailors no longer have to grit their teeth on hardtack and salt pork, although Navy-bean soup has survived as a popular menu item. A typical chow line today always includes a separate salad bar. Good food is

important for crew morale, and meal times represent the social high point of a day at sea. An officer is customarily detailed to join the enlisted mess to sample the choices offered. Often the officer is chagrined to discover that the enlisted seamen eat a greater variety of tastier food than is available in the officers' mess. The annual Ney Award to the best enlisted mess is one of the most sought after awards in the Navy, and a ship values its reputation as "a feeder."

As for drink, in early days sailors were given a ration of rum. To deter drunkenness, the rum was watered down and served as grog. A General Order eliminated this ration for enlisted men in 1862. For years the United States Navy was known as a "dry Navy." However, with long deployments to the Arabian Sea without port calls in the 1980s, Navy leaders sought to boost morale of sailors assigned to this arduous duty by allocating a beer ration of two beers for every forty-five days of consecutive steaming. The restrictions have been further loosened to allow wine or beer to be served in wardrooms when hosting dignitaries.

Throughout most of the twentieth century, film was a popular form of enter-tainment on Navy ships as the crew mustered on the mess decks in the evening to view a motion picture. Over a long deployment, ships exchanged films, and the ability of the designated movie officer to secure popular films was subject to acute observation by the rest of the ship's company. Recently the custom of movie call has faded away as crew members can watch individual videocassettes and sometimes can even see live broadcast television on TV monitors placed in the berthing spaces.

Technology also has lessened the impact of mail call, two words long associ-ated with an instant morale boost. On many ships, sailors can now contact family regularly by phone or e-mail while at sea. This communications revolution may threaten the custom of the "Mail Buoy Watch." Often, seamen on their first cruise are assigned to search for the mythical buoy that supposedly contains a cache of

On special occasions, such as a Sunday, holidays, or a transit through the Suez or Panama canals, the mess decks and wardroom are secured and the crew enjoys a barbecue on "steel beach." Seamen Roman Lacson prepares skewers for the crew of USS Bunker Hill *(CG 52).*

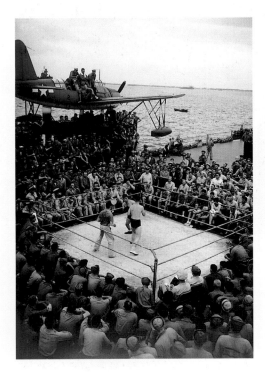

Right: *The evening movie plays at the forward end of the hangar deck on USS* Yorktown *(CV 10), while ordnancemen work on bombs for the next day's raid. Movies were the entertainment highlight, and before video machines multiplied offerings, the performance of the movie officer was a subject of close examination by the crew. (Photo: National Archives)*

Above: *USS* Iowa *(BB 61) holds a "smoker" while in port awaiting the start of the Marianas campaign in 1944. In years past, boxing matches or amateur theatricals were regular events in a ship's routine. The advent of movies reduced the popularity of these amateur shows. Today, sailors on large deck ships like aircraft carriers are more likely to play basketball, volleyball, or even football. (Photo: National Archives)*

The chief ceremonial addition that makes a wedding "military" is the exit honors rendered by the ushers formation of an arch of drawn swords. The act comes from medieval days and symbolizes the protection that the groom's friends promise to the new family. The Naval Academy chapel is the site of a large number of weddings immediately after graduation, because midshipmen are not permitted to marry while attending the academy.

ship's mail. Most understand it as a friendly initiation, but don raincoat, goggles, helmet, and signal flags to stand up on the bow to look out for the mythical mail buoy—for it certainly beats cleaning heads. This and other stunts, such as hunting for six feet of waterline or finding the hyphaducinator pump, continue to liven up life at sea regardless of the advances of technology.

There are few places that embrace and maintain the service's customs as intensely as the Naval Academy. John Paul Jones is buried and enshrined in the chapel. However, change is a constant even at this institution. Customs once universally accepted and carried out with élan and precision must be adapted to social changes. The custom of requiring midshipman to attend religious services on Sunday ended in 1972 when compulsory chapel attendance was declared to be unconstitutional by the U.S. Court of Appeals on the grounds that it represented "the establishment of a religion" in violation of the first amendment. While the midshipmen no longer parade to chapel, the customary inspirational services continue, well attended and open to the public.

Ceremonies that evolved from servility, which originated in fear and awe, are accepted today in military organizations as dignified gestures of respect to the symbols of the state and the state's officials. Ceremonies are a function of discipline. It follows that if the respect for lawful authority and the symbolism of the flag are worthy of preservation, they must be revered by their defenders: half measures will not do.

Years add glamour to the courageous or heroic acts of those who have gone. Mankind tends generally to weave some embroidery on the fabric of the actual event. Often romantic or sentimental traditions may hold little truth, yet they may have commendable inspirational value as folklore.

There is also a practical justification for fostering customs. Early customs become established traditions and exact regulations. Mahan in his essay, "Military Rule of Obedience," wrote, "The value of tradition to the social body is immense. The veneration for practices, or for authority, consecrated by long acceptance, has a reserve of strength which cannot be obtained by any novel device."

In a desire to emulate the progenitors of tradition, one becomes imbued with some of the spirit that prompted the original words and deeds. This factor is so imponderable but vital an influence on morale that men often die without

complaint in full knowledge that they have done their duty for country and unit, as did those who went before. "Don't give up the ship"; "Fight her till she sinks"; "Damn the torpedoes! Full speed ahead"; "Surrender? I have not yet begun to fight"; "We are ready now"; and "Take her down" are not mere words of sound and fury but carry lofty connotations—majestic overtones—of valor, self-sacrifice, and proud glory. They are the essence of priceless tradition.

The final words of a commendation for heroism, gallantry, or exemplary service contain the greatest praise that can be paid in the U.S. Navy—that the deed cited is in "the highest traditions of the naval service".

Above and above left: *"I do solemnly swear to support and defend the Constitution of the United States" begins the oath of enlistment. While officers serve at the pleasure of the president, enlisted personnel obligate themselves for finite periods. Reenlistments occur thousands of times a year, but always with due ceremony, whether the official administering the oath is a former president of the United States or a junior officer selected by the sailor re-enlisting.*

Left: *One of the Navy's most joyous ceremonies is graduation day at the Naval Academy, punctuated with the "tossing of the hats." As newly commissioned officers, these men and women will carry on the traditions and customs passed down from their predecessors. (Photo: Sandy Schaeffer, MAI)*

Above: *All traditions have a beginning. Going to an examination in Rickover Hall, the engineering building at the Naval Academy, midshipmen rub the nose on the bust of Admiral H. G. Rickover at the entrance for good luck.*

Lest We Forget
Museums and Memorials

Rear Admiral Henry C. McKinney, USN (Ret)

Memorials honor our nation's heroes who paid the ultimate sacrifice in defense of their country. Memorials have been around for as long as man has fought wars. Creators of memorials want us to sense the past, to be transported into the fury of the event remembered, and to imagine how it was back then. Battlefield memorials provide an excellent sense of the actual battle, the terrain, and the disposition of forces. At Gettysburg, we can hear the rumble and repulse of Pickett's charge and we can walk the fields where thousands of men lost their lives as they charged the Union lines on Cemetery Hill. At Normandy, we can scuff our feet in the sand and run our hands over the shell-pocked embattlements and wonder anew at the great sacrifices wrought on a June day.

Battles fought at sea—on, above, or under it—are different. With the exception of a few beached derelict ships, there is no trace of the Battle of Midway. True, Navy scientist and underwater explorer Robert Ballard has found the remains of several ships sunk during the battle, but even these lost ships do not give a true picture of this epic battle. There are no plaques in place to mark the scope of the battle of Coral Sea. One cannot appreciate the losses sustained to the crews of the ships on the floor of "Iron Bottom Sound." Even the milestones of our peacetime Navy are passed over by a sea that is uninhabitable by the student or the tourist. The places where naval history was made go unmarked and must be remembered remotely, ashore.

Museums

Museums are an important resource for honoring, preserving, and celebrating America's rich naval heritage. Far more than passive storage facilities, America's naval museums ably collect and display the artifacts of naval history and, most importantly, keep alive the story of America's historic reliance on naval power. There are eleven Navy-sponsored museums located throughout the country. The following are particularly noteworthy:

Above: *In this ceremony honoring the crew of USS* Drexler *(DD 741), sunk in a kamikaze attack off Okinawa in 1945, the children of Seaman Elmer M. Lewis, lost during the attack, present a wreath at the Navy Memorial in Washington. The sailors participating in the ceremony are from the Navy Ceremonial Guard and Navy Band, both stationed at the Washington Navy Yard. The reunion of the survivors of the ship itself and of the children and grandchildren of those killed is a major event at memorial sites.*

Opposite: *Honoring all who ever served in the naval services, the U.S. Navy Memorial is located on Pennsylvania Avenue midway between the White House and the Capitol. The memorial contains the largest map of the world, fountains and pools, and bronze relief sculptures. The* Lone Sailor *statue stands in the upper left quadrant of the granite map. The Naval Heritage Center, the memorial's visitor center, is located in the building on the right.*

U.S. Navy Museums

United States Navy Museum
Washington, D.C.

Naval War College Museum
Newport, Rhode Island

Submarine Force Museum
Groton, Connecticut

U.S. Naval Academy Museum
Annapolis, Maryland

**Patuxent River
Naval Air Museum**
Patuxent River, Maryland

Hampton Roads Naval Museum
Norfolk, Virginia

U.S. Navy Supply Corps Museum
Athens, Georgia

**National Museum of
Naval Aviation**
Pensacola, Florida

**Civil Engineer Corps /
Seabee Museum**
Port Hueneme, California

**Civil Engineer Corps /
Seabee Museum
Gulfport Branch**
Gulfport, Mississippi

Naval Undersea Museum
Keyport, Washington

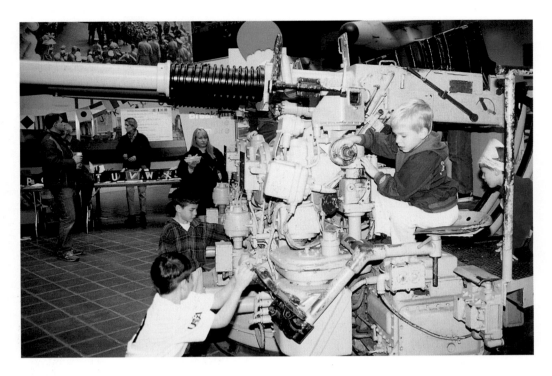

UNITED STATES NAVY MUSEUM, Washington, D.C., exhibits ship models, uniforms, ordnance, marine equipment, and fine art in the former Breech Mechanism Shop of the Naval Gun Factory. The exhibits span the Navy's history from the Revolution to the Gulf War and feature the fully rigged fighting top of USS *Constitution*, an F4U Corsair aircraft, a twin 5-inch gun mount, and a quad 40-millimeter anti-aircraft gun. The museum's gun mounts, submarine periscope, and other artifacts allow hands-on exploration by visitors. Although not on the Mall, the museum in the historic Washington Navy Yard is a must-see for any naval enthusiast.

SUBMARINE FORCE MUSEUM, Groton, Connecticut, part of the USS *Nautilus* (SSN 571) display, traces the history of the submarine force from the first U.S. submarine, USS *Holland* (SS 1) in 1900, to present-day nuclear attack and ballistic missile submarines. The museum has a world-renowned research library with an extensive collection of historical submarine documents.

NATIONAL MUSEUM OF NAVAL AVIATION, Pensacola, Florida, is one of the largest and most beautiful air and space museums in the world. It contains an exceptional display of naval aviation history. There are more than 130 carefully restored aircraft representing the Navy, Marine Corps, and Coast Guard. There is a remarkable display of four A-4 Skyhawks in a Blue Angels' diamond formation in the central seven-story glass and steel atrium. Flight simulators and an IMAX theater provide visitors with a sense of the "Magic of Flight." There is also an extensive exhibit devoted to World War II carrier aviation. One of the finest museums in the country, it is a prime attraction for all who are in the vicinity of Pensacola.

Top: *The Navy's official museum is in the Washington Navy Yard, D.C. Because many of the exhibits encourage "hands on," the U.S. Navy Museum ranks just behind the Smithsonian's Air and Space Museum in popularity surveys of those under eighteen.*

Center: *The world's first nuclear-powered submarine, USS* Nautilus *(SSN 571), is featured at the Submarine Force Museum, Groton, Connecticut. The museum is just outside the main gate to the Submarine Base along the banks of the Thames River. Modern submarines transit past the museum daily en route to or returning from their operating areas in the Atlantic Ocean to the south.*

HAMPTON ROADS NAVAL MUSEUM, Norfolk, Virginia, introduces the visitor to more than two centuries of naval activity in and around the great harbor of Hampton Roads, Virginia. From Revolutionary War battles to the historic first battle between the ironclads USS *Monitor* and CSS *Virginia*, Hampton Roads has played an important part in our country's naval history. Today it is the Navy's largest homeport.

USS *CONSTITUTION* MUSEUM, Boston, Massachusetts, is a private, nonprofit, educational museum located in the Charlestown Navy Yard next to USS *Constitution*. The museum's hands-on activities, artifacts, and art bring alive the life and chores of a sailor at sea in a nineteenth-century man-of-war. A visit to the museum enriches any tour of the ship.

ADMIRAL NIMITZ MUSEUM AND HISTORICAL CENTER, Fredericksburg, Texas, is a privately funded organization honoring Fleet Admiral Chester W. Nimitz. The Museum of the Pacific War highlights Nimitz's career and presents a chronology of World War II in the Pacific theater. The museum's George Bush Gallery hosts a tribute to the ten presidents who served in the war. Exhibits, many hands-on or audiovisual, display all types of artifacts used in Pacific campaigns.

SMITHSONIAN'S NATIONAL MUSEUM OF AMERICAN HISTORY, Washington, D.C., has opened a major exhibition on the role of the submarine in the Cold War as part of the celebration of the 100th anniversary of the submarine force in the year

2000. This exhibition gives visitors an inside look at submarine operations and the living conditions in a modern nuclear submarine.

Memorials

Over the years, but particularly since the end of World War II, retired Navy ships or parts of them have become the logical choice for memorials, and there are many across America. Often referred to as the "World's third largest fleet," four aircraft carriers, five battleships, two cruisers, ten destroyers, nineteen submarines, and assorted other craft are on display around the country. Interesting and attractive, each tells a story of what life was like at sea and of the sacrifices made by the men who manned these ships. Most of the ships, because of the battles in which they fought, have played a significant role in our nation's defense.

Ship memorials are impressive, especially for the former members of the ship's crew. These hardy mates stride the decks a little taller, and they see themselves and their shipmates in a context the casual visitors may not perceive. But ships are instructive even for the landlubber, their best purpose perhaps as an awakening to our nation's naval heritage. These great gray visual aids may not get us to Midway or to the Philippine Sea, but they offer worthwhile lessons from the past and give insight into the present.

Ships of the Memorial Fleet

AIRCRAFT CARRIERS. These ships revolutionized naval warfare in World War II. The four carriers on display, USS *Yorktown* (CV 10), USS *Intrepid* (CV 11), USS *Hornet* (CV 12), and USS *Lexington* (CV 16), each played a major role in the war in the Pacific. All are *Essex*-class carriers that formed the core of the fast carrier task forces that struck Japanese forces in the Pacific with devastating results. All of these ships were subsequently modernized for continued active service into the 1970s or later. Fighting in the Korean and Vietnam wars these aircraft carriers continued to serve with great distinction. Visits to these ships evoke not only echoes of World War II but also of the Cold War and our nation's continued commitment to maintain freedom of the seas.

SHIPS OF THE MEMORIAL FLEET:

AIRCRAFT CARRIERS
USS **YORKTOWN** *(CV 10)*—*Charleston, South Carolina*
USS **INTREPID** *(CV 11)*—*New York, New York*
USS **HORNET** *(CV 12)*—*Alameda, California*
USS **LEXINGTON** *(CV 16)*—*Corpus Christi, Texas*

BATTLESHIPS
USS **TEXAS** *(BB 35)*—*LaPorte, Texas*
USS **NORTH CAROLINA** *(BB 55)*—*Wilmington, North Carolina*
USS **MASSACHUSETTS** *(BB 59)*—*Fall River, Massachusetts*
USS **ALABAMA** *(BB 60)*—*Mobile, Alabama*
USS **MISSOURI** *(BB 63)*—*Pearl Harbor, Hawaii*

CRUISERS
USS **LITTLE ROCK** *(CL 92/CLG 4)* —*Buffalo, New York*
USS **SALEM** *(CA 139)*—*Quincy, Massachusetts*

DESTROYERS AND DESTROYER ESCORTS
USS **THE SULLIVANS** *(DD 537)*—*Buffalo, New York*
USS **KIDD** *(DD 661)*—*Baton Rouge, Louisiana*
USS **LAFFEY** *(DD 724)*—*Charleston, South Carolina*
USS **CASSIN YOUNG** *(DD 793)*—*Boston, Massachusetts*
USS **JOSEPH P. KENNEDY, JR.** *(DD 850)*—*Fall River, Massachusetts*
USS **BARRY** *(DD 933)*—*Washington, District of Colombia*
USS **EDSON** *(DD 946)*—*New York, New York*
USS **TURNER JOY** *(DD 951)*—*Bremerton, Washington*
USS **STEWART** *(DE 238)*—*Galveston, Texas*
USS **SLATER** *(DE 766)*—*Albany, New York*

SUBMARINES
USS **COD** *(SS 224)*—*Cleveland, Ohio*
USS **DRUM** *(SS 228)*—*Mobile, Alabama*
USS **SILVERSIDES** *(SS 236)*—*Muskegon, Michigan*
USS **CAVALLA** *(SS 244)*—*Galveston, Texas*
USS **COBIA** *(SS 245)*—*Manitowoc, Wisconsin*
USS **CROAKER** *(SS 246)*—*Buffalo, New York*
USS **BOWFIN** *(SS 287)*—*Pearl Harbor, Hawaii*
USS **LING** *(SS 297)*—*Hackensack, New Jersey*
USS **LIONFISH** *(SS 298)*—*Fall River, Massachusetts*
USS **BATFISH** *(SS 310)*—*Muskogee, Oklahoma*
USS **BECUNA** *(SS 319)*—*Philadelphia, Pennsylvania*
USS **CLAMAGORE** *(SS 343)*—*Charleston, South Carolina*
USS **PAMPANITO** *(SS 383)*—*San Francisco, California*
USS **TORSK** *(SS 423)*—*Baltimore, Maryland*
USS **REQUIN** *(SS 481)*—*Pittsburgh, Pennsylvania*
USS **ALBACORE** *(AGSS 569)*—*Portsmouth, New Hampshire*
USS **GROWLER** *(SSG 577)*—*New York, New York*
USS **BLUEBACK** *(SS 581)*—*Portland, Oregon*
USS **NAUTILUS** *(SSN 571)*—*Groton, Connecticut*

USS *Intrepid* (CV 11), the "Fighting I," is the centerpiece of the *Intrepid* Sea, Air, and Space Museum at Pier 86 in New York, New York. USS *Growler* (SSG 577), USS *Edson* (DD 946), and a supporting tug complete the museum. Thirty airplanes are on display on the carrier's flight and hangar decks.

BATTLESHIPS. Before the advent of carrier-based aircraft, confrontations at sea meant battleships dueling with their main batteries. The five battleships on display, USS *Texas* (BB 35), USS *North Carolina* (BB 55), USS *Massachusetts* (BB 59), USS *Alabama* (BB 60), and USS *Missouri* (BB 63), were designed for that mission. Although they did not participate in heavyweight slugging matches during World War II, these ships protected the fast carrier task forces from enemy air attack and conducting shore bombardment in both the Atlantic and Pacific. Amphibious landings were preceded by bombardments by battleships firing projectiles that weighed nearly two tons from their big guns. Visits to these behemoths are fascinating. The heavy armor to defend against attack by other battleships, and the size of the 16-inch gun turrets, are awe-inspiring sights. *Missouri* was the site of the formal surrender of Japan. Visiting both the *Arizona* Memorial and battleship *Missouri* in Pearl Harbor allows the visitor to see where the Pacific War started for America and where it ended.

USS Texas (BB 35) deployed to Scapa Flow in the British Isles in World War I and bombarded beaches at Normandy in World War II. (Photo: David A. Manning)

Top row (left to right):

USS Lexington *(CV 16), the "Blue Ghost," is moored in Corpus Christi, Texas. Hit twice by the enemy during the war, she participated in every major naval campaign in World War II from Tarawa to Tokyo.*

USS Hornet *(CV 12), an Essex-class carrier from World War II, is moored at Alameda, California, just across the bay from San Francisco. Only twenty-one months elapsed between the laying of her keel and her first engagement with the enemy.*

The namesake of the first modern battleship class, USS North Carolina *(BB 55) was nicknamed "The Showboat." Now open to visitors in Wilmington, North Carolina, she has the most extensive World War II battle record of any battleship, with fifteen battle stars for service from Guadalcanal to the actions against the home islands of Japan.*

Now a part of a state park, USS Alabama *(BB 60) served in both Atlantic and Pacific theaters in World War II earning a reputation for effectiveness in antiaircraft warfare while supporting amphibious landings.*

CRUISERS. Cruisers made important contributions in World War II, Korea, and Vietnam, both in antiaircraft warfare and shore bombardment. USS *Little Rock* (CL 92/CLG 4) commissioned late in World War II as a light cruiser, represents a class that saw extensive action against Japan. Converted to fire Talos surface-to-air missiles in the late 1950s, she was redesignated a guided missile ship. USS *Salem* (CA 139), commissioned in 1949, served as flagship of the U.S. Sixth Fleet for eight years. She was one of three in the *Des Moines* class, the last and most capable all-gun cruisers ever built.

DESTROYERS. The backbone of the Navy, these ships fulfilled many roles during World War II. Antiaircraft, anti-submarine, and surface warfare were principal missions. But these versatile ships also laid or swept mines, launched torpedoes and rockets, put landing parties ashore, and rescued downed pilots. The *Fletcher* class, designed in 1938 and the principal destroyer in World War II, is represented by USS *Kidd* (DD 661) in Baton Rouge, Louisiana. The subsequent *Gearing* class, with more firepower, is represented by USS *Laffey* (DD 724) at Patriot's Point in Charleston, South Carolina, and USS *Joseph P. Kennedy, Jr.* (DD 850) at Fall River, Massachusetts. Three destroyers on display as memorials represent the *Forrest Sherman* class from the Cold War era. A visit to a *Fletcher*-class destroyer is to take a step back in time and to gain an appreciation of the hardships of serving in a small combatant.

SUBMARINES. Submarines played a major role in the outcome of the war in the Pacific, and they paid a dear price. Suffering the highest casualty rate of any organization of our armed forces, fifty-two submarines and 3,617 submariners were lost at sea. Submarines sank 1,392 Japanese ships accounting for over five million tons of enemy shipping. In the war of attrition against Japan, these losses brought the Japanese war machine to its knees. A visit to a World War II diesel submarine such as USS *Bowfin* (SS 287) in Hawaii or USS *Cobia* (SS 245) in Manitowoc, Wisconsin, will convince even the greatest skeptic of the incredible courage it took to serve in this elite force. In addition to diesel submarines, the Memorial Fleet includes the world's first nuclear submarine, USS *Nautilus* (SSN 571), which is also the first ship to reach the North Pole.

Special Display Ships

USS *CONSTITUTION*, Boston, Massachusetts, "Old Ironsides," is the oldest commissioned warship afloat. *Constitution* was one of six ships ordered by President George Washington to protect America's growing maritime interests in the 1790s. *Constitution* soon earned widespread renown for her ability to punish French privateers in the Caribbean and thwart the Barbary corsairs in the Mediterranean. Her greatest glory came during the War of 1812 when she

Bottom row (left to right):

USS Missouri *(BB 63), seen here steaming into Pearl Harbor with her rails manned, is now moored just forward of the* Arizona Memorial. *Visitors here have a vivid demonstration of the beginning and end of World War II. The formal surrender ceremony on board* Missouri *on 2 September 1945 is pictured on page 141.*

USS Kidd *(DD 661) on display at Baton Rouge, Louisiana, is named for Rear Admiral Isaac C. Kidd, Jr., who was killed on board his flagship, USS* Arizona, *at Pearl Harbor, 7 December 1941.*

The USS Bowfin *(SS 287) Submarine Museum and Park in Pearl Harbor, Hawaii, is located next to the* Arizona *Memorial visitors' center.* Bowfin *completed nine war patrols in World War II.*

USS Cobia *(SS 245) at the Wisconsin Maritime Museum at Manitowoc is a memorial that keeps alive the heritage of the twenty-eight submarines built at Manitowoc during World War II.*

Right: *USS* Constitution *underway in Boston Harbor fires a twenty-one-gun salute to celebrate the nation's birthday. The frigate is "dressed" for the occasion with modern signal flags between the masts. The national colors flown at the mastheads are where they would be worn in battle to maximize visibility through the smoke from the gun powder.* Constitution's *crew, dressed in replica 1813 uniforms, demonstrate the skills and conduct of early nineteenth-century sailors.* Constitution *is open to the public.*

Below: *USS* Constellation *is a National Historic Landmark moored alongside Pier One in Baltimore, Maryland's Inner Harbor.*

On the riverfront in Philadelphia, Pennsylvania, sits USS Olympia *(C 6), Admiral Dewey's flagship at the Battle of Manila Bay in the Spanish-American War.* Olympia's *last official duty was to transport the body of the World War I Unknown Soldier from France to the United States for reburial in Arlington National Cemetery. USS* Becuna *(SS 319) is moored alongside and is also on exhibit.*

340

defeated four British ships. During the battle with HMS *Guerriere*, seamen watched British cannonballs bounce off her twenty-one-inch-thick oak sides, earning the vessel her nickname.

USS *CONSTELLATION*, Baltimore, Maryland, is the last existing Civil War-era naval vessel and the last sail-powered warship built by the U.S. Navy. In addition to service in the Civil War, *Constellation* was used extensively as a training ship for Naval Academy midshipmen, and during World War II she served as relief flagship for the admiral in charge of the Atlantic Fleet. She has recently been restored to the ship's 1861 configuration.

USS *OLYMPIA* (C 6), Philadelphia, Pennsylvania, is the oldest steel-hulled American warship afloat. She served as Commodore George Dewey's flagship during the Battle of Manila Bay on 1 May 1899, when he gave the now famous order to the captain of *Olympia*, "You may fire when ready, Gridley." In that engagement, Spanish naval forces in the Philippines were handed a smashing defeat, marking the emergence of the United States as a world power.

Memorials

USS *ARIZONA* (BB 39), Pearl Harbor, Hawaii, is dedicated to the 1,177 sailors who perished in the ship during the Japanese attack on Pearl Harbor. *Arizona's* magazines were pierced by a 1,760-pound bomb and the subsequent explosions

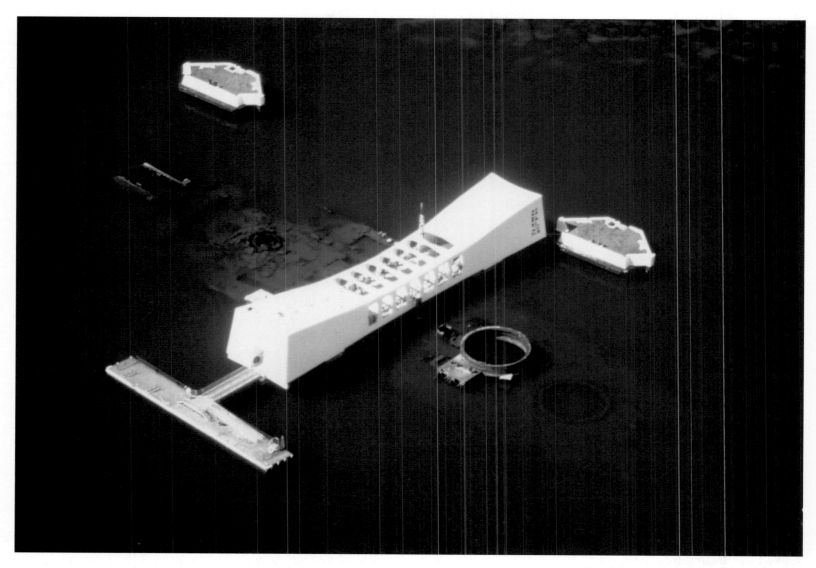

Above: *USS* Arizona *(BB 39) sits on the floor of Pearl Harbor, Hawaii, the tomb of hundreds of sailors who went down with their ship on Sunday morning, 7 December 1941. The memorial sits athwart the ship where the bridge superstructure was located. The round drum above the water to the right of the memorial is the barbette of the number two main battery turret. (Photo: National Park Service)*

Left: *A boat operated by the National Park Service ferries visitors from the park visitors' center to the* Arizona *Memorial. The names of those lost with the ship are inscribed on the walls of the memorial.*

shattered and sank the battleship in forty feet of water. *Arizona*'s burning superstructure and listing masts became one of the most reproduced scenes of the Pacific war as the nation rallied to the cry "Remember Pearl Harbor."

USS *INDIANAPOLIS* (CA 35), Indianapolis, Indiana, recalls a terrible ship disaster late in World War II. *Indianapolis* was sunk by a Japanese submarine on 30 July 1945 with a loss of 880 men. The memorial is a moving monument to these lost sailors, many of whom survived the sinking for several days in shark-infested waters before succumbing.

SUBMARINE MEMORIALS in Pearl Harbor, Hawaii, and Groton, Connecticut, accomplish the mission of the submarine veterans of World War II: "To perpetuate the memory of those shipmates who gave their lives in submarine warfare." The

Right: *This memorial in Indianapolis, Indiana, commemorates the bravery and sacrifice of the men on board the cruiser Indianapolis, sunk by a Japanese submarine near the end of World War II. The survivors of the sinking spent several days in the water before those who endured were rescued.*

Below and below, right: *The Submarine Veterans of World War II sponsor two national memorials, one at Pearl Harbor (below), the main base for the submarine campaign in the Central Pacific in World War II, and the second in Groton, Connecticut (below, right), home of the Submarine School and the Electric Boat Company, a major submarine builder. These and many smaller monuments commemorate the fifty-two submarines and their crews lost during the war.*

submarine force in World War II was critical to the victory in the Pacific Theater, but this success came at an enormous cost of life. These memorials are dedicated to the fifty-two U.S. submarines that were lost and the 3,617 men on "eternal patrol." A visit to either of these memorials is a moving experience.

UNITED STATES NAVY MEMORIAL, the privately funded Navy Memorial in Washington, D.C., unique among the museums and memorials, focuses on the people of the Navy, not the hardware, organizations, or systems of naval warfare. The emphasis is best symbolized, not by a decommissioned ship or expansive museum, but by the solitary statue of the *Lone Sailor*. Individuals, communities, and events in naval history are saluted here as are the Navy, Marine Corps, Coast Guard, and Merchant Marine. The Chief of Naval Operations flies his flag from the memorial's gaff. But the Navy Memorial is about American sailors—what they have done with their own skill and determination and their "honor, courage, and commitment." The tools of warfare at sea may change but not the hearts of people that America sends to sea.

Display ships and memorials perform important functions. Evoking memories, educating, inspiring, and providing places for reflection, like the Navy they commemorate, they should never be taken for granted. The vast majority are privately funded and manned by volunteers. Behind every memorial is a group of individuals working to preserve the legacy of the sailors they honor. They need volunteers and welcome financial contributions. Your help would be most appreciated.

THE LONE SAILOR: *A centerpiece of the Navy Memorial is Stanley Bleifield's compelling statue of the* **Lone Sailor,** *who maintains a silent vigil on a 100-foot diameter granite map of the world. The* **Lone Sailor** *represents a senior second class petty officer, twenty-five years old at most, who is fast becoming a seagoing veteran. He has done it all—fired his weapons in a dozen wars, weighed anchor from a thousand ports, repelled boarders, typed in quadruplicate, and mess cooked too. He has made "liberty call" in great cities and tiny villages, where he played tourist, ambassador, missionary to the poor, adventurer, souvenir shopper, and friend. His shipmates remember him with pride and tell their grandchildren stories, some of which, like him, are seven feet tall.*

Sculpted by Stanley Bleifield, the *Lone Sailor* represents all who have or will serve in the Navy. The seven-foot-tall bronze figure stands on the granite map of the world, which forms the center plaza of the Navy Memorial. Metal fragments from historic Navy ships were included in the bronze from which the statue is molded. Every day Navy veterans stop to pay their respects or honor departed shipmates in the presence of the *Lone Sailor* and thousands of active-duty sailors have chosen this site to reenlist in the Navy.

The Naval Academy at Annapolis, Maryland, holds many of the artifacts and memorials of the Navy. In addition to a fine museum and the chapel—with John Paul Jones's Crypt—colors and cannons captured in wars since 1798 are displayed in public areas of other buildings.

343

Acknowledgments

Most of the images in this book come from several collections rich in the heritage and lore of the United States Navy. The curators of these collections have been invaluable in selecting and procuring the best images on the subjects presented. The photographs in the historical chapters come primarily from the Naval Historical Center in the Washington Navy Yard. The Curator Branch of the Historical Center, especially Charles Haberlein, Edwin Finney, and Jack Green, were tireless in their response to the needs of the authors and editors. Gale Munro, curator of the Navy Art Collection, also was helpful and responsive. The vast collection of the U.S. Naval Institute, Annapolis, is another collection mined for both art and photographs. Paul Stillwell and Dawn Stitzel, manager of Library Services and Photographic Archives, were instrumental in taking advantage of this extensive collection. Images from the National Archives and Library of Congress were researched by Diane Hamilton. Finally, most of the photographs in the "Fleet Today" section come from the official Navy files at the Navy Still Media Center under Chris Madden's direction. There, Aviation Photographer's Mate Second Class Tim Altgedt was particularly helpful. Their web site was a constant source of fine images; the editors regret that more could not be used.

A number of Public Affairs Officers were most helpful. The enthusiastic response of Ms. Pam Warnken at the Naval Academy accounts for the many fine images of that institution which appear in the book. Chief Petty Officer Jon Hockersmith, PHC (AW), at the Naval War College also deserves mention for his responsiveness and artistic eye. Ensign Chuck Bell at the Mine Warfare Command deluged the editor with fine photos for that segment. Vice Admiral Yogi Kaufman, the premier photographer of naval subjects, provided his usual superb pictures in a number of areas, and Captain Bob Rositzke of Empire Video, Inc., filled in a number of vacancies at the last stages of the layout. The web site of Commander, Submarine Group Nine offered a wonderful source of internal submarine images.

Captain Charles T. Creekman, executive director of the Naval Historical Foundation, while not acknowledged in the editorial section, did yeoman work on the final layouts and captions. Alex Macensky, in the Foundation's Historical Services Section, took over image selection and reproduction near the end of the project, and without his diligence, the volume would have been much less rich. Finally, Sandra Doyle and Deborah Zindell struggled valiantly to keep the Editor-in-Chief's enthusiasm corralled and capitalization consistent, not always successfully.

344

Suggested Reading

Official histories, monographs, and bibliographies published by the Naval Historical Center are listed on the Center's website at www.history.navy.mil.

1775–1815
James Fenimore Cooper, *The History of the Navy of the United States of America* (1839)

Eugene S. Ferguson, *Truxtun of the Constellation: The Life of Commodore Thomas Truxtun, U.S. Navy, 1775–1822* (1956)

William M. Fowler, Jr., *Rebels Under Sail: The American Navy during the Revolution* (1976); *Jack Tars and Commodores: The American Navy, 1783–1815* (1984)

Robert Gardiner, ed., *Navies and the American Revolution, 1775–1783* (1997)

Linda M. Maloney, *The Captain from Connecticut: The Life and Naval Times of Isaac Hull* (1986)

Samuel Eliot Morison, *John Paul Jones, A Sailor's Biography* (1959)

Michael A. Palmer, *Stoddert's War: Naval Operations During the Quasi-War with France 1798–1801* (1987)

Theodore Roosevelt, *The Naval War of 1812* (1882)

Glenn Tucker, *Dawn Like Thunder: The Barbary Wars and the Birth of the U.S. Navy* (1963)

1816–1860
Herman Melville, *White-Jacket or, The World in a Man-of-War* (1850)

Samuel Eliot Morison, *"Old Bruin": Commodore Matthew C. Perry, 1794–1858* (1967)

Charles Nordoff, *Man-of-War Life: A Boy's Experience in the U.S. Navy* (1855)

CIVIL WAR
Bern Anderson, *By Sea and By River: The Naval History of the Civil War* (1962)

William C. Davis, *Duel Between the First Ironclads* (1975)

William M. Fowler, Jr., *Under Two Flags: The American Navy in the Civil War* (1990)

H. Allen Gosnell, *Guns on the Western Waters: The Story of River Gunboats in the Civil War* (1949)

Virgil C. Jones, *The Civil War at Sea* (3 volumes: 1960–1962)

Raimondo Luraghi, *A History of the Confederate Navy* (1995)

1865–1922
James C. Bradford, ed., *Admirals of the New Steel Navy: Makers of the American Naval Tradition, 1880–1930* (1990)

William R. Braisted, *The United States Navy in the Pacific, 1897–1909* (1958)

Mark Russell Shulman, *Navalism and the Emergence of American Sea Power: 1882–1893* (1995)

William S. Sims, *The Victory at Sea* (1920)

David F. Trask, *The War with Spain in 1898* (1981)

1922–1941
Cdr. Edward Ellsberg, *On the Bottom* (1929)

Marcus Goodrich, *Delilah* (1941)

Richard McKenna, *The Sand Pebbles* (1962)

Paul Stillwell, *Battleship Arizona: An Illustrated History* (1991)

WORLD WAR II
John T. Mason, Jr., *Atlantic War Remembered* (1990); *Pacific War Remembered* (1986)

Samuel Eliot Morison, *Two-Ocean War: A Short History of the United States Navy in the Second World War* (1963)

Herman Wouk, *The Caine Mutiny: A Novel of World War II* (1951)

1945–1991
George W. Baer, *One Hundred Years of Sea Power: The U.S. Navy, 1890–1990* (1994)

Stephen Howarth, *To Shining Sea: A History of the United States Navy, 1775–1991* (1991)

Edward J. Marolda, *By Sea, Air, and Land: An Illustrated History of the U.S. Navy and the War in Southeast Asia* (1994)

Edward J. Marolda and Robert J. Schneller, Jr., *Shield and Sword: The United States Navy and the Persian Gulf War* (1998)

Alan R. Millett and Peter Maslowski, *For the Common Defense: A Military History of the United States of America* (1994)

David F. Winkler, *Cold War at Sea* (2000)

SURFACE WARFARE
Malcolm Muir, Jr., *Black Shoes and Blue Water* (1996)

E. B. Potter, *Admiral Arleigh Burke* (1990)

CARRIER AVIATION WARFARE
Roy A. Grossnick, *United States Naval Aviation, 1910–1995* (1997)

Capt. Richard C. Knott, *A Heritage of Wings: An Illustrated History of Navy Aviation* (1997)

SUBMARINE WARFARE
Clay Blair, Jr., *Silent Victory: The U.S. Submarine War Against Japan* (1975)

Tom Clancy, *The Hunt for Red October* (1984)

Rear Adm. Corwin Mendenhall, *Submarine Diary* (1991)

Theodore Rockwell, *The Rickover Effect: How One Man Made a Difference* (1992)

AMPHIBIOUS WARFARE

Joseph H. Alexander, *Sea Soldiers in the Cold War: Amphibious Warfare, 1945–1991* (1994)

Merrill Bartlett, ed., *Assault from the Sea: Essays on the History of Amphibious Warfare* (1983)

Simon Foster, *Hit the Beach: The Drama of Amphibious Warfare* (1998)

Theodore L. Gatchel, *At the Water's Edge: Defending against the Modern Amphibious Assault* (1996)

SURVEILLANCE AND INTELLIGENCE

John Keegan, *The Price of Admiralty: The Evolution of Naval Warfare* (1989)

Office of Naval Intelligence monographs:

Worldwide Maritime Challenges (1997)

Worldwide Submarine Challenges (1997)

Worldwide Submarine Proliferation in the Coming Decade (1995)

MINE WARFARE

Malcolm W. Cagle and Frank A. Manson, *The Sea War in Korea* (1957)

Robert C. Duncan, *America's Use of Sea Mines* (1962)

Gregory K. Hartmann, with Scott C. Truver, *Weapons That Wait* (1991)

Edward J. Marolda, ed., *Operation End Sweep* (1993)

SEALs

Orr Kelly, *Never Fight Fair! Inside the Legendary U.S. Navy Seals: Their Own True Stories* (1996)

Capt. William H. McRave, *Spec Ops* (1998)

Susan L. Marquis, *Unconventional Warfare: Rebuilding U.S. Special Operations Forces* (1997)

SUPPORTING CAST

Rear Adm. Frank J. Allston, *Ready for Sea: The Bicentennial History of the U.S. Navy Supply Corps* (1995)

David P. Gray, *Many Specialties, One Corps* (1997)

Jan K. Herman, *Battle Station Sick-bay: Navy Medicine in World War II* (1997)

William Bradford Huie, *From Omaha to Okinawa; The Story of the Seabees* (1945)

Doris M. Sterner, *In and Out of Harm's Way: A History of the Navy Nurse Corps* (1996)

HERITAGE

Peter Kemp, ed., *The Oxford Companion to Ships & the Sea* (1976)

Vice Adm. William P. Mack, and Lt. Cdr. Royal W. Connell, *Naval Ceremonies, Customs, and Traditions* (1980)

Cedric W. Windas, *Traditions of the Navy* (1978)

Authors and Editors

DR. JAMES C. BRADFORD
(You May Fire When Ready, Gridley)
is associate professor of history at Texas A&M University specializing in early American and naval and maritime history. He received his Ph.D. from the University of Virginia, taught at the U.S. Naval Academy, and has been a visiting professor at the Air War College. The author or editor of a dozen books and articles including *Admirals of the New Empire* (1990) and *Crucible of Empire: The Spanish-American War & Its Aftermath* (1993), he currently edits *The Library of Naval Biography* for the Naval Institute Press.

DR. MICHAEL J. CRAWFORD
(Whose Flag Has Displayed in Distant Climes)
heads the Early History Branch of the Naval Historical Center. He edits the series *Naval Documents of the American Revolution* and *The Naval War of 1812: A Documentary History*. A native of St. Louis, Missouri, where he attended Washington University and received his B.A. and M.A. degrees, he earned his Ph.D. in American history at Boston University. He taught at Texas Tech University and subsequently served as a National Historical Publications and Records Commission Fellow with the Adams Papers at the Massachusetts Historical Society.

VICE ADMIRAL ROBERT F. DUNN, USN (RETIRED)
(Today's Fleet)
served thirty-eight years on active duty in destroyers, amphibious ships, and aircraft carriers. He flew combat in Vietnam, commanded the aircraft carrier USS *Saratoga* (CV 60), and at the time of his retirement was the Deputy Chief of Naval Operations for Air Warfare. He is the president of the Naval Historical Foundation.

DR. WILLIAM M. FOWLER, JR.
(We Have Met the Enemy and They Are Ours)
became the director of the Massachusetts Historical Society after teaching history for twenty-seven years at Northeastern University. A graduate of Northeastern University who earned his advanced degrees at the University of Notre Dame, Dr. Fowler has published eight books, most centered on early American maritime history, as well as more than two dozen essays in major scholarly and popular journals, magazines, and newspapers.

CAPTAIN GEORGE GALDORISI, USN (RETIRED)
(Land the Landing Force!)
recently retired from the United States Navy where he served numerous tours with the Amphibious Assault Navy, including Commanding Officer, USS *Cleveland* (LPD 7), and Commander, Amphibious Squadron 7. He holds master's degrees in oceanography from the Naval Postgraduate School and in international relations from the University of San Diego, and is a graduate of MIT Sloan School's Program for Senior Executives. He has published two textbooks on the law of the sea and two novels.

DR. THOMAS C. HONE
(A Navy Second to None)
is a member of the faculty of the Industrial College of the Armed Forces. He has also taught at the Naval War College and served as special assistant to Commander, Naval Air Systems Command. He is the author of *Power and Change: The Administrative History of the Office of the Chief of Naval Operations, 1946–1986,* and is the co-author of *American and British Aircraft Carrier Development, 1919–1941.*

REAR ADMIRAL CHARLES F. HORNE, USN (RETIRED)
(Weapons That Wait)
is chairman of the Mine Warfare Subcommittee of the National Defense Industrial Association's Expeditionary Warfare Committee and is the vice president of the Mine Warfare Association. He served as Commander, Mine Warfare Command (1979–1984) and as Commander, Naval Forces Korea (1984–1986), before retiring in 1987.

CAPTAIN JOHN EDWARD JACKSON, USN (RETIRED)
(The Supporting Cast)
served as a Navy Supply Corps officer afloat and ashore for over twenty-seven years. His final active-duty assignment was at the Naval War College in Newport, Rhode Island, where he holds the Frederick J. Horne Military Chair of Logistics and Sustainability and edits *Logistics Leadership Series* of books on logistical history and theory. He is a graduate of the Management Development Program at Harvard University, holds graduate degrees in education and management, and is a doctoral candidate at Salve Regina University in Newport, Rhode Island.

CAPTAIN ANDREW C. A. JAMPOLER, USN (RETIRED)
(Mare Nostrum: Ocean Surveillance)
deployed as a patrol plane commander during three maritime patrol squadron tours. He commanded Patrol Squadron 19 and Naval Air Station, Moffett Field. Retiring after twenty-four years of service, he has since held senior executive positions in international aerospace sales and marketing. He is a graduate of Columbia University's Columbia College and School of International Affairs.

CAPTAIN BRUCE R. LINDER, USN (RETIRED)
(Surface Action Starboard!)
commanded the guided missile frigate USS *Elrod* (FFG 55) and two major shore bases, Naval Training Center, San Diego, and the Fleet Antisubmarine Warfare Training Center, during more than twenty-six years of service. His articles and commentaries have appeared in magazines and other publications in the United States, Europe, and Japan. He continues to write on naval history topics including *San Diego's Navy*, a comprehensive history of the Navy in San Diego published by Naval Institute Press.

Vice Admiral William P. Mack, USN (Retired)
(Customs and Traditions)
graduated from the U.S. Naval Academy in 1937 and served in battleships, destroyers, and amphibious forces. His last two tours of duty were as Commander, Seventh Fleet during the mining of Haiphong Harbor and as Superintendent, U.S. Naval Academy. He is the author of *Naval Ceremonies, Customs, and Traditions* as well as ten editions of professional books and eight works of fiction.

Rear Admiral Alfred Thayer Mahan, USN
(The Prerogative of Sea Powers)
graduated from the Naval Academy in 1856, and served in the South Atlantic and West Gulf Blockading Squadrons during the Civil War, and in a number of ships thereafter. Teacher at and then president of the Naval War College, he wrote two books on seapower that made him the foremost naval authority of his time. He commanded the armored cruiser USS *Chicago* before retiring in 1896 after forty years of service. He continued to write and teach at the Naval War College after retirement and served on the Naval War Board during the Spanish American War.

Rear Admiral Henry C. McKinney, USN (Retired)
(Museums and Memorials)
grew up in LaGrange, Illinois, and attended Princeton University before entering the Navy in 1959. Serving in both destroyers and submarines, he commanded the nuclear attack submarine USS *Seahorse* (SSN 669), the submarine squadron in the Mediterranean, and the submarine force in the Pacific. He has continued his close association with the Navy after retirement as the president of the U.S. Navy Memorial Foundation.

Dr. Edward J. Marolda
(Cold War to Violent Peace)
is the Naval Historical Center's Senior Historian. He previously headed the Contemporary History Branch and in that capacity oversaw creation of the Contributions to Naval History and The U.S. Navy in the Modern World narrative history series. He has written or edited seven books, including *The Washington Navy Yard: An Illustrated History*, *Shield and Sword: The United States Navy and the Persian Gulf War* (with Robert J. Schneller), *FDR and the U.S. Navy*, and four works on the Navy in the Vietnam War. He is a veteran of that conflict and holds B.A., M.A., and Ph.D. degrees in history from Pennsylvania Military College, Georgetown University, and George Washington University.

Captain James H. Patton, USN (Retired)
(Dive! Dive!)
stumbled into the Submarine Service when, as a senior at the Naval Academy, he rose to the bait of applying for the first direct input to nuclear power training—advertised as absolutely not leading to submarines. At Nuclear Power School, when everyone else volunteered, so did he. After serving in USS *Scorpion* (SSN 589), he became addicted to the people. His service included tours on seven submarines including command of USS *Pargo* (SSN 650) as well as assignments at the Office of the Chief of Naval Operations, the Submarine School, Submarine Development Squadron 12, and the Naval War College.

Captain Rosario Rausa, USNR (Retired)
(Two Block Foxtrot!)
was a naval aviator who flew A1 Skyraiders, A4 Skyhawks, and A7 Corsairs. He served as editor of *Naval Aviation News* magazine and was head of the Naval Aviation History and Publications Division of the Naval Historical Center when he retired in 1988. Since then he has been editor of *Wings of Gold* magazine, the voice of the Association of Naval Aviation. He has written or co-authored seven non-fiction books on aviation subjects.

Paul Stillwell
(Winning a Two-Ocean War)
is the director of the History Division of the U.S. Naval Institute, Annapolis, Maryland. He spent thirty years in the Naval Reserve, including active duty in the late 1960s on board the tank landing ship USS *Washoe County* (LST 1165) and the battleship USS *New Jersey* (BB 62). He is the author or editor of several books, including *The Golden Thirteen: Recollections of the First Black Naval Officers*. He has done numerous oral history interviews, some of which he used in writing the World War II chapter of this book.

Dr. Craig L. Symonds
(Damn the Torpedoes! Full Speed Ahead!)
is professor of history at the U.S. Naval Academy where he has taught both naval history and Civil War history since 1976. He is the author of eight books including biographies of Joseph E. Johnston, Patrick Cleburne, and Franklin Buchanan, as well as the *Naval Institute's Historical Atlas of the U.S. Navy*.

Rear Admiral George R. Worthington, USN (Retired)
(Stealth from the Sea)
entered Underwater Demolition Team training after serving in destroyers. Subsequent assignments were in destroyers and a variety of SEAL assignments including command of SEAL Team One, Inshore Undersea Warfare Group One, and Naval Special Warfare Group One. He served as Deputy Secretary of Defense (Special Operations) and commanded the Naval Special Warfare Command until his retirement.

Editor-in-Chief
Rear Admiral W. J. Holland, Jr., USN (Retired)
served thirty-two years, thirteen in command, most in submarines. On retiring he became president of the Armed Forces Communications and Electronics Association's Educational Foundation. Author of over fifty professional essays and commentaries, he is a frequent contributor to the Naval Institute *Proceedings* and the *Naval Submarine Review* and has written for other professional journals.

Dr. David F. Winkler, *Editor,* received his Ph.D. from American University for his dissertation *Cold War at Sea,* subsequently published by the Naval Institute Press. A commander in the Naval Reserve, he is the director of programs with the Naval Historical Foundation.

David A. Manning, *Illustrations Editor,* received his B.A. in military history and design from the University of Maryland, and has worked both for historical organizations and in the photography industry. He is a data analyst and curator at the U.S. Army Center of Military History.

Index

Page numbers in *italics* indicate
    illustrations.

Aircraft, U.S.
  A3J, *158*
  A-4E, *176*
  A-6, 184, *188*, *196*, 197, 230–31
  A-7, 230–31, *230*, *234*
  AD, *148*, *150*
  AH-1E, *275*
  AH-6, 191
  AJ-1, 158
  AV-8B, 276, *277*
  B-1B, 183
  B-25, 104
  B-29, 135, 139
  E-6A, 257
  BT-1, 86
  C-47, 124
  C-130, 257
  CH-46, 274, 276, *300*
  CH-53, 274
  CH-53D, *187*
  CH-53E, 268, *275*
  CH-60, 287
  E-2C, 185, 244, 230, 232, *233*
  E-6A, 257
  EA-6B, 184, 230, *232*, 232–33,
    244, 247
  F/A-18, 184, 195, *202*, 230–31, 233,
    238, 244, 247
  F/A-18E, 244, *247*
  F-4, 169, *168*, *169*
  F-4J, 170
  F-8, 169
  F-14, 184–85, *186*, 188, 195, 230, *231*,
    234, 235, *236*, *237*, 244, 248, *249*
  F3F-2, *88*
  F4F, 104–105
  F4U, *150*, *155*
  F6F, 111, *119*, 130
  F9F, *155*
  HH-46D, *243*, *244*
  HH-60H, 244–45
  HSS-2, *163*
  HU-16, 169
  KA-6, *234*
  KC-135, 231
  MH-53E, 285
  MV-22, 270, 276
  N2S, 111
  N3N, *98*
  O2SU, 83, 136
  OH-58D, 197
  P-3, 193, 278, 280, 281, 283
  P2V, 156, *156*, *174*
  P4M, 156
  PB2Y, *86*
  PBY, *86*, 87, *97*, 97–98
  RH-53D, *183*
  S2F, *163*
  S-3B, 232, *233*, *241*
  SB2C, 111, *131*, 132, *132*
  SBD, 86–87, *104*
  SH-2, 213
  SH-3, 231, *231*
  SH-60, 197, 211–213, *214*, 230–31,
    231, 245, *245*
  T-1A, 244
  T-2C, 244
  T-34C, 244
  T-39, 244
  T3M, 87
  T-44, 244
  T-45, *243*, 244
  T4M 87
  TBD, 86
  TBF, *131*
  TH-57, 244
  U-2, 162
  UH-1B, 176, *176*
  UH-46, *175*

  WF-2, *163*
Abrams, Gen Creighton, 165
Achille Lauro, 188
Adams, John, *13*, *14*, 18
Adriatic Sea, operations in, 218, 239
Aeronautical Board, 81
Alden, Capt John, 58
Algiers, 16, 27
American Colonization Society, 37
"Anaconda Plan," 45, 49
Anglo-Japanese Naval Alliance
  of 1902, 72
Antisubmarine warfare, 251, 281
Anzio, landings at, 114
Arabian Peninsula, 191–92
Area Air Defense Command system, 222
Army-Navy Mobile Riverine Force, 177
Arthur, VAdm Stanley R., 195–97, *195*
Articles for Regulation of the Navy (*See
  also* "Rocks and Shoals"), 327–28
Ashworth, Cdr Dick, 139
Atlantic convoys, 109
Avalon deep submergence rescue vehicle,
  259

Bainbridge, Capt William, 20, *20*, 23;
  Commo, 27
Barbary War, 19–21
Barclay, Capt Robert, RN, 24–25
Barry, Capt John, *18*
Battle of Coral Sea, *102*, 102–103, 333
Battle of Jutland, 70, 122
Battle of Midway, 333
Battle of Mobile Bay, 55, *57*, 58–59, 317
Battle of Savo Island, 106
Battle of Sunda Strait, *100*
Battle of the Atlantic, 117
Battle of the Sibuyan Sea, 130
Beinecke, Lt Bill, 139
Benson, Adm William, 71
Bergner, Ens Hans, 124
Biddle, Commo James, 39
Bien, Capt Lyle, 234
Black sailors, 89, 125–26
Blanco, Gen Ramon, 68
Board of Navy Commissioners, 30
Board of Provisions and Clothing, 30
Boomer, LtGen Walter, USMC, 193, 198
Bosnia-Herzegovina, 218, 239
Boston Navy Yard, 108
Bridgeton, 191
British East India Company, 27
Brooke, Capt Philip Vere, RN, 24
Brooke, Lt John M., 54
Broughton, Nicholas, 14
Brown, Ens Jesse, 151–52, *151*
Bryant, Emory A., 297
"Bubiyan Turkey Shoot," 197
Buchanan, Capt Franklin, 54, *58*, 58–59
Buckner, Gen Simon B., 50
Bulkeley, Cdr John, 122, 124
Burial at sea, *325*, 325–26
Burke, Capt Arleigh, 319; Adm, 160, *160*
Burke, Cornelius Aloysius, 121–22
Bush, George, 132, 191, 195
Butler, MajGen Benjamin, 52

Cam Ranh Bay, 168,183
Cambodia, 165, 173, 177–78
Capodanno, Lt Vincent Robert, 304–305
Carpenter, Capt Scott, 189
Carson, RAdm Joseph M., *164*
Cassara, Capt Richard, 197
Castillo, 67
Cavite Navy Yard, 66, 99
Central Pacific Campaign, 119, 126–29
Cervera y Topete, RAdm Pascual, 67–68
Chaplain Corps, 302–305
Charleston, South Carolina, 53–54, 58
Chauncey, Isaac, 24
Chosin Reservoir, 151
Church, Lt Al, 106, 108

Churchill, Winston, *145*
Civil Engineer Corps, 305–306
Clark, Lt Eugene F., 148–49
Coffee, Lt Gerald, *164*
Colors, the, 321
Combat demolition units, 289
Confederate States Ships
  Alabama, 56, *56*, 300
  Chicora, 54, *55*
  Florida, 56
  H.L. Hunley (noncommissioned), 55
  Nashville, 46
  Palmetto State, 54–55
  Shenandoah, 56, 59
  Tennessee, 57–58
  Virginia, 45, *53*, 54, *54*
Continental Congress, 14, 293, 304
Continental Navy, Articles of, 320
Coolidge, Calvin, 85
Cooper, George, 125
Cooperative Engagement Capability,
  222
Corregidor, 100, 122
Counterdrug operations, 218
Cristobal Colon, 68
Crossing the Equator ceremony, 324
Cruiser and Transport Service, 70
Cruiser Conversion Program, 222
Cuba, 63, 66, 162, 164; intervention, 69
Cuban Missile Crisis, 162–64
Cumberland River, 49–50
Cunningham, Lt Randall H., *169*, 170
Cutter, Lt Slade, 101, *101*, 117; Cdr, 140

Dacros, Capt James, RN, 23
Dahlgren, Cdr John A., 36, 57
Dale, Commo Richard, 19
Dale, Lt Richard, 315
Dalton, John H., *226*
Damone, Vic, *175*
Danang, 165, 175
Daniels, Josephus, *70*, 71, 81–83, 96
Dare, Cdr James A., 153
Data fusion centers, 281
Dayton (Ohio) Peace Accords, 239–40
Dealey, Sam, 118
Decatur, Capt Stephen, *20*, 23; Commo,
  27, *315*
De Lôme, Ambassador Dupuy, 65
Dental Corps, established, 297
Department of Navy bureaus
  Aeronautics, 81, 84–85
  Construction and Repair, 78–79
  Construction, Equipment, & Repair, 30
  Engineering, 81
  Medicine & Surgery, 30, 81, 293–94
  Naval Personnel, 126
  Navigation, 80
  Navy Yards and Docks, 30
  Ordnance, 80, 88
  Ordnance and Hydrography, 30
  Provisions and Clothing, 299
  Ships, 114
  Supplies and Accounts, 81
  Yards and Docks, 305
Desoto Patrol, 166
Dewey, Commo George, 66, *318*,
  318–19
Dickinson, Jim, 118–19
Diego Garcia, 193, 223, 229
Dien Bien Phu, 157
Dixie Station, 167
Dixon, LCdr Bob, 103
Dominican Republic, 69
Don Antonio de Ulloa, 67
Donnelly, Cdr William N., 169
Doolittle, LtCol Jimmy, USA, 104
Doremus, LCdr Robert B., 169
Dornin, Dusty, 117
Downie, Capt George, RN, 25–26
Driscoll, Lt (jg) William P., *169*, 170
Drydock No. 1, New York Navy Yard, *35*

Du Pont, Flag Officer Samuel Francis,
  48, *48*, 55, 57
Duerk, RAdm Alene B., 181
Dutch East Indies, 100–101
Dyer, Capt Thomas H., 102, *102*, 103

Easter Offensive of 1972, 171, 178
Ecker, Cdr William B., 162
Edwards, LCdr Fred, 114–15
Eisenhower, Dwight D., 122, 157–59
Engen, Lt (jg) Don, 132
English Channel, 123
Enola Gay, bombing of Hiroshima, 139
Ericsson, John 54, *54*
Evan, Sydney Key, 302
Evans, Cdr Ernest E., 133
Exercise Okean 75, 183
Exercise Tiger, 122
Explosive Ordnance Disposal teams, 286

Fahey, James, 136
Farragut, Flag Officer David Glasgow,
  51–52, 58–59, *59*; Adm, *317*
Fast Sealift Ships, 193
Fauks, Paul, 123–24
Faylaka, 198
Field Medical Surveillance System, 296
Fillmore, Millard, 40
Five-Power Pact, 72–73, 75
Fleet Battle Experiments, 219
Fleet Problem IX, 86
Floyd, John B., 50
Foote, Flag Officer Andrew Hull, 49, 50
Formosa, 111
Forrestal, James, 134
Fort Beauregard, *49*
Fort Donelson, 50
Fort Fisher, 59, *59*
Fort Gaines, 58
Fort Henry, 50
Fort Jackson, 51
Fort McHenry, 26
Fort Morgan, *57*, 58
Fort Pierce, Florida, 127
Fort St. Philip, 51
Fort Sumter, 45–47, *47*
Fort Wagner, Morris Island, 57
Forward Air Controllers Airborne, 248
Four-Power Pact, 72
Fox, Gustavus Vasa, 45, *45*
Fox, LCdr Mark I., *19*, 196
Francis, Tench, *299*
Franklin, Benjamin, 15
Free-flooding SEAL delivery vehicle, 291
Freedom 7, 161
Friendship, 38
Friendship 7, 161
"From the Sea," 9, 237
Fulton, Robert, 35

General Board, 77
Gilbert Islands 119
Gilmore, Gen Quincy Adams, 57
Glenn, LtCol John H., Jr., 161
Globkar, Lt Susan, *193*
Glorie 54
Glover, Col John, 13
"Golden Thirteen," *125*, 125
Goodman, Lt Robert O., 186
Grant, Gen Ulysses S., 50, 53, 57–58;
  President, 63
Gravely, RAdm Samuel L., 181, *182*
"Great Black Fleet," 254
Great White Fleet, 69, *69*
Grenada, 187
Gridley, Capt Charles V., 66, 318
Guadalcanal, 105–106, 319
Guam, 127, 157; transferred to U.S., 68
Gulf of Tonkin, 166–70, 172
Gulf War, 191–99, 215, 229–39, 258,
  267–69
Gun salutes, 326–27

Haiphong, 178
Haiti, 217
Halsey, Adm William, 132–34, 140–41
Hampton Roads Naval Museum, 335, *335*
Hannah, 13, 13–14
Hanoi, 157, 159, 166, 173
Harralson, Radioman Dick, 99
Harris, Cdr Jack, 168
Harrison, Joseph, 293
Harrison, Gen William Henry, 25
Hart, Capt Thomas C., 78; Adm, 99
Hawaii, 65, 108; annexed, 68
Hay, John 66
Hayward, Adm Thomas B., *184,* 184
Hebert, Capt Ed, 226
Herrick, Capt John J., 166
Hewitt, RAdm Kent, 111
Hill, RAdm Harry, 128
Hiroshima, 139
HMAS *Darwin,* 195
HMCS *Athabascan, 147*
HMS *Alert,* 22
HMS *Amazon,* 19
HMS *Black Swan,* 146
HMS *Cherub, 23*
HMS *Countess of Scarborough,* 15
HMS *Cyane,* 26,
HMS *Detroit,* 25
HMS *Gloucester,* 199
HMS *Guerriere,* 23
HMS *Java,* 23
HMS *Levant,* 26
HMS *Macedonian;* 23, figurehead, *24*
HMS *Margaretta,* 12
HMS *Phoebe, 23*
HMS *Serapis, 10–11,* 15, *16,* 315
HMS *Shannon,* 23, 316
HMS *Triumph, 147*
HMS *Warrior,* 54
Ho Chi Minh Trail, 164, 173
Holloway, Lt (jg) James L., 130, 132;
    Adm, *182,* 183
Hoover, Herbert, *83*
Hopkins, Esek, 14, 16
Hopper, RAdm Grace Murray, 181
Hospital Corps, 298
Hudner, Lt (jg) Thomas, 151–52
Hue, 171–72, 175
Hughes, LCdr Massie, 97–98
Hull, Capt Isaac, *20,* 21–23
Humphreys, Joshua, 16
Hungnam, Korea, 152
Hunter, Alvah, 47–48
Hussein, Saddam, 191, 195, 198, 229
Hutchins, Lt Charles, 117

Il, Adm Sohn Wun, 147–48
Imperial Japanese Navy, 76–78; ships,
    Ayanami, 108
    Hyuga, 132
    Kirishima, 108
    Musashi, 130
    Shoha, 103
    Yamato, 139
    Zuikako, 132
Impressment of sailors, issue of, 21
Inchon, Korea, 148, 150
Indian Ocean, 191, 193, 229, 239
Iran, 190–91
Iraq, 191, 196, 217–19, 229
Iraqi Republic Guard Forces, 196, 199
"Iron Bottom Sound," 333
Island No. 10, 51, 53
Isthmus of Darien, 41
Istiqlal, 197
Iwo Jima, battle of, 134–35, 295

Jackson, Gen Andrew, 26; President, 29
James, Cdr Ralph, 133
Japan, 29; planned invasion, 140
Jeannette Memorial, USNA, *38*
Jefferson, Thomas, 18, 21
Johnson, Lyndon B., 165, 178
Joint Army-Navy agencies, 81
Joint Board of the Army and Navy, 81, 84
Joint Chiefs of Staff, 162
Jones, John Paul, *15,*15–16, 33, 315–16
Judge Advocate General Corps, 307

Kai-shek, Chiang, 145–46, 157
Kamikazes, 135
Kauffman, LCdr Draper, 127–28

Kelso, VAdm Frank B., II, *188;* Adm, 286
Kennedy, John F., 159, 162, 320; Lt, *322*
Kernan, Aviation Ordnanceman Alvin,
    108, 121, 140
Khomeini, Ayatollah, 190
Khrushchev, Nikita, 162, 164
Kimpo Airfield, Korea, 150
King George VI, 122
King, Yeoman Cecil, 99–100
King, Adm Ernest J., 105; FAdm, 139,
    300
King, Lt Jerry, 136–37
Kings Bay, Georgia, 257
Kleemann, Cdr Henry M., 184–85, *186*
Klinghofer, Leon, 188
Knott, Capt Richard, 237–38
Korean War, 146–55, 290
Kosovo, air campaign against, 247
Krulak, Gen Charles C., USMC, 270
Kuwait, 190–91, 193, 195–96, 198, 199,
    229, 268; invasion of, 229

L'Insurgente, 18, 18
La Vengeance, 18
Lake Champlain, 24–25
Lake Erie, 24, 317
Lake Ontario, 24
Landing craft
    Advanced Amphibious Assault
        Vehicles, 276–77
    Amphibian tractors, *17* 128, *135*
    Landing Craft, Air Cushion, 204, *267,
        268, 273,*274–75, *276,* 287
    Landing craft, mechanized, *17*
    Landing craft, medium, 137, *201, 301*
    Landing craft, utility, *271*
    Landing craft, vehicle, personnel, *122,
        124, 136,* 137
    Sea Shadow experimental stealth test
        craft, *224*
    Tank landing ships, *99, 113,* 114,
        122–23, *150,* 274, *301*
Landing Signal Officers, 237
Laos, 159, 164–65, 168
Lawrence, Capt James, *20,* 24, 316
Lawrence, VAdm William, 229
Layton, LCdr Eddie, 104
Leahy, FAdm William D., *145*
Lebanon, 158, 186
Lee, Fitzhugh, 65
Lee, Kent, 110–11
Lee, Gen Robert E., 53, 59
Lee, RAdm Willis A., Jr., 106, *106*
Leenhouts, Cdr John "Lites," 231
Lehman, John F., Jr., 184, *185*
Levy, Commo Uriah, *33*
Leyte, 129–30, 132
Liberty ships, 121
Libya, 184, 188–89, 192
Lincoln, Abraham, 45–46
Lindbergh, Charles A., *85*
Lloyd George, David, 70
Lockwood, RAdm Charles, 117
Logue, Ed, 110
London Naval Disarmament
    Conference, 1930, 86
London Treaty of 1930, 79
Lone Sailor, the, *343*
Long, John D., 66
Lopez, First Lt Baldomero, USMC, *149*
Luce, Adm Stephen B., 63
Luosey, Cdr Michael J., 147, *147*
Luzon, 130

MacArthur, Gen Douglas, 100, 122, 129,
    141, *148,* 150–51
MacDonough, Lt Thomas, *20,* 25–26
Macon, 76
Madison, James, 21, 27
Mahan, Capt Alfred Thayer, 63, 330;
    RAdm, *8*
Maher, Fire Controlman Bob, 108, 117
Mallory, Stephen R., *53,* 54, 56
Manhattan Project, 139
Manila Bay, 67, 76, 100, 318–19
Manus, Admiralty Islands, 133
Marine Corps units and commands
    I Marine Expeditionary Force, 193, 198
    III Amphibious Force, 165
    7th Marine Expeditionary Brigade, 192
    1st Marine Division, 149–50, 151, 198
    2d Marine Division, 198

4th Marine Brigade, 294, 297
5th Marines, 149
Marblehead Regiment, 13
Margaretta, 13
Maria Crisina, 66
Maria Theresa, 68
Mariannas, 129; invasion of, 126–27
"Mariannas Turkey Shoot," 127
Maritime Interception Force, 193
Maritime interdiction and blockade,
    Navy tasks of, 215
Maritime Strategy, 183–184
Marine Expeditionary Units (Special
    Operations Capable), 269, 272, 274
Marshall Islands, 101; invasion of, 126
Marshall Plan, 145
Martin, Graham, 125
Mason, Ted, 96
Matsu Island, 157, 159
Maury, Matthew Fontaine, *4,* 40
Mauz, VAdm Henry H., Jr., 193, 195
Mayaguez, 178; retaking of, 178
McAfee, Mildred, 126
McCampbell, Cdr David, 111, 130, *130*
McClusky, LCdr Wade, 104
McGonagle, Cdr William L., 180, *180*
McKinley, William, 65–66
McNamara, Robert S., 165
Medical Corps, 294
Medical Service Corps, 298–99
Mekong Delta, 175, 177–78, 289
Merchant marine, 121; Act of, 89
Meshuda, 27, *27*
Metcalf, VAdm Joseph, III, 187
Mexican Monument, USNA, *42*
Mexican War, 42–43
Midway Island, 104–105, 108
Military Airlift Command, 191, 193
Military Sea Transportation Service, 148
Miller, Cdr George, 133
Miller, Capt Harold B. "Min," 134
Mine warfare, 284–87
Minh, Ho Chi, 145, 157, 159, 164–65
Mississippi River, 49, 51
Mitchell, Gen William "Billy," 84–85
Mischer, VAdm Marc "Pete," *127*
Mobile, Alabama, 53, 58
Moffett, RAdm William A., 84–85
Mongilardi, Cdr Pete, 169
Mongillo, Lt Nick, 196
Monroe Doctrine, 69
Montojo y Parasón, RAdm Patricio, 66
Moorer, Adm Thomas H., *165*
Moreel, Adm Ben, Chief of Naval
    Engineers, 306
Morral, Cdr Dennis G., 197
Morris, Commo Richard Valentine, 19
Morton, "Mush," 117
Mount Suribachi, 135
Muczynski, Lt Lawrence M., 184–86
Muffit, Capt John, 56
Munitions Board, 81

Nagasaki, Japan, 139
Nassau, Bahamas, raided, 14
Nasty-class fast patrol boats, *166*
National Museum of American History,
    Smithsonian Institution, 255, 335
National Museum of Naval Aviation,
    Pensacola, Florida, 334, *335*
NATO, 146, 158, 238, 247
NATO Standing Naval Forces,
    Mediterranean, 218
Naval Air Station, Miami, Florida, 111
Naval Air Station, Miramar, California,
    170
Naval Air Station North Island, San
    Diego, California, 243
Naval Air Station Patuxent River,
    Maryland, 243
Naval Air Training Command, 243
Naval Authorization of 1938, 89
Naval blockade, 45–49
Naval Efficiency Board (*See also* Plucking
    Board), 31
Naval Hospital, Pensacola, Florida, 296
Naval Observatory, Washington, D.C., 40
Naval Postgraduate School, Monterey,
    California, 309
Naval Reactors Branch, 257
Naval Strike & Air Warfare Center,
    236–37

Naval Strike Warfare Center, 236
Naval Submarine Base, Bangor,
    Washington, 257–58, *265*
Naval Submarine School, 255, 257
Naval Training Station, Great Lakes,
    125, 309
Naval War College, 63, 81, 85, 252, *308,*
    309
Navy Astronautics Group, 189
Navy Programming Languages Group,
    181–82
"Navy Regulations," 14
Navy units and commands
    Afloat Prepositioning Force, 223
    African Squadron, 37
    Amphibious Ready Groups, 269, 272,
        286–87
    Armed guards, 121
    Asiatic Fleet, 66, 99–100
    Asiatic Squadron, 318
    Attack Squadron 153, 169
    Attack Squadron 155, 168
    Battleship Division 9, 71
    Blockade Task Force, 155
    Boxer Amphibious Ready Group, 275
    Brazil Squadron, 37
    Carrier Air Wing 8, 247
    Destroyer Division 8, 70, 319
    East Gulf Squadron, 48
    East India Squadron, 39
    Fifth Fleet, 286
    Fighter Squadron 21, 169
    Fighter Squadron 96, 170
    Fighter Squadron 154, 169
    Helicopter Attack (Light) Squadron 3,
        176
    Light Photographic Squadron 62, 162
    Maritime Prepositioning Squadron 2,
        193
    Military Sealift Command, 175,
        191–93, 223, 311; Special Mission
        Program, 223
    "Mosquito Fleet," 41
    Naval Forces, Vietnam, 175, 177
    Naval Special Warfare Group One, 198
    North Atlantic Squadron, 48
    Seabee battalions, 175, 192
    SEAL naval special forces, 176, 187,
        192, 197–98, 232, 245, 259, 289
    SEAL Delivery Vehicle Teams, 289
    SEAL Team 1, 29
    SEAL Team 2, 289
    Service Squadron 10, 133
    Seventh Fleet, 146–47, 157, 159,
        165–67, 171–72, 178, 180, 285,
        324
    Sixth Fleet, 146, 158, 182, 186,
        188–89, 338
    Sixth Task Force, 146
    South Atlantic Blockading Squadron, 55
    South Atlantic Squadron, 48
    Special Boat Squadrons, 289
    Special Operations Commands, 289
    Submarine Force, Pacific, 117
    Task Force 38, 91–92, 134
    Task Force 64,106
    Task Force 65, 183
    Task Force 77, 167, 170
    Task Force 90, 152
    Task Force 95, 155
    Task Force 135, 162
    Task Force 136, 162
    Task Force Mike, 198
    Task Group 21.14, 117
    Third Fleet, 132, 140–41
    Underwater demolition teams, 127,
        153, 289
    VA-72, 231
    Very Shallow Water detachment, 286
    West Gulf Squadron, 48
    West Indies Squadron, 36
Nelson, Adm Lord Horatio, 20
Nesby, Airman Brian, *219*
"Neutrality Patrol," 96
New London, Connecticut, 257
New Orleans, Louisiana, 26, 49, 51–52
Newport News Shipbuilding, 245
Ney Award, the, 329
Nicaragua, intervention in, 69
Nichols, Cdr John C., *109*
Nimitz, Adm Chester, 103–104, 184;
    Museum and Historical Center, 335

Nine-Power Pact, 72
Nixon, Richard M., 178, 182
Noble, Cdr Richard, 197
Norfolk Navy Yard, 54
Norfolk, Virginia, 111, 257
Normandy invasion, 122–24, 137
North Africa, landings in, 111
North Korean People's Army, 150
North Sea Mine Barrage, 72
North Vietnam, 165–68, 178, 183
North Vietnamese Army, 171, 177
Nowell, Senior Chief Radarman Larry, 170, 170
Nuclear Power School, 255
Nurse Corps, established, 297

O'Brien, Jeremiah, 13
O'Callahan, Cdr Joseph Timothy, 304
Office of Naval Communications, 78
Office of Naval Intelligence, 78
Ogden, Lt Jim, 97
Ogier, Cdr Herbert L., 166
O'Grady, Capt Scott, USAF, 272, 273
O'Hare, Cdr Edward H. "Butch," 119, 121, 140
O'Kane, Cdr Richard, 117, 118
Okinawa, 157; invasion of, 135–36
Oldendorf, RAdm Jesse, 130, 132
Omaha Beach, 123, 124
Open Door Notes, 68; policy, 72
Operations
    Allied Force, 219
    Decoy, 15
    Desert Fox, 219
    Desert Storm, 196–97, 234, 267
    El Dorado Canyon, 188
    Game Warden, 175
    Joint Endeavor, 218
    Linebacker, 168, 170, 178
    Market Time, 172
    Passage to Freedom, 157
    Restore Hope, 217
    Rolling Thunder, 168, 170
    Sharp Guard, 218
    Silver Wake, 218
    Starlite, 171
    Support Democracy, 217
    Sustaining Hope, 217
    34A, 166
    Uphold Democracy, 217
Oquendo, 68
O'Quin, Chief Quartermaster Herb, 129
Osborne, Lt (jg) Weed, 298
Ostfriesdland, 84
Owens, Adm William A., 215

Page, Cdr Louis C., 169
Panama, 65; intervention in, 69
Parker, Fireman Jackson K., 109–10
Parks, Cdr Lew, 101, 101
Parsons, Capt William S. "Deak," 139
Patriot's Point, South Carolina, 338
Patterson, George, 47
Pay Corps, 299, 300
PC-565, 116
Pearl Harbor, 77, 87, 98, 109, 257; attack on, 96, 319
Pearson, Capt Richard, RN, 15–16
Peleliu, Palau Islands, 128–29
Pemberton, LtGen John C., 53
People's Liberation Army, 151
People's Republic of China, 147, 151
Perry, Capt Oliver Hazard, 24–26, 317
Perry, Commo Matthew C., 37, 39, 40
Pershing, Gen John J., 84
Persian Gulf, 190–91, 195–96, 218–19, 229–30, 239, 286
Petty, Lt Orlando Henderson, 294
Philippines, 76, 134; war plans for, 99
Phillips, LCdr John, 119
Plattsburg Bay, 26
Pleiku, Vietnam 167
Plucking Board (See also Naval Efficiency Board), 31
Pnomh Penh, Cambodia, 178
Pond, Fire Controlman Jesse, 116
Pope, MajGen John B., 51
Porter, Capt David, 20, 22–23, 52, 58; Acting RAdm, 52–53
Porter, John, 54
Port Moresby, 103
Port Royal Sound, 48, 51, 53

Power projection, 215
Pratt, Adm William V., 85
Preble, Commo Edward, 19, 19
Prepositioning Program, 223
Prevost, Gen George, 25–26
Project Mercury, 161
Propulsion Examining Board, 210
Puerto Rico, transferred to U.S., 69
Puget Sound Navy Yard, 115
Pusan, Korea, 148; Perimeter at, 150
Pyongyang, North Korea, 147

Qaddafi, Muammar, 184, 186, 188–89
Quallah Battoo, Sumatra, 38
Quasi War with France, 16–19
Queenstown, Ireland, 70, 319
Quemoy Island, 157, 159
Quick, Ens Winifred, 126

Raborn, RAdm William "Red," 160
Ramsdell, Capt Steve, 233
Ray, Hospital Corpsman Second Class David R., 172
Reagan, Ronald, 183, 186, 191
Red Sea, 191, 195–96, 218, 229–30, 233
Reed, Ens Bob, 108
Reeves, Cdr Joseph M., 323; Capt, 85; RAdm, 85, 86
Reprisal, 15
Republic of Korea Navy, 147
Republic of Vietnam, 157, 164; navy, 165
Revolutionary War, 13–16
Rhee, Syngman, 145
Rickover, RAdm Hyman G., 158
River Patrol Boat 105, 175
Rochefort, Cdr Joe, 102–104
"Rocks and Shoals" (See also Articles for Regulation of the Navy), 327–28
Republic of Korea I and II Corps, 151
Roosevelt, Franklin D., 96, 141, 145
Roosevelt, Lt Franklin D., Jr, 114
Roosevelt, Theodore, 64, 66
Rosenthal, Joseph, 135
Royal Australian Navy, 171
Royal Navy, 21, 78
Rules for the Regulation of the Navy of the United Colonies of the United States, 293
Rules of Engagement, 239
Rushing, Lt (jg) Roy, 130

Sackett's Harbor, New York, 24
Sahand, 190
Saigon, 165, 167, 175, 178
Saipan, 127
Salerno, landings at, 114
Samoa, 68
Sampson, Radm William T., 67–68
San Bernardino Strait, 132–33
San Diego, California, 79, 257
Santiago, 68
Sargent, Cdr Nathan, 64
Saudi Arabia, 191–92, 229
Schley, Commo Winfield Scott, 67
Schwarzkopf, Gen Norman H., Jr., USA, 191, 195–96, 199, 229
Scott, Gen Winfield, USA, 42, 45, 49
Sea of Japan, 180, 279
Seabee battalions, 306; Memorial, 306
SEALORDS, 177–78
Seminole War, 29; Second, 41
Semmes, Capt Raphael, 56, 56
Shatner, MajGen William R., USA, 67–68
"Shellbacks," 324
Shepard, Cdr Alan, 161, 189
Sherman, Gen William T., 57
Shigemitsu, Mamoru, 141
Ships of the Memorial Fleet, 337
Sicily, 113–4, 188
Sims, RAdm William S., 70, 81
"600-ship Navy," 184
Slapton Sands, England, 122
Slave Trade Act of 1819, 37
"Slot," the, 319
Smith, LCdr John C. Smith, 169
Smith, Capt Ray, 198
Smoot, Capt Roland, 135
Snyder, Cdr Robert, 246
Soley, James Russell, 53, 64
Somalia, 217, 239
Somers, Lt Richard, 21
Sons of Liberty, 12, 13

South China Sea, 102, 159
South Seas Exploring Expedition, 40
South Vietnam Navy, 171
Spanish-American War, 66–68
Spruance, RAdm Raymond, 104
Stalin, Joseph, 145, 145, 146
Stephens, Ens Bill, 136
Stethem, Petty Officer Robert D., 188
Stewart, Capt Charles, 20, 26, 30
Still, William N., Jr., 48
Stockton, Commo Robert F., 37, 37
Stoddert, Benjamin, 17, 18
Strait of Hormuz, 191, 229, 252
Strait of Taiwan, 159
Straits of Messina, 114
Straits of Sunda, 26
Strategic Air Command, 257
Stringham, Flag Officer Silas, 48
Subic Bay, 146, 157
Submarine Force Dolphin insignia, 257
Submarine Force Museum, Groton, Connecticut, 334
Submarine memorials, 341–42
Submarines, 250–65; classes, 78–79
Suez Canal, 183, 191; crisis, 158
Sung, Kim Il, 145–46
Supply Corps, 300, 302
Surface Warfare missions, 214–19
Surigao Strait, 130
Suzuya Maru, 117

Taiwan, 147, 157, 239
Takasayo Maru, 139
Tanker War, 190–91
Tarawa, 119, 127, 289
Taussig, Cdr Joseph K., 70, 319
Taussig, Ens Joseph, 98
Teaser, 46
Tennessee River, 49–50
Tet Offensive of 1968, 172
Thach, LCdr Jimmy, 104–105
Thailand, 159
Theater Ballistic Missile Defense, 220
Theater High Altitude Air Defense, 222
Tilghman, BGen Lloyd, 50
Tinian, 127
Tokyo Bay, 40, 141
Tokyo, bombing of, 104, 135
Tonkin Gulf, 165; Resolution, 167
Top Dome, 236
Top Gun School, 170, 236
Treaty of Ghent, 26
Treaty of Kanagawa, 40
Tripoli, 16, 21, 189
Truman, Harry S., 140, 145–47
Tse-tung, Mao, 145, 157, 159
Tulagi, 105

U.S. Central Command, 191, 229, 234
U.S. Coast Guard, 173, 173, 192–93
U.S. Marine Corps, established, 14
U.S. Naval Academy, 21, 31, 81, 84, 181, 309, 330; established, 32; rebuilt and expanded, 69
U.S. Naval Forces, Central Command, 193
U.S. Naval Forces, Vietnam, 165
U.S. Naval Institute, 63
U.S. Navy ships
    Adroit, 197
    Akron, 87
    Alabama, 337, 338
    Alaska, 251, 321
    Alfred, 293
    Algol, 223
    America, 188, 197, 230, 233, 239, 299
    Arctic 299
    Argus, 19
    Arleigh Burke-class, 211, 220
    Arizona, 74, 98, 340–41; memorial 337, 341
    Atlanta, 63, 64
    Augusta, 80, 99, 113, 144
    Austin, 274; class, 276
    Avenger, 197; class, 285
    Bainbridge, 161
    Baltimore, 63
    Barb, 118
    Barry, 117
    Becuna, 115
    Benfold, 207–209

Bennion, 130, 132
Billfish, 251
Birmingham, 69
Blackhawk, 53
Boise, 144
Bonhomme Richard, 10–11, 15, 16
Bon Homme Richard (CV 31), 105, 315
Borie, 108, 116–17
Boston, 64, 304
Bowfin, 339, 339
Brandywine, 36
Bream, 129
Brooklyn, 58, 81, 113
Buffalo, 260
Bunker Hill, 191, 211
Cahaba, 292
Cairo, 51
California, 81, 96
Caloosahatchee, 157
Cambria, 128
Card, 117
Carl Vinson, 247
Carney, 206, 211
Carondelet, 50–51
Cassin, 115
Chesapeake, 24, 316
Chew, 116
Cheyenne, 261
Chicago, 63, 64, 170,
Chosin, 213
Cimarron, 213
Cleveland, 275
Cobia, 339, 339
Cochino, 155, 156
Columbus, 44, 144, 258
Comfort, 192, 223, 223
Congress, 29, 54
Connecticut, 251
Constellation, 17–18, 18, 27, 37, 167, 170, 340
Constitution, 17, 19, 21, 22, 23, 23, 26, 36, 312–13, 316, 339, 340
Constitution Museum, 335
Coral Sea, 168, 178, 188
Cowpens, 222
Cumberland, 54
Cyane, 42
Dace, 129
Dale, 8, 80
Darter, 129
Decatur, 222
Delaware, 71
Detroit, 215, 218
Dewey, 89
Dolphin, 64, 79
Douglas H. Fox, 153–54
Downes, 115
Dwight D. Eisenhower, 191, 229, 239
Edson, 337
Elliot, 207, 209
Emmons, 123
Enterprise, 85, 104, 108, 141, 161, 161–62, 167, 247
Erie, 36
Essex, 22–23, 23, 111, 130, 163
Fanning, 70
Fife, 212
Fletcher-class, 115, 338
Florida, 71
Forest-Sherman-class, 38
Forrestal, 157, 158
Franklin, 304
Franks, 133
Fulton, 35; II, 35
George Washington, 159, 160, 161, 245, 245
Germantown, 300
Gonzalez, 218
Grapple, 217, 217
Grasp, 217
Grayling, 79
Growler, 337
Guam, 187
Guardfish, 117, 259
Guerriere, 27
Gunston Hall, 267
Hancock, 168–69
Harpers Ferry, 275
Harry S. Truman, 245
Hartford, 58
Hector, 146
Henry B. Wilson, 178

Holland, 79
Hornet, 104, *338*; museum, 336
Housatonic, 55
Houston, 89, *91*, 99–101, 133
Hunchback, *47*
Inchon, 286
Independence, 27
Independence (CV 62), 162, 187, 191, 195, 229–30, 239, *239*, 245, 341
Indiana-class, 64
Indianapolis, 341
Intrepid, 20, 20–21, *337*; museum, 336
Iowa, 9, *145*, 184, *292*
Isabel, *81*
Jarrett, 191
Jimmy Carter, 251
John C. Calhoun, *263*
John C. Stennis, 245
John F. Kennedy, 196, *200–201*, 230, 230–31
John L. Hall, *210*
John R. Pierce, 164
Johnston, 13
Joseph P. Kennedy, Jr., 164, 320, 338
Juneau, 146, *205*
Kalinin Bay, *325*
Kansas, 8
Kearsarge, 56, *56*
Kearsarge (LHD 3), *268*, 300
Kidd, 338; class, 213
Laffey, 338
Lake Champlain, 161
Lake Erie, 213
Langley, 77, 85–87, 89, 100–101
Laramie, *223*
LaSalle, *193*
Lawrence, 24–25
Leutze, 135
Levant, 42
Lexington, 86–87, 90, 103, 103, 119, *338*; museum, 336
Leyte, *146*, 151
Liberty, 180, *180*
Little Rock, 183, 338
Lloyd Thomas, *182*
Long Beach, *161*
Los Angeles-class, 184, 251
LST-282, 123
LST-372, 123
Ludlow, 111, 113
Macedonian, 27, 29
Macon, 87
Maddox, *166*
Mahan, 65
Maine, 64–65
Maryland, 87
Massachusetts, 68, 113, *134*, 337
Mayrant, 114
McKee, *321*
Memphis, 80
Mercy, 192, 223, *295*
Merrimack, 54
Mervine, 109–10
Midway, 196–97, 230, 233
Minneapolis-St. Paul, 258
Minnesota, 54
Mississippi, 35, *35*, *38*
Mississippi (CGN 40), *230*
Missouri, 35
Missouri (BB 63), 140–41, *145*, 146, 152, 184, 191, 197, 199, 337, *339*
Mitscher, *215*
Mobile, 136
Monaghan, *80*
Monitor, 54, *54*
Monrovia, *110*
Monterey, 144
Montpelier, 136
Mount Hood, *213*
Murray, 139
Nahant, *47*
Narwahl, *79*
Nautilus, 19, 27, *79*
Nautilus (SSN 571), 158, *159*, 339
Nebraska, *263*
Nevada (BB 36), 71, 98
Nevada (SSBN 773), *255*
New Ironsides, 55, 57
New Jersey, 9, 171, 184, 186, *186*

New York, *63*, 64, 68, 71, *82*, 111
Newcomb, 135, *135*
Niagara, 25, *25*
Nicholas, 197
Nicholson, 70, 216
Nimitz, *185*; class, 184, 245
Noa, 161, 171
Normandy, 219, 230
North Carolina, 36, 114, 337, 338
O'Kane, *117*
Ohio, *8*, 184
Oklahoma, 71
Oklahoma City, 324
Oliver Hazard Perry-class, 213
Olympia, 64, 66, *67*, 318, 340, *340*
Ontario, 36
Oregon, 66
Oriskany, *168*
Oscar Austin, 212; class, 220
Patuxent, 134
PC-1129, 129
Peacock, 26–27
Peary, 100–101
Pennsylvania, 29, 75, 80, *89*
Perry, 7
Philadelphia, 19, *19*, 20
Philippine Sea, 151, *215*, 219, 230
Pike, *79*
Pintado, 7
Pittsburg, 51
Pollock, *259*
Pompano, 101–102, 140
Porpoise, 79
Porter, 23
Portland, 89
Potomac, 38
Preble, 230
Preston, 108
Princeton, 35, *35–36*
Princeton (CG 59), 151, 197, 285
Proteus, *161*
PT-504, 122, 124
Pueblo, 180
Puffer, 118–19
Ranger, 78, 113, 196–97
Reasoner, 195
Red Rover, *293*
Requin, 140
Resolute, *258*
Rochester, 146
Ronald Reagan, 245
Sacramento, *175*
St. Paul, 152, *170*
Salem, 338
Salt Lake City, *83*
Samuel B. Roberts, 191
San Antonio, 274; class, 276
San Diego, 72
San Jacinto, 39, 230
Saratoga, 84, 86–87, 188, 196, 233, 239, 230
Savannah, 42
Scorpion, 181, *181*
Seahorse, 102
Seawolf, *250*, 251; class, 276
Shangri-La, *292*
Shark, *79*
Shenandoah, 85
Shugart, 223
Siren, 19
South Dakota, 106
Spruance-class, 212
Stark, 190, 191
Sturgeon, 100
Susquehanna, 29
Tarpon, 79
Tecumseh, 55, *57*, 58
Tennessee, *135*
Texas, 64, 71, *73*, 337, *337*, *124*
The Sullivans, *105*
Theodore Roosevelt, 196, 197, 230, 233, 239, *245*, 247
Thomas S. Gates, *230*
Thresher, 180, 254
Ticonderoga, 166–67, 210; class, 213
Tide, 124
Tripoli, 197, 285
Triton, 161
Trout, 99
Turner Joy, 166

Tusk, 155
Tutuila, 77
United States, 17, *17*, 23, *24*, 316
Utah, 71
Valley Forge, *146*, 146–47, 151
Vermont, *8*
Vesole, 164
Vincennes, *40*, 191
Virginia, 264–65, 326
Vixen, 19
W.S. Sims, 327
Washington, 106, *107*, *111*
Wasp (CV 7), 92–93
Wasp (LHD 1), *269*
West Virginia, 115–16
Whidbey Island, 275
Will Rogers, 17
William V. Pratt, 230
Wisconsin, *133*, *152*, 184, 197, *199*
Worden, 80
Wyoming, 71
Yorktown, *85*, 103–105; museum, 336
U-405, 117
Uniform Code of Military Justice, 328
United States Navy Memorial, *332*, *333*, 342–43
United States Navy Museum, Washington, D.C., 334, *334*
Unity, 12, 14
Utah Beach, 123–24

Venlet, Lt David J., 184–85
Veracruz, Mexico, 42, 49; occupied, 69
Vicksburg, 52–53
Victory ships, 121
Viet Cong, 164–65, 171, 175–77
Vietnam War, 164–78, 185–86, 289
Vinson, Carl, 96
Virginius, 63
Volgoes, 164

Waddell, Capt James, 56, 59
Waheed, *187*
Wake Island, 68, 139
Walke, Cdr Henry, 51, 53
Walker, Cdr Edward, 114
Walker, John Grimes, *30*
War of 1812, 21–27, 30, 316
Ward, Norville G. "Bub," 117
Warfield, LCdr Bud, 231
Warren, James, 14
Warrington, Capt Lewis, 27
Washington, George, 13, 16
Washington Navy Yard, 21, 334
Washington Treaty, 75–77, 86–88
Watkins, Adm James D., 184, *184*
WAVEs, 126
Weapons, weapon systems
  3-inch battery, 80, *127*
  4-inch deck gun, *121*
  5-inch guns, 130, 135, 213
  5-inch/62 guns, 220
  6-inch guns, 78, 136, 171
  8-inch guns, 73, 80, 99, 170–71, 213
  9-inch smoothbore cannon, 36
  11-inch smoothbore cannon, 36
  16-inch guns, 73, 87–88, 106, 152, 184, 186
  18.1-inch guns, 130
  20-millimeter antiaircraft guns, *121*
  .50-caliber machine guns, 130, 174
  76mm gun, 213
  81mm mortar, *174*
  88mm gun, 124
  Abrams main battle tanks, 183, 193
  Advanced Swimmer Delivery Vehicles, 255
  Aegis Area TBMD system, 222
  Aegis battle management system, 192, 210–11, 216,
  Aegis vertical launchers, 220
  AGM-114B Hellfire missile, *214*
  AIM Sidewinder heat-seeking missiles, 185
  AIM-7F Sparrow radar-guided missiles, 185
  Airborne Mine Neutralization System, 287
  Airborne Warning and Control System 208, 231

  Army Advance Tactical Missile System, 259
  ASROC system 213
  Bradley armored fighting vehicle, 193
  Close-In Weapons System, *203*
  Cruise missiles, 216, 258
  Electronic Surveillance Measures System, 233
  Extended Range Guided Munitions, 220
  Forward Looking Infrared system, 239
  Harpoon antiship missile, 184, 212–13
  Hellfire laser guided missiles, 197, 213
  High-Speed Anti-Radiation Missiles, 232, 247
  Hypersonic theater ballistic missiles, 216
  Inverse Synthetic Aperture Radar, 232
  Joint Direct Attack Munition, 247
  Joint Stand-Off Weapon, 247–48
  Land Attack Standard Missile, 220
  Laser guided bombs, 197
  Lightweight Exoatmospheric Projectile warhead, 222
  Medium-range surface-to-air missiles, 213
  MK Vertical Launching System, 211
  MK-37 director, 130
  MK-48 torpedo, *252*
  MK-82, 231
  MK-83 bomb, *236*
  Organic Air Surface Influence System, 287
  Patriot Hawk missile, 222
  Penguin missile, 213
  Pershing II theater missiles, 183
  Polaris missile, 160, *161*, 162
  Remote Mine Hunting System, 287
  SA-2 missile, *168*
  SH-60B LAMPS III helicopter, 197
  Sidewinder air-to-air missile, 198, *238*
  Silkworm missiles, 199
  SM-2 missile, 222
  Sparrow air-to-air missile, 169, 196
  Standard (SM-2) surface-to-air missile, 220
  Standoff Land Attack Missile-Extended Range, 247
  Tactical Air Launched Decoys, 233
  Tactical Air Reconnaissance Pod System, 231
  Talos surface-to-air missiles, 338
  Tomahawk Land Attack Cruise Missile, *142–43*, 184, *194*, 196, 207, *208*, 209, 211, 213, 214–17, *218*, 219–20, 254–55, 258
  Torpedoes, 87, 101, 317
  Trident I missiles, 184; II, 255
Webber, Lt Gordon, 121–22
"Webfoot Regiment," 13
Webster-Ashburton Treaty, 37
"Weekend War" with Korea, 65
Welles, Gideon, 45, *45*
West, Cdr Michael, 226
Westmoreland, Gen William C., 165
Whipple, Abraham, 16, *16*
Wickes, Lambert, 15–16
Wilkes, Charles, 40–41
William Tyler Page, 121
Wilson, Woodrow, 70–72
Winslow, Capt John A., 56, *57*
Wise, Lt Dan, 231
Wolmi Do island, 149, *149*
Wonsan, 151–53; mines at, 285
Woodbury, Levi, 33
Worden, Lt John, 54
Wotje, 101

Yalu River, 150
Yamamoto, Adm Isoruku, 96, 104
Yankee Station, 167
Yazoo River, 53
"Yeomanettes," *72*, 126
Yom Kippur War, 182
Yucka, Gunner's Mate Walt, 141

Zumwalt, VAdm Elmo R., Jr., 177; Adm, 181, *181*